# Curating Research Data

## Volume Two: A Handbook of Current Practice

*by Lisa R. Johnston*

with 30 case studies contributed
by practitioners in the field

*Association of College and Research Libraries*
*A division of the American Library Association*
*Chicago, Illinois 2017*

The paper used in this publication meets the minimum requirements of American National Standard for Information Sciences–Permanence of Paper for Printed Library Materials, ANSI Z39.48-1992. ∞

Cataloging-in-Publication data is on file with the Library of Congress

Printed in the United States of America.

21 20 19 18 17 5 4 3 2 1

# Table of Contents

# Acknowledgments

*Curating Research Data, Volume Two: A Handbook of Current Practice* is a reality because of the steadfast commitment of each and every contributing case study author who has generously shared their perspectives, research findings, and best practices for data curation. Their optimism and unwavering dedication easily made the effort of writing this volume a true labor of love. In addition I'd like to thank the review board of the American College and Research Libraries for seeing the potential of this topic, the ACRL publication editors Kathryn Deiss and Erin Nevius for expertly overseeing the process, our eagle-eyed copyeditor Judith Lauber for her invisible yet greatly valued contributions, and our peer-reviewers for their thoughtful opinions and levelheaded advice. Finally, this work would not have been possible without the excellent staff at the University of Minnesota Libraries who have shaped my thinking around data management and curation over the last nine years. Thanks in particular to the libraries' 2014–2015 Data Management and Curation Initiative sponsor John Butler and members— Caitlin Bakker, Carolyn Bishoff, Josh Bishoff, Steven Braun, Francine Dupont Crocker, Kevin Dyke, Stephen Hearn, Alicia Hofelich-Mohr, Carol Kussmann, Eric Larson, Erik Moore, Alice Motes, Arvid Nelsen, Jon Nichols, Justin Schell, Nancy Sims, Bill Tantzen, and Amy West—these individuals represent the "we" behind any mention of the workflows, technology, policies, and procedures created for the Data Repository for the University of Minnesota and I whole-heartedly thank each of you!

# Foreword

*Curating Research Data, Volume Two: A Handbook of Current Practice* aims to guide you through the practical strategies and techniques for curating research data in a digital repository setting. The data curation steps for receiving, appraising, selecting, ingesting, transforming, describing, contextualizing, disseminating, and preserving digital research data are explored. Yet, what does it mean to actually apply these concepts to actual data? In this handbook, theory is supplemented with detailed case studies written by forty international practitioners from national, disciplinary, and institutional data repositories based in the United States, the United Kingdom, Canada, and Australia. Together we present actionable techniques that can be immediately applied at your home institution, such as appraising incoming digital data files, detecting personally identifiable information, and transforming proprietary software files into archival formats for long-term preservation. These timely examples may focus specifically on digital research data sets, yet they draw from existing theory and practice in the digital curation and archives communities and aim not to recreate the wheel, but to provide a solid base from which to build. By sharing our current strategies, we hope that this dissemination will lead to wider adoption of data curation best practices and encourage experimentation and dialogue in order to develop new and improved processes for curating research data.

Building from the introductory base established in *Curating Research Data, Volume One: Practical Strategies for Your Digital Repository*, which explores the concepts of research data and the drivers for establishing digital data repositories, the steps in Volume Two will detail the sequential actions that you might take to curate a data set from receiving the data (*Step 1*) to eventual reuse (*Step 8*). Notably, this handbook focuses on the data curation practices and techniques taken by curation staff in a digital repository setting, yet these steps will be valuable for anyone facilitating data management support for research data, regardless of the final destination of the data (e.g., long-term archiving). Therefore data curators, archivists, research data management specialists, subject librarians, institutional repository managers, and digital library staff will benefit from these current and practical approaches to data curation.

# Data Curation across the Data Life Cycle

Data curation cannot happen without implementing good data management practice early on and throughout the research life cycle. In practice, this means that research projects must be conceptualized and data collected, described, and managed with data archiving and reuse in mind. Sometimes this is not the case. Rather, repositories, digital libraries, and archives receive data that was not well-managed from the beginning stages and our curation challenge is to work with the data authors and providers to resolve any potential problems that a potential user may encounter further down the life cycle of data reuse. These concepts of data management, data curation, and data reuse form an interlinked conceptual model of the research data life cycle (see figure F.1). For example, the steps of creating, storing, analyzing, sharing, and even publishing research data typically are taken by the researcher (represented here by the 'data management' phase). Most often, reuse of the data beyond the data management phase is not a priority. This is where data curation services can prove invaluable.

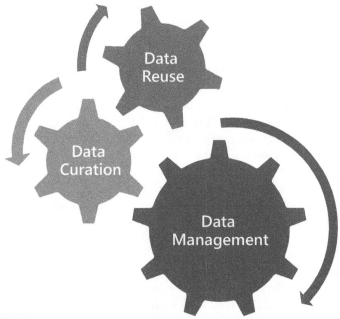

**FIGURE F.1**

Conceptual model of the research data life cycle with intersections between data management (researcher actions), data curation (repository actions), and data reuse.

The steps in the data curation handbook are adapted from the Digital Curation Centre's (DCC) Curation Lifecycle Model.[1] The visual of the model is quite complex and builds on an earlier model that helped establish the DCC as a center of expertise in the United Kingdom.[2] However, the sequential stages and various actions that form the data curation workflow have stood up to various critiques.[3] Table F.1 presents the stages of this handbook mapped to the sequential actions presented of the DCC model with the roles and actions taken at the various steps.

## TABLE F.1

Researcher and Curator Roles in the Stages of the Data Curation Life Cycle (adapted from the DCC's Curation Lifecycle Model)

| DCC Curation Lifecycle Model Sequential Actions | *Curating Research Data*, Volume Two Steps | Roles and Actions Taken in This Step |
| --- | --- | --- |
| Conceptualize | Step 0: Establish Your Service | Data curation services should be sustained through appropriate staffing and business models. |
| Create or Receive | Step 1: Receive the Data | Enable data creators to submit their data for deposit into a data repository (institutional or disciplinary). |
| Appraise and Select | Step 2: Appraise and Select | Include a review of data submissions to allow for selection and rejection of data that does not meet collection policy and mitigate known risk inherent to digital data. |
| Preservation Actions | Step 3: Processing and Treatment Actions | Include processing actions for all data deposited in order to best arrange, transform, and prepare the data according to established procedures. |
| Ingest<br><br>Store | Step 4: Ingest and Store | Ingest and store data in secure locations using appropriate repository infrastructure. |
| n/a | Step 5: Descriptive Metadata | Apply appropriate descriptive metadata and enhance author submitted metadata to best facilitate discovery. |
| Access, Use, Reuse | Step 6: Access | Facilitate access through discovery, dissemination, retrieval, and download functionality. |

**TABLE F.1** (continued)

| DCC Curation Lifecycle Model Sequential Actions | *Curating Research Data*, Volume Two Steps | Roles and Actions Taken in This Step |
|---|---|---|
| Transform | Step 7: Preserve | Preserve data in many forms for as long as the data is useful and adhere to policy-driven decisions for how long the data must be retained. |
| Reappraise and/or dispose | Step 8: Reuse | Evaluate the impact or value of the data and determine whether to keep or dispose. |

Note: Highlighted areas are the focus of the data curation handbook. An annotated list of the multistep actions involved in each curation step is presented as an appendix at the end of this foreword.

# Recommended Further Reading

Some necessary choices were made in the selection and scoping of content for this handbook. First, the focus on *digital* research data allows for a targeted discussion of emerging practice. For additional guidance on the handling *physical data collections*, such as specimen and sample collections, please consult publications such as the Society for the Preservation of Natural History Collections How-To series.[4] Second, *Curating Research Data Volume Two* focuses on curation steps taken by digital curation staff after the data has been received. Therefore this book takes a narrower approach by not focusing on all stages of the research data life cycle. Earlier stages taken by data creators, with the help of data stewards, such as planning, creating, storing, analyzing, and sharing data are key steps for producing valuable and usable data, but are not the focus here. These data management aspects have been effectively covered by other sources aimed at helping researchers (generally, as well as for those in specific disciplines such as the sciences and digital humanities) to better manage their data and prepare their data for sharing. Some recommended further reading on the topic of data management techniques for data creators and researchers include

- Kristin Briney's 2015 book *Data Management for Researchers. Organize, Maintain and Share Your Data for Research Success.*[5] Former researcher turned academic data librarian, Briney shares her easy-to-follow data management solutions for researchers in the United States on topics such as documentation, improving data analysis, managing sensitive data, storage and backups, as well as data reuse and "restarting the data lifecycle."

- The UK Data Archive's 2011 guide *Managing and Sharing Data: Best Practice for Researchers.*[6] Van den Eynden, Corti, Woollard, Bishop, and Horton from the UK Data Archive include concise case study examples from a wide range of mainly European data repositories in addition to their own best practices. Advice on topics speaking directly to the researcher include the importance of data management plans, documentation techniques, file-naming conventions, safe storage options, legal and ethical issues for sharing data, rights related to data, collaborative data management techniques, and "making use of other people's data."
- Australian National University Library's 2016 *Data Management Manual: Managing Digital Research Data at the Australian National University. Data Service Data Literacy Guide.*[7] In this guide, now in its tenth edition, the ANU presents best practices for researchers as well as training material that Australian libraries use for implementing their information literacy programs on data management.
- The Inter-university Consortium for Political and Social Research (ICPSR) 2012 *Guide to Social Science Data Preparation and Archiving: Best Practice throughout the Data Life Cycle* (5th ed.).[8] The ICPSR provides an excellent guide from an archives perspective that reflects tasks across research data life cycle, from the grant proposal–writing stage, project start-up, data collection and file creation, data analysis, preparing for data sharing, and data deposit. Applicable to researchers from disciplines beyond the social sciences focus of the archive, the guide includes contributions by curators that have written case studies for this handbook (relevant case studies are found in *Step 1*, *Step 2*, and *Step 8*).
- Arie Shoshani and Doron Rotem's 2010 *Scientific Data Management: Challenges, Technology, and Deployment,* CRC Press, 2010.[9] Shoshani and Rotem bring the scientists' perspective in this edited volume focusing around the "five main aspects and techniques of managing data during the scientific exploration process that scientists typically encounter," which they label as data storage and access, data transfer, databases and retrieval systems, data analysis, and scientific workflow or process management. Readers of this handbook may find their chapter 12, "Metadata and Provenance Management," particularly useful.
- Arjun Sabharwal's 2015 book *Digital Curation in the Digital Humanities: Preserving and Promoting Archival and Special Collections.*[10] Sabharwal applies the DCC Curation Lifecycle model to data in the digital humanities and presents several relevant digital humanities projects and their curation challenges. Also, addressed more to library

and archives specialists than the researchers and scholars themselves, the *DH Curation Guide* presents some of the legal issues with creating digital humanities collections as well as some examples from physical digitization projects, file format issues, and metadata standards used in the humanities.[11]

Finally, data curation as a service is just one component of the range of research data services offered by academic libraries and other target audiences for this book—for example, services such as data management planning support (e.g., writing quality data management plans or DMPs), assisting researchers in creating sufficient data documentation, and applying metadata standards or research ontologies to prepare data for eventual sharing and reuse. No doubt fueling this growth, several books and guides have recently focused on helping libraries develop their services to support research data management:

- Joyce M. Ray's edited 2014 book *Research Data Management: Practical Strategies for Information Professionals.*[12] With a US perspective, Ray brings together chapters by prominent experts in the information and library science field on a range of topics such as policy and data governance issues, copyright and licenses for data, metadata standards that are relevant to data management best practices, as well as case studies from four US university libraries on how they developed their research data management services at Cornell University, Purdue University, Rice University, and the University of Oregon.

- Graham Pryor, Sarah Jones, and Angus Whyte's 2014 book *Delivering Research Data Management Services: Fundamentals of Good Practice.*[13] The UK Digital Curation Centre staff members Prior, Jones, and Whyte combine their how-to guide know-how for delivering research data management services with effective case studies written by individuals providing these services at Johns Hopkins University, University of Southampton, Monash University, and the UK Data Service, as well as providing results of the Jisc-funded Managing Research Data program.

- Chuck Humphrey's blog (last updated January 6, 2015) *Preserving Research Data in Canada: The Long Tale of Data.*[14] Humphrey presents a view of research data management from the perspective of Canadian research policies and mandates. Topics cover data management plans, building data repositories, repository certification, national data infrastructure, and case studies for establishing research data management services in Canada.

- Lynda Kellam and K. Thompson's 2016 *Databrarianship: The Academic Data Librarian in Theory and Practice.*[15] Kellam and Thompson package a number of chapters on a variety of "databrarian" services offered by academic libraries. Particularly related to data curation issues are the chapters "Technical Data Skills for Reproducible Data Research" by Harrison Dekker and Paula Lackie, "Restricted Data Access and Libraries" by Jennifer Darragh, and "Appraisal and Selection of Digital Research Data" by Christopher Eaker.

- Laura Krier and Carly A. Strasser's 2013 *Data Management for Libraries: A Lita Guide.*[16] This guidebook by Krier and Strasser focuses on how libraries might develop and grow their data management services. It details the activities involved with providing data management plan consultations and addresses questions around ownership, intellectual property, sharing and access, metadata, and preservation.
- The Association of Research Libraries' 2013 *Research Data Management Services, SPEC Kit 334.*[17] This ARL SPEC Kit by Fearon and colleagues includes their survey findings of activities in this space with relevant examples of research data policies, data retention policies, DMP tools, job descriptions, needs assessment tools, and links to institution webpages.

# Appendix F1: Summary of *Curating Research Data: A Handbook of Current Practice*

**Preliminary Step 0: Establish Your Service**. Data curation services should be sustained through appropriate staffing and business models.

    0.1  Mission: As an organization, acknowledge the institutional commitment (e.g., resources, staff) to providing data curation services at a level appropriate for your goals.

    0.2  Policies: Define the scope of what data will be curated and establish written policies (e.g., criteria for acceptance and rejection).

    0.3  Target Audience: Perform a market analysis (e.g., user needs assessment, gap analysis of existing services, stakeholder analyses) to better understand the target audience needs and motivations for using the curation service.

    0.4  Costs: Understand and plan for the costs involved with staffing, resourcing, launching, and maintaining the curation service.

    0.5  Staffing: Define and allocate the organizational infrastructure to provide the data curation services at the level appropriate for your organization.

    0.6  Technological Infrastructure: Develop (or secure from a third party) the repository infrastructure to securely house and store the data.

**Step 1.0: Receive the Data**. Data curation services should enable data creators to submit their data for deposit into a data repository (institutional or disciplinary).

    1.1  Recruit Data for Your Service: Potential submitters learn of your services through successful recruitment strategies and a robust communications plan that engages your target audiences.

    1.2  Negotiate Deposit: The repository and the submitter come to a clear understanding and agreement of the terms of deposit for data into the repository (e.g., policies and conditions for access and reuse are known and well communicated).

    1.3  Obtain Author Deposit Agreements: A rights transfer agreement is signed by the data author (or authorized submitter), and any conditions involving legally protected or restricted use data are well understood.

    1.4  Facilitate Transfer of the Data: The data files are transferred to the repository in a secure manner that protects the integrity and authenticity of the data.

    1.5  Obtain Metadata and Documentation: The repository collects the author-generated metadata and supporting documentation necessary to use and understand the data. This information will be included in the curation process as part of the data submission.

1.6 Receive Notification of Data Arrival: The appropriate repository staff are alerted that a new data submission was received and is ready for curation.

**Step 2.0: Appraise and Select.** Data curation services should include a review of data submissions to allow for selection and rejection of data that does not meet collection policy and mitigate known risk inherent to digital data.

2.1 Appraise the Files: Determine that the repository is the appropriate home for this data (e.g., the data meets all collection policies) and, with appropriate curation, there is a potential long-term value for reuse.

2.2 Consider Any Risk Factors: The repository has clear understanding of the types of data (e.g., federally protected data, sensitive information, copyright violations) that should not be accepted and has protocols in place to reject or facilitate remediation of data that should not have been transferred to the repository.

2.3 Inventory the Submission: The data submission is inspected and the number, file types, and file sizes of the data are understood and documented. Identify any missing, duplicate, or corrupt (e.g., unable to open) files. Capture the organization of the files and any technical metadata (e.g., date last modified). Request more information from the author if necessary.

2.4 Select: The data submission is accepted or rejected based on the above actions. If accepted, determine if any additional information or files need to be acquired from the author before moving to the next step. This step may include the deselection and removal of any duplicate or unnecessary files.

2.5 Assign the Submission: Accept the data submission for inclusion in the repository and assign curation responsibility to the appropriate data curator based on subject and format expertise required.

**Step 3.0: Processing and Treatment Actions for Data**. Data curation services should include processing actions for all data deposited in order to best arrange, transform, and prepare the data according to established procedures.

3.1 Secure the Files: Create a working copy of the files in order to protect the originals when making any changes or additions to the submission during *Step 3*.

3.2 Start a Curation Log: Track any changes to the data in a curation log in order to keep a record of the correspondence (e.g., e-mails) between the repository and the submitter.

3.3 Inspect the File Representation and Organization: Understand the directory structures, file relationships, and any naming conventions used. Preserve any relationships in the files or generate documentation to help others understand how the files relate.

3.4 Inspect the Data: Review the content of the data files (e.g., open and run the files). Check for quality and usability issues such as missing data, ambiguous headings, code execution failures, and data presentation concerns. Try to detect and extract any "hidden documentation" inherent to the data files that may facilitate reuse. Generate a list of questions for the data author to fix any errors or issues.

3.5 Work with the Author to Enhance the Data Submission: Verify all metadata provided by the author and review the available documentation. Determine if this description of the data is sufficient for a user with similar qualifications to the author's to understand and reuse the data. If not, seek out or create additional documentation (e.g., use a readme.txt template).

3.6 Consider File Formats: Identify specialized file formats and their restrictions (e.g., Is the software freely available? Link to it or archive it alongside the data). Verify technical metadata (min resolution, audio/video codec) that would optimize the files for reuse. Transform files into open, nonproprietary file formats that broaden the potential audience for reuse and ensure that preservation actions might be taken by the repository in later steps. Retain original files if data transfer is not perfect.

3.7 Arrangement and Description: Organize and rename the files to optimize their meaning, and display them in a way that might facilitate reuse (e.g., Which files are the primary object and which are supplementary? Too many files, consider repackaging for display.)

**Step 4.0: Ingest and Store Data in Your Repository.** Data curation services should ingest and store data in secure locations using appropriate repository infrastructure.

4.1 Ingest the Data Files: Transfer the processed data files to the repository while maintaining integrity and verifying fixity throughout the process (e.g., generate file checksums).

4.2 Store the Assets Securely: Add the ingested files to a well-configured (in terms of hardware and software) archival storage environment. Perform routine checks and provide disaster recovery capabilities as needed.

4.3 Develop Trust in Your Repository: Become a trusted digital repository for data by applying for accreditation and growing your reputation locally and beyond.

**Step 5.0: Descriptive Metadata.** Data curation services should apply appropriate descriptive metadata and enhance author submitted metadata to best facilitate discovery.

5.1 Create and Apply Descriptive Metadata: Structure author-generated metadata into the metadata schema used by your repository in order to maximize search and discovery functionality. Create and apply new metadata for the data record, including technical and provenance metadata.

5.2 Consider Metadata Standards for Disciplinary Data: When appropriate, structure and present metadata in multiple schemas to facilitate discovery and future integration into other systems.

**Step 6.0: Access**. Data curation services should facilitate access through discovery, dissemination, retrieval, and download functionality.

6.1 Determine Appropriate Access Conditions: Determine what level of access is required and how target audiences for reuse may be affected by this condition (e.g., a terms of use).

6.2 Apply the Terms of Use and Any Relevant Licenses and Copyright Notices for the Data: Work with the author to choose to apply any specific reuse conditions (e.g., a terms of use agreement), and if appropriate, apply a license, such as Creative Commons Licenses.

6.3 Contextualize the Data: The discovery and access environment for the data should convey the possibilities of reusing the data. This can be done by visualizing the data, showcasing the primary data file contents to convey meaning, and linking to articles and projects that successfully reused the data.

6.4 Enhance the Submission to Increase Exposure and Discovery: Work directly and indirectly with third-party indexers to disseminate your repository holdings. For example, web search engines and services, such as Google, Bing, and Yahoo, rely heavily on text-based information to facilitate discovery. If possible, enhance the data submission for discovery purposes by generating search-engine-optimized formats of the data (e.g., full-text index).

6.5 Apply Any Necessary Access Controls: Depending on the conditions for access and reuse, place access restrictions on some or all data files.

6.6 Ensure Persistent Access: Generate a persistent identifier (e.g., a DOI) to help facilitate reliable long-term access to the data (e.g., via bibliographic citation).

6.7 Release Data for Access and Notify Author: Finalize the data submission by allowing the metadata of the data set to "go live" for discovery and access. Notify the author of this event and any further obligations that might be required of them (e.g., responding to requests for access).

**Step 7.0: Preservation of Data for the Long Term**. Data curation services should preserve data in many forms for as long as the data is useful and adhere to policy-driven decisions for how long the data must be retained.

7.1 Plan for Long-Term Reuse: The delivery and use of the data will rely on long-term preservation planning that anticipates format obsolescence and storage failures.

7.2 Monitor Preservation Needs and Take Action: Actively monitor the integrity and reusability of the data files using appropriate software, and apply digital preservation strategies.

**Step 8.0: Reuse.** Data curation services evaluate the impact or value of the data and determine whether to keep or dispose.

8.1 Monitor Data Rese: Track any requests for access, file downloads, data set citations, and other factors that might indicate the reuse value of data over time.

8.2 Consider Post-ingest Review Techniques: Allow others, public or experts, to provide feedback on the data in order to provide additional post-ingest quality control. Consider peer-review mechanisms to track input and provide quality measures for data housed in your repository.

8.3 Provide Ongoing Support as Long as Necessary: Provide services that meet the evolving needs of the data over the anticipated life or usefulness of the data, such as new versions, supplemental file additions, and user-generated documentation.

8.4 Cease Data Curation: Plan for any contingencies that will ultimately terminate access to the data, such as loss of funding for the repository. For example, how will you respond to takedown requests and deselection (e.g., provide tombstones)?

# Notes

1. Sarah Higgins. "The DCC Curation Lifecycle Model." *International Journal of Digital Curation* 3, no. 1 (2008): 134–40, doi:10.2218/ijdc.v3i1.48.

2. See the earlier model presented in Philip Lord, Alison Macdonald, Liz Lyon, and David Giaretta, "From Data Deluge to Data Curation," in *Proceedings of the UK e-Science All Hands Meeting 2004*, ed. Simon J. Cox, (Swindon, UK: EPSRC, 2004), 371–75, http://www.allhands.org.uk/2004/proceedings/papers/150.pdf.

3. P. Bryan Heidorn, "The Emerging Role of Libraries in Data Curation and E-science," *Journal of Library Administration* 51, no. 7–8 (2011): 662–72. doi:10.1080/01930826.2011.601269; Jake R. Carlson, "The Use of Life Cycle Models in Developing and Supporting Data Services," in *Research Data Management: Practical Strategies for Information Professionals*, ed. Joyce M. Ray (West Lafayette, IN: Purdue University Press, 2014), 63–86.

4. The Society for the Preservation of Natural History Collections publications are available online at http://www.spnhc.org/19/publications.

5. Kristin Briney, *Data Management for Researchers: Organize, Maintain and Share Your Data for Research Success* (Exeter, UK: Pelagic Publishing, 2015).

6. Veerle Van den Eynden, Louise Corti, Matthew Woollard, Libby Bishop, and Laurence Horton. *Managing and Sharing Data*, 3rd ed. (Colchester: UK Data Archive, University of Essex, 2011), http://www.data-archive.ac.uk/media/2894/managingsharing.pdf.

7. Australian National University Library. *Data Management Manual*, 10th ed., Data Service Data Literacy Guide (Canberra: Australian National University, 2016), https://services.anu.edu.au/files/DataManagement.pdf.

8.  Inter-university Consortium for Political and Social Research (ICPSR), *Guide to Social Science Data Preparation and Archiving: Best Practice throughout the Data Life Cycle,* 5th ed. (Ann Arbor, MI: ICPSR, 2012), http://www.icpsr.umich.edu/files/deposit/dataprep.pdf.

9.  Arie Shoshani and Doron Rotem, eds., *Scientific Data Management* (Boca Raton, FL: CRC Press, 2010).

10. Arjun Sabharwal, *Digital Curation in the Digital Humanities* (Cambridge: Chandos Publishing, 2015).

11. Digital Humanities Data Curation, "DH Curation Guide," accessed April 5, 2016, http://guide.dhcuration.org/contents.

12. Joyce M. Ray, ed., *Research Data Management: Practical Strategies for Information Professionals* (West Lafayette, IN: Purdue University Press, 2014).

13. Graham Pryor, Sarah Jones, and Angus Whyte eds., *Delivering Research Data Management Services: Fundamentals of Good Practice* (London: Facet Publishing, 2014).

14. Chuck Humphrey, "Canada's Long Tale of Data," Preserving Research Data in Canada: The Long Tale of Data, December, 2012, http://preservingresearchdataincanada.net/category/introduction.

15. Lynda Kellam and Kristi Thompson, eds., *Databrarianship: The Academic Data Librarian in Theory and Practice* (Chicago: American College and Research Libraries, 2016).

16. Laura Krier and Carly A. Strasser. *Data Management for Libraries: A Lita Guide* (Chicago: ALA TechSource, 2013).

17. David Fearon Jr., Betsy Gunia, Barbara E. Pralle, Sherry Lake, and Andrew L. Sallans, *Research Data Management Services: SPEC Kit 334* (Washington, DC: Association of Research Libraries, 2013), http://publications.arl.org/Research-Data-Management-Services-SPEC-Kit-334.

# Bibliography

Australian National University Library. *Data Management Manual: Managing Digital Research Data at the Australian National University*, 10th ed. Data Service Data Literacy guide. Canberra: Australian National University, 2016. https://services.anu.edu.au/files/DataManagement.pdf.

Briney, Kristin. *Data Management for Researchers: Organize, Maintain and Share Your Data for Research Success.* Exeter, UK: Pelagic Publishing, 2015.

Carlson, Jake R. "The Use of Life Cycle Models in Developing and Supporting Data Services." In *Research Data Management: Practical Strategies for Information Professionals.* Edited by Joyce M. Ray, 63–86. West Lafayette, IN: Purdue University Press, 2014.

Digital Humanities Data Curation. "DH Curation Guide." Accessed April 5, 2016. http://guide.dhcuration.org/contents.

Fearon, David Jr., Betsy Gunia, Barbara E. Pralle, Sherry Lake, and Andrew L. Sallans. *Research Data Management Services: SPEC Kit 334*. Washington, DC: Association of Research Libraries, 2013. http://publications.arl.org/Research-Data-Management-Services-SPEC-Kit-334.

Heidorn, P. Bryan. "The Emerging Role of Libraries in Data Curation and E-science." *Journal of Library Administration* 51, no. 7–8 (2011): 662–72. doi:10.1080/01930826.2011.601269.

Higgins, Sarah. "The DCC Curation Lifecycle Model." *International Journal of Digital Curation* 3, no. 1 (2008): 134–40. doi:10.2218/ijdc.v3i1.48.

Humphrey, Chuck. "Canada's Long Tale of Data." Preserving Research Data in Canada: The Long Tale of Data. December 5, 2012. http://preservingresearchdataincanada.net/category/introduction.

Inter-university Consortium for Political and Social Research (ICPSR). *Guide to Social Science Data Preparation and Archiving: Best Practice throughout the Data Life Cycle,* 5th ed. Ann Arbor, MI: ICPSR, 2012. http://www.icpsr.umich.edu/files/deposit/dataprep.pdf.

Kellam, Lynda, and Kristi Thompson, eds. *Databrarianship: The Academic Data Librarian in Theory and Practice.* Chicago: American College and Research Libraries, 2016.

Krier, Laura, and Carly A. Strasser. *Data Management for Libraries: A Lita Guide.* Chicago: ALA TechSource, 2013.

Lord, Philip, Alison Macdonald, Liz Lyon, and David Giaretta. "From Data Deluge to Data Curation." In *Proceedings of the UK e-Science All Hands Meeting 2004.* Edited by Simon J. Cox, 371–75. Swindon, UK: EPSRC, 2004. http://www.allhands.org.uk/2004/proceedings/papers/150.pdf.

Pryor, Graham, Sarah Jones, and Angus Whyte, eds. *Delivering Research Data Management Services: Fundamentals of Good Practice.* London: Facet Publishing, 2014.

Ray, Joyce M., ed., *Research Data Management: Practical Strategies for Information Professionals.* West Lafayette, IN: Purdue University Press, 2014.

Sabharwal, Arjun. *Digital Curation in the Digital Humanities: Preserving and Promoting Archival and Special Collections.* Cambridge: Chandos Publishing, 2015.

Shoshani, Arie, and Doron Rotem, eds. *Scientific Data Management: Challenges, Technology, and Deployment.* Boca Raton, FL: CRC Press, 2010.

Society for the Preservation of Natural History Collections. "Publications." Accessed April 5, 2016. http://www.spnhc.org/19/publications.

Van den Eynden, Veerle, Louise Corti, Matthew Woollard, Libby Bishop, and Laurence Horton. *Managing and Sharing Data: Best Practice for Researchers,* 3rd ed., Colchester: UK Data Archive, University of Essex, 2011. http://www.data-archive.ac.uk/media/2894/managingsharing.pdf.

# Establish Your Data Curation Service

Each of the data curation steps outlined in the following chapters must be complemented by a skilled staff and an overarching commitment (e.g., organizational support, dedicated budget, infrastructure, etc.) to the long-term stewardship of the digital data accepted by the service. The actions taken in this preliminary step mirrors the activities involved with establishing an institutional repository (IR), and several guides detail that topic (see for example Gibbons and SUNScholar).[1] However, despite some of the challenges that the heterogeneity of research data will bring to institutional repositories, IRs have shown great potential to be extended to successful data repositories.[2] The DCC's online guide by Jones, Pryor, and Whyte titled *How to Develop Research Data Management Services* provides a comprehensive and well-presented overview of the issues that will engage beyond their primary UK-based audience.[3] Generally, your data curation services should be established with a mission and purpose in mind, as well as a functional service model (with scoping policies) in place, implemented with appropriate staffing and infrastructure, and sustained through financial business models that take into account your long-term goals and values as an organization.

*Defining the mission and purpose.* Your intended data curation service should meet a purpose and a well-defined need. Demonstrating this need and obtaining the long-term commitment required for sustaining data curation services from your organization is key. Lynch explains that budget cuts and lack of sustained support may endanger your repository from carrying out its long-term mission and therefore warms that the establishment of such services should not be taken lightly.[4] Similarly, the Open Access Scholarly Information SourceBook (OASIS) stresses the importance of defining the mission and purpose of the repository and provides links to resources that may help when making the business case for a data repository to your institution.[5] It is worth noting that this OASIS resource, aimed at academic libraries, draws from a guide published by MIT library staff and based on their development and implementation of DSpace, the popular open-source repository software.[6] Finally, the Digital Repository Audit Method Based on Risk Assessment (DRAMBORA, http://www.repositoryaudit.eu), developed by the Digital Curation Centre (DCC) and DigitalPreservationEurope (DPE), is considered by Corrado and Moulaison to be another useful tool for assessing risk before launching your digital repository.[7]

---

In chapter 6, "Research Data Services Maturity in Academic Libraries," in *Curating Research Data, Volume One,* Inna Kouper, Kathleen Fear, Mayu Ishida, Christine Kollen, and Sarah C. Williams describe a range of basic, intermediate, and advanced research data services, which they derived from the frequency with which these services were observed in their research of academic research library offerings in the United States and Canada.

---

*Service models for curation.* Many institutions increasingly offer research data services (an umbrella under which data curation services might fall). Briney, Goben, and Zilinski found that half of the 206 large US research universities they studied had library research data services in 2014, a jump from only about 20 percent observed by an earlier study in 2011.[8] Other sources for useful data services model are found in Ray's 2014 edited volume, where case studies from Cornell University, Purdue University, Rice University, and the University of Oregon demonstrate how data curation service developed at each of their organizations.[9] Starr and colleagues at the University of California notably presented their data services as they mapped to the data management life cycle.[10] Similarly, Raboin, Reznik-Zellen, and Salo discussed the services of three institutions—the University of Wisconsin-Madison, the University of Massachusetts-Amherst, and Tufts University—under one article.[11] Finally, the steps involved with establishing the data curation services at my own institution, the University of Minnesota, are published in our 2015 business and service model.[12]

---

In chapter 2 of *Curating Research Data, Volume One* Kristin Briney, Abigail Goben, and Lisa Zilinski describe their research of the current landscape of federal-funder mandates for data as well as other top-down drivers for curation services such as institutional research data policies in "Institutional, Funder, and Journal Data Policies."

---

*Staffing and skills sets needed for data curation.* The staffing models required for running a data repository and delivering its services are still unfolding. Sherpa outlined the staffing and skill sets needed for an IR, which acknowledged the role that repositories *may* have with data curation, but this skill was listed only under current awareness and professional development.[13] Practical data curation skills combine professional digital curation expertise with domain-specific knowledge and, according to Henry in 2012, "there are currently no effective ways to prepare people for that hybrid role."[14] Recently a CLIR report outlined several LIS programs as well as a handful of professional development opportunities focused on data curation.[15] One notable example is the DigCCurr Professional Institute program, created by Helen Tibbo and Christopher Lee at the University of North Carolina-Chapel Hill that has been presented since 2010.[16] Costello and Brown presented a helpful overview of that first year's experience and demonstrated the potential for extending this post-career education approach.[17]

Faced with the changing nature of special collections, the archival community has taken action to translate curator skills from analog to digital through programs such as the Digital Archives Specialist (DAS) Certificate Program, which began in May 2011, and the National Digital Stewardship Residency, which kicked off in 2013 by the Library of Congress with support from the IMLS.[18] More recently, in 2015 a US National Research Council committee released the report *Preparing the Workforce for Digital Curation*, which outlined the skills needed for digital curators and the challenges of preparing staff to handle the wide variety of digital objects (including data).[19] These and other programs will undoubtedly help shore up this need for a skilled data curator workforce.

*Implementations of various data repository infrastructure and technology:* There are many infrastructure options for building your data repository, including open-source software (e.g., DSpace, Fedora, Hydra) and web-hosted solutions (e.g., Dataverse, figShare). Some notable descriptions of the technological infrastructure supporting their data repositories include Purdue University Research Repository (PURR) and JHU Data Conservancy.[20] Some IRs that accept data include: Penn State—ScholarSphere, the Stanford Digital Repository, and Columbia University—Academic Commons.[21] Technical approaches for developing and implementing data repositories, on the other hand, are more often found in conference presentations such as at the Open Repositories conference and Code4Lib. For example, past presentations by the University of Edinburgh's DataShare and the Purdue University Research Repository described their technical approaches.[22] More detail on the underlying software involved with data repositories is covered in *Step 4*: Ingest and Store Data in Your Repository.

*Financial and business models for paying for the costs of data curation.* Funding a data repository is another critical topic still emerging in the literature. For the general IR case, there are resources available to help you understand the business models for supporting an open-access repository.[23] For data specifically, Erway and Rinehart described seven ways to fund data management services as "obtaining institutional budgetary support, adding to grant budgets, charging data depositors, charging data users, establishing an endowment, using existing funding for data repository development, and making do with existing budgets."[24] Finally, disciplinary data repositories have been grappling with how to maintain financial support that goes beyond the initial start-up grant funding many of these repositories receive. Ember and colleagues evaluated the current disciplinary data repository funding models and found that each model has their advantages and disadvantages.[25]

---

Financial and business models for developing data repository services are further explored in *Curating Research Data, Volume One,* chapter 8, "Beyond Cost Recovery: Revenue Models and Practices for Data Repositories in Academia" by Karl Nilsen.

---

# Summary of Step 0: Establish Your Data Curation Service

0.1 Mission: As an organization, acknowledge the institutional commitment (e.g., resources, staff) to providing data curation services at a level appropriate for your goals.

0.2 Policies: Define the scope of what data will be curated and establish written policies (e.g., criteria for acceptance and rejection).

0.3 Target Audience: Perform a market analysis (e.g., user needs assessment, gap analysis of existing services, stakeholder analyses) to better understand the target audience needs and motivations for using the curation service

0.4 Costs: Understand and plan for the costs involved with staffing, resourcing, launching and maintaining the curation service.

0.5 Staffing: Define and allocate the organizational infrastructure to provide the data curation services at the level appropriate for your organization.

0.6 Technological Infrastructure: Develop (or secure from a third party) the needed repository infrastructure to securely house and store the data.

# Notes

1. Susan Gibbons, "Establishing an Institutional Repository," *Library Technology Reports* 40, no. 4 (July/August 2004), doi:10.5860/ltr.40n4; "SUNScholar's Practical Guidelines for Starting an Institutional Repository (IR)," Libopedia wiki, accessed March 14, 2016, http://wiki.lib.sun.ac.za/index.php/SUNScholar/Practical_guidelines_for_starting_an_institutional_repository_(IR).

2. Chuck Humphrey, "The Long Tail of Data Wagging the Institutional Repository," (slides for presentation, Open Repositories Conference, Charlottetown, Prince Edward

Island, Canada, July 8–12, 2013), http://or2013.net/sites/or2013.net/files/slides/OR2013_Workshop_Humphrey_0/index.pdf.

3.   Sarah Jones, Graham Pryor, and Angus Whyte, *How to Develop Research Data Management Services: A Guide for HEIs*, DCC How-to Guides (Edinburgh, UK: Digital Curation Centre, 2013), http://www.dcc.ac.uk/resources/how-guides/how-develop-rdm-services.

4.   Clifford A. Lynch, "Institutional Repositories: Essential Infrastructure for Scholarship in the Digital Age," *ARL Bimonthly Report,* no. 226 (February 2003), 1–7, http://www.arl.org/storage/documents/publications/arl-br-226.pdf.

5.   OpenOASIS, "Establishing a Repository," accessed March 14, 2015, http://www.openoasis.org/index.php?option=com_content&view=article&id=161&Itemid=354.

6.   Mary R. Barton and Margaret M. Waters, *Creating an Institutional Repository* (Cambridge, MA: MIT Press, 2004), http://hdl.handle.net/1721.1/26698.

7.   Discussed in chapter 6 of Edward M. Corrado and Heather Lea Moulaison, *Digital Preservation for Libraries, Archives, and Museums* (Lanham, MD: Rowman & Littlefield, 2014).

8.   Kristin Briney, Abigail Goben, and Lisa Zilinski, "Do You Have an Institutional Data Policy? A Review of the Current Landscape of Library Data Services and Institutional Data Policies," *Journal of Librarianship and Scholarly Communication* 3, no. 2 (2015): eP1232, eP1232, doi:10.7710/2162-3309.1232.

9.   Joyce M. Ray, ed., *Research Data Management* (West Lafayette, IN: Purdue University Press, 2014).

10.  Joan Starr, Perry Willett, Lisa Federer, Claudia Horning, and Mary Linn Bergstrom, "A Collaborative Framework for Data Management Services: The Experience of the University of California," *Journal of eScience Librarianship* 1, no. 2 (2012): e1014, http://escholarship.umassmed.edu/jeslib/vol1/iss2/7.

11.  Regina Raboin, Rebecca C. Reznik-Zellen, and Dorothea Salo, "Forging New Service Paths: Institutional Approaches to Providing Research Data Management Services," *Journal of eScience Librarianship* 1, no. 3 (2013): e1021, doi:10.7191/jeslib.2012.1021.

12.  University of Minnesota Libraries, "The Supporting Documentation for Implementing the Data Repository for the University of Minnesota (DRUM): A Business Model, Functional Requirements, and Metadata Schema," University of Minnesota Digital Conservancy, 2015, http://hdl.handle.net/11299/171761.

13.  Sherpa Briefing paper updated in 2011 on repository staffing and skill sets needed: Jackie Wickham, "Institutional Repositories: Staff and Skills Set," draft RSP document, 3rd ed., October 5, 2011, http://www.rsp.ac.uk/documents/Repository_Staff_and_Skills_Set_2011.pdf.

14.  Charles Henry, "Introduction," in *The Problem of Data* by Lori Jahnke, Andrew Asher, and Spencer D. C. Keralis, 1–2, CLIR publication no. 154 (Washington, DC: Council on Library and Information Resources, 2012), http://www.clir.org/pubs/reports/pub154/pub154.pdf.

15.  Chapter of the same CLIR report: Spencer D. C. Keralis, "Data Curation Education: A Snapshot," in *The Problem of Data* by Lori Jahnke, Andrew Asher, and Spencer D. C. Keralis, 32–43, CLIR publication no. 154 (Washington, DC: Council on Library and Information Resources, 2012), http://www.clir.org/pubs/reports/pub154/pub154.pdf.

16.  University of North Carolina, "DigCCurr Professional Institute: Curation Practices for the Digital Object Lifecycle," accessed March 14, 2016, http://ils.unc.edu/digccurr/institute.html.

17. Kaitlin Light Costello and Michael E. Brown, "Preliminary Report on the 2010–2011 DigCCurr Professional Institute: Curation Practices for the Digital Object Lifecycle," *D-Lib Magazine* 16, no. 11/12 (November/December 2010): 6, http://www.dlib.org/dlib/november10/costello/11costello.html.

18. Society of American Archivists. "Digital Archives Specialist (DAS) Curriculum and Certificate Program." Accessed March 14, 2016. http://www2.archivists.org/prof-education/das; Library of Congress, "National Digital Stewardship Residency," Digital Preservation, accessed March 14, 2016, http://www.digitalpreservation.gov/ndsr.

19. Committee on Future Career Opportunities and Educational Requirements for Digital Curation; Board on Research Data and Information; Policy and Global Affairs; National Research Council, *Preparing the Workforce for Digital Curation* (Washington DC: National Academies Press, 2015), http://www.nap.edu/catalog.php?record_id=18590.

20. Carly C. Dearborn, Amy J. Barton, and Neal A. Harmeyer, "The Purdue University Research Repository: HUBzero Customization for Dataset Publication and Digital Preservation," *OCLC Systems and Services* 30, no. 1 (2014): 15–27, doi:10.1108/OCLC-07-2013-0022; Matthew Mayernik, G. Sayeed Choudhury, Tim DiLauro, Elliot Metsger, Barbara Pralle, Mike Rippin, and Ruth Duerr, "The Data Conservancy Instance: Infrastructure and Organizational Services for Research Data Curation," *D-Lib Magazine* 18, no. 9/10 (September/October 2012): 2, doi:10.1045/september2012-mayernik.

21. Dan Coughlin and Mike Giarlo, "Architecting ScholarSphere: How We Built a Repository App That Doesn't Feel Like Yet Another Janky Old Repository App" (presentation, code{4}lib conference, Chicago, IL, February 11–14, 2013), http://code4lib.org/conference/2013/coughlin-giarlo; Stanford University Libraries, "Stanford Digital Repository," accessed March 14, 2016, https://library.stanford.edu/research/stanford-digital-repository; Columbia University, "Academic Commons," accessed March 14, 2016, http://academiccommons.columbia.edu.

22. Robin Rice, "On Being a Cog Rather Than Inventing the Wheel: Edinburgh DataShare as a Key Service in the University of Edinburgh's RDM Initiative" (slides from workshop: Institutional Repositories Dealing with Research Data, hosted by the DCC, IASSIST, and COAR, Open Repositories conference, Charlottetown, Prince Edward Island, Canada, July 8, 2013), http://www.slideshare.net/edinadocumentationofficer/or2013-workshoprice-0; Courtney Earl Matthews and Michael Witt, "The Purdue University Research Repository (PURR): An Institutional Data Management Service with a Virtual Research Environment, Data Publication, and Archiving" (poster presented at Open Repositories conference, Helsinki, Finland, June 10–12, 2014), http://docs.lib.purdue.edu/lib_fspres/52.

23. Alma Swan, "The Business of Digital Repositories," in *A DRIVER's Guide to European Repositories,* ed. Kasja Weenink, Loe Waaijers, and Karen van Godtsenhoven (Amsterdam, Netherlands: Amsterdam University Press, 2007), 14–26.

24. Ricky Erway and Amanda Rinehart, *If You Build It, Will They Fund?* (Dublin, OH: OCLC, 2016), http://www.oclc.org/content/dam/research/publications/2016/oclcresearch-making-research-data-management-sustainable-2016.pdf.

25. Carol Ember, Robert Hanisch, George Alter, Helen Berman, Margaret Hedstrom, and Mary Vardigan, "Sustaining Domain Repositories for Digital Data: A White Paper," December 11, 2013, 10–11, http://datacommunity.icpsr.umich.edu/sites/default/files/WhitePaper_ICPSR_SDRDD_121113.pdf.

# Bibliography

Barton, Mary R., and Margaret M. Waters. *Creating an Institutional Repository: LEADIRS Workbook.* Cambridge, MA: MIT Press, 2004. http://hdl.handle.net/1721.1/26698.

Briney, Kristin, Abigail Goben, and Lisa Zilinski. "Do You Have an Institutional Data Policy? A Review of the Current Landscape of Library Data Services and Institutional Data Policies." *Journal of Librarianship and Scholarly Communication* 3, no. 2 (2015): eP1232. doi:10.7710/2162-3309.1232.

Columbia University. "Academic Commons." Accessed March 14, 2016. http://academic-commons.columbia.edu.

Committee on Future Career Opportunities and Educational Requirements for Digital Curation; Board on Research Data and Information; Policy and Global Affairs; National Research Council. *Preparing the Workforce for Digital Curation.* Washington, DC: National Academies Press, 2015. http://www.nap.edu/catalog.php?record_id=18590.

Corrado, Edward M., and Heather Lea Moulaison. *Digital Preservation for Libraries, Archives, and Museums.* Lanham, MD: Rowman & Littlefield, 2014.

Costello, Kaitlin Light, and Michael E. Brown. "Preliminary Report on the 2010–2011 DigCCurr Professional Institute: Curation Practices for the Digital Object Lifecycle." *D-Lib Magazine* 16, no. 11/12 (November/December 2010): 6. http://www.dlib.org/dlib/november10/costello/11costello.html.

Coughlin, Dan, and Mike Giarlo. "Architecting ScholarSphere: How We Built a Repository App That Doesn't Feel Like Yet Another Janky Old Repository App." Presentation, code{4}lib conference, Chicago, IL, February 11–14, 2013. http://code4lib.org/conference/2013/coughlin-giarlo.

Dearborn, Carly C., Amy J. Barton, and Neal A. Harmeyer. "The Purdue University Research Repository: HUBzero Customization for Dataset Publication and Digital Preservation." *OCLC Systems and Services* 30, no. 1 (2014): 15–27. doi:10.1108/OCLC-07-2013-0022.

Ember, Carol, Robert Hanisch, George Alter, Helen Berman, Margaret Hedstrom, and Mary Vardigan. "Sustaining Domain Repositories for Digital Data: A White Paper." December 11, 2013. http://datacommunity.icpsr.umich.edu/sites/default/files/White-Paper_ICPSR_SDRDD_121113.pdf.

Erway, Ricky, and Amanda Rinehart. *If You Build It, Will They Fund? Making Research Data Management Sustainable.* Dublin, OH: OCLC, 2016. http://www.oclc.org/content/dam/research/publications/2016/oclcresearch-making-research-data-management-sustainable-2016.pdf.

Gibbons, Susan. "Establishing an Institutional Repository." *Library Technology Reports* 40, no. 4 (July/August 2004). doi:10.5860/ltr.40n4.

Henry, Charles. "Introduction." In *The Problem of Data,* by Lori Jahnke, Andrew Asher, and Spencer D. C. Keralis, 1–2. CLIR publication no. 154. Washington, DC: Council on Library and Information Resources, 2012. http://www.clir.org/pubs/reports/pub154/pub154.pdf.

Humphrey, Chuck. "The Long Tail of Data Wagging the Institutional Repository." Slides for presentation, Open Repositories Conference, Charlottetown, Prince Edward Island, Canada, July 8–12, 2013. http://or2013.net/sites/or2013.net/files/slides/OR2013_Workshop_Humphrey_0/index.pdf.

Jones, Sarah, Graham Pryor, and Angus Whyte. *How to Develop Research Data Management Services: A Guide for HEIs*. DCC How-to Guides. Edinburgh, UK: Digital Curation Centre, 2013. http://www.dcc.ac.uk/resources/how-guides/how-develop-rdm-services.

Keralis, Spencer D. C. "Data Curation Education: A Snapshot." In *The Problem of Data*, by Lori Jahnke, Andrew Asher, and Spencer D. C. Keralis, 32–43. CLIR publication no. 154. Washington, DC: Council on Library and Information Resources, 2012. http://www.clir.org/pubs/reports/pub154/pub154.pdf.

Lynch, Clifford A. "Institutional Repositories: Essential Infrastructure for Scholarship in the Digital Age." *ARL Bimonthly Report*, no. 226 (February 2003): 1–7. http://www.arl.org/storage/documents/publications/arl-br-226.pdf.

Matthews, Courtney Earl, and Michael Witt. "The Purdue University Research Repository (PURR): An Institutional Data Management Service with a Virtual Research Environment, Data Publication, and Archiving." Poster presented at Open Repositories conference, Helsinki, Finland, June 10–12, 2014. http://docs.lib.purdue.edu/lib_fspres/52.

Mayernik, Matthew, G. Sayeed Choudhury, Tim DiLauro, Elliot Metsger, Barbara Pralle, Mike Rippin, and Ruth Duerr. "The Data Conservancy Instance: Infrastructure and Organizational Services for Research Data Curation." *D-Lib Magazine* 18, no. 9/10 (September/October 2012): 2. doi:10.1045/september2012-mayernik.

Library of Congress. "National Digital Stewardship Residency." Digital Preservation. Accessed March 14, 2016. http://www.digitalpreservation.gov/ndsr.

OpenOASIS. "Establishing a Repository." Accessed March 14, 2016. http://www.openoasis.org/index.php?option=com_content&view=article&id=161&Itemid=354.

Raboin, Regina, Rebecca C. Reznik-Zellen, and Dorothea Salo. "Forging New Service Paths: Institutional Approaches to Providing Research Data Management Services." *Journal of eScience Librarianship* 1, no. 3 (2013): e1021. doi:10.7191/jeslib.2012.1021.

Ray, Joyce M., ed. *Research Data Management: Practical Strategies for Information Professionals*. West Lafayette, IN: Purdue University Press, 2014.

Rice, Robin. "On Being a Cog Rather Than Inventing the Wheel: Edinburgh DataShare as a Key Service in the University of Edinburgh's RDM Initiative." Workshop: Institutional Repositories Dealing with Research Data, hosted by the DCC, IASSIST, and COAR. Open Repositories conference, Charlottetown, Prince Edward Island, Canada, July 8, 2013. http://www.slideshare.net/edinadocumentationofficer/or2013-workshoprice-0.

Society of American Archivists. "Digital Archives Specialist (DAS) Curriculum and Certificate Program." Accessed March 14, 2016. http://www2.archivists.org/prof-education/das.

Stanford University Libraries. "Stanford Digital Repository." Accessed March 14, 2016. https://library.stanford.edu/research/stanford-digital-repository.

Starr, Joan, Perry Willett, Lisa Federer, Claudia Horning, and Mary Linn Bergstrom. "A Collaborative Framework for Data Management Services: The Experience of the University of California." *Journal of eScience Librarianship* 1, no. 2 (2012): e1014. http://escholarship.umassmed.edu/jeslib/vol1/iss2/7.

"SUNScholar/Practical Guidelines for Starting an Institutional Repository (IR)." Libopedia wiki. Accessed March 14, 2016. http://wiki.lib.sun.ac.za/index.php/SUNScholar/Practical_guidelines_for_starting_an_institutional_repository_(IR).

Swan, Alma. "The Business of Digital Repositories." In *A DRIVER's Guide to European Repositories*. Edited by Kasja Weenink, Loe Waaijers, and Karen van Godtsenhoven, 14–26. Amsterdam: Amsterdam University Press, 2007.

University of Minnesota Libraries. "The Supporting Documentation for Implementing the Data Repository for the University of Minnesota (DRUM): A Business Model, Functional Requirements, and Metadata Schema." University of Minnesota Digital Conservancy, 2015. http://hdl.handle.net/11299/171761.

University of North Carolina. "DigCCurr Professional Institute: Curation Practices for the Digital Object Lifecycle." Accessed March 14, 2016. http://ils.unc.edu/digccurr/institute.html.

Wickham, Jackie. "Institutional Repositories: Staff and Skills Set." Draft RSP Document, 3rd ed. October 5, 2011. http://www.rsp.ac.uk/documents/Repository_Staff_and_Skills_Set_2011.pdf.

# Receive the Data

In the life cycle model of data curation, the receiving step looks deceptively simple: *poof*, data is received. However, in reality, facilitating positive interactions with data authors in the steps that precede data transfer is a critical step. Successful strategies for obtaining the data, along with appropriate user-generated metadata and documentation, are explored in this chapter, and several web-based data submission forms will give you examples of how other repositories are successful in the Receiving the Data Step.

## 1.1 Recruit Data for Your Curation Service

In order to receive data, you must advertise your service and recruit data for deposit from a data provider (which may or may not be the data author, or creator of the data). This requires a good understanding of your target audiences and their (sometimes divergent) needs. First, understand the potential drivers for why a researcher would want to seek out data curation services. There may already be requirements (institutional or disciplinary) in place for researchers to share their data; however, there will be other factors as well. Data providers will want to meet requirements, but they also will weigh other factors, such as the time involved, as they evaluate whether or not to use your service. As you develop your recruitment strategies, consider all the possible roles and needs that a potential data provider might have (see table 1.1). Focusing on the most pressing needs of data providers, rather than the ideals of the data repository, is key to a successful and targeted promotion for data recruitment.

||||||||||||||||||||||||||||||||||||||||||||||||||||||||||||||||||||||||||||||||||||||||||||||||||||||||||

> Chapter 2 in *Curating Research Data, Volume One*, "Institutional, Funder, and Journal Data Policies" by Kristin Briney, Abigail Goben, and Lisa Zilinski goes into further detail on the many requirements and motivational drivers for researchers to share their data."

||||||||||||||||||||||||||||||||||||||||||||||||||||||||||||||||||||||||||||||||||||||||||||||||||||||||||

**TABLE 1.1**
Roles and needs to consider when recruiting data.

| Role of Individual | Possible Data-Related Needs |
| --- | --- |
| Principal investigator for a federal grant | Meet requirements to share data publicly; get future grant funding; get published; time constraints |
| Assistant rank faculty member at an institution with a data-sharing policy | Meet sharing expectations of institution; get published; not to release data prior to publication; time constraints |
| Graduate student in a university | Collect and analyze data to support dissertation; not to release data without advisor approval; time constraints |
| Researcher at a private company | Meet company expectations for data nondisclosure; time constraints |
| Researcher in a discipline with a subject data repository | Meet peer expectations with sharing data in subject data repository; time constraints |

# Develop a Communications Plan

Another step toward recruitment for your data curation service is to develop a communications plan. Your communications plan should detail any primary and secondary audiences of your communications, document the messages (driven by their needs and motivations) that you want to deliver, and identify any channels of communication that may be available to reach these audiences.

*Primary audiences* are just that, the direct users of the service. They could be different types of data providers (e.g., researchers, lab technicians, students) that are grouped into categories based on their motivations or needs. For example, researchers at a university may have differing needs from researchers employed by private or corporate institutions. Principal investigators (PIs) will have data repository sharing requirements by their grant that post-docs and research staff may not be aware of.

*Secondary audiences* may require different strategies as these individuals and groups may not become direct users of your service, but rather point potential users to your service. For example, a university administrator may need to understand the value proposition of data curation services before recommending the service to a primary user (or approving any continued funding!). Secondary audiences might include instructors and training staff, staff in other related units, and external audiences such as repository staff at other institutions.

A data curation service communications plan might include

1. Goals of your communication plan (Include any in-scope and out-of-scope aspects.)

2. Target audiences (broken into primary and secondary audiences) with
   a. Messages customized for that audience.
   b. Communication vehicles that might effectively deliver your messages.
   c. Evaluation plans for each communication vehicle (e.g., How will you know they got the message?).
   d. Any foreseeable contingencies that may impact the receipt of your communication (e.g., Academic researchers are less likely to read their e-mail during winter break, etc.).
3. A time-line view of your marketing plans for the foreseeable future.
4. Blurbs or example communication messages that can be used as new opportunities arise.

Communication strategies should be continuously monitored and evaluated for success. For example, mass e-mail delivery tools, such as MailChimp (http://mailchimp.com), will track how often recipients open your e-mail, track the click rate for any embedded URLs, and help you determine if your subject lines, URL hypertext, and sent-from e-mail accounts are resonating with your audiences. Other communication vehicles provide immediate feedback, such as how many times your recruitment Tweet is retweeted after a posting. Build these feedback opportunities into your communications plan for ongoing evaluation.

# Communication Vehicles to Reach Your Target Audiences

Next, establish several mechanisms for your audiences, data authors, and providers to easily reach out to you and get more information about your service. Data curation services might be a new concept for some researchers, and they may have questions before they are willing to deposit. You might also track the number of new inquires to demonstrate interest in your service. Some simple and essential recruitment tools for a data curation service include

- A website clearly listing what your data curation service provides, associated fees, policies, and any limiting factors such as eligibility or collection scope of your repository
- An e-mail contact address that is checked often
- A contact form that collects information about a user's need (which may also perform double duty as a request tracking form for any phone, e-mail, or in-person contacts, as shown in figure 1.1)
- Social media presence (such as Twitter, Facebook, Tumblr, Instagram, etc.) to help get the word out

New or dedicated social media accounts for your data curation service may not be necessary if you can rely on institutional accounts for promotion. For example, the University of Minnesota Libraries has an active Facebook page (https://www.facebook.com/umnlib) that already has an established web presence. A targeted message promoting the data curation service will have a broader impact than creating a new account that may go unused over time.

**FIGURE 1.1**

A contact form for your data curation services also works double duty when staff use it as a tracking form to monitor and assess the impact of your recruitment techniques, like the one shown here for the data services at the University of Minnesota.

# Marketing Strategies for Your Repository

Promotion and recruitment of your service to data authors and providers is an ongoing activity. As your service matures, continue to promote your repository in new and targeted ways. For example, from the IR literature, the JISC-funded Supporting Repositories project presents four top-down and four bottom-up approaches to promoting repositories, and Gierveld proposes a four-pronged strategy for getting researchers to see the value in your service.[1] Some data-centric ideas include

- Publishing success stories of recent data curation submissions
- Partnering with past data authors as co-presenters and advocates for recruiting new data

- Seeking out research groups and labs that post their data to a project website and offer them a more stable approach
- Working with your grants administration office to periodically reach out to grant awardees throughout the life of the project
- Monitoring which researchers are publishing in a journal that requires data sharing and offer curation services for data related to their next publication

Each data repository will have its own recruitment opportunities and challenges. The key is to understand your audience and provide ways to measure and respond to their feedback. For more, see *Curating Research Data, Volume One*, chapter 9, "Current Outreach and Marketing Practices for Research Data Repositories," where Katherine J. Gerwig presents survey results of current data repository promotional activities in order to provide data repository managers with example outreach and marketing strategies that are used to promote the data repository.

# 1.2 Negotiate Deposit

Before receiving data from providers, it is important that both parties have a clear understanding of the terms of deposit. For data authors, this includes an understanding of what types of data will be accepted, how long the data will be retained, and under what conditions the data will be made available. Your data curation service terms can help data authors find the right "home" for their data.

The negotiation of deposit may happen as a literal conversation or asynchronously via a web guide. The goal is to provide potential depositors with clear information that defines the mission and scope of the collection, noting any grounds for refusal to accept data, and establishes how the data will be managed once accepted (e.g., a preservation policy, an end-user access policy). Another way to help potential depositors understand your service is to provide a checklist for preparing data for deposit. For example the University of Edinburgh and the Data Repository for the University of Minnesota (presented in figure 1.2) have guides to walk users through the upload submission process using targeted questions that can help address any concerns prior to deposit.[2]

### Is Your Data Right for DRUM?
☐ Does your dataset meet the requirement for submission to DRUM? - Authored by at least one University of Minnesota - Twin Cities researcher - Does NOT contain any private, confidential, or other legally protected information - Ready for public access and reuse?

☐ Is there a more appropriate data repository in your field?

### Data Preparation:
☐ Would it make sense to break your data into multiple submissions?

☐ Are your data files grouped in a meaningful way?

☐ Is your data labelled consistently (e.g., data headers, file naming, etc.)?

☐ Have you avoided using proprietary software wherever possible?

### Data Documentation:
☐ Do you have documentation for your data? If not, have you prepared a README file to describe the dataset?

☐ Are all acronyms/abbreviations spelled out in the documentation?

☐ Is your data collection methodology included in the documentation?

☐ Would someone else be able to understand your dataset using the documentation?

### Deposit Rights
☐ Do you have all the necessary copyright permissions to make the data available on DRUM?

☐ Have all collaborators, advisors, or other interested parties agreed on sharing publicly via DRUM?

☐ Are you aware of the rights you are granting DRUM by depositing your data?

### Sharing and Permissions:
☐ Do you have any specific data sharing requirements (e.g., from funding agencies)?

☐ Is the data anonymized to protect any personally identifiable information?

☐ Do you wish to manage access to your data (e.g., place an embargo)?

☐ Have you made note of any special software that would be required to access your data?

### Licensing
☐ Have you considered applying an open license to your dataset?

☐ What constraints, if any, would you like to add to the license (e.g., non-commercial use only, attribution required, etc.)?

## FIGURE 1.2
Checklist for preparing data for deposit in the Data Repository for the University of Minnesota. Download at https://www.lib.umn.edu/datamanagement/drum.

Sometimes is it important to ask appraisal questions prior to the data's arrival. For example, your data repository may not be the best fit for the data and consultation may provide an opportunity to direct the user to a more appropriate home. Questions that should be raised by data curation staff in the negotiation with researchers for data deposit can be reused in a pre-deposit interview protocol.

# Questions to Address in a Pre-Deposit Interview

1. General aspects of the data set
   a. How many files?
   b. Total size (in bytes) of the data set.
   c. File formats and software needed to open the files.
   d. Stage of data (e.g., raw, processed, etc.).
   e. Is there documentation available? Describe.
   f. Who owns the copyrights for this work?
   g. What metadata standards are commonly used in the data or the field in general?
2. Sharing concerns
   a. Who are the coauthors of the data?
   b. Who funded this research, and are there agency requirements for sharing?
   c. What are the institutional obligations for data release?
   d. Is there potentially patentable information, and what licenses, if any, would the data be released under?
   e. Are there sharing concerns, such as protecting the identity of human subjects?
   f. What are the goals for dissemination (e.g., world wide access, researcher-only access)?
   g. Are there existing repositories in the field that you find and download data from?
3. Long-term value
   a. Are there existing publications that make use of or cite the data?
   b. Will the data change or be added to over time? How often?
   c. Are there alternative file formats recommended for deposit? (e.g., the data curator may recommend a format for preservation purposes.)
   d. Is the data easy or difficult to reproduce and why?
   e. What is the reuse potential of this data?
   f. When, if ever, should the data be withdrawn or destroyed?

## Pre-Deposit Interview in Action

Qianjin Zhang and Sara Scheib present a case study on how academic librarians conducted in-depth interviews with faculty researchers to better understand their data management needs.

# A Case Study for Organizing and Documenting Research Data

*Qianjin (Marina) Zhang and Sara Scheib**

## PROJECT SUMMARY

The University of Iowa Libraries, like many other academic libraries, is dedicated to the development of research data services. From 2012 to 2014, we ran an environmental scan on campus data management resources that assessed research data needs and identified gaps in existing research data services.[3] Based on the outcomes of the environmental scan and assessment, we formed a working group to create a guide for researchers and campus service providers on data management resources in August 2014. To explore good practices in research data services and establish a long-term partnership with researchers, faculty, and students, two subject specialist librarians from the group started a case study for organizing and documenting research data.

In consideration of the researcher's specific data generation, collection, and analysis methods, we developed a data organization scheme based on the ISA-Tab metadata standard and applied it as the data was migrated to secure storage. As a result, the organized data is not only more accessible to the researcher, her students, and collaborators but also easily understood by newcomers to their laboratory.

## CHALLENGE AND PROBLEM

In this case study, we worked with a researcher in the field of chemical and biochemical engineering and her graduate students to help them organize and document their research data resulting from an NSF-funded project. We conducted

---

in-depth interviews to better understand their data management needs. The researcher's data was stored on a variety of digital media, including personal computers, laboratory computers, commercial cloud-based storage, removable flash drives, and hard drives. Recently, our university's information technology unit began providing access to secure storage via remote server access for researchers, faculty, and students. The researcher contacted us to help prepare their data for migration to the secure storage and therefore organize and document their data in the process. In preparation for the first interview, we asked to review a sample of their data and the data management plan as submitted to the NSF.

In November 2014, we conducted our first in-person interview with the researcher and her graduate students. This conversation helped us understand her research project and their data process throughout the data life cycle. The interview questions were based on a questionnaire from the 2014 University of Iowa Libraries' report on campus research data needs.[4] The results of our first interview suggested that they needed a data organization scheme and an appropriate metadata standard for their data.

# APPROACH AND SOLUTION

After the first interview, we analyzed how the researcher and her graduate students did research. Their research project included multiple small projects. Each small project employed several types of instruments and technologies. We investigated existing metadata standards listed on Digital Curation Centre (DCC) and found the ISA-Tab metadata standard. The ISA-Tab metadata standard stands for the Investigation/Study/Assay tab-delimited format metadata standard.[5] In this standard, the investigation, study, and assay are organized in a hierarchical structure. This structure fits well with their data flow: the investigation corresponded to their research project, the study corresponded to a small project, and the assay corresponded to an instrument or technology employed.

A few weeks later, we conducted a second interview with the researcher and her graduate students to ensure that the ISA-Tab metadata standard could be adapted to meet their data organization and documentation expectations. In consideration of their specific laboratory equipment, materials, and measurements, we selected particular elements from the ISA-Tab metadata standard, customized these elements, and developed a data organization scheme in a hierarchical outline format as well as a visual map format (see figure 1.3).

Over the next two months, the researcher and her graduate students created their folder structure (see appendix 1.0 A on page 45) and sorted their files based on the data organization scheme. We also recommended some best practices on file-naming conventions, file version control, and data documentation. We answered clarifying questions about the data organization scheme via e-mail.

After completing this process, the researcher and her graduate students gave us positive feedback that they were satisfied with the data organization scheme and best practices on data documentation. In future projects, it may be wise to conduct a final wrap-up meeting with all participants at the conclusion of the project to solicit more detailed feedback.

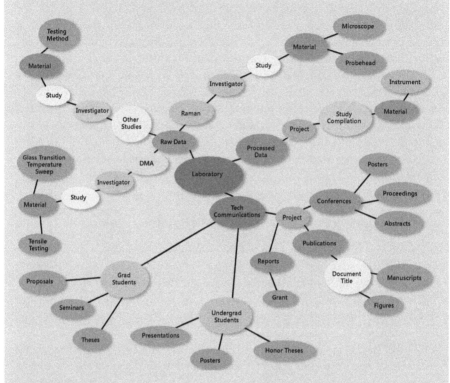

**FIGURE 1.3**
Data organization scheme.

# FUTURE WORK

We plan to share the data organization scheme and best practices on data documentation with other researchers in the same field and apply them to other fields. This case study can be used as an example to help researchers use best practices to manage their data throughout the data life cycle.

# 1.3 Transfer Rights and Deposit Agreements

A deposit agreement enables a repository to obtain the written permissions necessary to share or transfer the rights associated with a data set. A case study from ICPSR data curator Kaye Marz will illustrate some of the "Legal Agreements for Acquiring Restricted-Use Research Data" later in this section on page 24.

At its core, a deposit agreement states that *I, the depositor, own the rights to this content. I am sharing those rights with you, the repository, in order for you to do repository-like things.* Using more official language, the University of Minnesota's deposit agreement is displayed in figure 1.4.[6] The ICPSR's electronic deposit agreement states: "I give my permission to ICPSR to enhance, transform and/ or rearrange to the Data Collection, including the data and metadata, for any of the following purposes: Protect respondent confidentiality. Improve usability," and further defines the type of actions that the repository may take including

- To redisseminate copies of the Data Collection in a variety of media formats
- To promote and advertise the Data Collection in any publicity (in any form) for ICPSR
- To describe, catalog, validate and document the Data Collection
- To store, translate, copy or re-format the Data Collection in any way to ensure its future preservation and accessibility
- To incorporate metadata or documentation in the Data Collection into public access catalogues[7]

## *Addressing Legal Issues in Deposit Agreements*

In addition to rights transfer, there are a number of other legal issues that deposit agreements may also address; though this format may not the best place to clearly explain them, deposit agreements often do. For example, a deposit agreement might require the data provider to certify that they are following collection policies, such as not uploading legally protected information. For example, the Stanford Digital Repository Terms of Deposit includes several examples of protected information and restricted information in this statement:

> Depositor further warrants that the Work does not violate any law or agreement or infringe upon anyone's publicity, privacy or confidentiality rights, including but not limited to privacy

rights protected by HIPAA or FERPA. Depositor warrants that the Work does not contain any Restricted or Prohibited Data, such as Social Security Numbers, Driver's License Numbers or bank account information.[8]

A deposit agreement may go further to remove any potential liabilities should the content contain sensitive information. For example the data deposit form for the Odum Institute for Social Sciences Research includes the statement: "I further agree to release and hold harmless the Odum Institute and the University of North Carolina at Chapel Hill from any and all liability from claims arising out of any legal action concerning identification of research subjects, breaches of confidentiality, or invasion of privacy by or on behalf of said subjects. I also acknowledge that the Odum Institute is not liable for any loss of or damage to deposited data collections."[9]

Data ownership and copyright are often addressed in deposit agreements with little explanation and to confuse matters further, copyright laws may not provide clear ownership for non-creative works. In the article "Sharing Research Data and Intellectual Property Law: A Primer" American University law professor Michael W. Carroll describes some of the copyright fundamentals for sharing data.[10] For example, data deposit agreements typically ask the data provider to certify that they have the rights to transfer the content to the repository. This requires that the provider understand copyright law surrounding research data and the associated legal obligations of the sponsoring bodies related to the data's creation (e.g., any funder contracts, institutional ownership rights, etc.). This is not always the case, and a clear role for the data curator is to help donors understand the ownership considerations for their data. For example, a data author may not understand that any secondary data use may require the permission of the original creator to deposit any derivative of that data. To address this issue, the University of Minnesota's deposit agreement (see figure 1.4) includes the following language: "To the extent that any portions of the Content are not my own creation, they are used with the copyright holder's express permission or as permitted by law."[11]

---

By depositing this Content ("Content") in the University Digital Conservancy ("Digital Conservancy"), I agree that I am solely responsible for any consequences of uploading this Content to the Digital Conservancy and making it publicly available, and I represent and warrant that:

- I am **either** the sole creator and the owner of the copyrights and all other rights in the Content; **or**, without obtaining another's permission, I have the right to deposit the Content in an archive such as the Digital Conservancy.

To the extent that any portions of the Content are not my own creation, they are used with the copyright holder's express permission or as permitted by law. Additionally, the Content does not infringe the copyrights or other intellectual property rights of another, nor does the Content violate any laws or another's rights of privacy or publicity.

- The Content contains no restricted, private, confidential, or otherwise protected data or information that should not be publicly shared.

I understand that the Digital Conservancy will do its best to provide perpetual access to my Content. In order to support these efforts, I grant the Regents of the University of Minnesota ("University"), through its Digital Conservancy, the following non-exclusive, perpetual, royalty-free, world-wide rights and licenses:

- to access, reproduce, distribute and publicly display the Content, in whole or in part, in order to secure, preserve and make it publicly available, and

- to make derivative works based upon the Content in order to migrate the Content to other media or formats, or to preserve its public access.

These terms do not transfer ownership of the copyright(s) in the Content. These terms only grant to the University the limited license outlined above.

---

**FIGURE 1.4**
Example deposit agreement for the University of Minnesota's data repository housed in the University Digital Conservancy.

---

# Deposit Agreements in Action

A case study from Kaye Marz of the ICPSR illustrates how legal agreements for restricted-use research data can be put into action.

# Legal Agreements for Acquiring Restricted-Use Research Data

*Kaye Marz*[*]

The methods for sharing restricted-use data implemented by the Inter-university Consortium for Political and Social Research (ICPSR) were adapted to address changes in the research and technology environments over the last eighteen years. Described here are the secure infrastructure needed to handle such data, the legal agreement signed by depositor's institution to cover the transfer of data with human subject confidentiality concerns to the repository, and the associated legal agreement signed by the lead researcher and a representative of the researcher's institution to cover access to this data to the researcher through the repository.

## BACKGROUND

For thirty-five years, ICPSR at the University of Michigan (U-M) distributed only public-use files (PUFs), data sets for which the risk of disclosing confidential information about the research subjects is very small.[12] Almost all ICPSR data users were researchers at large universities that were consortium members of ICPSR and, prior to the Internet era, data was sent out on 9-track magnetic tape. In 1997, ICPSR initiated Web access to PUFs, allowing researchers at member institutions to download PUFs from anywhere in the world. Public access is also provided to PUFs from ICPSR's topical archives for which the supporting federal agencies and foundations cover the cost of access.

Concurrently, advancements in statistics and computing technology increased the amount and extent of data collected in the field. This large increase in the number of data items collected made creating public-use files difficult, and in some instances impossible, without severely reducing the analytic value of the data set. Such data sets need to retain most data items to be analytically useful, even if some items can indirectly pose confidentiality concerns.

## OBJECTIVE

In response, ICPSR designed a secure computing infrastructure and instituted

---

procedures to legally and ethically ingest and disseminate data sets that cannot be downloaded from the Web as public-use files (PUFs)[13] but need to be accessed as restricted-use files (RUFs) under controlled conditions.

## SECURE INFRASTRUCTURE

To ingest and disseminate RUFs, ICPSR modified its PUF-based infrastructure in these ways:

- Established connections to a legal advisor to set up base legal agreements designed to apply to the vast majority of institutional needs and to negotiate modification requests by depositing or receiving institutions if needed for their institutional or state requirements
- Created a secure computing environment, that is, encrypted connections for ingest through the online deposit form, processing of data sets on a virtual desktop created at login that is deleted when staff log off, transfer of content outside of the secure environment only through two audited gateways that require supervisor approval, storage of release versions of RUFs separate from release versions of PUFs to prevent accidental public exposure of the RUFs and to provide user access to RUFs via the Virtual Data Enclave
- Configured a physical data enclave for access to RUFs requiring extensive security protections
- Designed appropriate security plans for various methods of RUF access; all secure dissemination options require the researcher's computing system to prevent access or use of the RUFs by those not listed in the DUA (see table 1.2)
- Allocated funding to cover costs for ICPSR staff management of incoming, active, and terminated agreements for researcher access to RUFs
- Developed an online system for researchers to apply for data access and to be notified of events (e.g., access renewal or termination) and to store signed legal agreements and submitted application materials
- Developed resources for depositors to give to their institutional review boards about ICPSR's confidentiality policies, model informed consent language, informed consent services, and ICPSR's procedures for handling and sharing RUFs[14]
- Developed resources (e.g., webpages, PDF documents, video tutorials) to enable researchers to understand the legal and security requirements

Details are available on the ICPSR website in the Restricted Data section on the Find & Analyze Data webpage (http://www.icpsr.umich.edu/icpsrweb/content/ICPSR/access/restricted/index.html) and on the ICPSR's National Addiction & HIV Data Archive Program Website under the Deposit Data tab (http://www.icpsr.umich.edu/icpsrweb/content/NAHDAP/deposit/index.html).

## TABLE 1.2

Security plans for method of RUF access.

| Method of Access | Type of Security Plan | Definition of Security Plan |
|---|---|---|
| ***Secure Dissemination*** Researchers use RUFs in their own computing environment. Some ICPSR repositories do not offer the networked security plans. | Non-networked computer | RUFs are stored and analyzed on a stand-alone desktop computer, i.e., a computer in no way connected to another computer or networked device such as a switch or router. |
| | Private network | RUFs are stored and analyzed on a private network of two or more desktop computers and/or network devices (e.g., printer, switch, router) that are not connected in any way to the Internet or a LAN. |
| | Networked server | RUFs are stored on a file server connected to a network through which researchers access and analyze the data using their own computer. |
| | Networked personal computer | Researchers store and analyze RUFs on desktop computer(s) at their workplace that are connected to a network of two or more computers and/or network devices (e.g., printer, switch, router) connected to the Internet or a LAN. |
| ***Data Enclave*** Researchers use data in ICPSR's computing environment; any files researchers want to access outside the enclave are first vetted for disclosure by ICPSR staff or other designee and then sent to the researcher. | ICPSR Virtual Enclave | RUFs are stored on ICPSR's file servers, and researchers access and analyze the data using a virtual desktop computer. |
| | ICPSR Physical Enclave[a] | RUFs are stored on a non-networked desktop computer in the physical enclave in Ann Arbor, and researchers come in person to analyze the RUF. |

a. For an example, see the application for use of the ICPSR data enclave at http://www.icpsr.umich.edu/files/ICPSR/access/restricted/enclave.pdf.

Generally, the method of access is related to the level of risk of subject reidentification and potential for harm to the subject if information about him or her is disclosed. The ICPSR enclave options are for RUFs requiring more security, with the physical enclave in the most secure environment and used only under supervision of ICPSR staff. The method designated to an RUF may be determined by the funding agency or in discussion with the depositor.

## AGREEMENT TO TRANSFER RUF TO ICPSR

ICPSR and the U-M Office of Research and Sponsored Projects (ORSP) developed a Restricted-Use Data Deposit and Dissemination Agreement (RUDDDA), a bilateral legal agreement between U-M and the depositor's institution that covers the transfer, processing, and dissemination of the RUF.[15] No current legislation in the United States requires a RUDDDA be used. Depositing institutions have the option to execute a RUDDDA (or other material transfer form) to protect the data owners or data providers, ICPSR, and the University of Michigan.

Among others, the RUDDDA specifies these essential elements:
- Description of the RUF that covers current and future deposits
- Requirement that direct identifiers be removed by the depositor prior to deposit
- Resolution of the RUF's ownership
- Security for the RUF in ICPSR computing system
- What ICPSR can and cannot do with the RUF
- Period of the agreement
- Remedies if a breach of the RUDDDA occurs by U-M/ICPSR
- Options to depositors regarding data access (e.g., security plans allowed; student researchers, with or without sponsor; number of backup copies allowed; and access time frame)

## AGREEMENT TO ACCESS RUF FROM ICPSR

ICPSR and U-M ORSP also developed Restricted Data Use Agreements (RDUA) that legally addresses researcher access to RUFs.[16] Since the Secure Dissemination and Data Enclave access options involve different computing environments, separate RDUAs are used.[17] Most RDUAs are approved by U-M ORSP and are unilateral agreements signed by the lead researcher and an institutional representative (e.g., a dean or higher at a university or someone in the Office of Research or Contracts Office) able to sign binding legal agreements on behalf of the institution. ICPSR staff review and approve RUF access requests as an independent party. This avoids a perception of conflict of interest by the original researchers or funding agencies that could be asserted if either had been the approvers or disapprovers.

The RDUA includes these data-related components:

- Description of disclosure risk and disclosure risk remediation guidelines
- Requirements and qualifications of the lead researcher and institution
- ICPSR obligation to timely provide data, corresponding documentation, and user support
- Obligations of the researcher, research team, and institution
- Requirement that the RUF be used for statistical or research purposes only and that the RUF will not be merged with other data sets without prior approval
- Legal options if a violation occurs by anyone on the research team
- Publication restrictions
- Period of data access
- IRB document from researcher's institution approving or exempting described research
- Data Security Plan

## SUMMARY

The ingest and reuse of restricted-use data is possible, but doing so requires a more secure infrastructure than needed to share public-use data. A repository should develop a legal agreement to cover sharing of the RUF with other researchers (such as the RDUA presented here), and a legal agreement to ingest RUF data is recommended (such as the RUDDDA) if desired by the submitter's institution. These changes have cost implications in terms of additional security requirements and staff time to manage the legal agreements and the RUF request process. Although more complicated, the sharing and reuse of RUFs through the ICPSR offers a valuable service for the social science research community.

# 1.4 Facilitate Data Transfer

The acquisition of data may happen through a variety of mechanisms: for example, your institution may choose to receive data through digital repository software or, if institutional policy allows, the data may be transferred to third-party cloud-based storage (e.g., Dropbox or Google Drive). *Step 4*: Ingest and Store Data will go into more details on these types of mechanisms. Acquisition of sensitive data requires special handling and protocols.

Data will need to be transferred from the creator to the repository in a secure and reliable way (see table 1.3). Some data will be too large to transfer across the web, and the use of big data transfer software, like the Globus secure file sharing tool (https://www.globus.org) and Bagit, are emerging; yet the use of physical media (e.g., hard drives and flash drives) for data transfer is not uncommon.[18] Precautions may be taken, depending on the nature of the deposit, to isolate the files on a non-networked computer and run virus-checking software before opening any files that might compromise the local storage environment.

Additionally, you may use write-blocker software to read the files directly from the device without damaging the authenticity or structural metadata of the files (e.g., last opened date). Generally, however, forensic toolkits and computing environments, such as BitCurator, and tools that securely move files with writing over "last modified" dates, such as TeraCopy and Exactly, may be overly cumbersome for little gain in a data repository.[19]

## TABLE 1.3

Secure data transfer into a secure staging repository for further curation.

| Transfer Mechanism | Ideal | Acceptable (Real World) |
|---|---|---|
| Physical media device (e.g., flash drive, external hard drive) | Use write-blocker software to read the files directly from the device without damaging the authenticity or structural metadata of the files (e.g., last opened date). | Copy the files to a non-networked computer and run a virus check before opening on the local workstation. |
| Cloud-based transfer (e.g., Dropbox, Google Drive) | Do not use third-party storage. | Preview the files using the native viewer prior to download. |
| Secure FTP | Use a key-based encryption password system to enable protect access. | Only allow trustworthy donors to access your SFTP location. |
| File transfer software tools | Use tools that automatically capture the checksum of the digital file and verify that the file was perfectly moved to the new location. | Manually run checksums yourself, before and after migration. |
| Web-based submission form | | Ingest data into a staging repository that is not publically web-accessible until after curatorial review. |

Authentication is anther important factor for data transfer in data archives and will help to track the provenance of the data handoff. Questions such as: who is uploading the data and when can be captured systematically using a web-based submission tool and a credential logging system. For example, a password-protected submission interface will verify credentials of the person who is submitting the data.

# 1.5 Obtain Available Metadata and Documentation

Descriptive and structural metadata about the data set can be collected at the point of data transfer. This metadata, often generated by the data author via a submission form, will facilitate later curation steps. Here are two case studies that provide different approaches for acquiring metadata in a data curation service.

# Strategies for Acquiring Metadata That Facilitates Sharing and Long-Term Reuse of Research Data

*Ho Jung S. Yoo, Juliane Schneider, and Arwen Hutt**

This case study illustrates tools and processes used by curators to acquire rich metadata from researchers depositing data into the University of California San Diego (UC San Diego) Library Digital Collections (DC) repository. Our overarching goal is to enable discovery and maximize reuse of research data generated on campus. This repository is capable of handling complex digital objects, and data deposit is mediated completely by curators; that is, there is no self-deposit functionality. The actors in our example include the data provider, the DC project manager, and the DC metadata specialist. For this case study, we assume that the data has already been collected and finalized by the data provider and is ready for deposit.

# SETTING THE STAGE FOR A PRODUCTIVE INITIAL CONSULTATION

A data curation project is initiated when a data provider either submits a consultation request form (http://lib.ucsd.edu/rdcp-consult-request) through the Research Data Curation Program (RDCP) website (http://libraries.ucsd.edu/services/data-curation), expresses interest at one of our outreach events, or sends an e-mail to our program's group address. If initial contact occurs via e-mail or in person, data providers are encouraged to fill out the consultation request form. This form requests basic information about data ownership and the scope and content of the dataset (appendix 1.0 B on page 46). Questions on the form also prompt the data provider to consider the potential audience that may reuse the data. Once we receive the form, the next step is to schedule an in-person consultation. Here, we typically request that the data provider bring a snapshot of their folder structure or a sample of their files to the first meeting in order to expedite concrete discussions.

# INFORMATION EXCHANGE AT THE TABLE

At the initial consultation, the data provider, project manager, and metadata specialist discuss the current organization of the data files, potential ways in which the data can be reorganized for access through the repository, any external dependencies such as software and scripts that need to be described or included, access requirements, and the copyright status of the files. If the data is in a structured format or a database, a data dictionary or codebook is requested. We ascertain the amount and format of existing metadata, if any, that is available. We accept submission of file-level metadata in text, spreadsheet, or markup language format to make documentation and metadata creation as easy as possible for researchers. We also provide a link to our collection description form, a web form by which data providers can submit collection-level metadata such as description, attributions, and keywords (appendix 1.0 C on page 47).

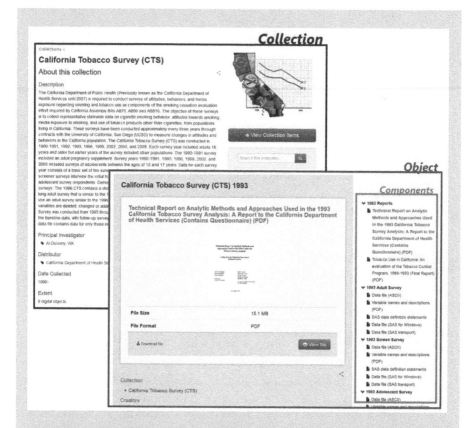

**FIGURE 1.5**

Hierarchical organization of collection, object (equivalent to "Collection Item" in the UI), and components in the UC San Diego Library Digital Collections.

During the consultation, a clear explanation of our repository's collection structure is critical. The DC is structured as a hierarchy of nested digital entities, which we refer to, in descending order, as collections, objects (referred to as "Collection Items" in the UI), components, and sub-components (figure 1.5). This hierarchical organization allows us to bundle the various files and documents such that the data is logically grouped, the intended context of the research is conveyed, and the downloadable files are packaged with the end user in mind. This structure frees us from the limitations of presenting collections as a flat list of data files, but does require curators to clearly establish a common vocabulary (e.g., landing page, collection, object-level metadata, component tree) with data providers. After a common understanding of the basic collection structure is established, we collaboratively discuss specific potential configurations of the provider's data within the DC. Aside from a core set of critical terms, we avoid using library-specific terminology as much as possible.

# READY, GET SET, INGEST!

After the consultation, a summary e-mail is sent to RDCP staff requesting informal review and approval of the project through "lazy consensus" (implicit assent if no explicit objections or issues are raised). If there are no concerns regarding appropriateness of the data for the DC or scoping of the workload for our team, we contact the provider via e-mail to initiate data deposit to the library. Since curation does not begin in earnest until we have the data in hand, it's important to maintain momentum after the initial consultation by facilitating early data transfer from the provider. Once all of the data and metadata have been received (DC data transfer tools are described in detail in the section on *Step 4* in our case study on ingest on page 147), the metadata specialist will populate the metadata template we built using Microsoft Excel. The template includes all available structural and descriptive metadata fields, helper text, validation on controlled values, and example values (*Step 4*, fig 4.2). The spreadsheet is customized for each particular collection by the metadata specialist and reviewed by the project manager.

Next, the metadata specialist creates a visual example of a digital object in the collection. A subset of the data is ingested into our DC test environment and screenshots of the UI are captured. The visuals are sent to the data provider with a list of follow-up questions or requests for additional information. The visuals also allow all parties to more easily detect gaps in the descriptive metadata and therefore minimize metadata or organizational issues before ingest. If needed, a second meeting is held to finalize the collection structure and the metadata. After the project manager and metadata specialist have determined that the collection is ready for ingest, the data provider is notified, and ingest of the collection begins.

# CONCLUDING REMARKS

Our lesson learned: use tools to collect standard metadata and conversation for everything else. The web-based forms and spreadsheet template that we have developed to acquire and wrangle metadata are based on standard information found across disciplines and collections. Nevertheless, face-to-face conversation and sometimes detailed e-mails remain crucial for eliciting useful metadata and external documentation that maximize reusability of research data collections. The relationships built during these conversations are invaluable to the quality of the collection and increase the likelihood of word-of-mouth promotion of our curation service, thus building bridges on campus between researchers and the library.

# Challenges with Quality of Data Set Metadata in a Self-Submission Repository Model

*Amy Koshoffer, Carolyn Hansen, and Linda Newman*[*]

This use case will examine the challenges in acquiring quality metadata for the submission type *Data Set* in a self-submission institutional repository model and how the University of Cincinnati Libraries is responding to these challenges with modifications to the submission process and user education. Here we describe an effort to reduce barriers to data set submission by improving the repository's submission interface so that required and optional metadata fields provide adequate descriptive metadata for data set discoverability and reuse.

## INTRODUCTION

As journals and funding agencies increasingly require authors to make the data behind their publications available through archiving and sharing, the creation of high-quality metadata will be essential in order to maximize the discoverability and reuse of archived data sets for future researchers. Data sets present unique challenges for description, especially within the context of a general purpose institutional repository that archives diverse work types. Data sets can be structurally complex because data sets may vary in file type or number of files. For example data can be in a single table formatted as a spreadsheet or can be many files functioning together as a unit. A text or photograph may be self-explanatory, but the meaning of raw data, as well as the relationships between files in a data set, is more difficult to decipher without adequate descriptive metadata provided by the repository submitter. A self-submission repository model places the responsibility on the submitter to provide structured and unstructured descriptive metadata as well as contextual information that make the data set discoverable in the repository and comprehensible by other researchers.

Structured descriptive metadata for a data set can be generated through a submission form that guides the submitter through the process of metadata generation. Data set metadata, such as readme files containing protocols, data dictionaries, and explanations of file relationships, are equally important. However, the lack of uniform structure or standards for these documents may make the metadata difficult to collect through a structured mechanism such as a submission form. Researchers could formulate standard formats for machine-readable research reports, but individual researcher practices and local research group policies may generate variability in these documents.

# THE UNIVERSITY OF CINCINNATI SELF-SUBMISSION REPOSITORY MODEL

The University of Cincinnati (UC) Libraries and University of Cincinnati Information Technology unit (IT@UC) collaborate on the continued development of UC's institutional repository, Scholar@UC (https://scholar.uc.edu). The repository application is built on the Project Hydra framework (http://projecthydra. org), which utilizes Fedora Commons (http://www.fedora-commons.org) as the underlying repository. Project Hydra is a multi-institution collaboration to develop open-source repository solutions resulting in an "ecosystem of components" that allows partner institutions to customize their own repository solutions. Scholar@UC is a self-submission digital repository with the goal of preserving the scholarly output of UC researchers, such as preprints of articles, conference posters, images, and data sets. Scholar@UC went into production in September 2015, but software development and engagement with early adopters continues.

# UC RESEARCH COMMUNITY ENGAGEMENT

To set policies and guide repository implementation, UC Libraries and IT@UC formed the Digital Repository Task Force (DRTF). In order to engage the greater UC research community, the DRTF formed the Early Adopter Working Group, composed of library faculty and staff who served as subject liaisons or whose responsibilities involved research data support, to recruit researchers as early adopters. Early adopters were research and teaching faculty who agreed to submit content (including data sets), provide feedback, and suggest additional functionality before the repository was open to all potential submitters campus-wide. The goal of early adopter sessions was to test more than just usability; it was to discover what researchers wanted and needed from a repository. Members of the Early Adopter Working Group selected early adopters based on discipline, types of digital content, and availability to collaborate with the working group.

# EARLY ADOPTER FEEDBACK SESSIONS

As part of the pre-rollout development process, Early Adopter Working Group members engaged these early adopting research and teaching faculty in face-to-face sessions to obtain feedback on the usability of the system and to communicate what additional functionality was needed to describe and archive their scholarly output. Members of the Early Adopter Working Group documented the early adopters' comments as they contributed content such as data sets to Scholar@UC. When submitting content, the repository interface prompted early adopters to select a work type, upload their content, contribute metadata, select a license, request a DOI (digital object identifier), and set the level of access for their content. After submission, working group members asked early adopters to search for their content and browsed other contributed content. Scholar@UC currently supports the following work types: *Article, Image, Dataset, Document, Video* and *Generic Work*.

The first decision a submitter makes is which work type to select. We learned during these feedback sessions that this decision was not always intuitive, and that our assumptions about what constitutes a data set were challenged. Our work types are based on the function of a resource's content, as opposed to its physical or digital format. For example, the *Image* work type is designed for use with visual content such as art and has different descriptive focus than the *Dataset* work type, for which the content is viewed as research data. Our helper text on the work type selection page for *Image* is "Visual content: art, photographs, posters, graphics" and for *Dataset* is "Files containing collections of data, including: raw data, spreadsheets, logs, etc." In this case, a researcher has a choice to submit scanned index cards representing data as either an *Image* or as a *Dataset.* The submission process is designed to respect the researcher's decision, and example data sets where the data is represented within images exist in our repository.

By selecting a work type, the submitter prompts the system to populate the submission form with premapped metadata elements for that particular work type (appendix 1.0 D). For data sets, this included metadata fields to identify software that may be needed to view or open the data set as well as specifics about the format of the data set. Provided file format advice encouraged use of open over proprietary formats, and per our Terms of Use (TOU) agreement, library staff could create open formats at a later date. In the first version of Scholar@UC tested by early adopters, if a submitter chose the *Dataset* work type, every possible premapped metadata field for the *Dataset* work type would appear in the submission form, regardless of whether the field's input was required or optional. As a result, the submission form contained up to twenty-five metadata fields, which submitters found excessive and confusing. Submitters also found it difficult to tell if a field was required or optional; then failure to complete required fields prevented the submitter from finishing the submission.

# METADATA CHALLENGES

Librarians and developers attending feedback sessions documented early adopters' comments and identified many metadata issues. Early adopters did not routinely supply extensive metadata when submitting a data set to the repository. In some cases, these researchers thought that sufficient descriptive information was contained within basic, required repository metadata fields or summary findings published in a journal unaccompanied by supporting data.[20] Many early adopters did not consider how the quality of metadata impacted data set discoverability and reusability while others found the input forms unclear, thereby preventing the submission of quality metadata.[21]

Early adopters commented that some metadata elements were unclear to them or that they were unsure what information was needed. For example, some early adopters interpreted the metadata field *Title* as an individual's academic title, not the work's title (early adopter comment in feedback session). Other early adopters entered metadata that was irrelevant or useless such as "p.txt" for a data set title, while others left optional fields blank because they did not want to complete so many fields. We were not clear if this misunderstanding suggests that data sets are usually only given descriptions rather than specific titles. Some early adopters also had multiple files or related works and desired the functionality to reuse metadata from previous submissions to save time.

We used these feedback sessions to educate early adopters about data curation best practices and creating more complete metadata to improve the discoverability of their specific data set. However, we also learned what aspects of selection and metadata were unclear to our submitters and needed significant improvement in order to sustain the vision of a repository designed for faculty submitting data sets without librarian mediation.

# USE CASES

Based on early adopter comments, library faculty developed use cases to describe the metadata changes that research and teaching faculty desired. Use cases were recorded and are available at https://github.com/uclibs/scholar_use_cases/blob/master/submission/submission_use_cases.md. Additionally, the source code for the UC repository can be accessed at https://github.com/uclibs/scholar_uc, and significant changes to the interface are summarized in a change log at https://github.com/uclibs/scholar_uc/blob/develop/CHANGELOG.md.

# THE NEW SUBMISSION FORM

The new submission process presents submitters with a streamlined form (for a comparison see original form in figure 1.6). Researchers upload their data set first and then are prompted to complete only the core or required metadata elements (see figure 1.7). Submitters have the ability to show additional optional elements by clicking the Show Additional Description link (see figure 1.8). Metadata element descriptions and examples were added to the submission form to clarify the desired input. For example, to clarify the metadata desired for the field *Title*, the example text says "Enter the title of your dataset. If the Dataset doesn't have a title, please enter a brief descriptive label."

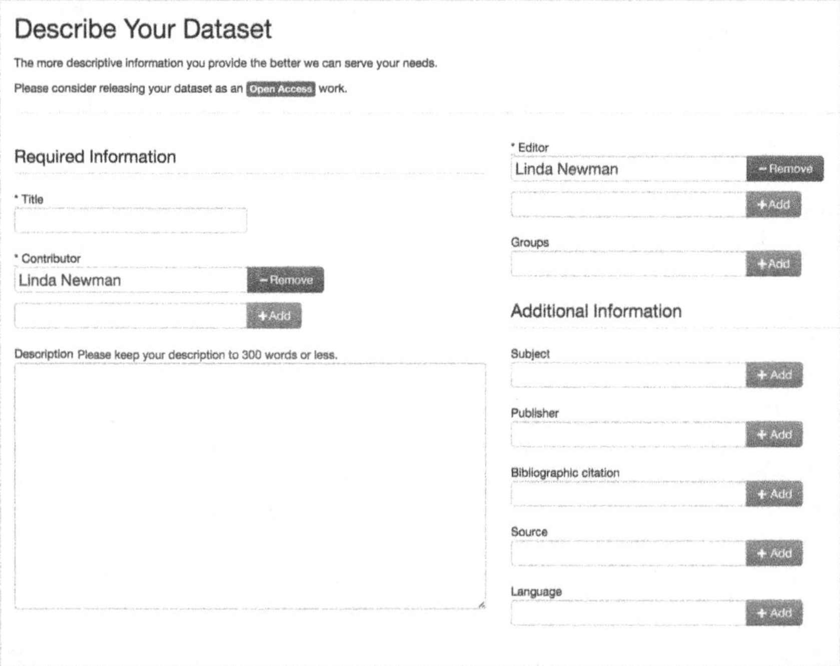

**FIGURE 1.6**
Our starting point with a "vanilla/generic" version of software inherited from other Hydra participants. Before we redesigned the form as shown in figures 1.7 and 1.8, we added fields for Required Software, Alternate Title, Geographic Subject, Time Period, Date Created, Note, and others, making this a very long form without any help information for metadata, and with permissions fields such as Editor Assignment intermixed with description.

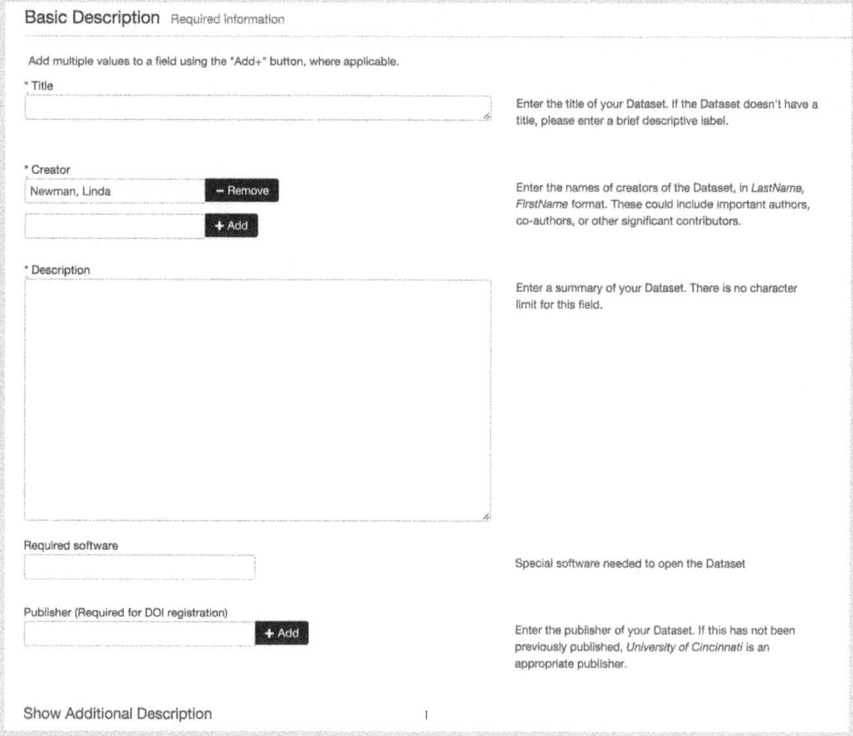

**Basic Description** Required information

Add multiple values to a field using the "Add+" button, where applicable.

* Title

Enter the title of your Dataset. If the Dataset doesn't have a title, please enter a brief descriptive label.

* Creator

Newman, Linda ‒ Remove

+ Add

Enter the names of creators of the Dataset, in *LastName, FirstName* format. These could include important authors, co-authors, or other significant contributors.

* Description

Enter a summary of your Dataset. There is no character limit for this field.

Required software

Special software needed to open the Dataset

Publisher (Required for DOI registration)

+ Add

Enter the publisher of your Dataset. If this has not been previously published, *University of Cincinnati* is an appropriate publisher.

Show Additional Description

**FIGURE 1.7**
Screenshot showing only the required metadata that must be completed to submit a data set to the repository, with brief help information next to each field on the right. Fields for file upload, Creative Commons licenses, access rights, DOIs, permissions such as editor and group assignment, and the depositor agreement have been moved to be distinct from the Basic Description.

The early adopters gave positive feedback about the new streamlined form. Now that we have achieved our initial rollout ("Scholar@UC 1.0"), developers are continuing to add functionality designed to encourage submitters to input sufficient metadata. This includes recommending the inclusion of unstructured metadata (attaching documentation such as readme files and data dictionaries). We are also investigating going beyond currently offered metrics from Google Analytics to provide submitters with metrics about accesses and downloads of their content and to include altmetrics-style data about citations. Our untested theory is that if submitters see evidence that metadata quality impacts their work's discoverability through social media outlets such as Twitter or projects like ORCID (http://orcid.org), through search engines such as Google, and avenues other than publisher-indexed databases, submitters would provide more descriptive metadata during submission. Future enhancements, such as a submission dashboard, will enable uploading groups of records with a common template for shared metadata. These ideas are based on suggestions by the use cases that focused more on submission than discovery, which is helpful at this stage in the repository development.

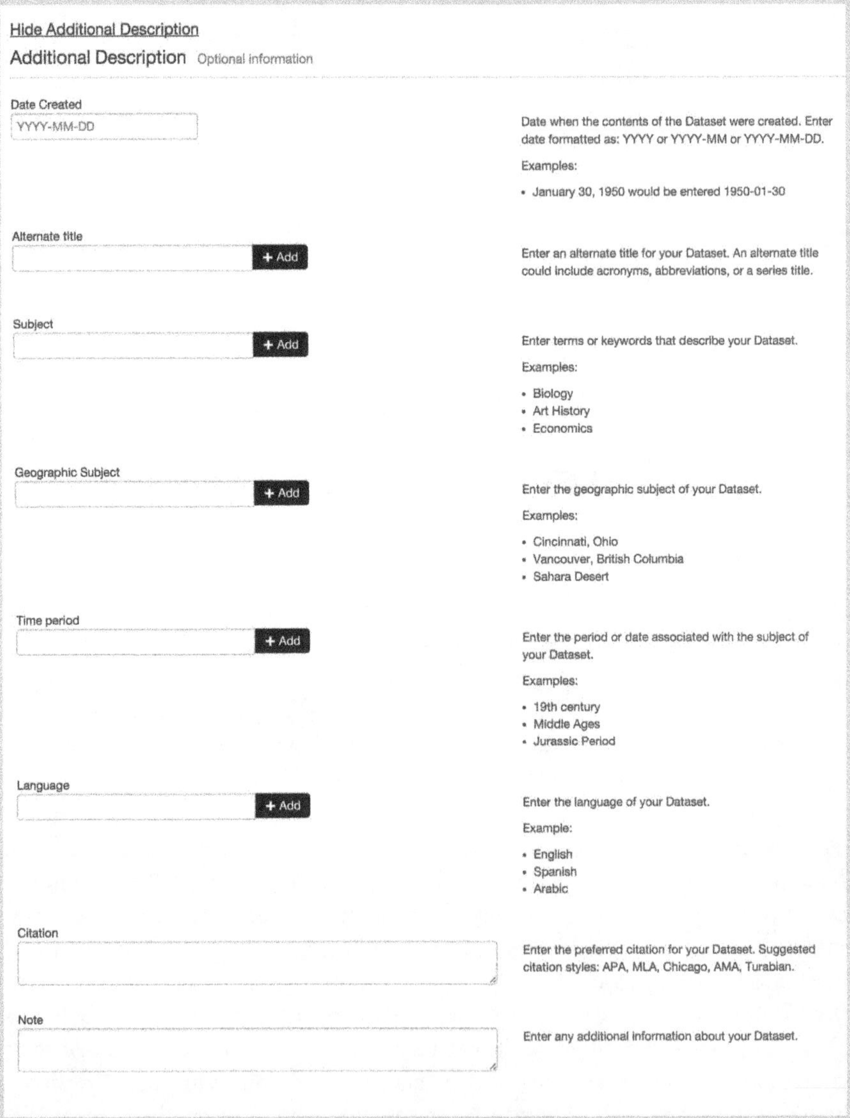

Hide Additional Description
**Additional Description**  Optional information

Date Created

YYYY-MM-DD

Date when the contents of the Dataset were created. Enter date formatted as: YYYY or YYYY-MM or YYYY-MM-DD.

Examples:

• January 30, 1950 would be entered 1950-01-30

Alternate title

+ Add

Enter an alternate title for your Dataset. An alternate title could include acronyms, abbreviations, or a series title.

Subject

+ Add

Enter terms or keywords that describe your Dataset.

Examples:

• Biology
• Art History
• Economics

Geographic Subject

+ Add

Enter the geographic subject of your Dataset.

Examples:

• Cincinnati, Ohio
• Vancouver, British Columbia
• Sahara Desert

Time period

+ Add

Enter the period or date associated with the subject of your Dataset.

Examples:

• 19th century
• Middle Ages
• Jurassic Period

Language

+ Add

Enter the language of your Dataset.

Example:

• English
• Spanish
• Arabic

Citation

Enter the preferred citation for your Dataset. Suggested citation styles: APA, MLA, Chicago, AMA, Turabian.

Note

Enter any additional information about your Dataset.

**FIGURE 1.8**
Screenshot showing Additional, Optional Metadata, with brief help information on the right.

# NEXT STEPS

Primary responsibility for inputting complete and accurate metadata resides with researchers now that the repository has been released to the UC community. What steps can the library take to ensure that submitters provide complete metadata? And for data sets in particular, how do we convey the importance of including documentation about research protocols and data dictionaries? How can the library help researchers understand the value of this description and documentation? UC Libraries is working hard to find a balance between what metadata a repository submitter will incorporate into their records and what support the library can feasibly provide. For example, the nonexclusive distribution license that users must agree to when submitting content to Scholar@UC states that UC Libraries reserves the right to preserve, transform, or enhance metadata. However, the goal is to respect the autonomy of the content submitter and the metadata created.

UC Libraries faculty and staff will continue to educate repository users on the value of metadata, especially as it is related to increasing citations to their data.[22] This involves educating researchers about the process of data curation and archiving data in the repository and the impact of metadata on data dissemination and discovery. Education can take the form of workshops on data curation and preservation, particularly using Scholar@UC, and providing best practices for both structured descriptive metadata and unstructured metadata for reuse such as a readme file with file relationship explanation, file-naming conventions, protocols, variable explanations, and researcher contact information. Since researchers may not submit data documentation in structured format, encouraging the use of templates for protocols and data formats could also aid in discovery and reuse. In the data management workshops we offer, we teach the principle of file-naming conventions. We suggest researchers implement a convention that explains relationship between associated files where titles would be assigned to projects and experiments and by extension to the data set that would be generated by the projects and experiments. Education opportunities can include stand-alone educational tools, one-on-one consultations, and partnering with research group principal investigators. Consultations during our early adopter sessions suggest that we can persuade researchers that quality metadata is the conduit to discovery of their content by demonstrating how a data set submitted to the repository with extensive and complete metadata could result in increased data citations and data reuse.[23] We also learned from these sessions that we would get poor or no metadata without a simpler and self-explanatory input interface. By both streamlining the submission process and educating our researchers on the need for complete and quality metadata, we will provide a better service that is easy to use and benefits researchers in the long run.

Commuting Data for Hamilton County, 2010   (Dataset)

Attributes

| Attribute Name | Values |
| --- | --- |
| Description | This data includes socio-economic-geographic attributes in Hamilton County by Census tracts of year 2010. |
| Creator(s) | Kim, Changjoo |
| Date Created | 2015-02-02 |
| Geographic Subject | Cincinnati, OH<br>Hamilton County, OH |
| Time Period | 2010 |
| Software Requirements | SPSS |
| Language | English |
| Subject | Commuting, Transportation |
| Publisher | University of Cincinnati |
| Note | If you need extended area or time, please contact Changjoo Kim. |
| Access Rights | Open Access |
| Content License | CC0 1.0 Universal |

**FIGURE 1.9**
Example of metadata generated by system for submitter content.

# 1.6 Receive Notification of Data Arrival

Repository staff should get an alert once the data has arrived at the repository. This can be in the form of an alert or notification of new objects in the submission staging area. Note that if one staff member is in charge of receiving these notifications that there are mechanisms in place to forward alerts due to absence or other busy times. For example, use a general e-mail account that several staff members are able to log into or receive forwarded e-mails to maintain consistent service during busy or understaffed periods.

A notification should be also given to the data author that their data was received (see figure 1.10). This notification may happen automatically by the system. The submission tool may also indicate what stage the data submission is in to keep the author up-to-date on the data curation progress. The systems used by publishers for article submissions (ie. bePress software's editorial submission workflow) are a good example for monitoring how your submission is moving through the process: received and pending review, under review, accepted pending recommended changes, author changes, finalized for publication, and so on.

---

Subject: Your submission to the Data Repository for the University of Minnesota (DRUM) in the University Digital Conservancy

Dear <Submitter Name>,

Thank you for your submission. In a separate email you will receive an approval from the Digital Conservancy indicating that your data submission has been accepted for inclusion into the Data Repository for the U of M (DRUM).

**But, there is one more step before your submission can be completed:** A digital curator will review your data to enrich your submission for reuse and discoverability. Within two business days our curation staff may ask you for additional information about your data and notify you of any curation actions that we may take (e.g., adding additional description or transforming file formats). We will also provide your data with a DOI that can be used to cite your data in your scholarly work.

Please respond to the curator's questions and provide any additional information, so that we may finalize your submission to the Data Repository.

Sincerely,

Staff at the Data Repository for U of M (DRUM)

---

**FIGURE 1.10**
A pre-acceptance e-mail is sent to data submitters to explain the curation process before the DSpace-based repository accept/reject step is used.

---

# Summary of Step 1.0: Receive the Data

1.1 Recruit Data for Your Service: Potential submitters learn of your services through successful recruitment strategies and a robust communications plan that engages targeted audiences.

1.2 Negotiate Deposit: The repository and the submitter come to a clear understanding and agreement of the terms of deposit for data into the repository (e.g., policies and conditions for access and reuse are known and well communicated).

1.3 Obtain Author Deposit Agreement: A rights transfer agreement is signed by the data author (or authorized submitter), and any conditions involving legally protected or restricted use data are well understood.

1.4 Facilitate Transfer of the Data: The data files are transferred to the repository in a secure manner that protects the integrity and authenticity of the data.

1.5 Obtain Metadata and Documentation: The repository collects the author-generated metadata and supporting documentation necessary to use and understand the data. This information will be included in the curation process as part of the data submission.

1.6 Receive Notification of Data Arrival: The appropriate repository staff are alerted that a new data submission was received and is ready for curation.

# Appendix 1.0 A: Directory Structure Used in "A Case Study for Organizing and Documenting Research Data"

*Qianjin (Marina) Zhang and Sara Scheib*

```
1. Raw Data
   1.1   Raman
         1.1.1.   Investigator
                  1.1.1.1.   Study
                             1.1.1.1.1.   Materials
                                          1.1.1.1.1.1.   Microscope
                                          1.1.1.1.1.2.   Probehead
   1.2   DMA
         1.2.1   Investigator
                 1.2.1.1.   Study
                            1.2.1.1.1.   Materials
                                         1.2.1.1.1.1.   Glass transition temperature
                                                        sweep
                                         1.2.1.1.1.2    Tensile testing
   1.3   Other studies
         1.3.1   Investigator
                 1.3.1.1.   Study
                            1.3.1.1.1.   Materials
                                         1.3.1.1.1.1.   Testing method
2. Processed Data
   2.1.  Project (funding agency or grant)
         2.1.1.   Study compilations
                  2.1.1.1.   Materials
                             2.1.1.1.1.   Instrument
3. Technical Communications
   3.1   Project
         3.1.1.   Conferences
                  3.1.1.1.   Posters (by date, conference acronym)
                  3.1.1.2.   Proceedings (by date, conference acronym)
                  3.1.1.3.   Abstracts (by date, conference acronym)
         3.1.2.   Publications
                  3.1.2.1.   Document Title
                             3.1.2.1.1.   Manuscripts
                             3.1.2.1.2.   Figures (Excel & JPG)
         3.1.3.   Reports (by date, funding agency acronym)
                  3.1.3.1.   Grant (include date in file name)
   3.2.  Graduate Students
         3.2.1.   Proposals
         3.2.2.   Seminar
         3.2.3.   Theses
   3.3.  Undergraduate Students
         3.3.1.   Posters
         3.3.2.   Presentations
         3.3.3.   Honors Theses
```

# Appendix 1.0 B: Sampling of Information Requested in the Consultation Request Form from "Strategies for Acquiring Metadata That Facilitates Sharing and Long-Term Reuse of Research Data"

*Ho Jung S. Yoo, Juliane Schneider, and Arwen Hutt*

- Name
- Contact information
- Working project title
- Brief abstract (2–4 sentences describing the purpose and content of the data)
- Who is the potential audience for your data? (Check all that apply: Researchers within my discipline; Researchers outside of my discipline; College-level educators or students; Public; etc.)
- What are ways in which the audience might use your data? (Check all that apply: To ask new research questions; To verify results in publications; As a teaching or training aid; To develop research tools; etc.)
- Is the data already associated with any of the following contributions to your field or community? (Check all that apply: Publications; Awarded grants; Dissertation or thesis research; Museum collections or archives; Educational institutions; Policy development; Media coverage; etc.)
- Does sharing of this data comply with an existing mandate from its funding agency, institution, or publisher?
- Approximately how many files are in your collection?
- Describe the types (e.g., spreadsheets, images) and formats (e.g., .csv, .tif) of your files.
- What is the maximum disk space required to store the data?
- If you have a data collection that you anticipate will grow after the initial ingest, please estimate its growth.
- Did you create or compile all of the data you plan to submit?
- Do you have permission to share the data that was not created by you?
- Does the data involve human subjects or contain other sensitive information?
- If yes, how will the data be anonymized prior to submission?

# Appendix 1.0 C: Sampling of Metadata Requested in the Collection Description Form from "Strategies for Acquiring Metadata That Facilitates Sharing and Long-Term Reuse of Research Data"

*Ho Jung S. Yoo, Juliane Schneider, and Arwen Hutt*

- Collection title
- Personnel names, identifiers, and roles (Roles has a drop-down menu with controlled vocabulary.)
- Range of dates over which the data was generated, collected, or compiled
- Keywords/topics
- Full collection description (links to two examples provided)
- Brief collection description (255 characters maximum)
- Identifiers: Do you already have identifiers for your data? Do you want DOIs to be assigned to each object?
- Related resources (funding sources, external links, associated publications)
- Licensing preferences (Creative Commons Attribution, CC BY, is encouraged, but alternatives can be discussed.)
- Embargo period
- Takedown date requested, if any

# Appendix 1.0 D: Descriptive Metadata for a Data Set Using Resource Description Framework (RDF) from "Challenges with Quality of Data Set Metadata in a Self-Submission Repository Model"

*Amy Koshoffer, Carolyn Hansen, and Linda Newman*

The model and standards at UC allow us to assign namespaces from different metadata standards for different types of work. For example, our *Image* work type includes some metadata elements with a Dublin Core namespace and some with a Visual Resource Association (VRA) namespace.[24] For the *Dataset* work type, however, all elements are from Dublin Core.

The Friend of a friend (FOAF) namespace is used for information about a submitter that is stored in their user profile.[25] In Scholar@UC, the only required metadata fields on the *Dataset* work type input form are Title, Creator, Description and Rights (Creative Commons Content License, [http://creativecommons. org] on the submission form. The Content License defaults to "All rights reserved.") The system will supply the name of the submitter as the Creator, but the submitter can remove their name and insert another creator name if applicable. In addition, the system supplies two date fields, dateSubmitted and Modified. When the submitter selects the Dataset input form, the system supplies the type field value as Dataset. The list below shows all metadata field content that could be generated in the submission process for an example data set.

The example below is descriptive metadata based on the record available at https://scholar.uc.edu/show/dr26xx804 and shown in figure 1.9.

```
<info:fedora/sufia:dr26xx804> <http://purl.org/dc/terms/type>
"Dataset" .

<info:fedora/sufia:dr26xx804> <http://purl.org/dc/terms/date-
Submitted>   "2015-08-05Z"^^<http://www.w3.org/2001/XMLSchema#-
date> .

<info:fedora/sufia:dr26xx804>   <http://purl.org/dc/terms/ti-
tle> "Commuting Data for Hamilton County, 2010" .

<info:fedora/sufia:dr26xx804>   <http://purl.org/dc/terms/cre-
ator> " Kim, Changjoo" .
```

```
    <info:fedora/sufia:dr26xx804>      <http://purl.org/dc/terms/de-
scription>  "This data includes socio-economic-geographic attri-
butes in Hamilton County by Census tracts of year 2010." .

    <info:fedora/sufia:dr26xx804> <http://purl.org/dc/terms/iden-
tifier>  "doi:10.7945/C29G68" .

    <info:fedora/sufia:dr26xx804>  <http://purl.org/dc/terms/re-
quires>  "SPSS" .

    <info:fedora/sufia:dr26xx804>  <http://purl.org/dc/terms/pub-
lisher>  "University of Cincinnati" .

    <info:fedora/sufia:dr26xx804>        <http://purl.org/dc/terms/
date#created>  "2015-02-02" .

    <info:fedora/sufia:dr26xx804>       <http://purl.org/dc/terms/ti-
tle#alternate>  "Commuting Data" .

    <info:fedora/sufia:dr26xx804>  <http://purl.org/dc/terms/sub-
ject>  "Commuting" .

    <info:fedora/sufia:dr26xx804>  <http://purl.org/dc/terms/sub-
ject>  "Transportation" .

    <info:fedora/sufia:dr26xx804>  <http://purl.org/dc/terms/cov-
erage#spatial>  "Cincinnati, OH" .

    <info:fedora/sufia:dr26xx804>  <http://purl.org/dc/terms/cov-
erage#spatial>  "Hamilton County, OH" .

    <info:fedora/sufia:dr26xx804>  <http://purl.org/dc/terms/cov-
erage#temporal>  "2010" .

    <info:fedora/sufia:dr26xx804>  <http://purl.org/dc/terms/lan-
guage>  "English" .

    <info:fedora/sufia:dr26xx804>  <http://purl.org/dc/terms/bib-
liographicCitation>  "Kim, C. (n.d.). Commuting Data for Hamilton
County, 2010 // Dataset [dr26xx804] // Scholar@UC. http://doi.
org/10.7945/C29G68".

    <info:fedora/sufia:dr26xx804>      <http://purl.org/dc/terms/de-
scription#note>  "If you need extended area or time, please con-
tact Changjoo Kim." .

    <info:fedora/sufia:dr26xx804>        <http://purl.org/dc/terms/
rights>  "CCO 1.0 Universal" .

    <info:fedora/sufia:dr26xx804>  <http://purl.org/dc/terms/mod-
ified>  "2015-08-05Z"^^<http://www.w3.org/2001/XMLSchema#date> .
```

# Notes

1.　Supporting Repositories Project, "Promotion of Repositories," 2011, http://www.rsp.
ac.uk/documents/briefing-papers/repoadmin-promotion.pdf; Heleen Gierveld, "Considering a Marketing and Communications Approach for an Institutional Repository,"
*Ariadne,* no. 49 (2006), http://www.ariadne.ac.uk/issue49/gierveld.

2.　University of Edinburgh, "Checklist for Deposit," accessed March 14, 2016, http://
www.ed.ac.uk/information-services/research-support/data-library/data-repository/
checklist; University of Minnesota Libraries, "Submission Checklist for DRUM,"
accessed August 6, 2016, https://www.lib.umn.edu/datamanagement/drum.

3.　Shawn Averkamp, Xiaomei Gu, and Ben Rogers, "Data Management at the University
of Iowa: A University Libraries Report on Campus Research Data Needs," annual report, February 28, 2014, University of Iowa Libraries Staff Publications. http://ir.uiowa.
edu/lib_pubs/153.

4.　Ibid.

5.　Philippe Rocca-Serra, Susanna-Assunta Sansone, and Marco Brandizi, "Specification
Documentation: Release Candidate 1, ISA-TAB 1.0," 2008, http://isatab.sourceforge.
net/docs/ISA-TAB_release-candidate-1_v1.0_24nov08.pdf.

6.　Adapted from the University of Minnesota's institutional repository: University of
Minnesota Libraries Digital Conservancy, "Deposit License," in "DRUM Policies and
Terms of Use," accessed March 14, 2016, https://conservancy.umn.edu/pages/drum/
policies/#deposit-license.

7.　See an example of a data deposit form from ICPSR: Inter-university Consortium for
Political and Social Research, "Data Deposit Form," accessed March 14, 2016, https://
www.icpsr.umich.edu/cgi-bin/ddf2?inbox=NAHDAP.

8.　Stanford University Libraries, "Stanford Digital Repository Terms of Deposit," accessed
January 10, 2016, http://www.stanford.edu/group/sdr/SDR-Terms-of-Deposit-v13.pdf.
More information about Stanford data security classifications is available at Stanford
University, "Data Classification, Access, Transmittal, and Storage," accessed March 14,
2016, https://uit.stanford.edu/security/dataclass.

9.　Odum Institute for Research in Social Science, "Data Deposit Form," accessed July 8,
2016, http://www.odum.unc.edu/content/pdf/OdumDepositForm.pdf.

10.　Michael W. Carroll, "Sharing Research Data and Intellectual Property Law: A Primer,"
*PLOS Biology* 13, no. 8 (2015): e1002235, http://journals.plos.org/plosbiology/article?id=10.1371/journal.pbio.1002235.

11.　University of Minnesota Libraries Digital Conservancy, "Deposit License" in "DRUM
Policies and Terms of Use," accessed July 8, 2016, http://conservancy.umn.edu/pages/
drum/policies/#deposit-license.

12.　Federal Committee on Statistical Methodology, *Statistical Policy Working Paper 22 (Second Version, 2005): Report on Statistical Disclosure Limitation Methodology* (Washington,
DC: Office of Management and Budget, 2005).

13.　See the case study "Considerations for Restricted-Use Research Data" on page 66.

14.　For examples, see National Addiction & HIV Data Archive Program (NAHDAP), "IRBs
and Data Sharing," accessed June 17, 2016, http://www.icpsr.umich.edu/files/NAHDAP/
irbs-data-sharing.pdf, and National Addiction & HIV Data Archive Program (NAHDAP),
*Restricted-Use Data Deposit and Dissemination Procedures,* October 2015, http://www.icpsr.
umich.edu/files/NAHDAP/NAHDAP-RestrictedDataProcedures_Revised_Oct2015.pdf.

15. A copy of a standard customizable RUDDDA is available upon request from the author. Contact ICPSR User Support at 734-647-2200. Depositors can elect to deposit RUFs using ICPSR's online deposit form with secure file upload and standard Deposit Agreement terms, as no legislation demands use of an agreement such as the RUDDDA. The RUDDDA, however, does more clearly protect the providers of the RUF and U-M/ICPSR.

16. See Alex Kanous and Elaine Brock, "Model Data Sharing Agreement," customizable model created as part of the Building Community Engagement for Open Access to Data project, George Alter, principal investigator, August 31, 2015, doi:10.3886/ModelDataSharingAgreement. For a list of legal documents that can be used, see Alex Kanous and Elaine Brock, "Contractual Limitations on Data Sharing," report prepared for ICPSR as part of the Building Community Engagement for Open Access to Data project, George Alter, principal investigator, March 31, 2015, doi:10.3886/Contractual-LimitationsDataSharing.

17. A RDUA for Secure Dissemination options is available at National Addiction & HIV Data Archive Program (NAHDAP), "Restricted Data Use Agreement for Confidential Data," sample, accessed June 17, 2016, http://www.icpsr.umich.edu/files/NAHDAP/GenericRDAAgreement.pdf. A RUDA for the Virtual Data Enclave is available at National Addiction and HIV Data Archive Program (NAHDAP), "Restricted Data Use Agreement for Use of Confidential Data through the ICPSR Virtual Data Enclave," sample, accessed June 17, 2016, http://www.icpsr.umich.edu/files/NAHDAP/NAH-DAPGenericVDERDUA.pdf.

18. Bagit was developed by the Library of Congress to transfer and validate complex packages of digital information. The open-source software is available for download at Library of Congress, "Bagit-java," Github, accessed March 14, 2016, https://github.com/LibraryOfCongress/bagit-java.git. Watch a comprehensive ten-part video series on the use of Bagit at State Archives of North Carolina, "BagIt Tutorials," YouTube playlist, accessed March 14, 2016, https://www.youtube.com/playlist?list=PL1763D-432BE25663D.

19. BitCurator was created by a team led by Christopher Lee from the University of North Carolina Chapel Hill and brings together a suite of open-source digital forensics tools for use by archivists into one computing environment. The open-source tools are available for download at BitCurator homepage, accessed March 14, 2016, http://www.bitcurator.net. TeraCopy creates checksums for digital files for the purposes of moving them from one location to another in a fast, secure fashion. The software is available for download at Code Sector, "TeraCopy for Microsoft Windows," accessed March 14, 2016, http://www.codesector.com/teracopy. Exactly transfers digital files from a sender to a recipient via FTP, network, or third-party service such as Dropbox and Google Drive. Exactly was developed by the AVPreserve and the Louie B. Nunn Center for Oral History at the University of Kentucky Libraries and utilizes the BagIt File Packaging Format (https://tools.ietf.org/html/draft-kunze-bagit-12, developed by the Library of Congress and the California Digital Library). According to its website, Exactly "allows the recipient to create customized metadata templates for the sender to fill out before submission. Exactly can send email notifications with transfer data and manifests when files have been delivered to the archive." (AVPreserve, "Exactly," accessed March 14, 2016, https://www.avpreserve.com/tools/exactly.)

20. Carol Tenopir, Suzie Allard, Kimberly Douglass, Arsev Umur Aydinoglu, Lei Wu, Eleanor Read, Maribeth Manoff, and Mike Frame, "Data Sharing by Scientists:

Practices and Perceptions," *PLOS ONE* 6, no. 6 (2011): e21101, doi:10.1371/journal. pone.0021101; Karen Hanson, Alisa Surkis, and Karen Yacobucci, "Data Sharing and Management Snafu in Three Short Acts," YouTube video, 4:40, posted by New York University Health Sciences Library, December 19, 2012, https://www.youtube.com/watch?v=N2zK3sAtr-4.

21. Aaron Griffiths, "The Publication of Research Data: Researcher Attitudes and Behaviour," *International Journal of Digital Curation* 4, no. 1 (2009): 46–56.
22. Heather A. Piwowar and Todd J. Vision, "Data Reuse and the Open Data Citation Advantage," *PeerJ* 1 (2013): e175, doi:10.7717/peerj.175.
23. Heather A. Piwowar, Roger S. Day, and Douglas B. Fridsma, "Sharing Detailed Research Data Is Associated with Increased Citation Rate," *PLOS ONE* 2, no. 3 (2007): e308, doi:10.1371/journal.pone.0000308.
24. Dublin Core Metadata Initiative 2013, accessed August 7, 2016, http://purl.org/dc/terms; Library of Congress, "VRA Core Schemas and Documentation," accessed November 11, 2015, http://www.loc.gov/standards/vracore/schemas.html.
25. Dan Brickley and Libby Miller, "FOAF Vocabulary Specification 0.99," accessed November 11, 2015, http://xmlns.com/foaf/spec.

# Bibliography

Averkamp, Shawn, Xiaomei Gu, and Ben Rogers. "Data Management at the University of Iowa: A University Libraries Report on Campus Research Data Needs." Annual Report. February 28, 2014. University of Iowa Libraries Staff Publications. http://ir.uiowa.edu/lib_pubs/153.

AVPreserve. "Exactly." Accessed March 14, 2016. https://www.avpreserve.com/tools/exactly.

BitCurator homepage. Accessed March 14, 2016. http://www.bitcurator.net.

Brickley, Dan, and Libby Miller. "FOAF Vocabulary Specification 0.99." Accessed November 11, 2015. http://xmlns.com/foaf/spec/.

Carroll, Michael W. "Sharing Research Data and Intellectual Property Law: A Primer." *PLOS Biology* 13, no. 8 (2015): e1002235. http://journals.plos.org/plosbiology/article?id=10.1371/journal.pbio.1002235.

Code Sector. "TeraCopy for Microsoft Windows." Accessed March 14, 2016. http://www.codesector.com/teracopy.

Dublin Core Metadata Initiative homepage. Association for Information Science and Technology. Accessed November 11, 2015. http://dublincore.org/.

Federal Committee on Statistical Methodology. *Statistical Policy Working Paper 22 (Second Version, 2005): Report on Statistical Disclosure Limitation Methodology.* Washington, DC: Office of Management and Budget, 2005.

Gierveld, Heleen. "Considering a Marketing and Communications Approach for an Institutional Repository." *Ariadne*, no. 49 (2006). http://www.ariadne.ac.uk/issue49/gierveld.

Globus homepage. Accessed March 14, 2016. https://www.globus.org.

Griffiths, Aaron. "The Publication of Research Data: Researcher Attitudes and Behaviour." *International Journal of Digital Curation* 4, no. 1 (2009): 46–56.

Hanson, Karen, Alisa Surkis, and Karen Yacobucci. "Data Sharing and Management Snafu in Three Short Acts." YouTube video, 4:40. Posted by New York University Health

Sciences Library, December 19, 2012. https://www.youtube.com/watch?v=N2zK3sA-tr-4.

Inter-university Consortium for Political and Social Research. "Data Deposit Form." Accessed March 14, 2016. https://www.icpsr.umich.edu/cgi-bin/ddf2?inbox=NAHDAP.

Kanous, Alex, and Elaine Brock. "Contractual Limitations on Data Sharing." Report prepared for ICPSR as part of the Building Community Engagement for Open Access to Data project. George Alter, principal investigator. March 31, 2015. doi:10.3886/ContractualLimitationsDataSharing.

———. "Model Data Sharing Agreement." Customizable model created as part of the Building Community Engagement for Open Access to Data project. George Alter, principal investigator. August 31, 2015. doi:10.3886/ModelDataSharingAgreement.

Library of Congress. "Bagit-java." Github. Accessed March 14, 2016. https://github.com/LibraryOfCongress/bagit-java.git.

———. "VRA Core Schemas and Documentation." Accessed November 11, 2015. http://www.loc.gov/standards/vracore/schemas.html.

MailChimp homepage. Accessed March 14, 2016. http://mailchimp.com.

National Addiction & HIV Data Archive Program (NAHDAP). "IRBs and Data Sharing." Accessed June 17, 2016. http://www.icpsr.umich.edu/files/NAHDAP/irbs-data-sharing.pdf.

———. *Restricted-Use Data Deposit and Dissemination Procedures*, October 2015. http://www.icpsr.umich.edu/files/NAHDAP/NAHDAP-RestrictedDataProcedures_Revised_Oct2015.pdf.

———. "Restricted Data Use Agreement for Confidential Data." Accessed June 17, 2016. http://www.icpsr.umich.edu/files/NAHDAP/GenericRDAAgreement.pdf.

———. "Restricted Data Use Agreement for Use of Confidential Data through the ICPSR Virtual Data Enclave." Accessed June 17, 2016. http://www.icpsr.umich.edu/files/NAHDAP/NAHDAPGenericVDERDUA.pdf.

Odum Institute for Research in Social Science. "Data Deposit Form." Accessed July 8, 2016. http://www.odum.unc.edu/content/pdf/OdumDepositForm.pdf.

Piwowar, Heather A., Roger S. Day, and Douglas B. Fridsma. "Sharing Detailed Research Data is Associated with Increased Citation Rate." *PLOS ONE* 2, no. 3 (2007): e308. doi:10.1371/journal.pone.0000308.

Piwowar, Heather A., and Todd J. Vision. "Data Reuse and the Open Data Citation Advantage." *PeerJ* 1 (2013): e175. doi:10.7717/peerj.175.

Rocca-Serra, Philippe, Susanna-Assunta Sansone, and Marco Brandizi. "Specification Documentation: Release Candidate 1, ISA-TAB 1.0." 2008. http://isatab.sourceforge.net/docs/ISA-TAB_release-candidate-1_v1.0_24nov08.pdf.

Stanford University. "Data Classification, Access, Transmittal, and Storage." Accessed March 14, 2016. https://uit.stanford.edu/security/dataclass.

Stanford University Libraries. "Stanford Digital Repository Terms of Deposit." Accessed January 10, 2016. http://www.stanford.edu/group/sdr/SDR-Terms-of-Deposit-v13.pdf.

State Archives of North Carolina. "BagIt Tutorials." YouTube playlist. Accessed March 14, 2016. https://www.youtube.com/playlist?list=PL1763D432BE25663D.

Supporting Repositories Project. "Promotion of Repositories." 2011. http://www.rsp.ac.uk/documents/briefing-papers/repoadmin-promotion.pdf.

Tenopir, Carol, Suzie Allard, Kimberly Douglass, Arsev Umur Aydinoglu, Lei Wu, Eleanor Read, Maribeth Manoff, and Mike Frame. "Data Sharing by Scientists: Practices and Perceptions." *PLOS ONE* 6, no. 6 (2011): e21101. doi:10.1371/journal. pone.0021101.

University of Edinburgh. "Checklist for Deposit." Accessed March 14, 2016. http://www. ed.ac.uk/information-services/research-support/data-library/data-repository/checklist.

University of Minnesota Libraries. "Submission Checklist for DRUM." Accessed August 6, 2016. https://www.lib.umn.edu/datamanagement/drum.

University of Minnesota Libraries Digital Conservancy. "Deposit License." In "DRUM Policies and Terms of Use." Accessed March 14, 2016. https://conservancy.umn.edu/ pages/drum/policies/#deposit-license.

University of Minnesota Libraries Facebook page. Accessed March 14, 2016. https://www. facebook.com/umnlib.

# Appraisal and Selection Techniques That Mitigate Risks Inherent to Data

After receiving the data submission, the next step in the data curation process is to appraise and select the materials that are appropriate for curation in your repository. In this step, data should be housed in a non-networked, isolated environment where checks can be made to ensure that the data does not contain any hazardous or potentially unacceptable materials, such as viruses, or sensitive information that requires specific storage or access environments not handled by the repository (e.g., data with HIPAA or FERPA restrictions). Techniques such as detecting sensitive information (e.g., social security numbers) and creating an inventory, or file manifest, will enable your repository to review and appraise the files before selecting the submission for further curation.

## 2.1 Appraisal

Although well-established in print-based archives, appraisal and selection techniques for digital files are less defined and the properties of digital files (e.g., their format, contents, and value) will vary greatly. Therefore it can be difficult to define clear appraisal guidelines for determining which data sets should be accepted, or selected, for your digital repository. Harvey explained that these differences for digital appraisal techniques versus the traditional are due to a number of factors, such as the technical limitations for preserving the digital files, the higher costs of stewarding digital content, the complex intellectual property issues with digital files, and the difficult decisions that must be made regarding which contextual aspects of the data to capture on ingest for future use to be possible.[1]

The issues of determining appropriateness may not be perfectly understood for all data types. Our role as data curators is to monitor use and keep in close contact with the community of users to understand and refine our appraisal policies going forward. Additionally, Harvey suggested that "Research datasets may be an excellent case where re-appraisal at defined intervals is particularly applicable. Most could be initially kept, then re-appraisal occurs at defined intervals to test the dataset against agreed-upon criteria to establish whether it still meets the conditions for applying resources to its long-term retention."[2]

||||||||||||||||||||||||||||||||||||||||||||||||||||||||||||||||||||||||||||||||||||||||||||||||||||||||||||||||||||||||||||||||||||

Andrea Ogier, Natsuko Nicholls, and Ryan Speer further explore the reappraisal process for data in *Curating Research Data, Volume One,* "Open Exit: Reaching the End of the Data Life Cycle."

||||||||||||||||||||||||||||||||||||||||||||||||||||||||||||||||||||||||||||||||||||||||||||||||||||||||||||||||||||||||||||||||||||

# Appraisal Questions to Consider

Appraising the files involves asking specific questions to determine if the data should be accepted into the repository. For example, Whyte and Wilson suggest the following five steps for deciding what data to keep:
- Consider the data's reuse potential. What purposes could the data serve?
- Identify data that must be kept do to legal or policy compliance.
- Identify which data should be kept because they have long-term value, are unique, may be too difficult/costly to replicate, and are of high quality.
- Weigh the costs of keeping the data versus not.
- Document your data appraisal process to reuse or refer back to when future decisions about this data arise.[3]

Reflecting on the information collected in the negotiation step (*Step 1.2*), consider the following questions and actions:
- Does the data meet your collection policies?
- Does the author has the necessary rights to deposit the data?
- Does the data contain any proprietary data or other copyrighted information not owned by the depositor?
- If the data contains human subjects data, request a copy the IRB-reviewed data-sharing agreement that all participants signed.
- Is there a more appropriate repository where this type of data might be deposited? If so, do we also accept a copy?

- Is this data set complete with all necessary documentation needed to understand the data (e.g., adequate documentation)?

Finally, if the data is deposited with restricted-use conditions, verify that any expectations for security or protection match your available services.

Based on these questions, additional actions may need to be taken. For example, you might ask the submitter for additional information or missing files; refer the data provider to another data repository (It might be useful to keep a list of related data repositories and contacts handy); or refer the data provider to other services in your organization, such as data deidentification or the technology commercialization (patents) office. Finally, rejection may be necessary if the submission does not meet your appraisal criteria (more on this in *Step 2.4:* Selection).

## Appraisal Criteria in Action

In the next case study John Faundeen from the US Geological Survey describes an appraisal process that uses a detailed questionnaire and sets the standard best practice for collection documentation used by the US National Archives and Records Administration and other US federal agencies.

# Scientific Records Appraisal Process: US Geological Survey Case Study

*John Faundeen*

In an archival context, *appraisal* is the process of determining whether records and other materials have permanent (archival) value.[4]

Determining the value of science records can be daunting and fraught with obstacles such as a lack of germane background information, knowledgeable and relevant staff willing to assign a future value, and organizational practices such as generally accepting all offers. Even technological advancements allowing more data to be retained at lower costs may work against conducting appraisals as some advocate to just *save everything*.[5]

The development of an appraisal process is foundational to a collecting repository and can be greatly aided by two key elements being present. An up-to-date mission statement is invaluable to an appraisal process by providing guidance to those conducting appraisals. Secondly, a well-written collection policy should clearly state what types of collections are desired and possibly what is not being considered (see USGS EROS Collection Policy at http://eros.usgs.gov/government/records/pl.php).

Even with those two policies in place, it can be difficult to put an appraisal policy into practice. Some practical justifications for proceeding include being able to assess conditions that may lead to preservation needs and improving overall collection management practices. Additionally, the practice of appraisal can help your organization determine if legacy records continue to align to your institution's mission. Such a process is also useful in justifying and documenting a negative response to potential donors.

In 2006, the US Geological Survey's (USGS) Earth Resources Observation and Science (EROS) Center implemented a formal appraisal process to address many of the justifications previously listed. Two concerns primarily drove us to develop the process. The first was to document the justification for collecting our current holdings and those offered, and the second was to create a meaningful way to respond to donors when their collections were not accepted. The appraisal process follows a how-to process through six main steps:

1. Form a review team.
2. Utilize a set of appraisal questions.
3. Engage stakeholders in the process.
4. Involve the day-to-day manager in the review.
5. Formulate a recommendation.
6. Obtain senior management approval.

Assembling an appraisal team is fairly straightforward. In our case, the archivist leads all appraisals while other members are engaged at relevant steps. The team always includes a scientist reviewer (a stakeholder), the day-to-day manager (who may expend resources toward preservation and access needs for collections), and possibly additional records management staff to research elements not documented sufficiently.

First, the archivist documents as much as possible on the collection being appraised. To capture this information, we created a records appraisal tool (an additional four questions if the collection contains analog film) to capture:

1. how a collection aligns to our mission statement and collection policy,
2. access and distribution characteristics,
3. why, where, and when the individual records were created,
4. the physical volume and media involved,
5. metadata availability, and
6. the expected costs to take on the collection.[6]

The documentation questions currently number forty-two and can be accessed online.[7] The US National Archives and Records Administration has repeatedly considered this documentation tool a best practice for US federal agencies.[8]

Next, we involve a stakeholder in the review process. At the EROS Center a scientist is provided the documentation and asked to review the collection. This reviewer must either have direct experience with the records under review or have worked with similar collections in the past. The scientist is free to comment on anything found in the question set document, but they must respond to the following three questions:

1.  **Is there another organization within the scientific community that might benefit from or have an interest in these records?** The answer to this question can be very informative to the appraisal process, as the scientist often knows institutions and repositories that may already possess the collection being reviewed. Contacting these sources can lead to USGS EROS not accepting an offer if other institutions are already in possession and are doing a good job of preserving and providing access to a collection.

2.  **What were the original scientific uses for these records?** With input from the scientist we can often better understand the context for the collection.

3.  **What may be future scientific uses of these records?** This question is the most subjective and causes the most difficulty for the scientist reviewer. It is understood that future use projections are theoretical and based on their own experience. However, the scientist is the best choice to provide these opinions based on their research community involvement.

With the question set documentation and the scientist responses in hand, we brief the day-to-day manager. Discussions focus on anticipated expenses to ingest, processing techniques, any necessary preservation work, and the state of the provided metadata. Based on this evidence, we develop a recommendation to either *Accept* or *Not Accept* a donor's offer. Alternatively, if the collection already exists in our archives, the recommendation would be to either *Retain* or *Dispose* of the collection.

From the briefing the archivist composes a recommendation for review by the EROS Center senior management. Following a two-week review period, the comments are assembled and delivered to the EROS Center Director, who makes the final decision and communicates that through a decision memorandum back to the senior management, the archivist, and the day-to-day manager.

The entire process is well documented; the question set, the scientist review, the recommendation memo to senior management, and the decision memo from the Center Director are retained to serve as justification for the decisions captured and as evidence for the process followed.

The USGS EROS Center is supported by taxpayer funds, and the appraisal process is one way for us to show accountability. Since 2006, over seventy collections have been appraised. Several collections have either been rejected from donors or disposed of from our archives based on the criteria established in the appraisal process. Disposing of collections begins an additional set of processes intended to find an institution willing and able to support the collection.

To summarize, the appraisal process described here helps to provide accountability for expenditures incurred for the ongoing preservation and access to science collections that meet the USGS EROS Center mission statement and collection policy. Refined over time, appraisals are now a required procedure for all collections offered to the center.

# 2.2 Risk Factors for Data Repositories

All repositories face certain risks when accepting content. Copyright violations, information too sensitive for unrestricted access, and personally identifiable information should be known and understood by the data curation staff prior to acceptance.[9] Particularly with data derived from human subjects, it will also be necessary to understand what level of disclosure risk the repository is willing to accept and how any data that poses such risks will be handled differently, once accepted.

*Copyright and Proprietary Data.* If the data includes information that is copyrighted by someone other than the submitter, there may be a risk for copyright violation. It is important to review the data and determine if the depositors have the necessary rights to deposit, and if not, the necessary permissions from the third-party.

*Sensitive Data.* Sensitive information, such as criminal or illegal behaviors like drug use, mental health information, sexual behaviors, and information about minors or other vulnerable populations may cause harm (legal or reputational) to the subjects if disclosed. Such data may or may not be legally protected. Additionally, information such as credit card numbers or passwords are too sensitive to share broadly and should be detected in the appraisal process. If accepted, these types of data will present an ongoing challenge for the repository for controlling and managing appropriate access, as two case studies will explore later in this chapter.

*Personally Identifiable Information (PII).* One of the challenges of accepting human subjects data is the risk that the data may identify an individual, either directly or indirectly. Additionally, the information in the data set may be legally protected (e.g., HIPAA regulated), which could lead to legal repercussions for you or bring harm to the individual if that information is released and linked to that individual's identity.

To look for disclosure risk, the data should be inspected for pieces of information that may identify an individual research participant or organization. Examples of disclosive information include:

- Direct identifiers or personally identifiable information (PII), such as name, address, social security number, and phone number (see table 2.1 for full list).

- Indirect identifiers, such as zip code, birth date, education, and race or ethnicity that could be used in combination to uniquely identify an individual.
- Information in a data set that can be linked with outside information, from sources such as social media, administrative data, or other public data sets, that may result in the identification of an individual.

It is important to note that even if all direct identifiers are removed from a data set, there may still be a risk of disclosure.

*Legally Protected Data.* In addition, some data may have legal restrictions due to how it was collected or who collected it. Certain classification of data may place additional restrictions on how data can be shared. Legally protected data classifications include:

- Family Education Rights and Privacy Act (FERPA) protected education records data, such as grades.
- Health Insurance Portability and Accountability Act (HIPAA) protected data that was collected by a medical or health care data organization.
- Federal Information Security Management Act (FISMA) protected data such as national defense and homeland security data.

Before accepting PII or legally protected data into a publicly accessible repository, the data set should be well understood and a determination made to accept, reject, or remove the potentially disclosive information, as the next section will explain.

# Detect Potential Disclosure Risk

There are many ways to detect PII, legally protected, and other sensitive information. Visually inspecting the data to look for direct identifiers, running detection software, and reviewing participant agreements for unique restrictions, and preventing deposit or not accepting some types of data are all valid approaches to consider for your appraisal process.

*Understand what sensitive information might be included.* Visual inspection of the data is one way to detect sensitive information. Things to look for include data derived from human subjects, such as survey forms and responses, columns headings that represent direct and indirect personal identifiers, such as age, height, address, or name, and information that may not have been created by the depositor, such as data generated by an external corporation or entity.

*Running detection software.* If there are many files, another approach is to run detection software on the data. Software like Identify Finder, Spider, Find_SSN and Bulk Extractor will look for well-structured information that may be sensitive. For example Storino compared two of these tools and reported that:

- "**Identify Finder** (http://www.identityfinder.com, ~60$/computer) searches a variety of file types that can be stored locally or remotely on file servers, network-attached storage devices, and desktops running Windows, Mac, and Linux. It looks for structured information such as social security numbers, bank account and routing information, driver's licenses, date of birth, phone numbers, addresses, and number strings that might represent passports, credit cards, medical records, or other national IDs. You can also use the tool to search for any custom string of information that you specify."

- **Bulk Extractor** (http://digitalcorpora.org/downloads/bulk_extractor, free download) scans a disk image, file, or directory that is stored locally or remotely (including hard drives, optical media, camera cards, or cell phones). It looks for a smaller set of information types, including credit card numbers and social security numbers, but also e-mail address, IP address, URLs, and GPS coordinates.[10]"

In practice, some information types will not be detectable by software if they are not uniformly structured. Also the free-text properties of human subjects such as name, age, or other sensitive freeform text will go unnoticed by these tools.

*Review participant agreements.* In addition to reviewing the contents of the data, if the data were derived from human subjects, you should review any agreements made with participants (see figure 2.1 for an example request) and verify that all participants signed such an agreement. These agreements, or "participant consent forms," must be approved by the local institutional review board (IRB), and they might include language that may limit the extent to which human subjects data can be released in order to maintain participant confidentiality.

When reviewing the consent form, look for language that describes how the data will be shared. Except in certain cases, overly restrictive language might include: "your responses will only be seen by the research team," "all data will be destroyed after project completion," or "your data will only be shared in aggregate form or in statistical tables." Instead, the ICPSR's *Guide to Social Science Data Preparation and Archiving* recommends better language that will allow more effective data sharing, including:

- "We will make our best effort to protect your statements and answers, so that no one will be able to connect them with you. These records will remain confidential. Federal or state laws may require us to show information to university or government officials [or sponsors], who are responsible for monitoring the safety of this study. Any personal information that could identify you will be removed or changed before files are shared with other researchers or results are made public."
- "The information in this study will only be used in ways that will not reveal who you are. You will not be identified in any publication from this study or in any data files shared with other researchers. Your participation in this study is confidential. Federal or state laws may require us

to show information to university or government officials [or sponsors], who are responsible for monitoring the safety of this study."[11]

Finally, it may be beneficial to retain a copy of the IRB consent form along with the data files, if accepted into the repository. This will provide context if questions about disclosure arise in the future.

---

Subject: Your submission to the Data Repository for the University of Minnesota (DRUM)

Dear <Submitter Name>,

Before I accept your submission to DRUM, I will need to review the form that informed participants of the future release of your data in a public repository like DRUM. Please do the following: 1) send me a copy of the IRB-approved form/agreement used in this project for our review, and 2) verify that you obtained consent from each participant whose data appears in your submission.

If you do not have such an agreement with your participants, we may not be able to accept your data into DRUM and recommend that you review the sample language on our website (https://www.lib.umn.edu/datamanagement/irb) for examples of how to maintain participant confidentiality without overly restricting future use of the data for next time.

Please let me know if you have any questions,

Lisa Johnston

Director of DRUM

---

**FIGURE 2.1**
IRB consent form agreement request e-mail template.

---

# Steps to Mitigate Disclosure Risk

Once data derived from human subjects is reviewed for direct identifiers, indirect identifiers, and violations of the data-sharing agreement, your next steps will be to determine what, if any, mitigating steps should be taken before accepting data with sensitive information or PII. These steps might include deidentification, redaction, or acceptance but with restricted access. Finally, safe removal should be considered for legally protected data that is not accepted into the repository.

**Deidentify the data set** by removing identifiers that may lead to participant disclosure and therefore create a "limited data set" for public distribution. A list of identifiers that may be considered for removal are displayed in table 2.1. There are several challenges with the deidentification process to consider.[12]

- If the data is deidentified, will it still retain its usefulness? For example, removing an identifier may impact the key components of research.
- Even with all personal identifiers removed, it may still be possible to detect participant identities using indirect identifiers or by combining outside information from sources like Facebook.
- A range of sensitivity can be found outside of human subjects, such as the geographic location of rare artifacts or endangered species.

**Digitally redact sensitive information** from files. If authenticity is a concern and you are unwilling to create a new version of the data, redaction techniques might be used. For example, Akgun and Hswe tested several redaction techniques for removing sensitive information from digital files housed in Penn State University's ScholarSphere digital repository.[13] They determined that manual redaction of physically blocking out sensitive information (with a black marker) on a physical printout, then scanning the document to generate a new optical character recognition (OCR) file was the best method. Other approaches, such as using the "Redact toolset" in Adobe Acrobat Pro, were not foolproof. And they warn: "Redaction using a rectangle tool to draw a filled black box— AVOID!" as the sensitive information will still be searchable in the document.[14] New techniques are needed, however, and a Mellon-funded project based at the University of Texas is developing a software tool to redact sensitive information more systematically for a project that aims to share paper-based hospital records digitally.[15]

**Restrict access indefinitely**: A final option to consider for mitigating disclosure risk is not sharing openly. For some repositories, this may present a challenge if you do not access deposits with indefinite access restrictions. However, some archives offer restricted access services, such as the Inter-university Consortium for Political and Social Research (ICPSR).[16]

**Reject and securely remove data**: If your data repository chooses to reject the data submission due to inherent risks in the content, safe removal techniques may be required. For example, if the data is HIPAA-protected, it cannot be stored on non-HIPAA-compliant storage, regardless of access conditions. Therefore, any sensitive information will need to be securely removed from its storage location within the repository. Indiana University (IU) describes some safe removal techniques for sensitive data that include:

- Wiping utilities, like the DBAN software tool (http://www.dban.org) that writes over the information with different information in order to securely remove the data.
- Destruction of the physical media to thoroughly prevent anyone from reading the device.
- Degaussing, which involves exposing the storage media to a powerful magnetic field in order to remove data on the media. IU notes that this method can be cost cost-prohibitive and is ineffective with optical

media such as DVDs and CDs.[17] (Incidentally, if you don't like your microwave, the destruction costs of such optical media can be greatly reduced! See YouTube for illustrative "DVD in microwave" videos.)

## TABLE 2.1
**List of personal identifiers for human subjects and detection methods.[18]**

| Direct Identifier | Example | Notes |
|---|---|---|
| Name | John M. Smith | |
| All geographic subdivisions smaller than a state | 5555 University Ave SW Minneapolis Hennepin County 4th Precinct 55455 | Zip code or equivalents must be removed, but can retain first 3 digits of the geographic unit to which the zip code applies if the zip code area contains more than 20,000 people. |
| Dates directly related to individuals | DOB: 01/01/1980 DOD: 05/07/2013 Admission date: 04/01/2013 Discharge date: 04/05/2013 | All elements of dates must be removed except year. |
| All ages over 89 or dates indicating such an age | DOB: 04/07/1922 Age: 96 | Ages over 89 may be removed, or you may have an aggregate category of individuals 90 and older. |
| Telephone number | 612-555-6111 | |
| Fax number | 612-555-4567 | |
| E-mail address | email001@umn.edu | |
| Social security number | 123-45-6789 | Find_SSNs and Bulk Extractor Tools can help detect SSN. |
| Health plan number | HVF123456789 | |
| Account numbers | 0000352783 | |
| Certificate or license numbers | S123-4567-8901-23 H019450127872 | |
| Vehicle identification/serial numbers, including license plate numbers | VIN: 1ZVHT82H485123456 License plate: PBE-314 | Could potentially use Bulk extractor or Spider for license plates. Both tools allow for creation of custom expressions for formatted numbers. |
| Device identification/ serial numbers | W78300NC77F | |

**TABLE 2.1** (continued)

| Direct Identifier | Example | Notes |
|---|---|---|
| Universal resource locators (URLs) | http:www.example.com/ | |
| Internet protocol (IP) addresses | 128.101.123.123 | |
| Biometric identifiers | Finger and voice prints | |
| Full face photographs and comparable images | Images and videos | Note: Some MRI 3-D brain scans have been shown to be visually identifiable[a] |
| Any other unique identifying number, characteristic or code | Credit card numbers 1234-4567-7891-1023 | |

a. Hidemasa Takao, Naoto Hayashi, and Kuni Ohtomo, "Brain Morphology Is Individual-Specific Information," *Magnetic Resonance Imaging* 33, no. 6 (2015): 816–21.

# Understanding Risk Factors: Two Case Studies

Two perspectives on understanding the risk factors for data curation services are presented. The first, by Kaye Marz, describes the history and evolution of how a well-established data archive manages restricted-use files (RUFs), with a specialized ingest workflow for secure file types. The second case study, by Christine Mayo and Erin Clary, describes how the Dryad repository approaches human subjects data, such as using deidentification techniques.

# Considerations for Restricted-Use Research Data

*Kaye Marz*[*]

The Inter-university Consortium for Political and Social Research (ICPSR) considers many issues when selecting and appraising restricted-use data for ingest. Restricted-use data retains more than minimal risk for reidentification of a research subject given the information in the data set and potential harm to the subject through the disclosure of that information.[19] ICPSR data managers must balance the scientific benefits likely to result from data reuse with the risk of disclosure and potential harm to a study's research subjects. Modifications made during the curation and processing procedures to address disclosure risk are done to preserve the data's analytic value as much as possible. Also, ICPSR weighs if the restricted-use data is expected to garner sufficient reuse to justify bearing the added costs for system security, staff training and workload, and development of resources for potential users to explore the data set when it cannot be accessed publicly and reserves the right to reject, if not.

# BACKGROUND

For its first thirty-five years, the Inter-university Consortium for Political and Social Research (ICPSR) distributed research microdata only as public-use files (PUFs), which are data sets for which the risk of disclosing confidential information about research subjects is very small.[20] However, subsequent advances in statistical methodology in social science research and computing technology have resulted in the collection of richer, more detailed data.[21] This detail makes the data valuable but also increases disclosure risk to research subjects due to the large amount of information collected about them that can make their record unique within the population or sample. Because researchers are eager to use this data, over fifteen years ago, ICPSR began to provide access to restricted-use files (RUFs).

# THE CHALLENGE

Human subjects research in the social sciences produces "a tension between privacy and releasing high-quality open data."[22] Additionally, the number of data sets has increased that are shared by government entities or collected by other researchers that can potentially be linked to a particular research data set using key data items such as geography of current residence, gender, race, exact age or birth date, city where born, and so on. Data providers, government agencies, researchers, and repositories alike recognize that not every research data set can ethically and responsibly be openly accessible for download via the web but can be shared with appropriate safeguards.[23]

ICPSR ingests social science data on sensitive topics (e.g., criminal justice, addiction, HIV, health care) and from vulnerable populations. In response to this challenge, ICPSR has developed a highly secure computing environment, legal agreements, and new procedures and services to enable RUFs to be reused and analyzed under controlled conditions.[24] This allows ICPSR to help data producers with federal grants to fulfill their data-sharing and archiving requirements and alleviates the burden of managing long-term restricted-use data storage and researcher access to RUFs.

# DATA SECURITY

All data is processed in ICPSR's secure data management environment (SDE). From intake to release, a data set is considered restricted-use unless staff determine it can be public-use. The ICPSR intake system is a collection of linked IT systems that transmits submissions over SSL-encrypted HTTP connections using a web server that enforces the use of strong ciphers, such as AES-256, and a storage system using a similarly strong cipher and encryption key while content is "at rest." Encrypted content is moved into ICPSR's SDE by an automated system and purged from the web server. Access to the SDE is restricted to ICPSR staff and systems administrators trained according to strict data management and disclosure review standards. All data management activities take place within the SDE using a virtual desktop created at login that is deleted when staff log off. Staff move content outside of the SDE only through two controlled gateways that require supervisor approval (i.e., release system for downloadable files and the less frequently used airlock with audit log if a file needs to be reviewed by someone who is outside of ICPSR, e.g., funding agency staff or data producer). Common data activities, such as file transfer or cut-and-paste to staff's desktop or outside the SDE and the attachment of files to e-mail are prohibited. Access to Internet applications is restricted to a processor-based intranet.[25]

# APPRAISAL

When assessing RUFs for ingest, ICPSR relies on its acquisition policy, which determines whether the data are in scope with ICPSR's mission.[26] One aspect of documented data set appraisal practice that is typically not described in detail is the evaluation for confidentiality or human subjects concerns.[27] In addition, commonly used appraisal methods by repositories either reject data with disclosure risk posed by indirect identifiers from ingest or expect that the data if accepted can be altered (e.g., anonymized via disclosure risk remediation techniques) to produce a public-use file without unduly comprising analytic utility.[28] Yet, anonymizing a data set can affect a user's ability to reproduce published findings and can also create uncertainty whether the future results of reuse are artifacts from deidentification.[29]

ICPSR staff are first users of the data for the wider research community, examining each data set from the viewpoint of a secondary analyst,[30] which involves examining the understandability of the content of each data item, comparing it to the submitted documentation, and considering how someone might use data items to reidentify a research subject. Upon request, ICPSR staff also review documentation and recommend changes to data elements prior to ingest. Conducting disclosure risk review is part art and part science. Much is learned through experience. ICPSR uses a two-level system. All processing staff are trained to recognize potential disclosure risk elements in a data set and are able to mask, recode, or remove data items that are potentially identifying but without analytic use (e.g., detailed administrative items). Supervisors then work with staff to apply measures to address disclosure risk. Although removing direct identifiers is straightforward,[31] it is a time-consuming task for data managers to take the necessary steps to evaluate and remediate indirect identifiers (e.g., detailed geography and demographics with exact date of events) that would be required prior to releasing a PUF. Staff must also do checks on the revised data set (e.g., cross tabulations) to verify the remediation was accurately done. Determining if the remediation was enough to address disclosure risk is a judgment call. For this second tier, supervising staff need additional expertise and technical skills to assess disclosure risk across several items, make complex remediation, and check the results for the effect on disclosure and also potential analyses.[32]

Therefore, preparing a RUF for reuse is easier than creating a PUF. Once ICPSR staff conduct a disclosure risk review to confirm that direct identifiers were removed prior to deposit, data with indirect identifiers can be shared through the controlled conditions established by ICPSR. Rather than be excluded from ingest, the appraisal process for human subjects data is largely to determine whether to ingest the RUF or not, and whether to release the data as RUF *and* PUF.[33] For some data sets, removing detailed or all geographic items alone is enough to allow all other variables to remain as submitted and be released as a PUF. When geography cannot be withheld, other data items need to be aggregated to broader categories so that no data value has a small number of cases. A data set with limited geographic and demographic information and mostly summary score or Likert-type items can often be released as a PUF. If a limited number of data items need to be modified for a PUF, but have great analytic usefulness for some analyses, then a RUF version is often also released. Typically longitudinal data sets on sensitive topics are not even considered for release as a PUF.

The cost trade-off is that RUFs are reused less than PUFs because use is restricted to approved researchers and because of the extra effort for them to apply for access, obtain legal signatures for the data use agreement, and implement required security measures at their workplace. For example, the National Comorbidity Survey baseline (NCS-1) and follow-up (NCS-2) data sets are available as both PUF and RUF. However, actual data access of the RUF is no more than 5 percent of the PUF (see table 2.2).

**TABLE 2.2**
Comparison of data use by type of data access.

| Study | Type of Access | Interested Only[a] | Accessed Data | Total |
|---|---|---|---|---|
| National Comorbity Survey (NCS-1) | PUF | 1,465 | 499 | 1,964 |
| National Comorbity Survey (NCS-1) | RUF | 11 | 6 | 17 |
| National Comorbity Survey (NCS-2) | PUF | 324 | 185 | 509 |
| National Comorbity Survey (NCS-2) | RUF | 54 | 10 | 64 |

a. Only accessed PUF documentation online but did not download the data set, or initiated but did not complete a RUF request.

# METADATA

To assist prospective users in determining if a RUF meets their research needs, ICPSR includes variable-level metadata (question text and univariate statistics) in web-accessible documentation (see a page from the NCS-2 codebook as figure 2.2. Staff may suppress some statistics for a RUF data set from public display in the data set's codebook if the values alone could be individually identifiable given the sample (e.g., outliers in continuous values such as age and income; full dates; free-text responses, etc.). In particular, staff look at items that would have needed to be modified to release the data set as a public-use file. The same metadata that ICPSR staff use to produce the web-accessible codebook is often imported into ICPSR's searchable "variables database" of data items to permit the online exploration of data items within a collection and across multiple data collections.

Study-level metadata for RUFs indicates
- Data modifications by the data producer or ICPSR before data release[34]
- Differences between the RUF and PUF, if both are available
- Limitations on how the data can be used, and instructions to apply for access to the data

# SUMMARY

Selecting and ingesting restricted-use data requires specialized skills and may carry significant costs with respect to providing appropriate data security, staffing, data review, and curation. Yet by making these investments, ICPSR is able to provide valuable, detailed data that still protects subject confidentiality.

**PEA40: True for you: I feel my emotions very strongly**

Now I am going to read a series of statements that people use to describe themselves.
I need you to tell me how true each statement is for you. The best answer is usually
the one that comes to your mind first, so don't take too much time thinking before
you answer.

When I feel emotions, I feel them very strongly.

| Value | Label | Unweighted Frequency | % |
|---|---|---|---|
| 1 | Very | 2134 | 42.7 % |
| 2 | Somewhat | 2239 | 44.8 % |
| 3 | Not Very | 489 | 9.8 % |
| 4 | Not at All | 132 | 2.6 % |
| | **Missing Data** | | |
| -9 | Missing | 4 | 0.1 % |
| -6 | Refused | 3 | 0.1 % |
| | Total | 5,001 | 100% |

Based upon 4,994 valid cases out of 5,001 total cases.

*Location:* 712-713 (width: 2; decimal: 0)
*Variable Type:* numeric
*(Range of) Missing Values:* -9 , -8 , -6

**PEA41: True for you: I get emotional very easily**

Now I am going to read a series of statements that people use to describe themselves.
I need you to tell me how true each statement is for you. The best answer is usually
the one that comes to your mind first, so don't take too much time thinking before
you answer.

I get emotional very easily.

| Value | Label | Unweighted Frequency | % |
|---|---|---|---|
| 1 | Very | 1316 | 26.3 % |
| 2 | Somewhat | 1777 | 35.5 % |
| 3 | Not Very | 1354 | 27.1 % |
| 4 | Not at All | 547 | 10.9 % |
| | **Missing Data** | | |
| -9 | Missing | 4 | 0.1 % |
| -6 | Refused | 3 | 0.1 % |
| | Total | 5,001 | 100% |

- 151 -

# FIGURE 2.2
NCS-2 codebook showing full question text and univariate statistics.

# Human Subjects Data in an Open Access Repository

*Christine Mayo and Erin Clary**

The research data transparency policies adopted by funders and publishers can pose a challenge to researchers and data repositories where human subjects data is concerned. Numerous national and international policies and laws, such as HIPAA and the EU Data Protection Directive, protect the rights and privacy of human subjects, which can make the prospect of publicly releasing these data seem daunting.[35] Yet the World Medical Association indicates that researchers and publishers are ethically obligated to disseminate the results of medical research, both positive and negative findings.[36] Additionally, the National Institutes of Health lists numerous reasons to share the results of human subjects studies, including transparency in science, a reduction in duplication of effort, and the possibility that the data may be used in novel ways.[37]

Established repositories in the social sciences, such as ICPSR, are set up to provide restricted access to human subjects datasets when necessary.[38] Dryad, as an interdisciplinary open-access data repository, is willing to accept and archive human subjects data associated with published research articles,[39] but only if the data can be made publicly available without restriction on use or reuse (i.e., placed in the public domain with a CC0 license[40]). Furthermore, any user may download data from Dryad without logging in or registering for an account. Thus, Dryad is able to accept only human subjects data that has been appropriately deidentified.

Following accepted deidentification practice, no data should be archived in an open repository with any direct identifier, such as name, date of birth, social security number, or other identifier that unambiguously refers to a single, specific person.[41] In addition to removing direct identifiers, Dryad asks authors to allow no more than three indirect identifiers, such as age, sex, education level, or income, to remain in the published data set. In theory, an informed consent document could include a statement granting permission for publication of personal details, but this has not yet arisen in practice.

Typically, when Dryad receives data files that do not meet the above requirements, curators work with authors to remove potential identifiers that are not vital to the analyses at hand. The deidentification process has removed information such as dates of medical procedures, locations and names of clinics,

---

unnecessary demographic information such as number and age of the subject's children, and more. With dates, it is recommended that authors switch from exact dates to using temporal durations, such as number of days or months between two procedures.

While these recommendations have been generally well received, deidentification is not always a straightforward process. Removing variables in order to properly anonymize a data set may impinge on the data's meaning or potential for reuse. At times, removing all human subject identifiers would prevent another researcher's ability to replicate the analyses. Additionally, the distinction between direct and indirect identifiers can blur depending on the size or composition of a data set.[42] For instance, ethnicity, sex, or age could directly identify an individual if that person was the only subject within the study representing that characteristic.

Although data packages with human subjects data make up a small percentage of Dryad's overall submissions (~5%), assessing their appropriateness for the public archive can be a challenge. In an internal study conducted at Dryad over a period of three-and-a-half months, we identified seventy-eight data packages that contained human subjects data. Of these, thirty-three data packages (approximately 42%) were returned to the submitter for further deidentification, and eleven of these data packages were returned more than once. Ultimately, sixty-two of the data packages (approximately 80%) were released.[43] On occasion, Dryad has declined to publish data that could not be deidentified without rendering it meaningless, as in cases where a researcher has analyzed interplay between numerous identifying characteristics such as residence, religion, caste, and income. In these cases, Dryad curators have offered the author information about organizations that may provide controlled access to the data with the identifiers intact (e.g., the Inter-university Consortium for Political and Social Research).

Very rarely, authors push back when asked to further deidentify their data, typically claiming that they already have IRB or ethical approval to publish the data in its current form. Requirements and policies in place to protect human subjects vary by nation, and researchers may not be aware of the applicable guidelines in their own country or the terms that Dryad must abide by as an organization based in the United States, including HIPAA. Authors may also worry that their journal will decline to publish the related article if they don't comply with the journal's mandatory data-archiving policy, not realizing that exceptions are granted in cases where sensitive data is concerned.[44]

As more authors become accustomed to archiving human subjects data in repositories, and as more authors plan for public archiving from study inception, we hope that the archiving process may become more streamlined.

# 2.3 Inventory

Sometimes there are too many files to get a good picture of what the data submission includes. For example, geospatial data sets may come with hundreds of files that are arranged in folder structures designed to run with proprietary software such as ArcGIS. In cases like these, it is useful to create an inventory of the contents of a data submission. Here you may want to identify file formats, analyze the number and size of the files, and obtain any technical metadata of the submission (e.g., checksums and MIME types).

To create an inventory of the files, try using open-source and free software that will capture and generate a report (xml-based or graphical interface) with detailed information and create custom metadata such as MD5 checksum values and validate file formats. Some good software options are Data Accessioner, DROID, and HashMyFiles, which are used by repository archivists to understand the overall scope of a submission, including the total number of files, the file sizes, and if there are any duplicate files.[45]

# 2.4 Selection

Once a data submission has been reviewed and appraised, the selection step will identify which data are ready to be curated for the repository. It is possible that some data repositories might want to notify the data submitter at this stage to inform them of the decision to select or reject (see example in figure 2.3). In the case of rejection, detail the reasons why a submission was rejected from the repository and if possible, offer to work with that author to better prepare their data to resubmit. In this case, additional staff, such as the library subject liaison, might be in the best position to work with the data author or researcher.

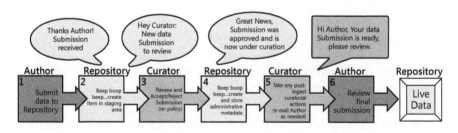

**FIGURE 2.3**
Illustrative example the sequential workflow steps for a data repository submission process by role: author, curator, and repository (machine).

# 2.5 Assign

After accepting the data submission for inclusion in the repository, the next step is to assign responsibility of the curation process to the appropriate data curator. This step assumes that data submissions to your repository may require specialized expertise that exists in your staffing model.

Assignments for data submissions will generally require an understanding of the various types of data, file format, and software needed to open and review the contents of the data files, as well as the expertise available and workloads of each data curator staff member. For example, a triage model for data curation among a group of staff might look like this:

1. First priority for data curation assignments determined by Type/Discipline of the data that matched to the corresponding data curator:
   a. Scientific Data Curator (e.g., tabular spreadsheets, Excel, instrument-readings, databases)
   b. Social Sciences Data Curator (e.g., qualitative, statistical packages such as SPSS, STATA)
   c. Geospatial Data Curator (e.g., ArcGIS files, shapefiles, Geodatabases)
   d. Digital Arts and Humanities Curator (e.g., video files, audio files, text-mining projects)
   e. Health Sciences/Human Subjects Data Curator (e.g., data derived from human subjects research, public health, and clinical trials)
   f. Unknown/Not Specified: Send to any available Data Curator for further research.
2. Second priority for data curation assignments determined by the workload of the appropriate data curator. For example, if the appropriate curator is handling one or two submissions currently, send to the next available data curator.
3. Additionally, the selected data submissions might be moved to a shared work space to allow for multiple staff to curate the data, anticipating unexpected staff outages, to avoid gaps in service.

Assignments should be tracked with date stamps of when the submission arrived, when the assignment was made to the appropriate data curator, and when the data submission was finalized and the author notified. These temporal metrics may be used to track and meet service level expectations. For example, if an author deposits their data on a Friday, how many hours, days, or weeks might be expected to process the new submission. This expectation will vary from institution to institution.

An accession tool might be used to track all incoming submissions and which curator they are assigned to. DRUM uses a Google Form for accessioning new data submissions, and the resulting assignment e-mail is shown in figure 2.4.

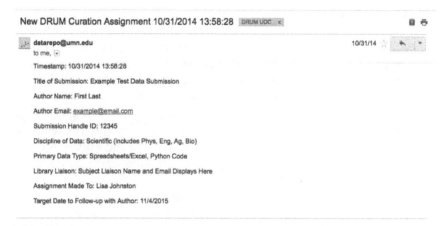

New DRUM Curation Assignment 10/31/2014 13:58:28  DRUM UDC  x

datarepo@umn.edu                                                        10/31/14
to me,

Timestamp: 10/31/2014 13:58:28

Title of Submission: Example Test Data Submission

Author Name: First Last

Author Email: example@email.com

Submission Handle ID: 12345

Discipline of Data: Scientific (includes Phys, Eng, Ag, Bio)

Primary Data Type: Spreadsheets/Excel, Python Code

Library Liaison: Subject Liaison Name and Email Displays Here

Assignment Made To: Lisa Johnston

Target Date to Follow-up with Author: 11/4/2015

**FIGURE 2.4**

E-mail generated via new Data Repository for the University of Minnesota submission form.

# Summary of Step 2.0: Appraise and Select

2.1 Appraise the Files: Determine that the repository is the appropriate home for this data (e.g., the data meets all collection policies) and, with appropriate curation, there is a potential long-term value for reuse.

2.2 Consider Any Risk Factors: The repository has clear understanding of the types of data (e.g., federally protected data, sensitive information, copyright violations) that should not be accepted and has protocols in place to reject or facilitate remediation of data that should not have been transferred to the repository.

2.3 Inventory the Submission: The data submission is inspected and the number, file types, and file sizes of the data are understood and documented. Identify any missing, duplicate, or corrupt (e.g., unable to open) files. Capture the organization of the files and any technical metadata (e.g., date last modified). Request more information from the author if necessary.

2.4 Select: The data submission is accepted or rejected based on the above actions. If accepted, determine if any additional information or files need to be acquired from the author before moving to the next step. This step may include the deselection and removal of any duplicate or unnecessary files.

2.5 Assign the Submission: Accept the data submission for inclusion in the repository and assign curation responsibility to the appropriate data curator based on subject and format expertise required.

# Notes

1.  Ross Harvey, "Appraisal and Selection," Curation Reference Manual, Digital Curation Centre, June 2006, http://www.dcc.ac.uk/resource/curation-manual/chapters/apprais-al-and-selection.

2.  Ibid., 25.

3.  Angus Whyte, "Five Steps to Decide What Data to Keep: A Checklist for Appraising Research Data," version 1, Edinburgh, UK: Digital Curation Centre, 2014, http://www.dcc.ac.uk/resources/how-guides/five-steps-decide-what-data-keep#sthash.Zrx3J3N3.dpuf.

4.  Richard Pearce-Moses, ed. *A Glossary of Archival and Records Terminology*, Chicago: Society of American Archivists, 2005, accessed May 8, 2015, http://www2.archivists.org/glossary/terms/a/appraisal.

5.  David Hunt, "'Save Everything' Data Retention: Why It's a Problem," *The C2C Blog*, July 1, 2013, https://web.archive.org/web/20150424052232/http://www.c2c.com/save-everything-data-retention-why-its-a-problem.

6.  US Geological Survey Earth Resources Observation and Science Center, "Records Appraisal Tool Questions," accessed June 15, 2015, http://eros.usgs.gov/government/ratool.

7.  Ibid.

8.  National Archives and Records Administration, "Toolkit for Managing Electronic Records," accessed June 15, 2015, http://www.archives.gov/records-mgmt/toolkit/#list.

9.  This section includes content written by Alicia Hofelich Mohr for the "Managing Sensitive Data" section of the University of Minnesota Libraries webpage "Managing Your Data," accessed March 11, 2016, https://www.lib.umn.edu/datamanagement/sensitive.

10. Christine M. Storino, "Identifying Sensitive, Private, or Legally Protected Data in DRUM Submissions," University of Minnesota Digital Conservancy, 2015, http://hdl.handle.net/11299/171825.

11. Inter-university Consortium for Political and Social Research (ICPSR), *Guide to Social Science Data Preparation and Archiving*, 5th ed. (Ann Arbor: ICPSR, University of Michigan, 2012), http://www.icpsr.umich.edu/files/ICPSR/access/dataprep.pdf.

12. For some arguments see Mark A. Rothstein, "Is Deidentification Sufficient to Protect Health Privacy in Research?" *American Journal of Bioethics* 10, no. 9 (2010): 3–11, doi:10.1080/15265161.2010.494215.

13. Mahir Akgun and Patricia Hswe, "A Tale of Redaction." *Digital Stewardship* (blog). December 1, 2015, http://stewardship.psu.edu/2015/12/01/a-tale-of-redaction.

14. Ibid.

15. University of Texas at Austin, "Information Researchers to Create Digital Archives from Central Lunatic Asylum for Colored Insane," UT News, news release, April 8, 2015, http://news.utexas.edu/2015/04/08/information-researchers-to-create-digital-archives.

16. Inter-university Consortium for Political and Social Research (ICPSR), "Restricted-Use Data Management at ICPSR," accessed March 14, 2016, http://www.icpsr.umich.edu/icpsrweb/content/icpsr/access/restricted/index.html.

17. Indiana University, "Secure Data Removal," accessed March 14, 2016, https://protect.iu.edu/online-safety/protect-data/data-removal.html.

18. Derived from the list of protected health information protected under the privacy rule: National Institutes of Health, "How Can Covered Entities Use and Disclose Protected

Health Information for Research and Comply with the Privacy Rule?" HIPAA Privacy Rule: Information for Researchers, accessed March 14, 2016, https://privacyruleandresearch.nih.gov/pr_08.asp)

19.  The two main issues with restricted-use data are the potential for the data to disclose information about the individual that would otherwise not normally be revealed, and the potential for harm to the individual because that information was disclosed. For example, some restricted-use data sets contain information on and individual's history with sensitive topics (e.g., health information, sexual behaviors, criminal records, etc.). However, data on sensitive topics can be in a public-use file as long as the information cannot be reasonably linked to specific individuals. In addition, some data may need to be restricted-use given promises made to the subjects to hold the information as confidential, even if the information is not about sensitive topics or because of third-party licensing, intellectual property rights, or other use agreements. Sensitivity of the information does factor into the level of harm to the subjects if their information was disclosed.

20.  Federal Committee on Statistical Methodology, *Statistical Policy Working Paper 22 (Second Version, 2005): Report on Statistical Disclosure Limitation Methodology* (Washington, DC: Office of Management and Budget, 2005).

21.  A study may use one or more of the following in order to measure a topic of interest in depth: multiple validated scales about attitudes and behaviors, multiple informants (subject, partner, caregiver, siblings, etc.); mix of quantitative and qualitative methods, links to official records, use of objective measures (e.g., urine testing, hair assays, buccal swabs, etc.), as well as longitudinal collection of these details from the same respondents over several time points.

22.  Jon P. Daries, Justin Reich, Jim Waldo, Elise M. Young, Jonathan Whittinghill, Daniel Thomas Seaton, Andrew Dean Ho, and Isaac Chuang, "Privacy, Anonymity, and Big Data in the Social Sciences," *acmqueue* 12, no. 7 (July 14, 2014), http://queue.acm.org/detail.cfm?id=2661641.

23.  See NIH Data Sharing FAQ 28 at US Department of Health and Human Services, "Frequently Asked Questions: Data Sharing," National Institutes of Health, Office of Extramural Research, revised February 16, 2004, http://grants.nih.gov/grants/policy/data_sharing/data_sharing_faqs.htm; Christopher Mackie and Norman Bradburn, eds., *Improving Access to and Confidentiality of Research Data* (Washington, DC: National Academies Press, 2000).

24.  For a case study about legal agreements for reuse of data with human subjects concerns, see "Legal Agreements for Acquiring Restricted-Use Research Data" on page 24.

25.  The National Addiction & HIV Data Archive Program (NAHDAP), a repository within ICPSR, funded by the National Institute on Drug Abuse, has an Authorization to Operate (ATO) under a Federal Information Security Management Act (FISMA) moderate rating for its Secure Data Environment (SDE) and a FISMA low rating for its public-facing website.

26.  See Inter-university Consortium for Political and Social Research (ICPSR), "ICPSR Collection Development Policy," accessed June 17, 2016, http://www.icpsr.umich.edu/icpsrweb/content/datamanagement/policies/colldev.html.

27.  GESIS, accessed July 8, 2016, http://www.gesis.org/en/services/archiving-and-registering/data-archiving; UK Data Service, *Collections Development Policy* (UK Data Service, January 19, 2016), https://www.ukdataservice.ac.uk/media/398725/cd227-collections-

developmentpolicy.pdf; Angus Whyte and Andrew Wilson, *How to Appraise and Select Research Data for Curation,* working level guide (Acton, Australia: Digital Curation Centre, Australian National Data Service, 2010); Myron P. Gutmann, Kevin Schürer, Darrel Donakowski, and Hilary Beedham, "The Selection, Appraisal, and Retention of Digital Social Science Data," *Data Science Journal* 3 (2006): 209–21. doi:10.2481/dsj.3.209.

28. Indirect identifiers are data items that when combined within the data set or with other information produce unique or nearly unique combinations that correspond to only one or an unacceptably small number of subjects in the data set (e.g., demographic items, small area geography, organizational memberships, exact occupation titles, exact dates of events [such as birth, arrest, graduation], and detailed income). No universal list of indirect identifiers exists. A data item may not be an indirect identifier in one data set, but may be in another based on the sample (e.g., a data set of octogenarians for which an age of 89 may not be unusual versus a general population data set for which few respondents are age 89).

29. Daries et al., "Privacy, Anonymity, and Big Data."

30. Staff also assess the files for completeness (that all needed data and documentation files have been submitted), for accuracy (that the data items and values are consistent with those expected given details known about the study and submitted documentation), and for understandability (that the study context is sufficient for analysts to use the data appropriately); Gutmann et al., "Selection, Appraisal, and Retention."

31. Direct identifiers are data items that point explicitly to a particular individual or unit solely based on the content of that one data item (e.g., names; postal, e-mail, and IP addresses; telephone and fax numbers; official identification numbers, etc.).

32. ICPSR rarely swaps records or adds noise to a data set to address disclosure risk. These are done only in consultation with the data producer, or more often by the data producer before submission of the data set.

33. Inter-university Consortium for Political and Social Research (ICPSR), "Disclosure Risk Training—For Public-Use or Not for Public Use, That Is the Question," YouTube video, 43:36, posted October 8, 2014 by ICPSR, https://www.youtube.com/watch?v=9vdWse-Lay9g&feature=youtu.be&list=PLqC9lrhW1VvaKgzk-S87WwrlSMHliHQo6%22.

34. For disclosure mediation options see Federal Committee on Statistical Methodology, *Statistical Policy Working Paper 22 (Second Version, 2005): Report on Statistical Disclosure Limitation Methodology* (Washington, DC: Office of Management and Budget, 2005).

35. US Department of Health and Human Services, Office for Civil Rights, "45 CFR Parts 160 and 164: Standards for Privacy of Individually Identifiable Health Information. Final Rule," *Federal Register* 67, no.157, August 14, 2002, DOCID:fr14au02-32, http://www.gpo.gov/fdsys/pkg/FR-2002-08-14/pdf/02-20554.pdf; European Parliament, Council of the European Union, "Directive 95/46/EC of the European Parliament and of the Council of 24 October 1995 on the Protection of Individuals with Regard to the Processing of Personal Data and on the Free Movement of Such Data," EUR Lex, accessed November 20, 2015, http://eur-lex.europa.eu/legal-content/EN/TXT/?uri=CELEX:31995L0046.

36. World Medical Association (WMA), *WMA Declaration of Helsinki: Ethical Principles for Medical Research Involving Human Subjects,* Fortaleza, Brazil: 64th WMA General Assembly, 2013, http://www.wma.net/en/30publications/10policies/b3.

37. US Department of Health and Human Services, "Frequently Asked Questions: Data Sharing."

38. Inter-university Consortium for Political and Social Research (ICPSR), "Preserving Respondent Confidentiality," accessed November 20, 2015, https://www.icpsr.umich.edu/icpsrweb/content/deposit/confidentiality.html.

39. Dryad Digital Repository homepage, last modified November 19, 2015, https://datadryad.org.

40. Creative Commons, "CC0 1.0 Universal (CC0 1.0): Public Domain Dedication," accessed November 20, 2015, https://creativecommons.org/publicdomain/zero/1.0.

41. US Department of Health and Human Services, "Health Information Privacy: Guidance Regarding Methods for De-identification of Protected Health Information in Accordance with the Health Insurance Portability and Accountability Act (HIPAA) Privacy Rule," Office of Civil Rights, accessed November 20, 2015, http://www.hhs.gov/ocr/privacy/hipaa/understanding/coveredentities/De-identification/guidance.html; Canadian Institutes of Health Research, *CIHR Best Practices for Protecting Privacy in Health Research* (Ottawa: Public Works and Government Services Canada, 2005), http://www.cihr-irsc.gc.ca/e/documents/et_pbp_nov05_sept2005_e.pdf; Inter-university Consortium for Political and Social Research (ICPSR), *Guide to Social Science Data Preparation and Archiving*; Sarah Olesen, *ANDS Guide to Publishing and Sharing Sensitive Data* (Melbourne, Australia: Australian National Data Service, 2014), http://ands.org.au/guides/sensitivedata.pdf; Veerle Van den Eynden, Louise Corti, Matthew Woollard, Libby Bishop, and Laurence Horton, *Managing and Sharing Data,* 3rd ed. (Essex: UK Data Archive, 2011), http://www.data-archive.ac.uk/media/2894/managingsharing.pdf.

42. Canadian Institutes of Health Research, *CIHR Best Practices*; Olesen, *ANDS Guide to Publishing,* 7.

43. These sixty-two data packages represented approximately 6 percent of total content archived over the same time period (i.e., 62 of approximately 1,032 data packages archived).

44. See for example, the author guidelines of The Royal Society (Royal Society, "Data Sharing and Mining: Open Data Policy," Publishing Ethics and Policies, accessed November 20, 2015, https://royalsociety.org/journals/ethics-policies/data-sharing-mining) and of *PLOS ONE* (PLOS ONE, "Guidelines for Specific Study Types: Human Subjects Research," Submission Guidelines, accessed November 20, 2015, http://journals.plos.org/plosone/s/submission-guidelines#loc-guidelines-for-specific-study-types).

45. The DataAccessioner was created at Duke University by Seth Shaw (Seth Shaw, "DataAccessioner," Github, accessed March 14, 2016, https://github.com/seth-shaw/DataAccessioner) and is now maintained by the POWRR Project (POWRR Project homepage, accessed March 14, 2016, http://digitalpowrr.niu.edu). The tool is available for download at http://www.dataaccessioner.org and uses FITS technology (File Information Tool Set [FITS], accessed March 14, 2016, http://projects.iq.harvard.edu/fits); Carol Kussmann provides a clear guide on how to use Hashmyfiles to run reports (Carol Kussmann, "HashMyFiles Evaluation," May 2012, Minnesota Historical Society, http://www.mnhs.org/preserve/records/legislativerecords/carol/docs_pdfs/HashMyFilesEvaluation.pdf).

# Bibliography

Akgun, Mahir, and Patricia Hswe. "A Tale of Redaction." *Digital Stewardship* (blog). December 1, 2015. http://stewardship.psu.edu/2015/12/01/a-tale-of-redaction.

Canadian Institutes of Health Research. *CIHR Best Practices for Protecting Privacy in Health Research.* Ottawa, Ontario: Public Works and Government Services Canada, 2005. http://www.cihr-irsc.gc.ca/e/documents/et_pbp_nov05_sept2005_e.pdf.

Creative Commons. "CC0 1.0 Universal (CC0 1.0): Public Domain Dedication." Accessed November 20, 2015. https://creativecommons.org/publicdomain/zero/1.0.

Daries, Jon P., Justin Reich, Jim Waldo, Elise M. Young, Jonathan Whittinghill, Daniel Thomas Seaton, Andrew Dean Ho, and Isaac Chuang. "Privacy, Anonymity, and Big Data in the Social Sciences." *acmqueue* 12, no. 7 (July 14, 2014). http://queue.acm.org/detail.cfm?id=2661641.

DataAccessioner homepage. Accessed March 14, 2016. http://www.dataaccessioner.org.

Dryad Digital Repository homepage. Last modified November 19, 2015. https://datadryad.org.

European Parliament, Council of the European Union. "Directive 95/46/EC of the European Parliament and of the Council of 24 October 1995 on the Protection of Individuals with Regard to the Processing of Personal Data and on the Free Movement of Such Data." EUR Lex. Accessed November 20, 2015. http://eur-lex.europa.eu/legal-content/EN/TXT/?uri=CELEX:31995L0046.

Federal Committee on Statistical Methodology. *Statistical Policy Working Paper 22 (Second Version, 2005): Report on Statistical Disclosure Limitation Methodology.* Washington, DC: Office of Management and Budget, 2005.

File Information Tool Set (FITS). Accessed March 14, 2016. http://projects.iq.harvard.edu/fits.

Gutmann, Myron P., Kevin Schürer, Darrel Donakowski, and Hilary Beedham. "The Selection, Appraisal, and Retention of Digital Social Science Data." *Data Science Journal* 3 (2006): 209–21. doi:10.2481/dsj.3.209.

Harvey, Ross. "Appraisal and Selection." Curation Reference Manual. Digital Curation Centre. June 2006. http://www.dcc.ac.uk/resource/curation-manual/chapters/appraisal-and-selection.

Hunt, David. "'Save Everything' Data Retention: Why It's a Problem." *The C2C Blog.* July 1, 2013. https://web.archive.org/web/20150424052232/http://www.c2c.com/save-everything-data-retention-why-its-a-problem/.

Indiana University. "Secure Data Removal." Accessed March 14, 2016. https://protect.iu.edu/online-safety/protect-data/data-removal.html.

Inter-university Consortium for Political and Social Research (ICPSR). *Guide to Social Science Data Preparation and Archiving: Best Practice throughout the Data Life Cycle,* 5th ed. Ann Arbor: ICPSR, University of Michigan, 2012. http://www.icpsr.umich.edu/files/ICPSR/access/dataprep.pdf.

———. "Disclosure Risk Training—For Public-Use or Not for Public Use, That Is the Question." YouTube video, 43:36, posted October 8, 2014. https://www.youtube.com/watch?v=9vdWseLay9g&feature=youtu.be&list=PLqC9lrhW1VvaKgzk-S87WwrlS-MHliHQo6%22.

———. "ICPSR Collection Development Policy." Accessed June 17, 2016, http://www.icpsr.umich.edu/icpsrweb/content/datamanagement/policies/colldev.html.

———. "Preserving Respondent Confidentiality." Accessed November 20, 2015. https://www.icpsr.umich.edu/icpsrweb/content/deposit/confidentiality.html.

———. "Restricted-Use Data Management at ICPSR." Accessed March 14, 2016. http://www.icpsr.umich.edu/icpsrweb/content/icpsr/access/restricted/index.html.

German Social Science Infrastructure Services (GESIS). Accessed July 8, 2016, http://www.gesis.org/en/services/archiving-and-registering/data-archiving.

Kussmann, Carol. "HashMyFiles Evaluation." May 2012. Minnesota Historical Society. http://www.mnhs.org/preserve/records/legislativerecords/carol/docs_pdfs/HashMy-FilesEvaluation.pdf.

Mackie, Christopher, and Norman Bradburn, eds. *Improving Access to and Confidentiality of Research Data: Report of a Workshop.* Washington, DC: National Academies Press, 2000.

National Archives and Records Administration. "Toolkit for Managing Electronic Records." Accessed June 15, 2015. http://www.archives.gov/records-mgmt/toolkit/#list.

National Institutes of Health. "How Can Covered Entities Use and Disclose Protected Health Information for Research and Comply with the Privacy Rule?" HIPAA Privacy Rule: Information for Researchers. Accessed March 14, 2016. https://privacyrule-andresearch.nih.gov/pr_08.asp.

Olesen, Sarah. *ANDS Guide to Publishing and Sharing Sensitive Data.* Melbourne, Australia: Australian National Data Service, 2014. http://ands.org.au/guides/sensitivedata.pdf.

Pearce-Moses, Richard, ed. *A Glossary of Archival and Records Terminology.* Chicago: Society of American Archivists, 2005. Accessed May 8, 2015, http://www2.archivists.org/glossary/terms/a/appraisal.

*PLOS ONE.* "Guidelines for Specific Study Types: Human Subjects Research." Submission Guidelines. Accessed November 20, 2015. http://journals.plos.org/plosone/s/submission-guidelines#loc-guidelines-for-specific-study-types.

POWRR Project homepage. Accessed March 14, 2016. http://digitalpowrr.niu.edu.

Rothstein, Mark A. "Is Deidentification Sufficient to Protect Health Privacy in Research?" *American Journal of Bioethics* 10, no. 9 (2010): 3–11. doi:10.1080/15265161.2010.494215.

Royal Society. "Data Sharing and Mining: Open Data Policy." Publishing Ethics and Policies. Accessed November 20, 2015. https://royalsociety.org/journals/ethics-policies/data-sharing-mining.

Shaw, Seth. "DataAccessioner." Github. Accessed March 14, 2016. https://github.com/seth-shaw/DataAccessioner.

Storino, Christine M. "Identifying Sensitive, Private, or Legally Protected Data in DRUM Submissions." University of Minnesota Digital Conservancy. 2015. http://hdl.handle.net/11299/171825.

Takao, Hidemasa, Naoto Hayashi, and Kuni Ohtomo. "Brain Morphology Is Individual-Specific Information." *Magnetic Resonance Imaging* 33, no. 6 (2015): 816–21. doi:10.1016/j.mri.2015.03.010.

UK Data Service. *Collections Development Policy.* January 19, 2016. https://www.ukdataservice.ac.uk/media/398725/cd227-collectionsdevelopmentpolicy.pdf.

University of Minnesota Libraries. "Managing Sensitive Data." Accessed March 11, 2016. https://www.lib.umn.edu/datamanagement/sensitive.

University of Texas at Austin. "Information Researchers to Create Digital Archives from Central Lunatic Asylum for Colored Insane." UT News, news release, April 8, 2015. http://news.utexas.edu/2015/04/08/information-researchers-to-create-digital-archives.

US Department of Health and Human Services. "Frequently Asked Questions: Data Sharing." National Institutes of Health, Office of Extramural Research. Revised February 16, 2004. http://grants.nih.gov/grants/policy/data_sharing/data_sharing_faqs.htm.

———. "Health Information Privacy: Guidance Regarding Methods for De-identification of Protected Health Information in Accordance with the Health Insurance Portability and Accountability Act (HIPAA) Privacy Rule." Office of Civil Rights. Accessed November 20, 2015. http://www.hhs.gov/ocr/privacy/hipaa/understanding/coveredentities/De-identification/guidance.html.

US Department of Health and Human Services, Office for Civil Rights. "45 CFR Parts 160 and 164: Standards for Privacy of Individually Identifiable Health Information. Final Rule." *Federal Register* 67, no.157. August 14, 2002. DOCID:fr14au02-32. http://www.gpo.gov/fdsys/pkg/FR-2002-08-14/pdf/02-20554.pdf.

US Geological Survey Earth Resources Observation and Science Center. "Records Appraisal Tool Questions." Accessed June 15, 2015. http://eros.usgs.gov/government/ratool.

Van den Eynden, Veerle, Louise Corti, Matthew Woollard, Libby Bishop, and Laurence Horton. *Managing and Sharing Data: Best Practice for Researchers*, 3rd ed. Essex: UK Data Archive, 2011. http://www.data-archive.ac.uk/media/2894/managingsharing.pdf.

Whyte, Angus. "Five Steps to Decide What Data to Keep: A Checklist for Appraising Research Data," version 1. Edinburgh, UK: Digital Curation Centre, 2014. http://www.dcc.ac.uk/resources/how-guides/five-steps-decide-what-data-keep#sthash.Zrx3J3N3.dpuf.

Whyte, Angus, and Andrew Wilson. *How to Appraise and Select Research Data for Curation*. Working level guide. Acton, Australia: Digital Curation Centre, Australian National Data Service, 2010.

World Medical Association (WMA). *WMA Declaration of Helsinki: Ethical Principles for Medical Research Involving Human Subjects*. Fortaleza, Brazil: 64th WMA General Assembly, 2013. http://www.wma.net/en/30publications/10policies/b3.

# Processing and Treatment Actions for Data

In this step we review the contents of the data to determine if the submission contains all the necessary information to sufficiently understand and reuse the data. If needed, we apply our skills as data curators to *optimize the data submission for reuse*. An important consideration for *Step 3* will be to document any changes that are made to the submission and keep track of all correspondence with the data author to maintain provenance.

## 3.1 Secure the Files

Before making any changes, we need to secure the files and protect the integrity of the original submission. This saves the original order, file content, and metadata of the submission so that later we can refer to or revert to the original if needed. First, create a new working copy of the files and any author-submitted metadata. This working copy might be saved to a shared staff drive (e.g., departmental remote access server) with an easily recognizable folder name, which allows for other curators to continue the work in case of unexpected staff outages. Here a file-naming schema can be applied to uniquely identify the project, such as CuratorLastName_YYYYMMDD_SubmissionID.

If there are many files (perhaps more than ten), you might use UNIX commands to recursively copy the files to the working directory (`cp -r originalFolder/* destinationFolder`) or, if you don't have direct access to the staging server location, use a browser-based tool such as DownloadThemAll (Firefox addon) or Download Master (Chrome Extension) to copy the files in one swift action.

# 3.2 Create a Log of Actions Taken

A curation log can be used to document all actions and changes that are made with the data submission as well as to capture any important correspondence with the author. A simple text-based log might combine any information collected from the file inventory in *Step 2*, including the original metadata, or your repository might use a more sophisticated tool, like a wiki or an Electronic Lab Notebook, to record this information. Use a template so that each log has the same structure and information (see example in figure 3.1). The log should be stored in a safe long-term location for future reference. For example, the Data Repository for the University of Minnesota (using DSpace loads a copy of the curation log to the finalized data record in our repository as a Metadata File, a content type that does not display publicly for download, but remains stored and perserved with the submission record.

---

CURATION LOG (save as plain .txt file)

Submission ID: <paste record ID here>

File Location: drive/CuratorLastName_YYYYMMDD_SubmissionID
   1. Inventory of Files Received
      a. List here
   2. Changes made to files
      a. List here
   3. Added Files
      a. List here
   4. Deleted Files
      a. List here
   5. Metadata Changes
      a. List metadata added, removed, why
   6. Correspondence Notes
      a. Questions asked of author
      b. Include email summaries or copy/paste responses to question.
   7. Other issues

**Original Metadata As Originally Submitted from Author (include timestamps)**

Paste repository generated <xml> here

---

**FIGURE 3.1**

Example curator's log template for the Data Repository for the University of Minnesota (DRUM).

# 3.3 Inspect the File Names and Structure

Take a moment to review the submission and understand any file relationships, directory structure, and naming conventions that might represent important metadata that could be helpful in understanding the data contents.

## *File Relationships and Directory Structure*

Some data files have dependencies on other files to run correctly. This typically becomes known when you try to execute a file and an error returns that the dependent file is not found. Some tools may help, such as PE Explorer, a tool used to reverse-engineer software, which includes a "Dependency Scanner" function that is intended to identify malware in an executable.[1] But this tool can also be "helpful in discovering missing or invalid modules, import/export mismatches, circular dependencies and other module-related problems, and in troubleshooting system errors caused by the loading or executing of modules."[2] A case study later in this step describes a more human approach to understanding the file directory structures—asking the data author. It is important to preserve any inherent relationships in the files (consider preserving directory structures in using compression tools such as the zip file format), and it might be necessary to generate documentation to help others understand how the files relate and incorporate this information into the documentation (discussed later in *Step 3.5*).

## *File-Naming Conventions*

Good data management practice suggests that using a consistent file-naming convention is one way to help researchers keep better track of their data. For example, file names may track the version of a data file (e.g., v001, v002 instead of USETHISONE, FINALFINAL), differentiate between various stages of analysis (e.g., "raw" data versus "processed" data), and track the evolution of the data using dates and other codes. However, some file-naming convention meanings are not easily apparent and must be explained in the documentation. See the example presented by Stanford University Libraries where the file named "FR3S.140623.129C.2653.W.JPG" has meaning only if the details of the creators' naming convention are known.[3] In this case, the file name indicates, "This was image 2,653 of whole, caged tile 129 from study site 3 in shallow water, taken on June 23, 2014."

If you detect that the author may be using a complex file-naming convention, ensure that this schema is described in the documentation along with an explanation of codes or number sequences used (e.g., "C" indicates "caged" in the above example).

## Understanding File Structures in Action

The next case study by Jennifer Thoegersen presents an easy-to-implement approach for understanding file-directory structures with the added benefit of direct liaison interaction between researcher and librarian.

# Just-in-Time Data Management Consultations

*Jennifer Thoegersen*[*]

While it is preferable to provide data management support to every researcher at an institution throughout the data life cycle, in practice this isn't always possible. Data sets may show up on your data repository's doorstep from researchers who had little data management training or have given little thought to optimizing their data's reusability. Files may be disorganized, poorly named, or lack documentation. In these cases, the University of Nebraska-Lincoln Libraries staff provides "just-in-time" data management consultations.

When the repository receives a data set, it gets reviewed by the data curation librarian. If the data set is difficult to navigate and understand, a consultation will be set up with the depositing researcher. The librarian will bring along a printed copy of the folder structure, including file names, of the entire data set in question. During the consultation, the librarian will ask the researcher to describe the data set while looking through the folder structure. Often, the researcher will begin to notice flaws in the folder structure, inadequate folder or file names, or extraneous or missing files. They will often begin making notes on the provided folder structure printout. They will discuss the creation of a README text file that provides descriptive information about the data set and explain the organizational structure and file-naming conventions of the data set. The librarian can also use this opportunity to discuss preferred file formats and file-naming conventions and encourage the researcher to transform data to these formats prior to resubmission, if possible.[4] The researcher and librarian will set a date for resubmission of the newly organized data set.

# FOLDER STRUCTURE PRINTOUT

Here is how we create a text file printout containing the folder structure (and all the files contained in the folders) of a data set.

## *INSTRUCTIONS FOR WINDOWS*

1. In Windows File Explorer, navigate to the top-level folder of the data set.
2. While holding the Shift key, right-click on the folder and select "Open command window here" from the menu.
3. Type `tree /f /a > tree.txt` and press Enter.
4. A text file called `tree.txt` will be created in the current folder, which you can then open and print.

## *INSTRUCTIONS FOR MAC*

1. Open Finder.
2. Go to Applications → Utilities, and then select Terminal. A command terminal will open.
3. Type `cd` in the terminal.
4. In Finder, navigate to the folder containing the data set.
5. Select the data set folder, and drag and drop it into the terminal window. This will make the full path to the data set appear on the command line. The full command should be
6. `cd full/path/to/dataset`
7. Press Enter.
8. Type `find . -print | sed -e 's;[^/]*/;|--;g;s;--| ;|;g' > tree.txt` and press Enter.
9. A text file called `tree.txt` will be created in the current folder, which you can then open and print.

Ideally, data management will permeate the entire data life cycle, resulting in well-structured and well-documented data sets. However, even when this is not the case, "just-in-time" data management consultations can improve the reusability and sustainability of data sets deposited in a data repository.

# 3.4 Inspect the Data

In order to review the content of the data, we must first open and run the files. This step will often require specialized software. Note that sometimes opening each file is not practical (in the case of large numbers of files or too many file types), and spot checks might suffice.

## *Software Needed by Data Curators*

The software needed by data curators will vary by the focus of the repository and the types of data collected. One question to address at this step: Do you need specialized software to open the files? If the specialized software needed to run the data, you might consider the following options:

- *Proprietary software and cost prohibitive*: Determine if the files can be converted to a non-proprietary file format that is more accessible (e.g., output proprietary ESRI GIS files as open standard shapefiles).
- *Open-source software or freeware available for download*: Include instructions on how to access the software in the documentation (with its version number, last accessed date, and a [persistent] URL).
- *Custom-built and not previously published software*: Invite the code author to deposit their source code as a separate data submission to your repository (and link the records together) or to an external open code repository such as GitHub or RunMyCode.[5]

Many data files will arrive in commonly used formats. Here are some examples of some software packages (in alphabetical order) that may be useful:

- **Adobe Acrobat Pro** (.pdf, .obj): Opens a range of files, including text and fixed images, but 3D models (OBJ versions) are also viewable in Adobe. Adobe Reader is the free version but may not have the tools included in Acrobat Pro needed to manipulate the files. More details at https://acrobat.adobe.com.
- **Adobe Photoshop** (.psd): Opens a range of visual file formats, including the proprietary Photoshop formats. More details at http://www.adobe.com/photoshop.
- **AliView** (.fa): Opens and visualizes sequence data (FASTA files). Free download at http://www.ormbunkar.se/aliview/#DOWNLOAD.
- **ArcGIS** (.shp, .e00): Opens GIS files such as shapefiles, geodatabases, CAD, and raster files. More details at https://www.arcgis.com.
- **Matlab** (.m): Programming language used for scientific and mathematical models. More details at http://www.mathworks.com/products/matlab.
- **Microsoft Excel** (.xls, .xlsx): Opens tabular data, delimiter-separated formats, XML-structured data, comma-separated values (.csv). More details at http://office.microsoft.com/en-us/excel.

- **MZmine**: Runs mass spectral data files (.raw) with a focus on LC-MS processing. Free download available at http://mzmine.github.io.
- **Omero**: A popular biological microscopic image software and file conversion tool. Free download available at https://www.openmicroscopy.org.
- **Statistical Software** (SPSS files such as .sav, .sas; R files such as .Rdata, .R, .Rnw): Statistical software packages such as the open-source R program (https://www.r-project.org) is prevalent, but many researchers also use proprietary packages such as SPSS (http://www.ibm.com/software/analytics/spss) or SAS (http://www.sas.com). Free download of RStudio available at https://www.rstudio.com.
- **TeX** (for LaTeX compiling): Many programs available to run TeX files such as MacTeX for MacOSX (https://tug.org/mactex), and proTeXt (https://www.tug.org/protext) for Windows.

# Attempt to Understand and Use the Data

This is one of the most important steps in the data curation process. Submissions to a data repository may lack key pieces of information or the documentation files may not be complete or comprehensive enough to allow for reuse. For example the study by Roche, Kruuk, Lanfear, and Binning found that over half of the 100 data sets that they studied, all published in Dryad between 2012 and 2013 due to the data-archiving policies of seven "leading journals" from the ecology and evolution field, were lacking critical information for reuse.[6] Their analysis addressed the "completeness" (Is all data supporting the findings available?) and "reusability" (How readily can the archived data be accessed and reused by third parties?) of each data set, and based on their criteria, they rated 56 percent incomplete (3 or less on a 5-point Likert scale) "because of missing data or insufficient metadata" and 64 percent lacking the essential metadata or using inadequate files formats ("non-machine-readable file formats, such as pdf, that require specialized software to read") that would prevent reuse.[7] Moreover, the study reports that nearly 40 percent of the "incomplete" data sets lacked only small amounts of data that might have been avoided or corrected with some help.

# Questions to Help Understand the Data

Shortly after submission is the best time to try to detect any quality or usability issues with the data; as time goes on, the data author may not be able or willing to address any questions about information that may be missing from the data submission. The long-term usability of the data will depend on a thorough review of the data contents, which involves opening each data file and attempting to understand the data as a potential user. In this way, by addressing any concerns with the author, a future user of the data may encounter fewer difficulties.

Questions and areas to look for when reviewing the data include

- Checking for overall quality and usability issues. Does the data appear consistent or logical? Are there gaps in the data that cannot be explained?
- Look at the presentation and note any apparent errors. Are the headers well aligned in the tabular data file, for example?
- Note how codes are explained. If there are "blank" data fields, verify that the documentation explains these null values and that other missing values are described.
- Run any software code and be sure that any dependent files are available.
- Look for missing units in the data. Units, such as the values and sizes of a measurement, often are not well described if the typical values are commonplace for the field. However, all information should be clearly defined and no assumptions made.

Things such as missing data, ambiguous headings, code execution failures, and organization concerns may be detected in this step and potentially corrected. Note any oddities or irregularities in the curation log, and generate a list of questions to bring to the data author who might quickly be able to resolve any errors or issues. Here are some examples of questions that could arise in a data repository:

- **Understanding the files**
  - ○ The folders contain many files. How were these files named? What is the significance of the numbers and the letters in the file names?
  - ○ What program(s) (and what versions) did you use to generate the data and process the data? Are these programs available for free download? Is there any other instrument-specific information needed to view or interpret the data?
- **Understanding the data**
  - ○ It is unclear what some of your variables are (e.g., OE; Pab, etc.). Do you already have a codebook that might be worth including in your submission?
  - ○ How do your column header codes translate? I've included a data dictionary template for you to fill out that defines each header column name.
  - ○ Some sites show values of "0"—what does this indicate for that value?
  - ○ Some data points show values of "–9999" could you please define what this means for your data. How is this code different from a blank cell?
  - ○ Some spaces are highlighted yellow in the Excel file. What do they signify?

- **Missing granularity**
  - I am unsure how to interpret the schematics provided in the documentation. Can you add more detail explaining what these schematics illustrate? Or would these be understood as-is by other researchers using this data?
  - Some date/time points have fractional seconds (e.g., "2014/8/6 15:40:5.625"). Can you note the sensitivity of the instruments used to collect data in your documentation?
  - Can you provide explicit units for all measurement types? Although units are given in shorthand (for example, $m$), a fuller description of exactly what units are being used in measurement ("m = abbreviation for meters") will be helpful.
  - I noticed that many packages are built under R3.0.2. Is this the version of R you used to do your analysis?
- **Missing Documentation**
  - In addition to the documentation you provide about the nomenclature used within the files, it would be helpful to have separate documentation about the file structures themselves such as: How do the files all relate to one another?
  - When was data collected? (At regularly timed intervals? Why these times?)
  - What was the methodology for creating the data? Please use the readme.txt template that I have attached to give you a start on filling out this information.
- **Missing Files**
  - When running the software code, I noticed a file missing that is called by a function used several times in your code. Please send this missing file or explained why it is no longer needed.
  - Would it be possible to get a copy of your survey questions by which this data was obtained? We prefer that the actual survey be included as part of the submission. This likely will be important to help people to understand your data.
  - Could you provide me with your R session info for running the R scripts? This can be included in the README file.

# Documenting Computational Environments

Scientific workflows are a form of published documentation that describes the environment and conditions of a computational analysis performed during research. Providing others with the detailed information necessary to fully replicate an experiment, in other words, a reproducible computing environment, is an emerging trend in scientific scholarship where best practices are being developed. Repositories such as MyExperiment (http://www.myexperiment.org) provide an openly accessible platform where these workflows can be shared and tested.[8] Similarly, tools that may help data submitters pull together a comprehensive submission also exist. For example, NYU has developed two tools to help with this: ReproZip (https://github.com/ViDA-NYU/reprozip) and VisTrails (http://www.vistrails.org/index.php/Downloads), which are open-source tools that allow researchers to capture their data files, code libraries, and coding environment settings in one "container" so that others may reproduce their results without having to re-engineer the environment. In cases of code deposit, it might be beneficial to ask the data submitter to capture their data submission using a tool like ReproZip to ensure that all the necessary components are captured.

## Detecting Hidden Documentation in Action

Some file formats tend to be more "self-describing" than others. For example, digital cameras often embed self-documenting types of information in the photos taken, such as geospatial coordinates and copyright information, and recommended software to open the file. Therefore, in this curation step, try to detect and extract any "hidden documentation" inherent to the data files that may facilitate reuse. Alicia Hofelich Mohr, from the University of Minnesota, provides examples in the next two case studies

# Finding Metadata in R: Where to Look

*Alicia Hofelich Mohr**

The software R is an increasingly popular tool for data analysis, statistical computing, and visualization.[9] It is free to download (https://cran.r-project.org) and highly extensible. Users can load and create extensions for the software, called "packages," that provide increased functionality through reusable functions and documentation.

Depending on how the data was loaded into R, any metadata about the data may or may not be included. For example, data can be loaded into R from

1. a delimited file format (e.g., .csv)
2. an .Rdata file
3. other statistical packages (e.g., SPSS or Stata files)
4. data that is embedded in packages
5. data from another R script

If the metadata exists, it may also be stored or associated with the data set in several different ways. Here are some tips on how to find the main documentation for a data set in R. These documentation elements include variable labels (what a variable is about), value labels (what the numbers in a variable mean), and missing values (what codes indicate nonvalid data).

# A DELIMITED DATA FILE

All R projects received for curation should include a script file (.R file) and, if reading in a delimited file (e.g., .csv file, .txt file, etc.), the data set as a separate file. In the R script, there will be a line of code that points to the location of the delimited data file on the user's computer to load it into R. Look for some of the following common commands early in the script (see figure 3.2):

- `setwd(mydirectory)`
- `read.delim()`
- `read.csv()`
- `read.table()`

The working directory can be set with `setwd()`, or it can be explicit in the location of the file in any of the `read` commands. To load the data file, the directory will have to match the location of the data file on the user's computer. To aid reuse, the curator may want to put a comment in (a line started with # in the script) directing a user to change the parts of the script that reference the working directory, if such comments were not included originally.

## *VARIABLE LABELS*

From a delimited data set, typically R captures no metadata beyond the column names, which are read in as the variable names for the data set. Variable labels can be supplied in the script to the data set (which may be done with commands like `attribute()` or `attr()`). However, because R allows variable names up to 10,000 bytes,[10] very explicit variable names may have been provided that negate the need for additional labels (use the `names()` command in R to see the full variable names). Variable labels may be included in the first or second line of the data file and not read into R as data. To determine if this is the case in a script, look for the `skip` argument in any of the `read` commands that loaded the data set, or for code that removes those lines after the data file is loaded (see figure 3.2). Either way, information on where to find the variable labels should be provided in a separate documentation file and referenced as a comment in the code.

```
##### Example R Script with Output ######

# Required packages
library(lme4)
library(tm)
library(foreign)

# Set working directory - change to match location of data
setwd("~/Desktop")

# Read in delimited datafile (skips first line of file, re-codes 9999 and
# 8888 as missing
data <- read.csv(file = "Dataset1.csv", header = T, na.strings = c("9999", "8888"),
    skip = 1)

# Load in a .Rdatafile that contains a data2 object with the second
# dataset
load("Dataset2.Rdata")
ls()

> [1] "data"  "data2"

# Read in an SPSS file
data3 <- read.spss(file = "Dataset3.sav", use.value.labels = FALSE, to.data.frame = TRUE)
head(data3)

>    ID Group Trialtype word  medRT
> 1 1491    1         1    1 1825.5
> 2 1560    1         1    1  610.0
> 3 1834    1         1    1  961.5
> 4 1997    1         1    1  848.0
> 5 2146    1         1    1  985.5
> 6 2200    1         1    1  870.5

attr(data3, "variable.labels")

>                            ID                           Group
> "Participant Random ID Number"         "High or Low Empathy"
>                     Trialtype                            word
>                  "Trial Type"                  "Word Shown"
>                         medRT
>    "Median RT to classify word"

attr(data3$word, "value.labels")

>    sad happy angry
>      3     2     1
```

**FIGURE 3.2**

Example R script illustrating relevant commands and output for identifying metadata in R.

## *VALUE LABELS*

Unlike other statistical packages, categorical variables in R do not need to be coded numerically, but rather can be textual labels for each group coded as a "factor." For example, in SPSS, a variable labeled Gender may have three values (0, 1, and 2), which require value labels such as 0="male"; 1="female"; 2="other." In R, the variable Gender can instead have values that *are* the labels—"male"; "female"; "other"—so there is no need for numeric value labels. However, additional documentation is needed if the codes or categories are unclear. Helpful commands to see this information in R include summary() and str().

## *MISSING VALUES*

Without using additional R packages, R has only one code to indicate a missing value (NA), which can limit how users distinguish between different kinds of missing data. Therefore, users may code other values to act like NA when the data is read into R by using the na.strings part of the read commands. For example, if the data set contains two types of missing values, coded as 8888 and 9999, the command read.csv(…, na.strings=c("8888", "9999") will recode both of these values as NA in R. Some R packages, such as *memisc* (https:// cran.r-project.org/web/packages/memisc), will allow more than one missing value.

## AN .RDATA FILE

Double clicking an .Rdata file will open it directly in R; otherwise, .Rdata files can be read in from the R console with the load() command. Once an .Rdata file is loaded, the data set will be present in current workspace but may not automatically appear in the console window. To confirm that it is present, type ls() in the command window to see a list of objects (the contents of the .Rdata file) loaded in R's workspace.* Note that the ls() command will display all objects currently loaded in R's workspace, so it will return any objects currently in the workspace along with any new data sets or objects brought in with the .Rdata file. To view the data set or object, type the name of the data set into the command window to view, or use the command head(), View(), or str() to view a subset or summary of the data.

Because .Rdata files may contain one or more data sets, information about the contents should be provided in the documentation or script files submitted with the .Rdata file. If not provided, a curator may wish to list the contents of the .Rdata file in the file description or project metadata.

---

* RStudio, a user interface for R, makes it easy for users to see objects loaded into the Workspace with the Environment tab.

## *VARIABLE LABELS*

Data set variable labels may be embedded as attributes for the entire data set or for individual variables. The `attribute()` command will return the names of all attributes embedded in the data set. To examine a specific attribute (for example, an attribute called "variable.labels" associated with a data set called "dataname"), use `attr(dataname, "variable.labels")`, which will return the metadata associated with that attribute. Because these attributes are embedded within the data, exporting the contents of the attributes, by writing them to a .csv or .txt file, would help enhance the data's discoverability when shared, as these file types are more likely to be exposed to full-text search in a repository. As with data loaded from delimited files, if no embedded metadata exists for variable labels, they should be specified in separate documentation.

## *VALUE LABELS*

The same principles for delimited files discussed above hold true for .Rdata files. However, it is possible that value labels are embedded either within the data set or within each variable. To examine whether variables have specific attributes associated with them, use the `attribute(dataname$Var1)` command.

# DATA FROM OTHER STATISTICAL SOFTWARE PACKAGES

R packages allow for reading in other kinds of data files. Some popular packages in the social sciences include *xlsx* (https://cran.r-project.org/web/packages/xlsx) for reading Microsoft Excel files and *foreign* (https://cran.r-project.org/web/packages/foreign) for reading in SPSS, SAS, or Stata files. Check the top of the file for the packages that are used in the code, for example, look for `library(xlsx)` or `require(xlsx)`.

## *VARIABLE AND VALUE LABELS*

Depending on the type of file, metadata may be captured in different ways. Excel files may be read in using the `read.xlsx()` command, which allows the user to specify which worksheets in the Excel workbook contain the data. It is possible that separate worksheets in the Excel file contain additional documentation about the variable or value labels. For SPSS .sav files that are read in using the *foreign* package, the variable and value labels present in the .sav file are stored as attributes of the R data object (named "dataspss", for example). Variable labels can be seen using the `attr(dataspss, "variable.labels")` command, and value labels can be seen using the `attr(dataspss$Var1, "value.labels")`. Similarly, for Stata .dba files that are read in using the *foreign* package (and assigned to the name "datastata"), use the `attr(datastata, "var.labels")` command to identify variable labels. The value labels are stored in a combination of two different attributes for Stata files: a list of value labels, `attr(datastata, "val.labels")`, which gives a table name for each variable, and the label table, `attr(datastata, "label.table")`, which gives the specific labels for each table referenced by the `val.labels` attribute.

# DATA EMBEDDED IN A PACKAGE OR LIBRARY

Some data may be embedded within packages, which users submit to the CRAN R repository (https://cran.r-project.org) for public use. Documentation submitted with the package can be found in a PDF document in the CRAN R repository or by using the `help()` command when using the package. Although these data sets are often included as examples for using a package function, they may also be submitted to a disciplinary or institutional repository as part of a script or other research documentation underlying a published paper. For curation, it is helpful to note which commands give the relevant metadata for the file (for example, `help(Orange)` provides documentation for R's built-in *Orange* dataset).

# DATA SOURCED FROM ANOTHER R SCRIPT

An R script may reference and run a different R script using the command `source()`. This is commonly used to run custom functions, but could also reference data that is simulated in another script. For curation, ensure that any supplementary sourced files are collected with the submission and archived with the data with adequate documentation; otherwise, the script that references them may not run correctly or reproduce the same results.

# Helpful Commands for Exporting Metadata from Statistical Software Packages SPSS, Stata, and R

*Alicia Hofelich Mohr**

Many statistical packages embed metadata within a data file. While this is help-ful for users of the data, this metadata is often lost when saving statistical files down into nonproprietary, more archival-friendly formats (such as .csv, .txt, or ascii). Additionally, if these data files were submitted to a repository with full-text searching, metadata within a data file would likely not be exposed to these search-es. Therefore, it may be helpful to export internal metadata stored in statistical data files to external files in readable formats for sharing and archival purposes.[†] This case study will describe how to do this in SPSS, Stata, and R.

## METADATA FROM SPSS FILES

First, open the .sav file in SPSS and open a new SPSS Syntax file. Then type and run the following commands:

```
DISPLAY DICTIONARY.
CODEBOOK.
EXECUTE.
```

This will print the data dictionary and codebook for that data file in the open SPSS output file (.spv). Because the .spv file requires SPSS to view, a better option is to save the output as a PDF document using the OMS command. First, you will need to change the outfile location to match where you want the file to be saved, then run the codebook command by typing and running the code below in the SPSS Syntax file:

```
OMS
/SELECT ALL
/DESTINATION FORMAT=PDF
OUTFILE="C:\Users\Documents\Data_Codebook.pdf".
```

---

† Most statistical programs offer several options for export formats, including PDF, TXT, and XML.

```
CODEBOOK
/VARINFO LABEL TYPE FORMAT MEASURE VALUELABELS MISSING
/OPTIONS VARORDER=VARLIST SORT=ASCENDING MAXCATS=200
/STATISTICS COUNT PERCENT MEAN STDDEV.

EXECUTE.

OMSEND.
```

The result will be a `Data_Codebook.pdf` file that is located in the specified directory. It will contain the variable labels, value labels, missing data codes, and summary statistics (count, percent, mean, and standard deviation) for each variable in the data file. By extracting this information, a data user will be able to learn more about the data without needing to open SPSS to view the data file (.sav) or the output file (.spv). It could also accompany an Excel or .csv version of the SPSS data to provide the relevant metadata for each variable.

## METADATA FROM STATA FILES

Open Stata, and then open a .dta file in the program. Once the data is loaded, type `codebook` into the command window. The codebook will then display in the command window. You may need to scroll to the bottom (or press the Enter or Return key) to see the entire output. As with SPSS, you may also want to export this information to a format that can be read outside of the Stata program. This can be done with the following syntax typed into the command window or a do-file:

```
set more off
sysuse auto
log using codebook.txt, text
codebook
log close
```

This will produce a plain-text codebook file named that will be saved in current working directory in Stata (you can retrieve the working directory by typing `pwd` in the command window or change the wording directory using the `cd` command).

## METADATA FROM R FILES

Unlike SPSS and Stata, R does not have a standard way of storing variable and value label metadata, nor does it have a standard way of extracting metadata. However, variable labels and value labels may be stored as attributes of a datafile in R, which is how this metadata is stored when an SPSS or Stata file is read in to R using the *foreign* package (https://cran.r-project.org/web/packages/foreign).

If this is the case, it is possible to export this metadata as a separate text file resembling a data dictionary, and I have written several functions in an R package called *datadictionary* that do this (https://github.com/ajhmohr/datadictionary). Because metadata may be stored in various ways in R, these functions may need to be customized for specific data (and attribute) structures.

Once a data set (.Rdata or other file) is loaded into R, named here as myda-ta, you may locate the attributes that contain relevant metadata (e.g., variable labels and value labels) by typing the following in the command window (see figure 3.3 for an example):

```
attributes(mydata)
attributes(mydata[,1])
```

```
##### Exporting Metadata from R #####

# load in R data file
load("~/Desktop/ExampleData.Rdata")
ls()

> [1] "mydata"

# look for attributes that may contain relevant metadata
attributes(mydata)

> $names
> [1] "ID"        "Group"      "Trialtype" "word"      "medRT"
>
> $row.names
> [1] ""
>
> $class
> [1] "data.frame"
>
> $variable.labels
>                         ID                       Group
> "Participant Random ID Number"     "High or Low Empathy"
>                  Trialtype                        word
>                "Trial Type"                "Word Shown"
>                      medRT
>    "Median RT to classify word"
>
> $codepage
> [1] 65001

attributes(mydata[, 1])

> NULL

attributes(mydata[, 2])

> $value.labels
>  low high
>   2    1

# The variable labels are stored as the 'variable.labels' attribute of the
# dataset
attr(mydata, "variable.labels")

>                         ID                       Group
> "Participant Random ID Number"     "High or Low Empathy"
>                  Trialtype                        word
>                "Trial Type"                "Word Shown"
>                      medRT
>    "Median RT to classify word"

# The value labels are stores as the 'value.labels' attribute of individual
# variables
attr(mydata[, 2], "value.labels")

>  low high
>   2    1

# install 'datadictionary' package from github
library(devtools)
install_github("ajhmohr/datadictionary")
library(datadictionary)

# Use DictionarySPSS to create data dictionary file
DictionarySPSS(mydata, file = "DataDictionary.txt")
```

**FIGURE 3.3**

Example R script showing ways to explore variable and value labels stored as attributes of an .Rdata file.

The first command will return all attributes associated with the data set. Look for the attributes that hold the variable label and value label information. In the example in figure 3.3, the variable labels are stored as an attribute of mydata called `variable.labels`. Sometimes, value labels are stored as attributes associated with each individual variable, rather than in attributes of the overall data set. In this case, use the second command, which will display attributes of the first (`[,1]`) column, or first variable, in the data. You may need to scan several columns by adjusting the number after the comma (i.e., `[,2]` or `[,3]`), as value labels may not be defined for all variables. In figure 3.3, you can see that the attribute `value.labels` is stored for each individual variable, and is null for the first variable, but takes the values of `1=high` and `2=low` for the second variable.

If the value labels are stored as in figure 3.3 (which is how SPSS files loaded into R with *foreign* are often structured), you can use the `DictionarySPSS()` function from the *datadictionary* package to write a data dictionary from the file. This function will extract the value labels from each variable, and then write a text file that contains a list of all the variables with the variable names, labels from the `variable.labels` attribute, and the value labels from `value.labels` attribute listed with each (see figure 3.4).

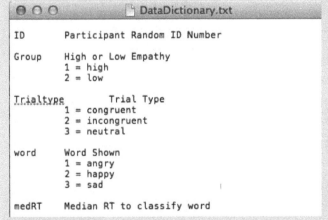

**FIGURE 3.4**
Example text codebook generated from the `DictionarySPSS()` function in the *datadictionary* R package.

If the value labels instead are stored in a combination of `label.table` and `val.label` attributes at the data level (as common for Stata files when loaded into R with *foreign*), then the `DictionaryStata()` function can be used to write a data dictionary from the file. This function first combines the information in `label.table` and `val.label` to create a single `value.label` attribute, and then writes the dictionary as in the `DictionarySPSS()` function.

If your data follows a different structure, or if you have lists of variable labels and value labels you would like to organize into a data dictionary, you can use the more generic `DataDictionary()` function. In this function, you will need to specify a list of variable labels and a list of value labels that are the same length as the number of variables (columns) in the data set. The order of each label should also correspond to the order of the variables in the data.

While these functions provide one way of creating a data dictionary from stored R attributes, there are other methods for extracting this data. For example, the package *memisc* (https://cran.r-project.org/web/packages/memisc) has built-in functions for creating codebooks and other documentation for survey data in R.

## SUMMARY

Whatever method you choose, finding ways to automatically extract metadata from these statistical packages make it easy for users and curators alike to create documentation files for data sets. Because these files do not require statistical packages to read, they increase accessibility and have the potential to expose more of the variable-level metadata to full-text searches when these documents are included with a data submission to a repository. It can also be useful documentation for R users, especially if they are working with data originally from SPSS or Stata, as variable-level metadata for these data files in R is not displayed as prominently as it is in the native statistical programs.

# 3.5 Work with Author to Enhance the Submission

Once you have inspected the data and noted any issues in your log, now is your chance to work with the author to resolve these issues. For example, data curation staff might e-mail the author a list of questions to resolve and then augment the files and documentation, as shown in figure 3.5. Another approach could be to schedule a time to meet with the data author to gain a shared understanding of the challenges encountered during the curation process.

Subject: Curation of Your Submission to DRUM

From: datarepo@umn.edu

Dear <submitter>,

Thank you for your submission to the Data Repository for the U of M (DRUM). I am in the process of reviewing your submission, and I have a few questions for you:

1.  Could you provide me with your R session info for running the scripts named file1.R and file2.R? Also, it would be great if I could get an approximate date that these files were finalized, if that is possible.

2.  I noticed some blank spaces in the file3.csv file. Does a blank space signify that no sampling was done at that location for that particular year? If not, what do they signify?

Please let me know if you have any questions or concerns. Thank you very much for your submission, and I look forward to hearing from you.

Sincerely,

<curator name>

DRUM Scientific Data Curator

~~~~~~~~~~~~~~~~~~~~~~~~~~~~~~~~~~~~~~~~~~~~~~~~~~~~~~~~~~

*Data Repository for U of M (DRUM)*

*Email: datarepo@umn.edu*

*Web: z.umn.edu/drum*

*One of several services for Data Management by the University Libraries*

*University of Minnesota–Twin Cities*

*http://lib.umn.edu/datamanagement*

---

**FIGURE 3.5**
Example e-mail to author requesting further information.

# Readme Files: Documentation for Any File Format

For data that does not have adequate descriptive documentation, the data curator may work with the author to draft a comprehensive "readme" file that details any aspects of the data needed to understand and use the data. A template can be used to help the author to consider what information might be needed. The completed readme file will make the data submission more comprehensive and therefore facilitate reuse.

Figure 3.6 shows an example readme.txt template, which can be downloaded from http://z.umn.edu/readme. This template was adapted from the readme file created by Wendy Kozlowski at Cornell University.[11] Additionally, this type of template could scale to a wide variety of data types or be customized for sending to authors based on the different types of data they produce.

---

This readme.txt file was generated on <YYYYMMDD> by <Name>

GENERAL INFORMATION
1. Title of Data set:
2. File Information:
   A. Filename:
   B. Short description:
   C. Filename:
   D. Short description
   E. Filename:
   F. Short description:
   G. If data set includes multiple files related to one another, include relationship here:
3. Principal Investigator Contact Information
   A. Name:           C. Address:
   B. Institution:    D. E-mail:
4. Associate or Co-investigator Contact Information
   A. Name:           C. Address:
   B. Institution:    D. E-mail:
5. Associate or Co-investigator Contact Information
   A. Name:           C. Address:
   B. Institution:    D. E-mail:
6. Date of data collection (single date, range, approximate date): <suggested format YYYYMMDD>
7. Geographic location of data collection (where was data collected?): n/a
8. Date files were created: <suggested format YYYYMMDD>
9. Are there multiple versions of the data set? yes/no
   A. If yes, list versions:
   B. Name of file that was updated:
      i. Why was the file updated?
      ii. When was the file updated?
   C. Name of file that was updated:
      i. Why was the file updated?
      ii. When was the file updated?

10. Information about funding sources that supported the collection of the data:

METHODOLOGICAL INFORMATION
1. Description of methods used for collection/generation of data:
   <Include links or references to publications or other documentation containing experimental design or protocols used in data collection>
2. Methods for processing the data:
3. Instrument-specific information needed to interpret the data:
4. Standards and calibration information, if appropriate:
5. Environmental/experimental conditions:
6. Describe any quality-assurance procedures performed on the data:
7. Codes or symbols used to note or characterize low quality/questionable outliers that people should be aware of
   A. Code/symbol:

B. Definition:
C. Code/symbol:
D. Definition:
8. People involved with sample collection, processing, analysis, and/or submission:

DATA-SPECIFIC INFORMATION
1. Parameters and/or variables used in the data set
   A. Name:
   B. Description:
   C. Units of measurement:
   D. Name:
   E. Description:
   F. Units of measurement:
   G. Name:
   H. Description:
   I. Units of measurement:
2. Column headings for tabular data
   A. Full name (spell out abbreviated words):
   B. Definition:
   C. Full name (spell out abbreviated words):
   D. Definition:
   E. Full name (spell out abbreviated words):
   F. Definition:
3. Codes or symbols used to record missing data
   A. Code/symbol:
   B. Definition:
   C. Code/symbol:
   D. Definition:
4. Other specialized formats or abbreviations used:
5. Additional related data collected that was not included in the current data package:

SHARING/ACCESS INFORMATION
1. Licenses/restrictions placed on the data:
2. Links to publications that cite or use the data:
3. Links to other publicly accessible locations of the data:
4. Links/relationships to ancillary data sets:
5. Was data derived from another source?
   A. List source(s):
6. Recommended citation for the data:

---

## FIGURE 3.6

Readme template (saved as a plain text or .txt format) such as this one can be a useful way to solicit descriptive information about a data set.

## *Working with Authors to Curate Their Data*

Andrew S. Gordon, Lisa Steiger, and Karen E. Adolph from the Databrary Project based at New York University provide an example of working with the author at this stage in the next case study.

# Losing Research Data Due to Lack of Curation and Preservation

*Andrew S. Gordon, Lisa Steiger, and Karen E. Adolph*

Child development researchers have a problem: Their primary source of data is video, a medium with boundless potential for reuse; but researchers lack the community practices and infrastructure to make reuse possible. Researchers lack tools and standard practices across labs and institutions for organizing, storing, and ensuring long-term preservation of their video data, thus precluding reuse. This case study describes how Databrary developed a solution to the problem of data loss by enabling child development researchers to curate and describe their own research videos in an online repository that allows for sharing and reuse and provides long-term preservation. More generally, the processes and strategies described here can inform active, researcher-driven curation in other academic disciplines.

## VIDEO DATA IN CHILD DEVELOPMENT RESEARCH

For most child development researchers, video recordings of children's behavior serve as the raw data for their research programs. Video is the medium of choice because it captures the richness and complexity of children's behavior easily and with high fidelity. Moreover, as a medium, video is especially well suited for analyzing behavior because it allows researchers to manipulate time. They can watch recorded behaviors unfold at various playback speeds, stop the video to focus on a particular event, and loop portions of the recording to better understand an event.

The general process is to record children's behavior and then score and analyze the recordings. The methods for collecting, annotating, and analyzing video footage are boundless. Videos can focus on experimental manipulations or natural, spontaneous expressions of behavior. Recordings can span a few seconds or several hours. Children can be observed once or across multiple time points. Observations can include a single child, multiple family members, peer groups, or entire school classrooms. With the recordings in hand, researchers then apply standard or user-defined tags to segments of the videos to generate quantitative data (e.g., frequency counts, rates, and durations) and qualitative data (e.g., ratings, ethnographic descriptions, conversation analyses, and narratives). Finally, researchers analyze the processed data to make inferences about child development.

Compared with other forms of research data (e.g., flat-file tabular data, imaging data, textual data), video offers unique potential for reuse. One aspect of research video that makes it eminently reusable is that important information about the raw data is directly accessible. The recordings convey visible and audible information about the original context in which they were collected. Viewers can see what is happening, what the researchers did, and what the children did. Thus, new investigators can reuse research videos with little additional information or documentation to perform integrative analyses or increase the diversity and size of their sample. A second related aspect of research video is the richness of the data that it contains. A close-up view of a child's face, for example, contains information about the child's facial expressions, vocalizations, and patterns of looking behavior, and how these various behaviors unfold over time. A wide shot view of a child at play could be used to study the development of walking or the development of social interaction. Thus, investigators can reuse existing raw research videos to explore entirely different phenomena and to ask new questions outside the scope of the original study.

Despite the unique advantages of video, video data sharing and reuse is not the norm in developmental science, and few platforms exist to motivate developmental researchers to publish their video data. Instead, most researchers collect videos for a single study and upon completion of the study, they allow the data to molder away on a hard drive or in a stack of DVDs in a cabinet. The process of collecting video data from children is expensive and time-consuming—data collection requires appropriate recording equipment, and lab staff must identify potential participants, schedule the appointments, run the data collection, and process the data. Thus, the field incurs a great loss when the use of a data set is limited to the scope of a single study in a single lab, and the life of a data set is only as long as the life of the media it is stored on.

Given the rich potential of video for research reuse and the importance of providing long-term preservation of these assets, we launched the Databrary repository in October 2014 to enable sharing, reuse, and indefinite preservation of raw research videos among child development researchers. Databrary is a Web-accessible repository, with access permissions set differently for authorized researchers and the public, depending on the data set and individual participant consent. The project—funded by the National Science Foundation (BCS-1238599) and the National Institute of Child Health and Human Development (U01-HD-076595)—is housed at New York University's Institute of Human Development and Social Change and collaborates closely with the university's libraries and the Information Technology Services.

## POST HOC CURATION VERSUS ACTIVE CURATION

Post hoc curation (i.e., curation after all of the data have been collected and analyzed) is the most common way that researchers contribute data to domain repositories. So we initially assumed that this would be the primary means of acquiring data in Databrary. However, post hoc curation is hugely time-consuming and cumbersome to the data contributor.[12] To prepare the data for deposit, researchers must revisit data that they have already collected, analyzed, and stored away and now organize and describe it for the purpose of sharing. We quickly learned that the required commitment of time and personnel exceeded what most researchers were willing to do. Moreover, researchers lacked the expertise to prepare the data for ingest, so information professionals were needed to process the collection for sharing.[13]

To preempt these barriers to sharing, Databrary implemented tools to enable researchers to actively curate their own data immediately following each data collection—to organize, describe, and store the data at an early phase of the research life cycle, rather than as a burdensome final step at the end of the project. To encourage researchers to use these tools to organize, describe, and share their data, we built them with a strong emphasis on integrating the language and interfaces that our intended community was already using.

## BUILDING A SYSTEM OF ACTIVE CURATION TO SUIT RESEARCHERS' NEEDS

Determining the best way to build active curation tools for the developmental science community required a clear understanding of researchers' workflows—in particular, the path from video data collection to storage of the video files and metadata. We started by interviewing a handful of representative researchers and their staff at NYU and other institutions who regularly collect video data and who represent the diversity of research in the developmental science community. The

interviews were unstructured and were intended to elicit details about researchers'
current data management workflows and practices. We hoped that the interviews
would inform us about what researchers might want from a service that would
help them to organize, manage, store, and eventually share their videos. However, the interview results were only minimally informative about what researchers
would want. Most researchers were not able to tell us how the various tasks of their
day-to-day data management amounted to an explicit workflow, and it was evident that many of them had not previously considered how to prepare their data
for sharing and reuse—in most cases, even for reuse within their own laboratories.

We realized that we needed information science professionals and domain
experts working together to observe researchers' current practices and the tools
they used (or lacked) in their labs. These observations allowed us to make inferences about the best ways to support active video curation for child development
researchers. To obtain an understanding of how researchers collect, organize, and
analyze their videos and metadata, we gathered a sample of data from each researcher we had originally interviewed to determine similarities and differences
among data sets and lab practices. We learned that child development research is
characterized by a wide diversity of data management practices, both within and
across labs. As a result, data sets are heterogeneously structured and organized,
which significantly increases the time required to prepare this data for post hoc
ingesting into a repository.

Despite this diversity, we observed that researchers across labs care about
emphasizing certain aspects of their research, such as what tasks were involved
in a data collection (e.g., toy play, book reading, answering a set of question,
watching displays on a computer monitor), whether the data collection was preliminary (i.e., intended to work the kinks out of the method) or part of the target
dataset, and whether a participant had to be excluded from analyses for particular
reasons (e.g., fussy or sleeping baby, equipment failure, experimenter error). Developing and implementing an approach to active curation required a focus on
the evident similarities across different data sets and lab practices to gain traction
with the intended research community.

Finally, we understood that our intended user group would require tangible
incentives for adopting new practices for managing and storing their research data
in a central repository. Notably, major disincentives include the cost to laboratories in terms of extra time and effort for post hoc curation and the financial cost
of storing and serving video files. Thus, Databrary eliminated the cost of post hoc
curation by replacing it with active curation tools that make trivial the cost of
uploading and managing video recordings. Databrary creates incentives for active
curation by providing free, unlimited storage; the repository acts as a convenient
lab server to facilitate communication among lab members and with collaborators
off site. After a study is complete and the contributors are ready to do so, sharing
the data with the entire Databrary community is as simple as the push of a button.

# ACTIVE CURATION IMPLEMENTED IN DATABRARY

## HOW RESEARCHERS VIEW THEIR DATA

Active curation reduces friction for researchers contributing to a repository by merging the effort of describing and storing videos for sharing and reuse with data collection and organization. But first the intended community of researchers needed a more standardized process for organizing and describing different types of data sets. To accomplish this goal, we designed Databrary from the beginning to be a user-facing data repository that accommodates the diversity of existing data management practices we observed. The system relies on a metadata schema that reflects how researchers already view the different components of their video data sets (participant demographics, study conditions and tasks, geographic location, language of the participant, and so on).

For active curation tools to make sense to our intended user base, we chose to adopt researchers' language and organizing principles.[14] Developmental researchers call the analytic units of their studies "sessions."[15] A session is essentially a recording period. Within each session, we assign the general term *record* to the metadata that describes a session. Records comprise the important information about participants, activities, and researcher-defined conditions and groups as outlined in the metadata schema. The predefined records available in the upload interface were drawn from what we observed to be the most common types of metadata used across multiple labs, the metadata required for reporting by journals, and the metadata required by the major granting agencies.

## INTERFACES THAT THE COMMUNITY ALREADY USES

Critically, to enable researchers to use our active curation service, we needed to craft interfaces that were easy to use and already familiar to the community. Spreadsheets are a common tool employed across labs to record session metadata. As a result, we designed a web application view that allows users to upload, modify, and manage session metadata into a spreadsheet, with features such as auto-completion, field pre-population, bulk editing, and suggested entries for convenience (figure 3.7). Rows of the spreadsheet correspond to individual sessions. The columns correspond to basic records describing the sessions, which helps researchers to manage their own data and assists other researchers in searching and finding videos of interest to them. Column categories in the spreadsheet are customizable and can be applied as needed to the researcher's study.

| 🗂 | session | | | participant | task | | context | file |
|---|---|---|---|---|---|---|---|---|
| | name ⬦ | test date ⬦ | release ⬦ | age ⬦ | description ⬦ | | setting ⬦ | name ⬦ |
| | | | | | *4 tasks* | | | |
| | | | | | Standard two option typical box task | | | |
| 📁 | 2014-XX-XX | ⬡+ | 4.6 yrs | 3 option unexpected contents with neutral box | | Lab | 3 files |
| | | | | | 3 option unexpected location task | | | |
| | | | | | 3 option unexpected contents with typical box | | | |
| 📁 | 2014-XX-XX | ⬡+ | 3.9 yrs | *4 tasks* | | Lab | 3 files |
| 📁 | 2014-XX-XX | ⬡+ | 4.6 yrs | *4 tasks* | | Lab | 3 files |
| 📁 | 2014-XX-XX | ⬡+ | 4.6 yrs | *4 tasks* | | Lab | 3 files |

**FIGURE 3.7**
Databrary metadata interface example. Spreadsheet metadata interface for a data set hosted on Databrary. Databrary exposes as much metadata about a study as possible without revealing sensitive or identifiable information (as determined by the participant and the data contributor). The availability of the metadata differs depending on the permission level of the user attempting access. Source: William Fabricius, "Absence of Construct Validity in Standard False Belief Tasks," Databrary, 2014, accessed November 10, 2015, doi:10.17910/B7Z300.

In addition to allowing researchers to add and modify record metadata through this interface, we provided tools to enhance researchers' ability to analyze their data. Allowing users to create, save, and share summaries of their metadata—such as number of participants by group, condition, or gender—gives them the power to quickly and easily gain insights into their data as they collect it (figure 3.8).

| 🗂 | task | session | | | |
|---|---|---|---|---|---|
| | description ⬦ | name ⬦ | test date ⬦ | release ⬦ | summary ⬦ |
| | 3 option unexpected contents with neutral box | | | *32 sessions* | |
| | 3 option unexpected location task | | | *32 sessions* | |
| | Standard two option typical box task | | | *32 sessions* | |
| | 3 option unexpected contents with typical box | | | *32 sessions* | |
| | No task | 📁 | 2014-XX-XX | ⬡+ | participant, context Lab |

**FIGURE 3.8**
Metadata summary view. Display of summary information for the metadata from a data set. (Source: Catherine Tamis-LeMonda, "Language, Cognitive, and Socio-emotional Skills from 9 Months until Their Transition to First Grade in U.S. Children from African-American, Dominican, Mexican, and Chinese backgrounds," Databrary, 2013, accessed November 16, 2015, doi:10.17910/B7CC74.) This example shows the number of sessions for several tasks. Users can drag and drop metadata records to explore their data sets at a higher level of analysis.

Finally, most researchers annotate their research videos with a set of user-defined codes using desktop coding software such as Databrary's Datavyu, The Language Archive's ELAN, Mangold's Interact, Noldus's Observer, or the University of Wisconsin's Transana.[16] Thus, we implemented a time line view for managing the videos and metadata within sessions that is similar to these commonly used desktop coding tools (figure 3.9). On the time line, researchers can stream video files and visualize how video data, session metadata, and other files relate to each other temporally and thematically. Researchers can also use this interface to annotate an entire video file, or specific segments of video, with keywords and tags. The time line and tagging functionality further enrich the metadata to help other researchers to find and make sense of the video data contained in Databrary on a granular level.

### FIGURE 3.9

Databrary time line interface example. Time line for one of the sessions in a data set hosted on Databrary. (Source: Karen E. Adolph, "Social and Motor Play on a Playground," Databrary, 2014, accessed November 10, 2015, https://nyu.databrary.org/volume/9/slot/6113/-?asset=9607, doi:10.17910/B77P4V.) Users can access video assets in the browser, and data owners can manage their data using the time line interface. Video Image License: http://creativecommons.org/licenses/by-nc-sa/4.0.

## POSSIBILITIES FOR ACTIVE CURATION AND PRESERVATION IN OTHER AREAS OF RESEARCH

In conceiving Databrary, we came to understand that valuable research data is susceptible to loss because it is not traditionally collected for the purposes of being preserved and shared with other researchers. We also knew that the task of preparing data toward these ends is cumbersome. Researchers need services, tools, and a centralized infrastructure to make preserving and sharing their research data a viable process. Our starting assumption that researchers are more motivated to use a service that is similar to their existing workflow allowed us to develop tools to facilitate and incentivize active curation so that researchers might prepare their own data for contribution to a repository that is a shared, community resource. Of course, child development is not the only discipline where video or audio data is central to the research workflow. Researchers in education, social anthropology, ethology, sociology, and linguistics also collect significant numbers of research video and audio files. Similar projects serving other fields may need to determine the metadata schema and interfaces that work best for their community. Other fields and institutions will also want to decide the scale at which they expect their repository solutions to function. Finally, they will also have to determine the ethical policies and protections (e.g., what to collect, what to share, with whom, and how) that best suit the nature of their research and the type of data they collect.

Different data types have different repository needs, but research video has specific needs and requirements for its curation and management. As a result, active curation may be possible in other fields of research with video or audio files at their center. The Databrary example demonstrates what is critical to this endeavor: Make curation similar to and seamless with researchers' current workflows; use language and interfaces that are based on researchers' current practices; and provide researchers with the infrastructure that allows them to organize, describe, manage, and store their data products so that they may be shared with their colleagues now and in the future. Most important, eliminate disincentives and build in incentives (e.g., centralized storage, collaborative tools, and curatorial assistance) for data sharing and reuse.

# 3.6 Consider the File Formats

In this step, identify all file formats in the data submission and note their restrictions. Curators may also want to verify the technical metadata of the files (e.g., resolution, audio/video codec) that may limit the files for various reuse purposes. When appropriate, curators may choose to transform the data files into open, nonproprietary formats that might broaden the potential audience for reuse and ensure that preservation actions might be taken by the repository in later steps (detailed in *Step 7*: Preservation of Data for the Long Term). Finally, your actions may impact the authenticity of the files; therefore, it will be necessary to determine if your repository should retain the original files, particularly if data transfer is not perfect.

Determine what, if any, actions need to be taken regarding file formats by asking the following questions:

- Are the file formats compatible with your repository preservation policy?
- Can they/Should they be converted to more preservation-friendly format? If so, should the original file formats be retained?
- Can the data be used widely in this format (e.g., by the general public vs. researchers in this particular field)? If not, to increase potential use, should we create an alternative access copy (e.g., proprietary software to an exportable XML)?
- What pros and cons exist if we retain the current format? How do alternative file formats mitigate risk in terms of reusability of these file formats?
- If you altered the format (e.g., for preservation), what would you lose? Is there information that will be lost in transferring files from proprietary formats (e.g., tables, formulas, color coding, etc.)? If so, do we keep both versions (the original and the alternative)?
- Is the software needed to open these files freely available? If not, consider linking to it or archive it alongside the data.

# Microsoft Excel: A Use Case in Format Preservation

A great use case for these questions comes from Microsoft Excel. A popular data format with academic researchers, Excel files contain much more information than simple tabular data. They may contain graphs, charts, pivot tables, and rich text formatting, and each cell may contain formulas that rely on the information in other cells. With all of this contextual value, it should be clear that conversion to a more simplified comma-delimited file format (.csv) would be detrimental, not to mention impractical since this conversion works for only one Microsoft Excel worksheet tab at a time (i.e., therefore, many tabs would be time-consuming to export).[17] Yet the proprietary nature of the Microsoft files and the costs of using the software may prevent broad reuse or future emulation.

To address this concern John McGrory, a graduate research assistant at the Data Repository for the University of Minnesota, developed the **Excel Archival**

**Tool**, available for free download from Github (http://z.umn.edu/exceltool). The Windows-based tool will scan a directory for any Excel files (allowing for batch conversions) and output a directory containing the converted files (a CSV file of the data plus any formulas, charts, and any visual formatting) along with a report with the following information:

- Name of file/folder that was converted
- Date and time of conversion
- Number of Excel files converted
- Number of .csv files generated
- Number of charts/figures exported as .png files
- Number of formula files generated[18]

# Proprietary File Formats Conversions

Many software tools allow for export of data in a variety of formats. Some additional conversion tools, however, might be needed to obtain a new copy of the data in a file format variant. Table 3.1 describes some of the file format conversion actions that might be taken on some common data file formats.

## TABLE 3.1
Preservation file transformations (by format).

| File Format | Conversion Format | Process | Notes |
|---|---|---|---|
| MS Word (.doc, .docx) | PDF | In **Microsoft Word**, Save as ...PDF | If file includes page breaks, this will result in multiple PDFs. Combine using Adobe Pro. |
| MS Excel (.xls) | CSV | Use the "**Excel Archival Tool**" to capture all contextual information along with the tabular data. | Works on Windows only. |
| MS Access (.accdb, .mdb) | XML | In **Microsoft Access** 2013, export data and entry relationship diagram (design of table relationships) to XML, XSD, and XSL. | Other database formats such as MySQL, PostgreSQL, and SQLServer may export as a database dump.[a] |
| Photoshop (.psd) | TIFF | In **Photoshop**, Save as ... | |

**TABLE 3.1** (continued)

| File Format | Conversion Format | Process | Notes |
|---|---|---|---|
| ESRI ArcGIS interchange file (.e00) | Shapefile, retain original | Use the **ArcGIS Quick Import Tool** from the Data Interoperability ToolKit to import file coverage into a file geodatabase, then export to shapefiles. | If the data of interest consists of points, it is best to add X and Y fields and export the table as plain text and save as a CSV. |
| SPSS (.sas, .spv) | .sav (.csv and syntax file) | Use Sledgehammer (http://www.mtna.us/#/products/sledgehammer) to output a fixed file and then output an SPSS script. Write code to convert to .sav. | The .sav can be read by nonproprietary statistical software such as R. The proprietary output can also be exported to text (PDF, Excel) or as data (using the OMS command), as tab-delimited text, PDF, XLS, HTML, XML. |
| Audiovisual | .mov, .wav, .mp4 | Evaluate size and resolution. Use **Handbreak** to compress videos into a smaller size (adjust resolution settings) | Evaluate if we need to transcode based on the standard vs proprietary codec used—Note: Evaluate resolution to see if we need compress for web viewing. |
| Sequence Data | .fa (ASCII based) | Use **AliView** for creating a visualization of the FASTA file if sequences are meant to be aligned. http://www.ormbunkar.se/aliview/.<br><br>IGV can create visualization for VCF files. Galaxy can be used for FASTQ file visualization. | All can be opened in text editors. |

**TABLE 3.1** (continued)

| File Format | Conversion Format | Process | Notes |
|---|---|---|---|
| Sweave (LaTeX, R) | .Rnw | Convert script to text (.txt), compile to TeX (.tex) | Open .Rnw file in a text editor, save as .txt. If using Sweave or knitr, load package in R/RStudio and compile—syntax in R: `knit(filename.Rnw)`— this will create a .tex file in the working directory. |

a. See also Sara Day Thomson, "Technical Solutions: Preserving Databases" in *Preserving Transactional Data*. DPC Technology Watch Report 16, May 2, 2016, http://dx.doi.org/10.7207/twr16-02, p25.

## Preserving Data Files in Action

The use of 3D images in research has grown in recent years creating a new and challenging research data object for curators to preserve. The next case study by curators at the UK-based Archaeology Data Service describes their process for managing and preserving these files types.

# Preserving 3D Data Sets: Workflows, Formats, and Considerations

## Archaeology Data Service*

The growing importance of 3D data is well documented.[19] Decreases in hardware costs alongside the development of faster and more cost-effective software has allowed 3D data capture to be applied to a wide range of materials, from cultural objects to built heritage, to archaeological stratigraphy. Technological advances have also allowed much more of this data to be accessible online, resulting in a growing number of project websites showcasing this data. Websites such as Scottish Ten, CyArk, and the Smithsonian X 3D site allow access to a variety of 3D digital surrogates,[20] and at the Archaeology Data Service we have also aimed to provide interactive access to such data alongside preservation of the underlying data set (figure 3.10).

**FIGURE 3.10**
Screenshot of a wooden head (object 38819) displayed in the online viewer from The Virtual Amarna Project (Source: Barry Kemp, The Virtual Amarna Project [York: Archaeology Data Service, 2011], doi:10.5284/1011330), Archaeology Data Service.

From an archival perspective, however, 3D data sets frequently present a challenge. Many projects are focused on an end "product" or deliverable such as an online gallery, interactive model, or video fly-through. While these digital objects characterize the conclusion of a project, in many cases they have limited reuse potential and do not represent the raw data or interpretative process that an archive aims to preserve and document.

# SOURCES OF 3D DATA

The majority of archaeological 3D data sets are the result of direct data acquisition using techniques such as aerial or terrestrial laser scanning or photography (for photogrammetry). Such capture techniques are described in detail in the 3D-ICONS Guidelines.[21] Cost, project scale, and required resolution all influence how and which techniques are used, but as technologies have evolved, similar, high-quality results can be obtained from a range of techniques.[22]

While the raw 3D data from nearly all these techniques is often easily preserved as ASCII point data, preservation planning can be complicated by the subsequent processing and interpretation of this raw data at various stages on its route to final project deliverables. Most importantly, such workflows can complicate the notion of a "raw data set." The creation of other outputs and deliverables (such as images and video) during a workflow can obscure the relationship between one or more raw data sets and subsequent derived products, making it difficult to determine if and how these products should be preserved.

# WORKFLOWS FOR 3D DATA

Workflows for 3D data sets are described generally by 3D-ICONS[23] and more specifically in the Archaeology Data Service/Digital Antiquity *Guides to Good Practice* sections for laser scanning and close-range photogrammetry.[24] Such workflows include phases of data collection, cleaning, and processing, and can branch off for the creation of data "products" such as images, video, or simplified (i.e., low-resolution) models (see figure 3.11). When considering preservation and dissemination strategies, these workflows can be broken down into a series of Preservation Intervention Points at which data is processed (e.g., meshed, decimated, or cleaned) and output, either as data sets to be processed further or as final deliverable products.[25] As some of these processes result in the gradual removal of elements from the raw data set, either in terms of data (e.g., noise) or functionality (e.g., the creation of still images or video), the identification of these points allows the assessment of a workflow in terms of

- **Data selection:** the point at which versions of the data should be selected for preservation (e.g., prior to decimation, noise removal, etc.) or for dissemination (e.g., prior to post-meshing).
- **Format selection:** the point at which data is most easily preserved. Certain 3D formats (e.g., OBJ or PLY) are more easily migrated than software-specific formats and have different capabilities in terms of what and how elements are stored.[26]
- **Metadata and documentation:** the point at which metadata and documentation should be created in relation to data processing and the creation of deliverables. As discussed below, in some cases suitable documentation might mitigate the need for preserving certain intermediate datasets.

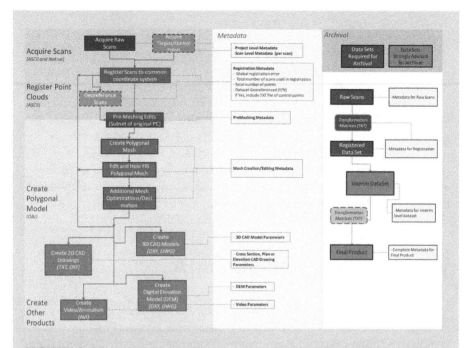

**FIGURE 3.11**
Example workflow for laser scan data (Source: Payne, Angie, "Laser Scanning for Archaeology: A Guide to Good Practice" in Guides to Good Practice 9, York: Archaeology Data Service, 2011], http://guides.archaeologydataservice. ac.uk/g2gp/LaserScan_1-1).

# IDENTIFYING "ORIGINAL DATA"

An important element of workflow examination, and the pinpointing of key points in the processing workflow, is the identification of "original data" for ingest and preservation. While for many projects this may simply be the raw data initially acquired in the field, subsequent processing steps such as cleaning, noise reduction, or merging with other data streams may render the raw data unsuitable for reuse. In such cases it is important to explore the possibility of storing versions of the "original data" from various points along the workflow. However, it is also important to consider the role that suitable documentation and metadata play in the recording of this processing. If software settings and processes are recorded and may be easily repeated on the raw data, then conversely it may not be necessary to store that particular resulting data-set.

## DISSEMINATING 3D DATA

While raw data is a key concern for a digital archive, it is often less valuable for the data producer and casual consumer. Detailed examination of the project workflow can aid in the identification of suitable dissemination products, many of which may have smaller file sizes and be more easily Web accessible than the original data.[27] In contrast to recognized preservation formats for 3D data (e.g., ASCII XYZ text files), formats used for disseminating 3D data change and new formats with different capabilities (e.g., X3D and U3D) have regularly emerged over the last ten years. A number of the formats described in the original Arts and Humanities Data Service Virtual Reality guide are now outdated[28] when compared to more recent surveys of formats.[29] Such format lifespans highlight the relatively transient nature of some dissemination deliverables and the importance of securing robust original data sets for preservation. This distinction between archival formats (the AIP) and dissemination formats (the DIP) follows the workflow implicit in the OAIS preservation standard.[30]

## IMPORTANCE OF DOCUMENTATION

Having identified original data and suitable dissemination products, examination and documentation of the entire data workflow from acquisition to the creation of deliverables are key to finalizing the effective preservation of 3D datasets. Documentation of workflow processes by the data creator is crucial to understanding what a final 3D model and any subsequent interpretations represent, and how they relate to the original raw data and intermediate processed data sets.

Through analysis of workflows, an awareness of the relative limitations of formats, and the various impacts of processing, it is possible for an archive to fulfill its own preservation and reuse requirements, as well as the needs of 3D data consumers for access to data sets that are complete, usable, and accessible.

# 3.7 File Arrangement and Description

Next, as necessary, organize or rename the files and their descriptions for optimal display and access. Consider which files are the primary object and which are supplementary, then order then to indicate these relationships. For their descriptions, consider using the function of the file first before indicating its format to allow for easier scanning across the files (e.g., "Metadata of R code" or "Primary

Data in R Code"), and keep a dictionary of terms used so that the repository can stay consistent in file name use. Here are some example sets of files:

- Example 1:
  o Map depicting the Bedrock Geology of Minnesota (PDF)
  o GIS Shapefiles for the Bedrock Geology of Minnesota (ZIP)
  o Metadata for GIS Shapefiles (XML)
  o Description of this Submission (TXT)
- Example 2:
  o Spreadsheet of the Legacy Carbon Emissions Effect Data (Excel)
  o Archival Version of the Excel File Data (CSV)
  o Video Model Depicting of the Carbon Emissions (MP4)

## Compression

Consider how the files will display in your data repository discovery interface. For example, if there are a large number of files (e.g., over ten), then the files may not be easily scanned by a potential user. In some cases, it might be worthwhile to repackage the data set for download, such as through one compressed zip. This approach will also help retain any file directory structure needed for some data to render as intended, such as in the case for related HTML files or GIS data. When zipping files, data curators must balance the downsides of this approach with the gains.[31] For example, compressed file packages will not be indexed by web crawlers therefore, any keywords or metadata information will be obscured. Additionally, some users may not want to download the compressed file without fully understanding the contents. One approach might be to document the file structure of the compressed package in an easy-to-access file outside of the zip file (e.g., readme file).

## Contextual Concerns with Data in Action

Understanding the context of a data set may involve several steps, or even a face-to-face conversation with the data author, as the next case study by Tina Qin demonstrates.

# Legacy Research Data Management for Librarians: A Case Study

*Tina Qin*

As science becomes more collaborative and data-intensive, academic libraries face challenges of organizing and preserving large amounts of data. In the summer of 2013, data management novice library school students at the Indiana University undertook the task of curating a legacy public health research data set. The staff took several steps to understand and manage the data set and addressed three main issues: contextualization of the data, file organization, and storage and access.[32]

A public health professor retired and asked the university librarians to preserve her legacy research data set that spanned several decades. The data set was created during the 1970s, 1980s, and early 1990s, and the collection included 854 data files in 15 folders and 2 descriptive documents. The project was finished by library students who have no formal data management training and possess few data management resources. When we first accessed the data, we identified the following problems:

- **Understanding the context:** The data files contained a series of numbers with no explanation about what these numbers meant. Without the original questionnaires or the background knowledge of the study, the data would not be understandable and therefore unusable.
- **Naming complexity:** Decoding the naming conventions for files would take time and require access to other documents or an additional interview with the data creator. Letters and numbers in the file name could potentially refer to locations, courses, collaborating researchers, topics and the years that the data was gathered, and other specific identifiers.
- **Difficulty understanding codes used within files:** The code in input files is supposed to be understood by the SPSS software. The professor created information in the file that related to her own research. The data creator's own code, which includes abbreviations for data categories in tables, was difficult to understand without a data dictionary or codebook.
- **Identifying Desiderata:** Some files may have been corrupted, contain uncorrected errors, be incomplete, be blank, or not have file extensions. Decisions of what to save should be according to the knowledge of the data code.

- **Software compatibility:** The files were created and modified with outdated versions of SPSS in a Unix computing environment. Newer computer operational systems, which run more recent versions of SPSS, had difficulty working with the files.

With all of these considerations, we focused our effort on three areas: providing context for the data, organizing the files, and identifying data storage and access options.

# CONTEXTUALIZING DATA

The questionnaires and articles that assisted with the data set informed the creation of some basic metadata. Using a metadata standard such as Dublin Core is advisable since these are widely used and compliant with many digital repositories. To decide the file format to store metadata, we recommended CSV because it is easy to generate, smaller in size, and simple to implement and parse.

# FILE ORGANIZATION

The files within a data set have a definable relationship to other files within the set that requires definition for context. In our case, SPSS data files containing survey results were understandable only when linked to the questionnaires. We decided that including this contextual information in our file-naming convention would be helpful. For example:

> folderName_originalName_sourceName_sourceFormat [questionnaire or data file]
> Examples:
> IndianaUniversityStudy2001_slisclass_PHQ_questionnaire
> IndianaUniversityStudy2001_sliswrit_slisclass_data

# STORAGE AND ACCESS PLATFORMS

To determine how to store the data set, our consideration is whether the storage platform is secured and backed up. In addition, we prefer the storage with the future access options for users. An institutional repository would be a good place to securely store, preserve, and provide access to the data set. Our university has the institutional repository that would be the storage platform we selected. An institutional repository may not be an option for all cases. Another option that provides storage, preservation, and accessibility, though with potential costs, might be a domain repository.

After determining a storage platform that handles data preservation, an important consideration is to determine how users will be able to access the data. We worked with public health data, which introduced special considerations of human subject implications. The researcher who created the data would be best able to determine whether there are any human subject implications, but if the researcher is unavailable, consult the institution's research ethics committee. Considering the software compatibility, we kept the original file format for further access.

By sharing our experience in this case study, we created general guidelines for managing legacy public health research data: contextualizing data, organizing files, and identifying storage and access. We hope sharing our experience helps librarians with data responsibilities and provides resources for data management training in library schools.

# Summary of Step 3.0: Processing and Treatment Actions for Data

3.1 Secure the Files: Create a working copy of the files in order to protect the originals when making any changes or additions to the submission during *Step 3*.

3.2 Start a Curation Log: Track any changes to the data in a curation log in order to keep a record of the correspondence (e.g., e-mails) between the repository and the submitter.

3.3 Inspect File Representation and Organization: Understand the directory structures, file relationships, and any naming conventions used. Preserve any relationships in the files or generate documentation to help others understand how the files relate.

3.4 Inspect the Data: Review the content of the data files (e.g., open and run the files). Check for quality and usability issues such as missing data, ambiguous headings, code execution failures, and data presentation concerns. Try to detect and extract any "hidden documentation" inherent to the data files that may facilitate reuse. Generate a list of questions for the data author to fix any errors or issues.

3.5 Work with the Author to Enhance the Data Submission: Verify all metadata provided by the author and review the available documentation. Determine if this description of the data is sufficient for a user with similar qualifications to the author's to understand and reuse the data. If not, seek out or create additional documentation (e.g., use a readme.txt template).

3.6 Consider File Formats: Identify specialized file formats and their restrictions (e.g., Is the software freely available? Link to it or archive it alongside the data). Verify technical metadata (min resolution, audio/video codec) that would optimize the files for reuse. Transform files into open, nonproprietary file formats that broaden the potential audience for reuse and ensure that preservation actions might be taken by the repository in later steps. Retain original files if data transfer is not perfect.

3.7 Arrangement and Description: Organize and rename the files to optimize their meaning, and display them in a way that might facilitate reuse (e.g. Which files are the primary object and which are supplementary? Too many files, consider repackaging for display).

# Notes

1. Windows only. Download a free trial at PE Explorer download page, http://www.pe-explorer.com/peexplorer-download.htm.
2. Heaventools Software, "Malware Code Analysis Made Easy," PE Explorer data sheet, 2007, 5, http://www.heaventools.com/files/11hFgnI0s/PE.Explorer.datasheet.pdf.
3. Stanford University Libraries, "Case Study: File Naming Done Well," accessed March 14, 2016, https://library.stanford.edu/research/data-management-services/case-studies/case-study-file-naming-done-well.
4. Scott Brandt, "Data Management for Undergraduate Researchers: File Naming Conventions," Purdue Libraries, last modified December 8, 2015, http://guides.lib.purdue.edu/c.php?g=353013&p=2378293.
5. GitHub is a popular repository build for hosting publically accessible code available at https://github.com; RunMyCode is an online repository allowing people to share code and data associated with scientific publications (articles and working papers) available at http://www.runmycode.org.
6. Dominique G. Roche, Loeske E. B. Kruuk, Robert Lanfear, and Sandra A. Binning, "Public Data Archiving in Ecology and Evolution: How Well Are We Doing?" *PLOS Biology* 13, no. 11 (2015): e1002295, doi:10.1371/journal.pbio.1002295.
7. Ibid., 3 / 12.
8. Kristina M. Hettne, Katherine Wolstencroft, Khalid Belhajjame, Carole A. Goble, Eleni Mina, Harish Dharuri, David De Roure, Lourdes Verdes-Montenegro, Julián Garrido, and Marco Roos, "Best Practices for Workflow Design: How to Prevent Workflow Decay," in *SWAT4LS 2012: Semantic Web Applications and Tools for Life Sciences,* Proceedings of the 5th International Workshop on Semantic Web Applications and Tools for Life Sciences, Paris, November 28–30, 2012, ed. Adrian Paschke, Albert Burger, Paolo Romano, M. Scott Marshall, and Andrea Splendiani (Aachen, Germany: CEUR Workshops Proceedings, 2012), http://ceur-ws.org/Vol-952/paper_23.pdf.
9. Robert Muenchen, "The Popularity of Data Analysis Software," r4stats.com, last updated October 17, 2015, accessed November 6, 2015, http://r4stats.com/articles/popularity/.
10. R Core Team, R Project for Statistical Computing homepage, R Foundation for Statistical Computing, 2015, http://www.R-project.org.
11. Wendy Kozlowski, "Guidelines for Writing 'readme' Style Metadata," Research Data Management Services Group, Cornell University Library, last updated May 30, 2014, http://data.research.cornell.edu/sites/default/files/SciMD_ReadMe_Guidelines_v4_1_0.pdf.
12. Michael J. Giarlo, "Academic Libraries as Data Quality Hubs," *Journal of Librarianship and Scholarly Communication* 1, no. 3 (March 2013): 1–10, doi:10.7710/2162-3309.1059.

13. P. Bryan Heidorn, "The Emerging Role of Libraries in Data Curation and E-Science," *Journal of Library Administration* 51, no. 7/8 (October 2011): 662–72, doi:10.1080/01 930826.2011.601269; Lisa Federer, "The Librarian as Research Informationist: A Case Study," *Journal of the Medical Library Association* 101, no. 4 (January 2013): 298–302.

14. Luis Martinez-Uribe and Stuart MacDonald, "User Engagement in Research Data Curation," in *Research and Advanced Technology for Digital Libraries*, Lecture Notes in Computer Science, vol. 5714, 309–14 (New York: Springer, 2009), doi:10.1007/978-3-642-04346-8_30.

15. Roger Bakeman and Vicenç Quera, "Behavioral Observation," in *APA Handbook of Research Methods in Psychology, Vol 1: Foundations, Planning, Measures, and Psychometrics*, ed. H. Cooper, P. M. Camic, D. L. Long, A. T. Panter, D. Rindskopf, and K. J. Sher, (Washington, DC: American Psychological Association, 2012), 207–25, doi:10.1037/13619-013.

16. Datavyu homepage, accessed November 16, 2015, http://www.datavyu.org; Language Archive, "ELAN," accessed November 16, 2015, https://tla.mpi.nl/tools/tla-tools/elan; Mangold International, "INTERACT: The Professional Software for Behavioral Research Studies," accessed November 16, 2015, http://www.mangold-international.com/software/interact/what-is-interact.html; Noldus, "Event Logging Software: The Observer XT," accessed November 16, 2015, http://www.noldus.com/human-behavior-research/products/the-observer-xt; Transana home page, accessed November 16, 2015, http://www.transana.org.

17. John McGrory, "Poster for 'Excel Archival Tool: Automating the Spreadsheet Conversion Process'" (presented at the 2015 Research Data Access and Preservation Summit, Minneapolis, MN, April 23, 2015), http://hdl.handle.net/11299/171966.

18. John McGrory, "Excel Archival Tool User Guide," Github, April 24, 2015, https://github.com/mcgrory/ExcelArchivalTool/blob/master/UserGuide.pdf.

19. For an overview of 3D data use see Robert Z. Selden Jr., Bernard K. Means, Jon C. Lohse, Charles Koenig, and Stephen. L. Black, "Beyond Documentation: 3D Data in Archaeology," *Texas Archaeology* 58, no. 4 (Fall 2014): 20–24.

20. Scottish Ten homepage, accessed June 18, 2016, http://www.scottishten.org; CyArk homepage, accessed June 18, 2016, http://www.cyark.org; Smithsonian X 3D homepage, accessed June 18, 2016, http://3d.si.edu.

21. 3D-ICONS, "Guidelines," 2014, http://3dicons-project.eu/eng/Guidelines-Case-Studies/Guidelines2.

22. Fabrizio, Galeazzi, Holley Moyes, and Mark Aldenderfer, "Defining Best 3D Practices in Archaeology: Comparing Laser Scanning and Dense Stereo Matching Techniques for 3D Intrasite Data Recording," *Advances in Archaeological Practice* 2, no. 4 (2014): 353–65, doi: 10.7183/2326-3768.2.4.353.

23. 3D-ICONS, "Guidelines," 18–26.

24. Archaeology Data Service/Digital Antiquity, "Data Selection: Preservation Intervention Points," in *Guides to Good Practice* (York, UK: Archaeology Data Service, 2011), http://guides.archaeologydataservice.ac.uk/g2gp/ArchivalStrat_1-3; Angie Payne, "Laser Scanning for Archaeology: A Guide to Good Practice," in *Guides to Good Practice* (York, UK: Archaeology Data Service, 2011), http://guides.archaeologydataservice.ac.uk/g2gp/LaserScan_1-1; Adam Barnes, "Close-Range Photogrammetry: A Guide to Good Practice," in *Guides to Good Practice* (York, UK: Archaeology Data Service, 2011), http://guides.archaeologydataservice.ac.uk/g2gp/Photogram_2-1.

25. Archaeology Data Service/Digital Antiquity, "Data Selection."
26. For detailed discussions of 3D formats, see IANUS, "3D und Virtual Reality," in *IANUS IT-Empfehlungen* (Berlin: Deutsches Archäologisches Institut, 2015), http://www.ianus-fdz.de/it-empfehlungen/3d (German language only); and Kenton McHenry and Peter Bajcsy, *An Overview of 3D Data Content, File Formats and Viewers*, technical report isda08-002 (Urbana, IL: National Center for Supercomputing Applications, 2008), http://isda.ncsa.illinois.edu/drupal/sites/default/files/NCSA-ISDA-2008-002.pdf.
27. For a discussion of 3D data as "Big Data," see Tony Austin and Jenny Mitcha, *Preservation and Management Strategies for Exceptionally Large Data Formats: "Big Data"* (York, UK: Archaeology Data Service, 2007), http://archaeologydataservice.ac.uk/research/bigData.
28. Kate Fernie and Julian D. Richards, eds., *Creating and Using Virtual Reality*, AHDS Guides to Good Practice (London: Arts and Humanities Data Service, 2002), http://www.vads.ac.uk/guides/vr_guide.
29. For examples, see McHenry and Bajcsy, *An Overview of 3D Data Content,* and IANUS, "3D und Virtual Reality."
30. Consultative Committee for Space Data Systems, *Reference Model for an Open Archival Information System (OAIS)* (Washington, DC: CCSDS Secretariat: 2012), http://public.ccsds.org/publications/archive/650x0m2.pdf.
31. Kristinn Sigurðsson, "To ZIP or Not to ZIP, That Is the (Web Archiving) Question," *Kris's blog,* January 28, 2016, http://kris-sigur.blogspot.ca/2016/01/to-zip-or-not-to-zip-that-is-web.html.
32. As discussed previously in Brianna Marshall, Katherine O'Bryan, Na Qin, and Rebecca Vernon, "Organizing, Contextualizing, and Storing Legacy Research Data: A Case Study of Data Management for Librarians," *Issues in Science and Technology Librarianship,* no. 74 (Fall 2013), doi:10.5062/F4K07270.

# Bibliography

Adolph, Karen E. "Social and Motor Play on a Playground." Databrary. 2014. Accessed November 10, 2015. doi:10.17910/B77P4V.

Archaeology Data Service/Digital Antiquity. "Data Selection: Preservation Intervention Points." In *Guides to Good Practice*. York, UK: Archaeology Data Service, 2011. http://guides.archaeologydataservice.ac.uk/g2gp/ArchivalStrat_1-3.

Austin, Tony, and Jenny Mitcham. *Preservation and Management Strategies for Exceptionally Large Data Formats: "Big Data."* York, UK: Archaeology Data Service, 2007. http://archaeologydataservice.ac.uk/research/bigData.

Bakeman, Roger, and Vicenç Quera. "Behavioral Observation." In *APA Handbook of Research Methods in Psychology, Vol 1: Foundations, Planning, Measures, and Psychometrics.* Edited by H. Cooper, P. M. Camic, D. L. Long, A. T. Panter, D. Rindskopf, and K. J. Sher, 207–25. Washington, DC: American Psychological Association, 2012. doi:10.1037/13619-013.

Barnes, Adam, "Close-Range Photogrammetry: A Guide to Good Practice." In *Guides to Good Practice.* York, UK: Archaeology Data Service, 2011. http://guides.archaeology-dataservice.ac.uk/g2gp/Photogram_2-1.

Brandt, Scott. "Data Management for Undergraduate Researchers: File Naming Conventions." Purdue Libraries, Last modified December 8, 2015. http://guides.lib.purdue.edu/c.php?g=353013&p=2378293.

Consultative Committee for Space Data Systems. *Reference Model for an Open Archival Information System (OAIS).* Washington, DC: CCSDS Secretariat: 2012. http://public. ccsds.org/publications/archive/650x0m2.pdf.

CyArk homepage. Accessed June 18, 2016. http://www.cyark.org/.

Datavyu homepage. Accessed November 16, 2015. http://www.datavyu.org/.

Fabricius, William. "Absence of Construct Validity in Standard False Belief Tasks." Databrary. 2014. Accessed November 10, 2015. doi: 10.17910/B7Z300.

Federer, Lisa. "The Librarian as Research Informationist: A Case Study." *Journal of the Medical Library Association* 101, no. 4 (January 2013): 298–302.

Fernie, Kate, and Julian D. Richards, eds. *Creating and Using Virtual Reality: A Guide for the Arts and Humanities.* AHDS Guides to Good Practice. London: Arts and Humanities Data Service, 2002. http://www.vads.ac.uk/guides/vr_guide/.

Galeazzi, Fabrizio, Holley Moyes, and Mark Aldenderfer. "Defining Best 3D Practices in Archaeology: Comparing Laser Scanning and Dense Stereo Matching Techniques for 3D Intrasite Data Recording." *Advances in Archaeological Practice* 2, no. 4 (2014): 353–65. doi: 10.7183/2326-3768.2.4.353.

Giarlo, Michael J. "Academic Libraries as Data Quality Hubs." *Journal of Librarianship and Scholarly Communication* 1, no. 3 (March 2013): 1–10. doi:10.7710/2162-3309.1059.

GitHub homepage. Accessed March 14, 2016. https://github.com.

HeavenTools Software. "Malware Code Analysis Made Easy." PE Explorer data sheet. 2007. http://www.heaventools.com/files/11hFgnI0s/PE.Explorer.datasheet.pdf.

Heidorn, P. Bryan. "The Emerging Role of Libraries in Data Curation and E-Science." *Journal of Library Administration* 51, no. 7/8 (October 2011): 662–72. doi:10.1080/0193 0826.2011.601269.

Hettne, Kristina M., Katherine Wolstencroft, Khalid Belhajjame, Carole A. Goble, Eleni Mina, Harish Dharuri, David De Roure, Lourdes Verdes-Montenegro, Julián Garrido, and Marco Roos. "Best Practices for Workflow Design: How to Prevent Workflow Decay." In *SWAT4LS 2012: Semantic Web Applications and Tools for Life Sciences.* Proceedings of the 5th International Workshop on Semantic Web Applications and Tools for Life Sciences, Paris, November 28–30, 2012. Edited by Adrian Paschke, Albert Burger, Paolo Romano, M. Scott Marshall, and Andrea Splendiani. Aachen, Germany: CEUR Workshops Proceedings, 2012. http://ceur-ws.org/Vol-952/paper_23.pdf.

IANUS. "3D und Virtual Reality." In *IANUS IT-Empfehlungen.* Berlin: Deutsches Archäologisches Institut, 2015. http://www.ianus-fdz.de/it-empfehlungen/3d.

Kozlowski, Wendy. "Guidelines for Writing 'readme' Style Metadata." Research Data Management Services Group, Cornell University Library. Last updated May 30, 2014. http://data.research.cornell.edu/sites/default/files/SciMD_ReadMe_Guidelines_v4_1_0.pdf.

Language Archive. "ELAN." Accessed November 16, 2015. https://tla.mpi.nl/tools/tla-tools/elan/.

Mangold International. "INTERACT: The Professional Software for Behavioral Research Studies." Accessed November 16, 2015. http://www.mangold-international.com/software/interact/what-is-interact.html.

Marshall, Brianna, Katherine O'Bryan, Na Qin, and Rebecca Vernon. "Organizing, Contextualizing, and Storing Legacy Research Data: A Case Study of Data Management for Librarians." *Issues in Science and Technology Librarianship,* no. 74 (Fall 2013). doi:10.5062/F4K07270.

Martinez-Uribe, Luis, and Stuart MacDonald. "User Engagement in Research Data Curation." In *Research and Advanced Technology for Digital Libraries*, Lecture Notes in Computer Science, vol. 5714, 309–14. New York: Springer, 2009. doi:10.1007/978-3-642-04346-8_30.

McGrory, John. "Excel Archival Tool User Guide." Github. April 24, 2015. https://github.com/mcgrory/ExcelArchivalTool/blob/master/UserGuide.pdf.

———. "Poster for 'Excel Archival Tool: Automating the Spreadsheet Conversion Process.'" Presented at the 2015 Research Data Access and Preservation Summit, Minneapolis, MN, April 23, 2015. http://hdl.handle.net/11299/171966.

McHenry, Kenton, and Peter Bajcsy. *An Overview of 3D Data Content, File Formats and Viewers*. Technical report isda08-002. Urbana, IL: National Center for Supercomputing Applications, 2008. http://isda.ncsa.illinois.edu/drupal/sites/default/files/NCSA-ISDA-2008-002.pdf.

Muenchen, Robert. "The Popularity of Data Analysis Software." r4stats.com. Last updated October 17, 2015. Accessed November 6, 2015. http://r4stats.com/articles/popularity/.

Noldus. "Event Logging Software: The Observer XT." Accessed November 16, 2015. http://www.noldus.com/human-behavior-research/products/the-observer-xt.

Payne, Angie, "Laser Scanning for Archaeology: A Guide to Good Practice." In *Guides to Good Practice*. York, UK: Archaeology Data Service, 2011. http://guides.archaeologydataservice.ac.uk/g2gp/LaserScan_1-1.

PE Explorer download page. Accessed March 14, 2016. http://www.pe-explorer.com/peexplorer-download.htm.

R Core Team. R Project for Statistical Computing homepage. R Foundation for Statistical Computing. 2015. http://www.R-project.org/.

Roche, Dominique G., Loeske E. B. Kruuk, Robert Lanfear, and Sandra A. Binning. "Public Data Archiving in Ecology and Evolution: How Well Are We Doing?" *PLOS Biology*13, no. 11 (2015): e1002295. doi:10.1371/journal.pbio.1002295.

RunMyCode homepage. Accessed March 14, 2016. http://www.runmycode.org.

Scottish Ten homepage. Accessed June 18, 2016. http://www.scottishten.org/.

Selden, Robert Z. Jr., Bernard K. Means, Jon C. Lohse, Charles Koenig, and Stephen. L. Black. "Beyond Documentation: 3D Data in Archaeology." *Texas Archaeology* 58, no. 4 (Fall 2014): 20–24.

Sigurðsson, Kristinn. "To ZIP or Not to ZIP, That Is the (Web Archiving) Question." *Kris's blog*, January 28, 2016. http://kris-sigur.blogspot.ca/2016/01/to-zip-or-not-to-zip-that-is-web.html.

Smithsonian X 3D homepage. Accessed June 18, 2016. http://3d.si.edu/.

Stanford University Libraries. "Case Study: File Naming Done Well." Accessed March 14, 2016. https://library.stanford.edu/research/data-management-services/case-studies/case-study-file-naming-done-well.

Tamis-LeMonda, Catherine. "Language, Cognitive, and Socio-emotional Skills from 9 Months until Their Transition to First Grade in U.S. Children from African-American, Dominican, Mexican, and Chinese Backgrounds." Databrary. October 2013. Accessed November 16, 2015. doi: 10.17910/B7CC74.

Thomson, Sara Day. "Technical Solutions: Preserving Databases." Preserving Transactional Data. DPC Technology Watch Report 16, May 2, 2016. http://dx.doi.org/10.7207/twr16-02.

3D-ICONS. "Guidelines." 2014. http://3dicons-project.eu/eng/Guidelines-Case-Studies/Guidelines2.

Transana home page. Accessed November 16, 2015. http://www.transana.org/.

# Ingest and Store Data in Your Repository

This step involves the transfer of the data to your secure storage environment—often contained within a digital repository infrastructure. The various software configurations, which allow you to better control the data for ingest, management, access, and preservation, are discussed. However, hosting a data repository can be costly and involve an enormous investment in the form of staffing resources and ongoing maintenance. Therefore, the variety and diversity of locally hosted and cloud-based data repository options will be explored in this step.

## 4.1 Ingest the Files

Once the data files have been optimized, arranged, and described, the data is ready for ingest into your digital repository environment. There are many existing software solutions for the underlying infrastructure to run a data repository. The international standard Reference Model for an Open Archival Information System (OAIS) demonstrates an ideal structure for a data repository and many digital repository technologies, or digital asset management systems, are built using this model. The technical aspects of data curation performed by an OAIS are the following:

- Ingest: receiving the information and preparing it for storage and management within the system
- Archival Storage: ensuring that the information is stored securely and appropriately for the purposes of retrieval
- Data Management: coordinating all descriptive information about the objects stored in the system
- Administration: managing the day-to-day operations of the system

- Preservation: monitoring the environment of the system to ensure that the information remains accessible and understandable over the long term
- Access: supporting end users in discovering, requesting, and receiving (e.g., delivery) information stored in the system.[1]

Additionally the OAIS model addresses the responsibilities of an archive to engage with designated audiences in order to ensure that data is understandable and usable by users.

# Digital Repository Infrastructure Options

Brinley and colleagues found that only 11 percent of the 204 American universities studied had dedicated data repositories, as compared with IRs that accept data (58%).[2] There is much to explore in the literature on the digital repository infrastructure as many institutions have shared their experiences with either building a digital repository or with implementing a hosted solution, and several how-to manuals and online guides are available that help further detail the process.[3] As a data curation service provider, your choices likely boil down to these options:

1. No Repository: Help data authors prepare their data for deposit into a domain-specific repository that is hosted elsewhere (e.g., national or subject repository hosted at another institution).

2. Custom Build: Develop custom architecture to meet your needs that performs the desired functionality of the OAIS model (e.g., ingest, management, and access). The benefits of a fully customized solution may come at a cost of ongoing time and development investment with no outside support.

3. Local Installation: Download and deploy an open-source repository software (e.g., DSpace, ePrints, Fedora/Hydra). The benefit here may be a strong developer community that is actively contributing new features to the core code base.

4. Hosted Service: Pay a provider for a hosted repository service (e.g., bepress, DSpace Direct). Customization options may be limited. However, user support is typically much stronger than with an open-source solution.

5. Mix-and-Match: Use a mixture of the above (e.g., pay a provider for cloud storage and preservation services, but run your own repository software or vice versa).

In the summer of 2015 Ricky Erway from OCLC did a "very informal" survey of American academic libraries running institutional data repositories.[4] Out of twenty responses from institutions with data repositories, eight of the institutions ran a stand-alone data repository, and twelve have a combination institutional repository and data repository. Six of the sites ran DSpace, six ran Hydra/Fedora systems, four had locally developed systems, and there was one each running Rosetta, Dataverse, SobekCM, and HUBzero. Several of these options and more are presented in table 4.1, along with some example implementations of the tools.

## TABLE 4.1
A selection of data repository software and hosted solutions.

| Software (Developer) | Availability (Software Download or Service Provider URLs) | Example Implementations |
|---|---|---|
| *Archivematica (Artefactual Systems)* | open-source download https://www.archivematica.org hosted service (fee-based) http://archivesdirect.org | Archives Canada, http://archivescanada.accesstomemory.ca |
| *Colectica Repository* | for-purchase software http://www.colectica.com/software/repository | CLOSER (longitudinal studies), http://www.closer.ac.uk |
| *Dataverse (Harvard)* | open-source download http://dataverse.org hosted service (free) https://dataverse.harvard.edu | Harvard-Smithsonian Center for Astrophysics (CfA) Dataverse, https://dataverse.harvard.edu/dataverse/cfa |
| *Digital Commons (Bepress)* | hosted service (fee-based) http://digitalcommons.bepress.com | Washington University St. Louis Open Scholarship, http://openscholarship.wustl.edu |
| *DSpace (DuraSpace)* | open-source download http://www.dspace.org hosted service (fee-based) http://www.dspacedirect.org | Dryad, https://datadryad.org Data Repository for the University of Minnesota (DRUM), http://hdl.handle.net/11299/166578 |
| *EPrints (U. of Southampton)* | open-source download http://www.eprints.org/uk hosted service also available | University of Bath Research Data Archive, http://researchdata.bath.ac.uk |

**TABLE 4.1** (continued)

| Software (Developer) | Availability (Software Download or Service Provider URLs) | Example Implementations |
|---|---|---|
| *Fedora (DuraSpace)* | open-source download http://fedorarepository.org | Rutgers University RUcore Research, https://rucore.libraries.rutgers.edu/research |
| *HUBzero (Purdue U.)* | open-source download https://hubzero.org hosted service available | NanoHub, https://nanohub.org Purdue University Research Repository (PURR), https://purr.purdue.edu |
| *Hydra* | open-source download http://projecthydra.org | Penn State University ScholarSphere, https://scholarsphere.psu.edu Stanford Digital Repository (SDR), http://sdr.stanford.edu |
| *Invenio (CERN)* | open-source download http://invenio-software.org hosted service (fee-based) https://tind.io | CERN Document Server, https://cds.cern.ch |
| *Islandora (U. PEI)* | open-source download http://islandora.ca hosted service (fee-based) http://www.discoverygarden.ca | Simon Fraser University's Research Data Repository, http://researchdata.sfu.ca[a] |
| *SobekCM (U. of Florida)* | open-source download http://sobekrepository.org/software/download | University of Florida Digital Collections (UFDC), http://ufdc.ufl.edu |

a. As described in manez, "Research Data in Islandora," Islandora blog, December 2, 2014, http://islandora.ca/content/research-data-islandora.

# Functional Requirements for a Data Repository

A list of functional requirements of your data repository will help you determine which software or hosted service will meet your needs. Some software comparisons and lists of repository functional requirements can be found online and may provide a good place to start before analyzing your particular needs. For example:

- The National Library of Medicine (NLM) published its well-structured report for building a data repository in 2007, which follows the OAIS model to define the functional requirements and minimum metadata requirements for a digital repository that can be applied to a data repository.[5]
- Although the Budapest Open Access Initiative's comparison of repository software published in 2004 is a over decade old, the features and functionality table on page 17 still provide a good baseline of things to look for when evaluating software.[6]
- The Oregon State University Libraries did a comparison of the features for Hydra, Digital Commons, and DSpace, concluding that a custom-built repository solution using Hydra was the best approach for them to handle complex objects such as research data.[7]
- The University of Minnesota Libraries published ninety-nine functional requirements for building the Data Repository for the University of Minnesota using the open-source DSpace software.[8]

# Data Curation without a Locally Hosted Repository

Many of the data curation steps outlined so far in this handbook can be used prior to depositing a data set into a repository external to your institution. Preparing data for ingest into a disciplinary data repository, for example, would be a great value for researchers in need of curation assistance. As the next case study by Baker and Duerr will demonstrate, there are many types of repositories open to deposit, including those hosted by institutions in the public and private sectors, as well as government-supported national data repositories. For example, the Registry of Research Data Repositories (http://www.re3data.org) lists over 1,400 data repositories worldwide and the features and trustworthiness of these repositories will vary. In 2015 Leahey and colleagues reviewed the functionality of thirty-two publically accessible online data repositories, including the well-established disciplinary data repositories Pangaea, ICPSR, Polar Data Catalogue, CESSDA, GEOSS portal, Archaeology Data Service, National Snow and Ice Data Centre, and 3TU.Datacentrum.[9] Many offered features such as minting stable URLs, and several (7 out of 32) were certified as a trusted repository (i.e., Data Seal of Approval). However, the study also found that their heterogeneous array of services and nomenclature could make navigating the submittal process very difficult.

Among the growing list of available domain repositories are several general-use data repositories (such as those presented in table 4.2). Commercial services like figshare have grown significantly in the last few years (e.g., figshare held 1,120,112 digital objects and 271,927 data sets in 2015 according to Leahey and collagues[10]) as a popular option due to their quick deposit process, often zero cost, and DOI minting capabilities for researchers who may not have a disciplinary or institutional data repository available.

**TABLE 4.2**
Example data repositories open to general deposit.

| Repository Name | Collection Focus | Website URL |
| --- | --- | --- |
| DataOne DASH | general (any discipline) | https://oneshare.cdlib.org |
| Dryad | sciences and medicine | https://datadryad.org |
| Figshare | general (any discipline) | https://figshare.com |
| Harvard Dataverse | general (any discipline) | https://dataverse.harvard.edu |
| Mendeley Data | general (any discipline) | https://data.mendeley.com |
| openICPSR | social sciences and humanities | https://www.openicpsr.org |
| Open Science Framework | general (any discipline) | https://osf.io |
| ScratchPads | general (any discipline) | http://scratchpads.eu |
| UK Data Archive | social sciences and humanities | http://www.data-archive.ac.uk |
| Zenodo | general (any discipline) | https://zenodo.org |

# The History of Digital Repositories for Data

To better understand the ecosystem in which data repositories have evolved, the next case study by Karen S. Baker and Ruth E. Duerr dives deeper into the history of managing digital data across a variety of domains.

# Data and a Diversity of Repositories

*Karen S. Baker and Ruth E. Duerr**

In looking across the research landscape today, there is a diversity of repositories that hold research data. They vary in their funding arrangements, scope, design, and legal basis; they are digital or nondigital, reside in academic and nonacademic locations, and may or may not be part of a coalition or a network. A repository's holdings may focus on a specific region (such as a national park), a professional domain (such as the field of ecology), a particular theme (such as the topic of war), content type (such as photographic images), or may contain data generated by members of an organization. Some repositories may be certified while others may provide selected data services.

Though definitions of *data* are the subject of ongoing discussion,[11] in this case study the term *data* is defined as recorded material believed to be factual that is commonly accepted in research communities as necessary to support or validate research findings—a variation of that found in the US "data sharing mandate" memo.[12] Though a large amount of data is generated in conjunction with research carried out in academia, a significant proportion of research in the United States is also conducted outside the halls of academia, through the work of tens of thousands of employees of federal, state, and local governments, as well as researchers working for nongovernmental organizations of all sorts including the private sector. Today, data-centric repositories are not only making more data available but also enabling access and fostering discussion across academic and nonacademic communities.

A basic working definition of *digital repository* is drawn from two evolving community dictionaries of terminology (RDA, CASRAI):[13] A digital repository is an organizational entity able to store, organize, manage, and maintain data objects as well as provide access to them. A growing number of repositories, generally focused on data rather than on documents, provide digital access via online public interfaces. Data access differs from traditional print publishing in that measurements are considered to be facts under the law, and therefore most observational science data is not amenable to copyright. Browsing and download of full and related versions of data are available. This digital access contrasts with the summary tables and selected findings typically found in the scholarly literature as well as with findings privately held or disseminated through nonacademic channels.

When a researcher needs data from several repositories, repository differences become a barrier. One response has been for domains to establish either domain-specific repositories containing worldwide holdings of data of a certain type (e.g., the Protein Data Bank [PDB], http://www.wwpdb.org) or discovery catalogs that register the holdings of potentially every repository that contains data on a particular topic (e.g., the Global Change Master Directory [GCMD], http://gcmd.nasa.gov). In other cases, law sets the holdings of a repository. For example, the US Code mandates that the United States Geologic Survey (USGS) maintain both an archive of geologic information as well as an archive of land remote-sensing data, among other types of data, and that the National Oceanographic and Atmospheric Administration (NOAA) archive a wide variety of data about fisheries, coastal regions, the ocean, weather events, and so on.[14] More recently, in response to the US mandate for open data access,[15] many US federal government agencies have initiated new approaches to collecting and managing data and documentation relevant to their respective missions. Requirements for data management plans and funding for research on information infrastructure development are stimulating change across the data landscape. The following provides a brief overview of the arenas of data and kinds of data repositories.

# INTERNATIONAL DATA ARENA

The total number of international research organizations—governmental, nongovernmental, and intergovernmental—is large, and many are associated with digital data repository systems. Global coordinating efforts include the International Council of Science (ICSU) with its World Data System, the International Social Science Council (ISSC), the International Society for Environmental Ethics (ISEE), and the Alliance of Digital Humanities Organizations (ADHO).[16] Missions for international organizations may be observationally oriented as with the World Meteorological Organization (WMO) and the Group on Earth Observations (GEO).[17] GEO is a voluntary partnership of governments and organizations that are building a Global Earth Observation System of Systems (GEOSS, http://www.geoportal.org) to make data about agriculture, biodiversity, climate, disasters, ecosystems, energy, health, water, and weather more easily discoverable and accessible for better-informed decision making. An international Registry of Research Data Repositories (re-3data, http://www.re3data.org) effort is underway with the aim of providing a comprehensive listing of data repositories. Partners are working to extend the re3data schema to support disciplinary distinctions that can support activities of other communities.

# US NATIONAL ARENA

The data repository landscape within the United States is complex and, in many cases, intertwined with international efforts. In the earth sciences, for example, the Global Change Master Directory (GCMD), operated by NASA and a component of an earth science International Directory Network (IDN, http://idn. ceos.org), includes in its mission the discovery, access, and use of earth science data and data-related services held anywhere in the world. Moreover, it is a resource for GEOSS as well as the US Global Change Research Program's (US-GCRP) Global Change Information System (GCIS, http://data.globalchange. gov), which connects each of the conclusions in the Third National Climate Assessment to the 2,195 journal articles, 172 books, 918 reports, 33 models, and 2,562 data sets upon which they were based. In turn, the GCIS feeds Data.gov (https://www.data.gov), a repository that contains not only federal data but also data sets from state and local governments, universities, and nonprofits, as well as a few commercial data sets. The situation with other agencies is similar. For example EarthCube (http://earthcube.org), an initiative funded by the National Science Foundation's Directorate for Geosciences and Division of Advanced Cyberinfrastructure, aims to support new approaches across the geosciences that facilitate data sharing. A federal effort, the National Data Service (NDS, http:// nationaldataservice.org), is emerging with a vision of serving scientists and researchers across all disciplines.

# KINDS OF REPOSITORIES

Expanding on earlier classifications of repositories,[18] table 4.3 illustrates the variety of kinds of data repositories in the United States. The categories are overlapping and contested; it is not clear which will survive or what form they will take as they evolve. Three alphabetized sections are shown. For each category, just a few examples are given. Each repository is further nuanced in its design, for instance in terms of access and use control policies.[19] Note that many repositories fall into more than one category. For instance, the National Snow and Ice Data Center (NSIDC, https://nsidc.org) is currently funded at the federal government level as a NASA Distributed Active Archive Center, with NOAA funding for data from operational communities, and as a shorter-term research repository with a theme of polar research. Finally, though aggregated systems often appear via a data portal that provides links to its multiple data systems, aggregations of data systems are not called out in the table as such (e.g., Interdisciplinary Earth Data Alliance [IEDA, http://www.iedadata.org], Worldwide Protein Data Bank [WWpdb, http://www.wwpdb.org]).

**TABLE 4.3**

Examples of kinds of data repositories found in the United States.

| Kind of Repository | Examples |
| --- | --- |
| Federally Funded Data Centers | NASA Distributed Active Archives (DAAC), NOAA National Centers for Environmental Information (NCEI), National Snow and Ice Data Center (NSIDC), USGS Earth Resources Observation Systems (EROS) Data Center (EDC) |
| Federally Funded Research and Development Centers (FFRDC) | National Center for Atmospheric Research (NCAR), Jet Propulsion Lab (JPL), Oak Ridge National Laboratory (ORNL) |
| National Libraries | National Library of Medicine (NLM), National Agricultural Library (NAL), Library of Congress (LOC) |
| State and Local Agencies | State geological surveys, County planning offices |
| Thematic Repository | Long Term Ecological Research Network Information System (LTER NIS), Andrews Forest LTER (AND), National Snow and Ice Data Center (NSIDC), Maria Rogers Oral History Program |
| Domain Repository | Global Biodiversity Information Facility (GBIF), Inter-university Consortium for Political and Social Research (ICPSR), DataOne, Interdisciplinary Earth Data Alliance (IEDA) |
| Institutional Repository | Purdue University Research Repository (PURR), Data Repository for the University of Minnesota (DRUM) |
| Replication Repository | Dryad Digital Repository, Pangaea Data Library |
| Software Repository | GitHub, SourceForge |
| Commercial Archives | DigitalGlobe, Aerial photography companies, Resource exploration companies, Figshare |
| Private Archives | Huntington Library, Getty Research Institute |

Entries in the top section of the table include those with long-term government funding. Federally Funded Data Centers (FFDC) are funded specifically to archive data, while Federally Funded Research and Development Centers (FFRDC) are funded to do research but by necessity have grown to archive their data in support of their missions. National libraries that exist for a few designated audiences play varying roles in the repository realm. Researchers in all domains often use state and local agency data (e.g., geologic maps, land-use categories, infrastructure locations, etc.).

The middle section includes different combinations of funding and scope. Themed repositories are generally bounded by topic or subject definition, while domain repositories are generally associated with a diversity of themes associated with a research field or discipline. In contrast, an institutional repository is generally not differentiated by topic or domain but rather is concerned solely with the outputs of members of the organization within which it resides. Software repositories began as distributed software version control systems but are rapidly evolving to include materials other than software. Though GitHub and SourceForge are repositories, it should be noted that their strengths are storage and version control, while ongoing preservation and curation of their contents are not part of their mission. Replication repositories, discussed further below, were developed to archive the data associated with a specific journal article.

The bottom section has two entries that are supported by private funding: commercial and private repositories. Commercial archives operate as profit-making organizations, while private archives are typically nonprofit. Figshare, now under commercial management, is a general repository that is undergoing change. Describing itself as a digital repository rather than a data repository, it provides cloud storage and institutional repository–like services.

One distinguishing feature of a repository is whether it collects data sets in support of or independent of a particular journal article. A majority of the repositories generally consider data and data compilations as objects worthy of preservation in their own right. Preservation of complete data collections facilitates reuse of data by making data sets more readily available for browsing regardless of whether some of the data appears in the scholarly literature. In the case of replication repositories, however, a direct link from a publication to the exact data that underlies its findings is provided. Note that although published papers are peer-reviewed, the data sets are often not peer-reviewed. Although the link to data contributes to transparency and validation, the data referenced may be only a fragment of a much larger and more comprehensive data collection. For example, a researcher may publish a summary table of monthly temperature in a lake during a time period where a special event occurs (e.g., El Niño). Summary data may appear in a replication repository, but the full data set consisting of a longer record of daily temperature data together with biological observations may be deposited in a domain repository.

# FINAL THOUGHTS

There is a diversity of kinds of repositories in the data landscape. Work is ongoing to understand the differences and similarities among them since data held in repositories is "necessary to validate research findings."[20] It is important to recognize and plan for this diversity. Repository relationships are an issue that will likely be addressed in the future via unique data set identifiers and metadata completeness. As distinctions between types of data objects appear or disappear and as repository boundaries blur or become more defined, many questions arise. For example, is a digital image considered data? And if it is data, who is responsible for it—the Library of Congress, the National Archives and Records Administration, or any of a large number of other players in the digital landscape? Answers depend on how the data is used. Such questions underscore the need to understand the complex, interdependent sets of data held in an ecosystem with repositories that differ in characteristics such as funding, scope, design, and legal basis.

# Repository Ingest Workflows for Data

There are different options for ingesting data into your repository. For example, the University of Minnesota considered three ways to design the ingest workflow for data into a DSpace-based repository (illustrated in figure 4.1a–c).

- Option 1: Non-mediated or self-deposit. This option functions like a typical institutional repository where data is deposited with no mediation (or curation) by repository staff. Option 1 was eliminated as (hopefully made abundantly clear by the contents of this handbook) we determined that the library should not accept data sets without some form of curatorial oversight that ensure that the data is complete and in the best condition for long-term reuse.

- Option 2: Self-deposit with post-ingest curation. This option allows authors (AU) to submit their data to a data repository collection in the IR where, using the built-in DSpace workflows for accept/reject/edit, curation staff will review and approve submissions prior to ingest. However, due to limitations of the software, curation staff are unable to make changes to the files while in review. Therefore, some curation actions must be taken post-ingest and a separate notification must be made to the author noting this process (see figure 1.9 in *Step 1*: Receiving Data).

- Option 3: Fully mediated deposit with pre-ingest curation: In this option, the author would submit data through a custom web form that would allow for the acquisition of the assets and metadata into a temporary staging repository, rather than the production repository. Curation staff could then review and process the submission and curate the data before the submission is submitted to DSpace by the data curation staff. This option would create an ideal environment, but was not chosen as it would require additional development work and staff time to build the custom staging area.

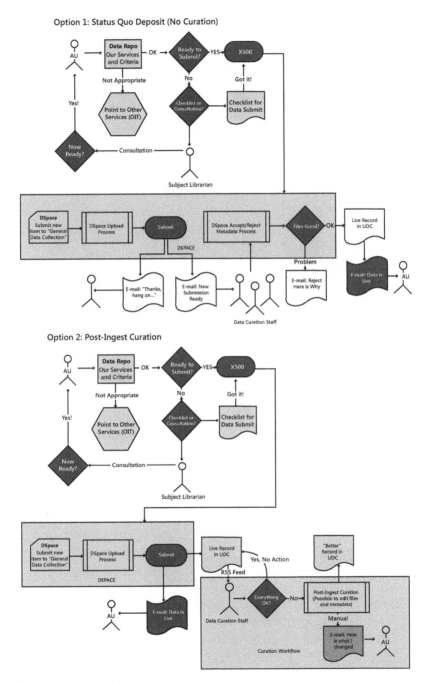

**FIGURE 4.1a&b**
Option 1 and 2 of 3 ingest workflow options considered by the Data Repository for the University of Minnesota.

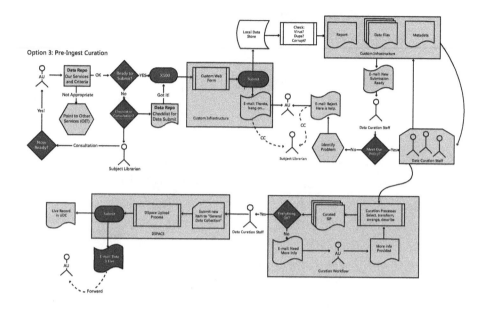

**FIGURE 4.1c**
Option 3 of 3 ingest workflow options considered by the Data Repository for the University of Minnesota.

# Repository Ingest Workflows in Action

In the next two case studies, a team from UC San Diego (Juliane Schneider, Arwen Hutt, and Ho Jung S. Yoo) and curators at Dryad (Erin Clary and Debra Fagan) each present their case studies describing the ingest workflows for "mediated deposit" and "self-deposit," showcasing how data repositories work directly with researchers in various ways.

Readers will find an additional example of an ingest workflow in Jon Wheeler's chapter 7 in *Curating Research Data, Volume One* detailing how the University of New Mexico uses a mirroring process to batch harvest data from disciplinary repositories into the library-run IR in "Extending Data Curation Service Models for Academic Library and Institutional Repositories".

# Standardization and Automation of Ingest Processes in a Fully Mediated Deposit Model

*Juliane Schneider, Arwen Hutt, and Ho Jung S. Yoo*[*]

This case study discusses the work done to automate and standardize a curation ingest process for improved consistency and efficiency. As mentioned in our first case study presented in *Step 1*: Receiving the Data, the University of California (UC)–San Diego Library Digital Collections repository is capable of handling complex digital objects, and data deposit is fully mediated by curators; that is, there is no self-deposit functionality.

## LEARNING THROUGH CUSTOM PILOT PROJECTS

During the early development of our research data curation services, we collaborated with researchers on highly complex and diverse pilot projects. The five pilot project data sets were intensely curated; the ingest processes leaned heavily on project-specific script and tool development, and specialized metadata fields were used to encode unique types of data. As might be expected, this level of custom design and coding was both time- and resource-intensive.

Yet, it was also very informative. The pilots helped us to identify a set of needs and requirements that crossed multiple data providers, collections, and research domains. These included research-specific metadata fields, levels of description for different audiences, core similarities in data structure, data transfer challenges, and the importance of clear citation information.

Building on these commonalities, and the need for improving the efficiency of our ingest process while maintaining our mediated curation model, we developed a suite of tools to standardize and automate our curation processes as much as possible.

---

# ALL THE METADATA: STANDARD AND NOT SO STANDARD

Microsoft Excel is a flexible tool that we use for ingesting standardized metadata. A metadata specialist, or sometimes even the data provider themselves, fills out an Excel template indicating the correct elements, properties, and hierarchical level of each metadata record (e.g., collection, object, component, sub-component).

Thus one Excel template contains both the descriptive metadata and the complex hierarchy of the collection (figure 4.2). Our metadata template includes drop-downs that allow a user to indicate controlled values for file use (e.g., document-service, image-source) and type of resource (e.g., text, data), as well as allowable metadata properties, including many of our research data–specific properties such as role (e.g., author, principal investigator, researcher, research team head), subject type (e.g., topic, geographic, anatomy, cruise, scientific name, common name), and note (e.g., methods, water depth). The identity of a metadata record within this template is represented by two properties, a unique object identifier and a categorical variable indicating the hierarchical level (i.e., object, component, or sub-component).

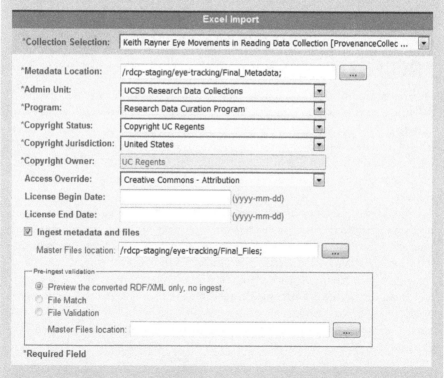

## FIGURE 4.2
Metadata template created in Microsoft Excel, for object and collection records.

In trying to achieve a balance between flexibility and efficiency, supplementary files can be included with the metadata, which goes beyond the level of detail supported within the database/data model. These supplementary files can be in the form of README TXT files, PDF documents, or encoded data formats, like XML. These are also keyword searchable through our system's full-text indexing functionality.

# PROVIDE FLEXIBLE (BUT WELL-DEFINED) OPTIONS FOR DATA TRANSFER

We offer several options to make data transfer as easy as possible for the diversity of deposit preferences we have seen on campus. For large data collections that require shared access and collaboration between the curator and the data provider, we have allocated multiple terabytes of staging space on a shared file server, which allows for folder-level access permissions. This staging area can be mounted as a drive by users with a campus account. Alternatively, for data not needing collaborative work, data providers can use a file transfer appliance to upload their data to a temporary space on a library server and send the download link directly to our e-mail accounts. This option has the advantage of requiring only a web browser and for one party to have a campus account. Any data on physical media, such as flash drives or portable hard drives, is readily accepted, as is transfer via a commercial cloud platform such as OneDrive, Dropbox, or Google Drive.

# INGEST: ONE FORM, MANY FUNCTIONS

Once the content is ready the ingest tool is used to bring the collection into our repository (figure 4.3). This internal, web-based tool performs a number of functions. Before ingest, a validation check is run to verify that the metadata in the Excel template agrees with the data model and system requirements, that the files are valid, and that all files represented in the metadata are present in the staging area. The ingest process then transforms the metadata from the Excel template into our local RDF data model format, including reconciliation of subject values against existing subject records in the repository, a library-built triplestore with a SOLR index and Hydra stack, an open-source repository software solution. The files are ingested into the repository, checksums generated, technical metadata extracted, and derivatives created. Locally minted ARKs (Archival Resource Keys) are assigned to items, subjects, files, and so on. Finally, indexing is performed and the materials are ready for the quality assurance process.

**FIGURE 4.3**
Standard ingest tool for importing files and metadata into the UCSD data repository.

# QUALITY ASSURANCE OF COLLECTIONS

The curators perform a quality assurance (QA) review on ingested collections before making the collection publicly available. This includes reviewing the metadata for completeness and accuracy and assessing that the collection is functioning as expected, for example, subjects are faceting correctly, file level access and download restrictions are working properly, and the hierarchical structure of the collection is correct. During the QA process, the collection's access levels are set so that only the curation staff may view the records until all critical issues are resolved. Issues are tracked in our workflow management system (Atlassian JIRA). Once the curators finish with the QA process, the collection is published and the data provider is notified.

# CITATIONS, DOIS, AND SHARING

For researchers, any citation of their scholarly output is a key metric of their research impact. To promote reuse and proper attribution of their data by end users, we display formatted citations on each collection's landing page and, at the request of the data provider, on each object's landing page within the collection. To facilitate the process of adding a persistent identifier to citations, we developed a Digital Object Identifier (DOI) minting tool within our repository's digital asset management system. A single click of the mint tool button on any collection or object landing page by the curator triggers three actions: (1) a new DOI is minted via EZID (http://ezid.cdlib.org), an identifier production service of the California Digital Library, (2) the DOI is appended to the end of the data citation, and (3) the metadata associated with the citation is pushed to the EZID registry via its API ((http://ezid.cdlib.org/doc/apidoc.html; figure 4.4). This third action helps to expose our collections to a wider potential audience than only those that use our repository, since EZID records are automatically pushed to the DataCite index (https://www.datacite.org/).

**FIGURE 4.4**
The mint DOI button, which is accessible only when a curator is logged into the system, generates a DOI, appends it to the end of the preferred citation, and pushes the metadata to the DataCite registry.

In addition to pushing our metadata to DataCite, our collections are indexed in Google, and there are efforts currently underway to push our metadata to the California Digital Library (http://www.cdlib.org), Digital Public Library of America (http://dp.la), and the Center for Open Science SHARE service (https://osf.io/share).

# Dryad Curation Workflows

*Erin Clary and Debra Fagan**

Dryad is a general-purpose, open-access repository for data that underlies scholarly publications.[21] A data package is a Dryad object that is associated with a scholarly publication, most often a journal article. Each archived data package has descriptive metadata, one or more data files, and a citation and URL link to the publication.[22] A data package with its data files travels through Dryad's workflow as one object. The journey that each data package takes is partly determined by whether the publisher has taken the necessary steps to partner with our service and integrate its manuscript submission process with Dryad's data submission process.[23] Submissions associated with nonintegrated publishers follow Dryad's basic workflow, while integrated submissions may include additional options for authors and publishers, such as the opportunity to review data alongside the manuscript, and consequently follow a more complex workflow.

## BASIC WORKFLOW FOR NONINTEGRATED PUBLISHERS

In the basic workflow, authors upload their data to Dryad after their manuscript has been accepted for publication or is already published. The author logs in to Dryad's Web-based submission system, enters basic bibliographic metadata about the publication, and then uploads and describes the associated data files.

Before it is accepted for the public archive, each submitted data package is reviewed by Dryad curators to verify that the data files can be opened and that the content complies with Dryad's terms of service.[24] For instance, curators will return for revision any data package that contains copyright or license statements, identifiable human subjects data, or location data for endangered species, although the ultimate responsibility for meeting the terms rests with the submitting author. Curators also check that the bibliographic metadata for the submission is valid, formatted correctly, and complete; they correct and update the metadata as needed. Once the data files and bibliographic metadata pass these steps, the data package is approved for the archive.[25]

At approval, a DOI is registered with the California Digital Library's EZID service through its Web application programming interface (API).[26] All approved data packages for nonintegrated publishers are held temporarily in "publication blackout." That is, data files and bibliographic metadata are not publicly released until the associated article has been published. When the publication appears online, the data package is released, and a citation with a link to the publication is added to the metadata.

# WORKFLOW FOR INTEGRATED PUBLISHERS

When publishers integrate the submission of manuscripts with the submission of data to Dryad, they are provided with a number of workflow options. Integration relies on a series of communications sent between the publisher and Dryad. The communication steps are achieved either through automated e-mail notifications sent to and from the journal or programmatically through Dryad's REST API.[27] The number of communications sent, and when they are sent, depend on which point in the manuscript submission process the publisher wishes to have authors upload data. Basic integration can be set up on most major manuscript processing systems without vendor customization needed.

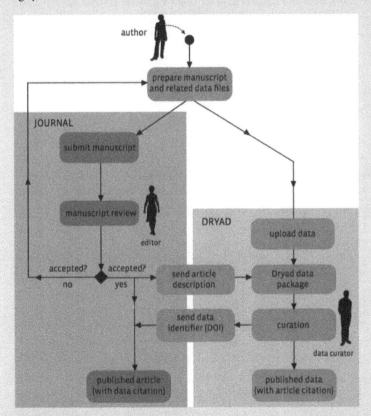

**FIGURE 4.5**

Illustration of the workflow for an integrated journal in which data submission is made upon acceptance of the publication.

The most basic integrated workflow is represented in figure 4.5, which describes a journal using e-mail communication. When a publisher accepts an article for publication, the journal automatically generates and sends an acceptance e-mail to the author. The e-mail contains a customized link to the Dryad submission system and includes metadata describing the article. A copy of the e-mail is also sent to Dryad, where the e-mail is automatically parsed and the metadata is written to an XML file.[28]

When an author accesses the Dryad submission system through the link in an acceptance e-mail, Dryad uses the associated XML file to prepopulate the submission form on the fly with the requisite bibliographic metadata for the data submission. The author may then upload and describe data files. As with nonintegrated submissions, Dryad's curation team next inspects the submitted files and metadata and either accepts the data package or returns it to the author's workspace for revision. On acceptance by Dryad, a DOI is registered with the California Digital Library's EZID service through its Web application programming interface (API),[29] and an automated notification is sent to the journal's editorial office with the Dryad DOI for inclusion in the text, and potentially the metadata, of the published article.

## DATA REVIEW

Integrated journals also have the option to use Dryad's "review" workflow. This workflow allows authors to upload data at the time of manuscript submission so that data is available for review alongside the manuscript. In this workflow, an author is invited to submit his or her data after the manuscript has been submitted, rather than after the manuscript is accepted. When data is received, a notification is sent from Dryad to the journal's editorial office with a "reviewer URL." This is a temporary URL that can be provided to peer reviewers for private and anonymous access to the data package.

In order to maintain the integrity of the review process, the changes that can be made to data packages while in review are limited. Authors can upload additional files without our intervention, but cannot remove files, and Dryad must assist authors who wish to make any other form of change. Dryad curators will remove superseded files from the data package prior to the public release of the data package.

Once the journal sends Dryad notification of an accepted manuscript, the data package automatically enters the queue for curation, and the workflow converges with that described previously: files are checked for compliance with Dryad's terms of service, superseded files are removed, and so on.

## *TIMING OF DATA PACKAGE RELEASE*

Unlike nonintegrated submissions, which are all held in publication blackout until the associated article is published, integrated journals may choose to opt out of publication blackout by allowing either the metadata alone or the metadata plus data files to be released immediately.

Some integrated journals give authors the additional option of placing a post publication download embargo on individual data files. When a file is embargoed, only the descriptive metadata for the file is publicly available at the time of release. Where journal policy allows, authors may embargo a file for one year after article publication, or longer with written permission from the editor. Dryad curators oversee the release of data packages and files according to these policies.

# 4.2 Store the Assets Securely

To store the assets securely, data files and metadata must be ingested into a well-configured archival storage environment. Your repository staff should perform routine checks on the integrity of the files (i.e., to avoid bitrot) and provide disaster recovery capabilities as needed. Additional repository administrative actions might be taken, such as generating and managing descriptive metadata (e.g., ingest dates and timestamps) and performing periodic audits of the assets and metadata to verify that they conform to archive standards (i.e., run URL link resolvers to check any URLs that appear in the metadata).

Some repositories have published their approach to data storage, which may provide helpful examples to learn from. For example, the HathiTrust states on its Technology Profile (https://www.hathitrust.org/technology) that it uses Isilon storage and that "Backup and restore functionality is provided at a system level and consists of a) file system backup and b) database backup. Backup services are currently provided by Tivoli Storage Manager."[30] In their data management plan template, Columbia University describes the storage solution for their institutional repository, Academic Commons:

> Files deposited in Academic Commons are written to an Isilon storage system with two copies, one local to Columbia University and one in Syracuse, NY; a third copy is stored on tape at Indiana University. The local Isilon cluster stores the data in such a way that the data can survive the loss of any two disks or any one node of the cluster. Within two hours of the initial write, data replication to the Syracuse Isilon cluster commences. The Syracuse cluster employs the same protections as the

local cluster, and both verify with a checksum procedure that data has not altered on write.[31]

Traditional file storage mechanisms are also being challenged with emerging techniques to store data more effectively, for example, as described by Rasheed and Mohideen on using Apache Hadoop distributed computing technology with Fedora.[32] However, their research notes that Hadoop still has a way to go when it comes to disaster recovery before it can be fully implemented in libraries.

# 4.3 Develop Trust in Your Digital Repository

Establishing trust with potential users of your digital repository is a key component of data curation services. The 2002 Research Libraries Group report *Trusted Digital Repositories: Attributes and Responsibilities* defines a trusted digital repository (TDR) as "one whose mission is to provide reliable, long-term access to managed digital resources to its designated community, now and in the future."[33] The TDR model is implied to go beyond secure ingest and storage. The International Association of Sound and Audiovisual Archives guidelines explain: "The technical specification of the digital storage environment is an important part of ensuring that the digital content that is managed is still accessible to researchers in the future. It is not of its own, however, enough to ensure that this will be achieved. The institution within which the digital archive resides has to be able to ensure that the content it manages is curated and maintained responsibly."[34] Therefore, trust implies that your repository also enjoys long-term organizational support, which will help ensure long-term success.

To further explore the role that trust plays in digital data repositories, see Ixchel M. Faniel and Elizabeth Yakel's chapter 4, "Practices Do Not Make Perfect: Disciplinary Data-Sharing and Reuse Practices and Their Implications for Repository Data Curation" in *Curating Research Data, Volume One*, which details with research on the "Trust Markers" for data reuses.

To further develop trust and build a positive reputation for your digital repository, you might apply for accreditation from one of the emerging certification bodies on data. Two options are presented below.

*Data Seal of Approval.* There is a growing awareness for the need to track and certify digital repositories as trusted services. The DSA (http://datasealofapproval.org) does this through an informal self-assessment application process that includes sixteen specific questions about the services and technology supporting the data repository. A review board then evaluates your submitted response application and determines if your answers meet the DSA Guidelines. Recently the DSA announced that it was working with the World Data System (https://www. icsu-wds.org) through the Research Data Alliance (RDA, https://rd-alliance.org) to "align the trust based questions which form part of process for WDS membership with the DSA Guidelines."[35]

*Trusted Repository Audit Certification (TRAC): Criteria and Checklist* (http:// www.crl.edu/PDF/trac.pdf). The Center for Research Libraries' TRAC program is an extensive multistep process to certify a digital repository as trustworthy. Since the criteria and checklist were first produced in 2007 (https://www.crl.edu/ sites/default/files/d6/attachments/pages/trac_0.pdf), only a handful of repositories have been successfully certified in the process: Canadiana.org, Chronopolis, CLOCKSS, HathiTrust, Portico, Scholars Portal. The certification steps developed for TRAC were adapted into an international standard in 2012 as ISO 16363/TDR.[36]

---

To read more about how Scholars Portal is being used for research data, see chapter 3, by Leanne Trimble, Amber Leahey, Larry Laliberté, and Eugene Barsky, titled "Collaborative Research Data Curation Services: A View from Canada" in *Curating Research Data, Volume One*.

---

# Additional Factors That Influence Trust in Digital Repositories

There are many reasons why a data author may choose to use one repository over another. Additionally, some policy makers, such as federal agencies or journals, might recommend that their stakeholders use a particular data repository for a variety of reasons. The next two case studies examine the benefits of hosting data in an institutional data repository (written by a team of IR managers and data librarians) or in a disciplinary data repository (written by Jared Lyle of the ICPSR).

# Making the Case for Institutional Data Repositories

*Cynthia R. H. Vitale, Jacob Carlson, Amy E. Hodge, Patricia Hswe, Erica Johns, Lisa R. Johnston, Wendy Kozlowski, Amy Nurnberger, Jonathan Petters, Elizabeth Rolando, Yasmeen Shorish, Juliane Schneider, and Lisa Zilinski**

Recent publisher and funder mandates, accompanied by an overall push toward enhanced rigor and reproducibility of research, have resulted in the required, or strongly recommended, sharing of research data in many scholarly disciplines and domains. To address these requirements, researchers have a number of data repository options available to them, many of which have varying levels of curation protocols and funding models. One of the more robust options available is the local institutional data repository, often supported by their institution's library. Unfortunately, many researchers, publishers, and funders may not be well aware of the benefits a local institutional data repository provides. What follows is an explanation of those benefits and reasons why libraries are a natural home for their institution's research data.

Libraries are an important fixture in the research process. They are leaders in information: its description, its accessibility, and its persistence. Regardless of whether that information is kept on paper or in a digital environment, libraries ensure that information lives on.

Librarians and information professionals believe strongly in preserving the scientific and historical record, in capturing and disseminating knowledge, and in supporting research and teaching efforts. For these reasons and many more, libraries are active in helping authors understand and comply with publisher and funder data-sharing policies, and work directly with publishers and funders to identify and enact good data-sharing practices.

Libraries recognize the challenge presented in managing and curating research data and are applying their knowledge, skills, and perspectives to address the issues faced by researchers. Libraries have offered support to researchers in the form of new staff, computing infrastructure, training programs, information portals, and many other activities, tools, and services. Over the past decade, this work has resulted in a large and growing community of research data management service providers at universities, colleges, and institutions worldwide.[37]

The academic library is a natural partner in the research life cycle. Libraries are an integral part of the research community at their institutions. They understand the ecosystems of scholarly communication and the differences between how information is shared and communicated within and between fields of study. Libraries are a visible presence in every college and university. Their mission is to ensure longevity and accessibility of key resources and to connect users to these resources in ways that are meaningful to their needs. Libraries include staff who understand technology and who are capable of developing, maintaining, and sustaining data repositories and tools for working with data. Libraries are in the unique position of being the one cross-platform, interdisciplinary, all-level arena that contain a cross-section of both intellectual work and hands-on, front-facing services.

Academic and research libraries are an important component of the data-archiving and -sharing landscape. Institutional data-archiving services are a viable, and proven, solution to providing long-term access to data sets and are an important complement to the growing list of domain and disciplinary repositories. A few examples of established data repositories include

- Purdue University Research Repository (PURR)
- Johns Hopkins University (JHU) Data Archive
- University of Nebraska–Lincoln (UNL) Data Repository
- Cornell University Geospatial Information Repository (CUGIR)
- Stanford Digital Repository
- Columbia University—Academic Commons
- University of Washington—ResearchWorks Archive Service
- University of Minnesota—Data Repository for U of M (DRUM)
- University of Michigan—Deep Blue
- Penn State University—ScholarSphere
- MIT—DSpace@MIT, Geodata Repository, HMDC/IQSS Dataverse Network
- Indiana University—IUScholarWorks
- University of British Columbia—Abacus Dataverse

In general, libraries and their data repositories are not competitors to domain repositories, but are another option to be equally recognized when guidance is provided to researchers on how they can promote and share their work, and also comply with data sharing policies or needs. Here are some reasons why:

*Libraries persist.* Libraries and publishers are changing and transitioning, but while disruptions in the economics of publishing put publishers in jeopardy of going out of business, libraries are a central fixture of the institutions they serve and as such, will persist as long as those institutions do. Encouraging authors to use services that rely on an uncertain business model in favor of established services with a consistent revenue stream puts these valuable materials at risk. Additionally, libraries and archives have been in the business of identifying, selecting, organizing, describing, preserving, and providing access to information materials for centuries. Many libraries and archives have offered digital data services for decades. The care of materials like data sets is central to their mission.

*Libraries are service-oriented.* Information professionals are able to offer in-person support that's difficult to duplicate virtually. Ready access to a dedicated expert is helpful when archiving data in an institutional data repository, and when researchers are preparing their data for deposit in disciplinary data repositories.

*Libraries preserve.* Many libraries have dedicated archival services enabling researchers to deposit their data for free or for a minimal charge. Many of these repositories offer mediated deposit or curation assistance to help with file format normalization, file organization, and documentation and metadata. Library archiving services are trusted by their institutions to preserve the important records of the institution or university, including items like theses and dissertations, published literature, student projects, and unique special collections.

*Libraries are neutral and interdisciplinary.* A nonaligned service is an important complement to the domain-focused services. Many research products are multi-disciplinary, contain diverse data types, or belong to the long tail of data. Those materials are best supported by a service that actively seeks to build connections between disparate communities.

*Libraries are local.* Academic and research libraries are fundamental parts of higher education organizations with stated missions focused on education, research, and the public good. In contrast to general-purpose and disciplinary repositories, institutional data repositories can provide services and resources in person, which makes navigating the changing requirements on data sharing easier for researchers.

*Libraries know rights.* Libraries are often home to intellectual property experts who deal with copyright or privacy, and those skills are important in making informed decisions on the complicated issues of how to ethically and responsibly share data. Many libraries have experience working with or supporting research that uses sensitive data and can help guide researchers tasked with managing and curating it.

*Libraries advance the sharing of scholarly outputs.* Libraries have spearheaded or directly supported faculty open-access policies at Harvard University, MIT, and the University of California, among others. Acting as the campus-wide home for scholarly communications, many libraries advise on open-access journal options and develop protocols for sharing research data. As collective organizations, we value openness and transparency in scholarly publishing by developing programs such as the ARL/ACRL Institute on Scholarly Communication and the ACRL Scholarly Communications Roadshow, to promote the development of library-led outreach on scholarly communication issues. Libraries push for open access and understand the significant impact and transformation that open-access articles and data can have upon our society.

*Libraries are leaders.* Libraries have been at the forefront in the development of policy and best practices pertaining to responsible data sharing and sustainable digital preservation. The Registry of Data Repositories (re3data), the Data Seal of Approval, and the Trusted Repository Audit Checklist are all efforts that came from libraries and information professionals. Free from proprietary concerns, libraries are able to focus on the big-picture, international challenges inherent in sharing versus ownership.

With the continued importance placed on the sharing and availability of well-documented research data, the need for these close partnerships between academic libraries and research data producers will not diminish. In keeping with the historical mission of libraries, information professionals continue to pursue and maintain the knowledge and perspectives and develop skills necessary to curate data, with the institutional support and resources to ensure the data's ongoing availability.

The future of these services are already in development. New models for institutional data repositories are being actively explored and include consortial approaches to technical repository development, institutional networks of curation, and the establishment of communities of practice around data curation. Libraries that provide this level of service are coalescing to leverage individual institutional strengths and are building services together to ensure long-lasting access to our data assets. Libraries are also being recognized as important collaborators in this area, partnering with publishers such as the Public Library of Science, nonprofits such as SHARE and the Center for Open Science, and others to lend their expertise to the curation of research data.

# ACKNOWLEDGMENTS

This essay was previously published as "An Open Letter to PLOS" available at https://datacurepublic.wordpress.com/open-letter-to-plos-libraries-role-in-data-curation/.

# Making the Case for Disciplinary Data Repositories

*Jared Lyle**

Many advantages come with depositing to a disciplinary repository to make original data available to other potential users. Disciplinary, or domain, repositories "serve a scientific community, which may be a traditional academic discipline, a subdiscipline, or an interdisciplinary network of scientists, united by a common focus."[38] In addition to their core functions of describing, curating, preserving, and providing access to data collections, "they seek to know what [their] community wants and expects in terms of content, format, delivery options, support, and training."[39]

This specialized service is a key differentiator. While institutional and general repositories serve a broad range of users and data, with metadata, access, and user support mechanisms geared to a heterogeneous and wide audience, a disciplinary repository can provide specialized data, services, and tools used and favored by a specific scientific community.

There are several advantages to submitting your data for stewardship in a disciplinary repository.

*Subject expertise.* "The specialized facility is more likely to know of the existence of important bodies of data relevant to its specialties. Its personnel are best equipped to make judgments as to priorities in data acquisition, as well as to necessary quality controls on new data."[40] Specialized personnel are also best equipped to provide support to reuse the data. The Qualitative Data Repository (QDR, https://qdr.syr.edu), for instance, is a dedicated archive for storing and sharing digital data (and accompanying documentation) generated or collected through qualitative and multi-method research in the social sciences. Trained staff, including international experts in qualitative methodology, administer the repository and understand the unique properties of qualitative and multi-method data.

*Customized metadata.* "[Disciplinary] archives are familiar with international standards for creating and storing metadata, which greatly enhances the usability, interoperability, and exchange of data."[41] Whereas general self-deposit repositories often solicit minimal metadata, disciplinary repositories can collect and enhance data documentation to ensure complete and self-explanatory collections.[42]

In the social sciences, for instance, many disciplinary repositories use the Data Documentation Initiative (DDI, http://www.ddialliance.org) metadata standard, which captures comprehensive methodological information and enables detailed discovery, including at the variable level. [43]

*Disclosure expertise*. If data has confidentiality or privacy issues, a disciplinary repository may be "familiar with the [statistical disclosure control] literature and can work with [investigators] to balance the trade-off between data utility and the protection of study participants."[44] For example, the social and behavioral sciences research data repository, the Inter-university Consortium for Political and Social Research (ICPSR, http://www.icpsr.umich.edu), reviews all data for disclosure risk and makes disclosive and sensitive data available through highly secure, highly controlled data access mechanisms, including virtual and physical data enclaves.[45] Likewise, the Digital Archaeological Record (tDAR, http://www.tdar.org), an international digital repository for the digital records of archaeological investigations, reviews and treats confidential and culturally sensitive digital content.[46]

*Customized curation and preservation*. Disciplinary repository personnel are experts at curating and preserving data, including conducting "data quality reviews" to organize, clean, enhance and preserve data, which "reduces threats to their long-term research value and mitigates the risk of digital obsolescence."[47] Disciplinary repositories are especially attuned to supporting subject-specific formats, which general repositories may not have the expertise or time to handle. For example, Green and Gutmann commented: "The level of long-term support for different kinds of content is an important issue for potential depositors and users of social science data. The ...experience of social science data archiving reveals that, while some core formats for datasets have persisted over time, many formats have not."[48] The UK Data Archive (UKDA, http://www.data-archive.ac.uk), the United Kingdom's largest collection of digital research data in the social sciences and humanities, follows a policy of active preservation of acquired content "to ensure the authenticity, reliability, and logical integrity of all resources entrusted to our care while providing usable versions for research, teaching or learning, in perpetuity."[49] In addition to the preservation actions, UK Data Archive acquisitions are curated, which includes data validation, enhanced labelling, grouping of survey variables, and the creation of user guides.

*Specialized tools*. Because data in disciplinary repositories is curated to a higher level, specialized tools can be offered to further enhance the user experience. At ICPSR, for instance, a Variables Database, containing nearly 4 million variables, enables users to examine and compare variables and questions across studies or series.[50] Users can download data in a wide array of formats (R, SAS, SPSS, Stata, tab-delimited), or they can view and analyze the data on the Web without downloading individual data files.[51] As a final example, ICPSR links each data collection to a list of publications that analyzed the data previously. Citations to these data-related publications are actively collected and managed in a bibliographic database.[52] These tools go above and beyond basic functionality found at a general repository.

*One-stop, focused collection of data.* Disciplinary repositories offer deep collections, making them one-stop sources of data. Similarly, in contrast to general repositories with a diversity of data types, disciplinary repositories "focus on data that benefit from being used in relation to, and in comparison with, other data in the collection."[53] The Archaeology Data Service (ADS, http://archaeologydataservice.ac.uk) in the United Kingdom, for instance, provides a vast catalog of high-quality digital data in archaeology. The Protein Data Bank (PDB, http://www.rcsb.org/pdb) archive is another example of a disciplinary repository as a single source of specialized information—in the PDB's case, 3-D structures of large biological molecules, including proteins and nucleic acids.

## SUMMARY

Researchers are fortunate to have so many options for depositing data. Depositing in any trustworthy repository benefits science. That said, disciplinary repositories offer unique and specialized data, services, and tools used and favored by a specific scientific domain and community. These include subject expertise, customized metadata, disclosure expertise, customized curation and preservation, specialized tools, and a one-stop, focused collection of data.

# Summary of Step 4.0: Ingest and Store Data in Your Repository

4.1 Ingest the Data Files: Transfer the processed data files to the repository while maintaining integrity and verifying fixity throughout the process (e.g., generate checksums of the files).

4.2 Store the Assets Securely: Add the ingested files to a well-configured (in terms of hardware and software) archival storage environment. Perform routine checks and provide disaster recovery capabilities as needed.

4.3 Develop Trust in Your Repository: Become a trusted digital repository for data by applying for accreditation and growing your reputation locally and beyond.

# Notes

1. These functions are described in useful detail from Magenta Book's Recommended Practice manual (Consultative Committee for Space Data Systems, *Reference Model for*

*an Open Archival Information System (OAIS)*, Recommended Practice, CCSDS 650.0-M-2, Magenta Book, Issue 2 [Washington, DC: CCSDS Secretariat, June 2012], http://public.ccsds.org/publications/archive/650x0m2.pdf.) For further reading, The OAIS standard ISO 14721:2012 is defined in International Organization for Standardization, "ISO 14721:2012: Space Data and Information Transfer Systems—Open Archival Information System (OAIS)—Reference Model," September 1, 2012, http://www.iso.org/iso/catalogue_detail.htm?csnumber=57284. An excellent history and background of the development of the OAIS is presented by Brian F. Lavoie in "The Open Archival Information System Reference Model: Introductory Guide," *Microform and Imaging Review* 33, no. 2 (2004): 68–81, doi:10.7207/twr14-02.

2.   Kristin Briney, Abigail Goben, and Lisa Zilinski, "Do You Have an Institutional Data Policy? A Review of the Current Landscape of Library Data Services and Institutional Data Policies," *Journal of Librarianship and Scholarly Communication* 3, no. 2 (2015): eP1232, doi:10.7710/2162-3309.1232.

3.   Karen Estlund and Anna Neatrour, "Utah Digital Repository Initiative: Building a Support System for Institutional Repositories," *D-Lib Magazine* 13, no. 11/12 (November/December 2007), http://www.dlib.org/dlib/november07/neatrour/11neatrour.html; Steven Van Tuyl, Hui Zhang, and Michael Boock, "Analysis of Challenges and Opportunities for Migrating ScholarsArchive@ OSU to a New Technical Platform: Requirements Analysis, Environmental Scan, and Recommended Next Steps," February 26, 2015, http://hdl.handle.net/1957/55221; Carol A. Watson, James M. Donovan, and Pamela Bluh, "Implementing BePress' Digital Commons Institutional Repository Solution: Two Views from the Trenches" (presentation at the 18th Conference for Law School Computing [CALI], University of Maryland School of Law, Baltimore, MD, June 19–21, 2008), http://digitalcommons.law.uga.edu/ir/4; Allison B. Zhang and Don Gourley, *Creating Digital Collections* (Oxford: Chandos Publishing, 2014); Ian H. Witten and David Bainbridge, *How to Build a Digital Library* (San Francisco: Morgan Kaufmann, 2003); Repositories Support Project, "Briefing Papers," accessed June 18, 2016, http://www.rsp.ac.uk/help/publications/#briefing-papers; Raym Crow, *SPARC Institutional Repository Checklist and Resource Guide* (Washington, DC: Scholarly Publishing and Academic Resources Coalition, 2002), http://sparcopen.org/wp-content/uploads/2016/01/IR_Guide__Checklist_v1_0.pdf.

4.   Summary of Ricky Erway's survey results is presented in the blog *Hanging Together*, and the blog comments reflect the informal nature of the survey (Ricky Erway, "What Is Actually Happening Out There in Terms of Institutional Data Repositories?" *Hangingtogether.org* [blog], July 27, 2015, http://hangingtogether.org/?p=5342).

5.   National Library of Medicine Digital Repository Working Group, "Digital Repository Policies and Functional Requirements," v. 1, revised March 16, 2007, https://www.nlm.nih.gov/digitalrepository/NLM-DigRep-Requirements-rev032007.pdf.

6.   Budapest Open Access Initiative, *Guide to Institutional Repository Software*, 3rd ed. (New York: Open Society Institute, August 2004), http://www.budapestopenaccessinitiative.org/pdf/OSI_Guide_to_IR_Software_v3.pdf.

7.   Van Tuyl et al., "Analysis of Challenges and Opportunities."

8.   University of Minnesota Libraries, *The Supporting Documentation for Implementing the Data Repository for the University of Minnesota (DRUM): A Business Model, Functional Requirements, and Metadata Schema* (University of Minnesota Libraries, 2015), http://hdl.handle.net/11299/171761.

9. Amber Leahey, Peter Webster, Claire Austin, Nancy Fong, Julie Friddell, Chuck Humphrey, Susan Brown, and Walter Stewart, "Research Data Repository Requirements and Features Review," v. 4, Standards and Interoperability Committee, February 24, 2015. http://hdl.handle.net/10864/10892.

10. Ibid., figures taken from the "Repository Requirements Features Review Spreadsheet."

11. Christine L. Borgman, *Big Data, Little Data, No Data* (Cambridge, MA: MIT Press, 2015), 18–30.

12. John P. Holdren, "Increasing Access to the Results of Federally Funded Scientific Research," Memorandum for the Heads of Executive Departments and Agencies, Office of Science and Technology Policy, Executive Office of the President, February 22, 2013, http://www.whitehouse.gov/sites/default/files/microsites/ostp/ostp_public_access_memo_2013.pdf.

13. Research Data Alliance Data Foundation and Terminology Working Group (RDA DFTWG) Definition of "digital repository," accessed July 9, 2016, http://smw-rda.esc.rzg.mpg.de/index.php/Special:FormEdit/RDA/digital_repository; Consortia Advancing Standards in Research Administration Information (CASRAI) definition of "repository," accessed July 9, 2016, http://dictionary.casrai.org/Repository.

14. Office of the Law Revision Counsel, United States Code, accessed June 18, 2016, http://uscode.house.gov: USGS archiving land remote sensing (Title 51, Section 60142), National geological preservation (Title 42, Section 15908), USGS maps (43 USC31f) and requirements (Title 15, Section 1534); NOAA archiving (Title 15, Section 1537), coastal mapping, ocean and coastal science (Title 33, Section 3501).

15. Holdren, "Increasing Access to the Results of Federally Funded Scientific Research."

16. International Council for Science World Data System (ICSU WDS) homepage, accessed June 18, 2016, https://www.icsu-wds.org; International Social Science Council (ISSC) homepage, accessed June 18, 2016, http://www.worldsocialscience.org; International Society for Environmental Ethics (ISEE) homepage, accessed June 18, 2016, http://enviroethics.org; Alliance of Digital Humanities Organizations (ADHO) homepage, accessed June 18, 2016, http://adho.org.

17. World Meteorological Organization (WMO) homepage, accessed June 18, 2016, https://www.wmo.int; Group on Earth Observations (GEO) homepage, accessed June 18, 2016, https://www.earthobservations.org.

18. Chris Armbruster and Laurent Romary, "Comparing Repository Types: Challenges and Barriers for Subject-Based Repositories, Research Repositories, National Repository Systems and Institutional Repositories in Serving Scholarly Communication," Social Science Research Network, November 23, 2009, http://ssrn.com/abstract=1506905.

19. Kristin R. Eschenfelder and Andrew Johnson, "Managing the Data Commons: Controlled Sharing of Scholarly Data," *Journal of the Association for Information Science and Technology* 65, no. 9 (2014): 1757–74.

20. Holdren, "Increasing Access to the Results of Federally Funded Scientific Research."

21. Dryad Digital Repository homepage, last modified November 19, 2015, https://datadryad.org.

22. Dryad Digital Repository, "Dryad Metadata Application Profile (Schema)," last modified February 27, 2013, http://wiki.datadryad.org/Metadata_Profile.

23. Dryad Digital Repository, "Submission Integration: Overview," last modified January 15, 2016, http://wiki.datadryad.org/Submission_Integration.

24. Dryad Digital Repository, "Terms of Service," last modified August 22, 2013, https://datadryad.org/pages/policies.

25. Dryad Digital Repository, "Dryad Metadata Application Profile (Schema)."

26. EZID, "The EZID API, Version 2," accessed February 10, 2015, http://ezid.cdlib.org/doc/apidoc.html.

27. Dryad Digital Repository, "Dryad REST API Technology," last modified November 10, 2015, http://wiki.datadryad.org/Dryad_REST_API_Technology.

28. Dryad Digital Repository, "Journal Metadata Processing Technology," last modified November 17, 2015, http://wiki.datadryad.org/Journal_Metadata_Processing_Technology.

29. EZID, "The EZID API, Version 2."

30. HathiTrust Digital Library, "Technological Profile," accessed July 9, 2016, https://www.hathitrust.org/technology.

31. Columbia University Libraries, "Depositing Data in Academic Commons," Accessed March 14, 2016, http://scholcomm.columbia.edu/data-management/depositing-data-in-academic-commons.

32. Abdul Rasheed and Mohamed Mohideen, "Fedora Commons with Apache Hadoop: A Research Study," *code4lib*, no. 22 (October 14, 2013), http://journal.code4lib.org/articles/8988.

33. Research Libraries Group, *Trusted Digital Repositories: Attributes and Responsibilities*, an RLG-OCLC report (Mountain View, CA: Research Libraries Group, May 2002), http://www.oclc.org/content/dam/research/activities/trustedrep/repositories.pdf.

34. Kevin Bradley, "Chapter 6.1.9: Trusted Digital Repositories (TDR) and Institutional Responsibility," *Guidelines on the Production and Preservation of Digital Audio Objects*, 2nd ed. (International Association of Sound and Audiovisual Archives, 2009), http://www.iasa-web.org/tc04/trusted-digital-repositories-tdr-and-institutional-responsibility.

35. Data Seal of Approval, "Extension to the Current Data Seal," news release, February 3, 2016, http://datasealofapproval.org/en/news-and-events/news/2016/2/3/extension-current-data-seal.

36. International Organization for Standardization, "ISO 16363:2012: Space Data and Information Transfer Systems—Audit and Certification of Trustworthy Digital Repositories," February 15, 2012, http://www.iso.org/iso/catalogue_detail.htm?csnumber=56510.

37. The American Research Libraries (ARL) E-science Task Force was charged in 2006 and the resulting "Agenda for Developing E-Science in Research Libraries" (2007) is available online: Joint Task Force on Library Support for E-Science, *Agenda for Developing E-science in Research Libraries*, final report and recommendations to the Scholarly Communication Steering Committee, the Public Policies Affecting Research Libraries Steering Committee, and the Research, Teaching, and Learning Steering Committee (Washington, DC: Association of Research Libraries, November 2007), http://www.arl.org/storage/documents/publications/arl-escience-agenda-nov07.pdf

38. Carol Ember and Robert Hanisch, "Sustaining Domain Repositories for Digital Data: A White Paper," output of the workshop "Sustaining Domain Repositories for Digital Data," Ann Arbor, MI, June 24–25, 2013, doi:10.3886/SustainingDomainRepositories-DigitalData.

39. Ann G. Green and Myron P. Gutmann, "Building Partnerships among Social Science Researchers, Institution-Based Repositories, and Domain Specific Data Archives," *OCLC Systems and Services: International Digital Library Perspectives* 23 (2007): 35–53, http://hdl.handle.net/2027.42/41214.

40. Philip E. Converse, "A Network of Data Archives for the Behavioral Sciences," *Public

*Opinion Quarterly* 28, no 2 (Summer 1964): 273–86, http://www.jstor.org/stable/2746992.

41. Jeremy J. Albright and Jared A. Lyle, "Data Preservation through Data Archives," *PS: Political Science and Politics* 43, no. 1 (January 2010):17–21, doi:10.1017/S1049096510990768.

42. A well-prepared data collection "contains information intended to be complete and self-explanatory" for future users. (Center for Human Resource Research, section 3.3, "NLSY97 Documentation," chapter 3, "Guide to the NLSY97 Data," in *NLSY97 User's Guide: A guide to the Rounds 1–3 Data, National Longitudinal Survey of Youth 1997* (Columbus: Ohio State University, 2001), https://web.archive.org/web/20100727011626/http://www.nlsinfo.org/nlsy97/97guide/chap3.htm.

43. See the DDI Alliance website: Data Documentation Initiative (DDI) homepage, accessed June 18, 2016, http://www.ddialliance.org.

44. Albright and Lyle, "Data Preservation through Data Archives."

45. See the ICPSR website: Inter-university Consortium for Political and Social Research (ICPSR), "Data Enclaves," accessed June 18, 2016, http://www.icpsr.umich.edu/icpsrweb/content/icpsr/access/restricted/enclave.html.

46. Joshua Watts, "Building tDAR: Review, Redaction, and Ingest of Two Reports Series," *Reports in Digital Archaeology,* no. 1 (June 2011), Center for Digital Antiquity, Arizona State University, Tempe, AZ, http://www.digitalantiquity.org/wp-uploads/2011/07/20110930-Building-tDAR.pdf.

47. Limor Peer, Ann Green, and Elizabeth Stephenson, "Committing to Data Quality Review," *International Journal of Digital Curation* 9, no. 1 (2014): 263–91, doi:10.2218/ijdc.v9i1.317; Digital Curation Centre, "What Is Digital Curation?" accessed June 14, 2016, http://www.dcc.ac.uk/digital-curation/what-digital-curation.

48. Green and Gutmann, "Building Partnerships." See also Ann Green, JoAnn Dionne, and Martin Dennis, *Preserving the Whole*, CLIR Publication 83 (Washington, DC: Council on Library and Information Resources, 1999), http://www.clir.org/pubs/reports/pub83/contents.html.

49. See UK Data Archive, "How We Curate Data: Our Preservation Policy," accessed June 18, 2016, http://www.data-archive.ac.uk/curate/preservation-policy.

50. See Inter-university Consortium for Political and Social Research (ICPSR), "Search/Compare Variables," accessed June 18, 2016, https://www.icpsr.umich.edu/icpsrweb/ICPSR/ssvd.

51. See Inter-university Consortium for Political and Social Research (ICPSR), "Additional ICPSR Services," accessed June 18, 2016, http://www.icpsr.umich.edu/icpsrweb/content/datamanagement/lifecycle/services.html.

52. See Inter-university Consortium for Political and Social Research (ICPSR), "Find Publications," accessed June 18, 2016, https://www.icpsr.umich.edu/icpsrweb/ICPSR/citations/index.jsp. See also Elizabeth Moss, Christin Cave, and Jared Lyle, "Sharing and Citing Research Data: A Repository's Perspective," *Big Data, Big Challenges in Evidence-Based Policy Making*, ed. H. Kumar Jayasuriya and Kathryn A. Ritcheske, American Casebook Series (St. Paul, MN: West Academic Publishing, 2015), Chapter 4, 1-17.

53. Ember and Hanisch, "Sustaining Domain Repositories for Digital Data."

# Bibliography

Albright, Jeremy J., and Jared A. Lyle. "Data Preservation through Data Archives."
*PS: Political Science and Politics* 43, no. 1 (January 2010):17–21. doi:10.1017/
S1049096510990768.

Alliance of Digital Humanities Organizations (ADHO) homepage. Accessed June 18, 2016.
http://adho.org.

Armbruster, Chris, and Laurent Romary. "Comparing Repository Types: Challenges and
Barriers for Subject-Based Repositories, Research Repositories, National Repository
Systems and Institutional Repositories in Serving Scholarly Communication." Social
Science Research Network. November 23, 2009. http://ssrn.com/abstract=1506905.

Borgman, Christine L. *Big Data, Little Data, No Data: Scholarship in the Networked World.*
Cambridge, MA: MIT Press, 2015.

Bradley, Kevin. "Chapter 6.1.9: Trusted Digital Repositories (TDR) and Institutional
Responsibility." *Guidelines on the Production and Preservation of Digital Audio Objects,*
2nd ed. International Association of Sound and Audiovisual Archives, 2009. http://
www.iasa-web.org/tc04/trusted-digital-repositories-tdr-and-institutional-responsibil-
ity.

Briney, Kristin, Abigail Goben, and Lisa Zilinski. "Do You Have an Institutional Data
Policy? A Review of the Current Landscape of Library Data Services and Institutional
Data Policies." *Journal of Librarianship and Scholarly Communication* 3, no. 2 (2015):
eP1232. doi:10.7710/2162-3309.1232.

Budapest Open Access Initiative. *Guide to Institutional Repository Software*, 3rd ed. New York:
Open Society Institute, August 2004. http://www.budapestopenaccessinitiative.org/
pdf/OSI_Guide_to_IR_Software_v3.pdf.

Center for Research Libraries (CRL) and Online Computer Library Center (OCLC). *Trustworthy Repositories Audit and Certification (TRAC): Criteria and Checklist.* Chicago:
CRL and Dublin, OH: OCLC, 2007. https://www.crl.edu/sites/default/files/d6/
attachments/pages/trac_0.pdf.

Columbia University Libraries. "Depositing Data in Academic Commons." Accessed March
14, 2016. http://scholcomm.columbia.edu/data-management/depositing-data-in-ac-
ademic-commons.

Consortia Advancing Standards in Research Administration Information (CASRAI). "Repository." Accessed July 9, 2016. http://dictionary.casrai.org/Repository.

Consultative Committee for Space Data Systems. *Audit and Certification of Trustworthy Digital Repositories.* Recommended Practice, CCSDS 652.0-M-1, Magenta Book, Issue
1 Washington, DC: CCSDS Secretariat, September 2011. http://public.ccsds.org/
publications/archive/652x0m1.pdf.

———. *Reference Model for an Open Archival Information System (OAIS).* Recommended
Practice, CCSDS 650.0-M-2, Magenta Book, Issue 2. Washington, DC: CCSDS
Secretariat, June 2012. http://public.ccsds.org/publications/archive/650x0m2.pdf.

Center for Human Resource Research. "Guide to the NLSY97 Data." in *NLSY97 User's Guide: A guide to the Rounds 1–3 Data, National Longitudinal Survey of
Youth 1997.* (Columbus: Ohio State University, 2001). https://web.archive.org/
web/20100727011626/http://www.nlsinfo.org/nlsy97/97guide/chap3.htm.

Converse, Philip E. "A Network of Data Archives for the Behavioral Sciences." *Public Opinion Quarterly* 28, no 2 (Summer 1964): 273–86. http://www.jstor.org/stable/2746992.

Crow, Raym. *SPARC Institutional Repository Checklist and Resource Guide.* Washington, DC: Scholarly Publishing and Academic Resources Coalition, 2002. http://sparcopen.org/wp-content/uploads/2016/01/IR_Guide__Checklist_v1_0.pdf.

Data Documentation Initiative (DDI) homepage. Accessed June 18, 2016. http://www.ddialliance.org.

Data Seal of Approval. "Extension to the Current Data Seal." News release, February 3, 2016. http://datasealofapproval.org/en/news-and-events/news/2016/2/3/extension-current-data-seal.

Digital Curation Centre. "What Is Digital Curation?" Accessed June 14, 2016. http://www.dcc.ac.uk/digital-curation/what-digital-curation.

Dryad Digital Repository. "Dryad Metadata Application Profile (Schema)." Last modified February 27, 2013. http://wiki.datadryad.org/Metadata_Profile.

———. "Dryad REST API Technology." Last modified November 10, 2015. http://wiki.datadryad.org/Dryad_REST_API_Technology.

———. "Journal Metadata Processing Technology." Last modified November 17, 2015. http://wiki.datadryad.org/Journal_Metadata_Processing_Technology.

———. "Submission Integration: Overview." Last modified January 15, 2016. http://wiki.datadryad.org/Submission_Integration.

———. "Terms of Service." Last modified August 22, 2013. https://datadryad.org/pages/policies.

Dryad Digital Repository homepage. Last modified November 19, 2015. https://datadryad.org.

Ember, Carol, and Robert Hanisch. "Sustaining Domain Repositories for Digital Data: A White Paper." Output of the workshop "Sustaining Domain Repositories for Digital Data," Ann Arbor, MI, June 24–25, 2013. doi:10.3886/SustainingDomainRepositoriesDigitalData.

Erway, Ricky. "What Is Actually Happening Out There in Terms of Institutional Data Repositories?" *Hangingtogether.org* (blog). July 27, 2015. http://hangingtogether.org/?p=5342.

Eschenfelder, Kristin R., and Andrew Johnson. "Managing the Data Commons: Controlled Sharing of Scholarly Data." *Journal of the Association for Information Science and Technology* 65, no. 9 (2014): 1757–74.

Estlund, Karen, and Anna Neatrour. "Utah Digital Repository Initiative: Building a Support System for Institutional Repositories." *D-Lib Magazine* 13, no. 11/12 (November/December 2007). http://www.dlib.org/dlib/november07/neatrour/11neatrour.html.

EZID. "The EZID API, Version 2." Accessed February 10, 2015. http://ezid.cdlib.org/doc/apidoc.html.

Green, Ann, JoAnn Dionne, and Martin Dennis. *Preserving the Whole: A Two-Track Approach to Rescuing Social Science Data and Metadata.* CLIR Publication 83. Washington, DC: Council on Library and Information Resources, 1999. http://www.clir.org/pubs/reports/pub83/contents.html.

Green, Ann G., and Myron P. Gutmann. "Building Partnerships among Social Science Researchers, Institution-Based Repositories, and Domain Specific Data Archives." *OCLC Systems and Services: International Digital Library Perspectives* 23 (2007): 35–53. http://hdl.handle.net/2027.42/41214.

Group on Earth Observations (GEO) homepage. Accessed June 18, 2016. https://www.earthobservations.org.

HathiTrust Digital Library. "Technological Profile." Accessed July 9, 2016. https://www.hathitrust.org/technology.

Holdren, John P. "Increasing Access to the Results of Federally Funded Scientific Research." Memorandum for the Heads of Executive Departments and Agencies, Office of Science and Technology Policy, Executive Office of the President, February 22, 2013. http://www.whitehouse.gov/sites/default/files/microsites/ostp/ostp_public_access_memo_2013.pdf.

International Organization for Standardization. "ISO 16363:2012: Space Data and Information Transfer Systems—Audit and Certification of Trustworthy Digital Repositories." February 15, 2012. http://www.iso.org/iso/catalogue_detail.htm?csnumber=56510.

———. "ISO 14721:2012: Space Data and Information Transfer Systems—Open Archival Information System (OAIS)—Reference Model." September 1, 2012. http://www.iso.org/iso/catalogue_detail.htm?csnumber=57284.

International Council for Science World Data System (ICSU WDS) homepage. Accessed June 18, 2016. https://www.icsu-wds.org.

International Social Science Council (ISSC) homepage. Accessed June 18, 2016. http://www.worldsocialscience.org.

International Society for Environmental Ethics (ISEE) homepage. Accessed June 18, 2016. http://enviroethics.org.

Inter-university Consortium for Political and Social Research (ICPSR). "Additional ICPSR Services." Accessed June 18, 2016. http://www.icpsr.umich.edu/icpsrweb/content/datamanagement/lifecycle/services.html.

———. "Data Enclaves." Accessed June 18, 2016. http://www.icpsr.umich.edu/icpsrweb/content/icpsr/access/restricted/enclave.html.

———. "Find Publications." Accessed June 18, 2016. https://www.icpsr.umich.edu/icpsrweb/ICPSR/citations/index.jsp.

———. "Search/Compare Variables." Accessed June 18, 2016. https://www.icpsr.umich.edu/icpsrweb/ICPSR/ssvd/.

Joint Task Force on Library Support for E-Science. *Agenda for Developing E-science in Research Libraries.* Final Report and Recommendations to the Scholarly Communication Steering Committee, the Public Policies Affecting Research Libraries Steering Committee, and the Research, Teaching, and Learning Steering Committee. Washington, DC: Association of Research Libraries, November 2007. http://www.arl.org/storage/documents/publications/arl-escience-agenda-nov07.pdf.

Lavoie, Brian F. "The Open Archival Information System Reference Model: Introductory Guide." *Microform and Imaging Review* 33, no. 2 (2004): 68–81. doi:10.7207/twr14-02.

Leahey, Amber, Peter Webster, Claire Austin, Nancy Fong, Julie Friddell, Chuck Humphrey, Susan Brown, and Walter Stewart. "Research Data Repository Requirements and Features Review," v. 4. Standards and Interoperability Committee. February 24, 2015. http://hdl.handle.net/10864/10892.

manez. "Research Data in Islandora." *Islandora* blog, December 2, 2014. http://islandora.ca/content/research-data-islandora.

Moss, Elizabeth, Christin Cave, and Jared Lyle. "Sharing and Citing Research Data: A Repository's Perspective." *Big Data, Big Challenges in Evidence-Based Policy Making.* Edited by H. Kumar Jayasuriya and Kathryn A. Ritcheske, Chapter 4, 1-17. American Casebook Series. St. Paul, MN: West Academic Publishing, 2015.

National Library of Medicine Digital Repository Working Group. "Digital Repository Policies and Functional Requirements," v. 1. Revised March 16, 2007. https://www.nlm.nih.gov/digitalrepository/NLM-DigRep-Requirements-rev032007.pdf.

Peer, Limor, Ann Green, and Elizabeth Stephenson. "Committing to Data Quality Review." *International Journal of Digital Curation* 9, no. 1 (2014): 263–91. doi:10.2218/ijdc.v9i1.317.

Rasheed, Abdul, and Mohamed Mohideen. "Fedora Commons with Apache Hadoop: A Research Study." *code4lib*, no. 22 (October 14, 2013). http://journal.code4lib.org/articles/8988.

Registry of Research Data Repositories homepage. Accessed March 14, 2016. http://www.re3data.org.

Repositories Support Project. "Briefing Papers." Accessed March 14, 2016. http://www.rsp.ac.uk/help/publications/#briefing-papers.

Research Data Alliance Data Foundation and Terminology Working Group (RDA DFT-WG). "Edit RDA: digital repository." Accessed July 9, 2016. http://smw-rda.esc.rzg.mpg.de/index.php/Special:FormEdit/RDA/digital_repository.

Research Libraries Group. *Trusted Digital Repositories: Attributes and Responsibilities.* An RLG-OCLC report. Mountain View, CA: Research Libraries Group, May 2002. http://www.oclc.org/content/dam/research/activities/trustedrep/repositories.pdf.

UK Data Archive. "How We Curate Data: Our Preservation Policy." Accessed June 18, 2016. http://www.data-archive.ac.uk/curate/preservation-policy.

University of Minnesota Libraries. *The Supporting Documentation for Implementing the Data Repository for the University of Minnesota (DRUM): A Business Model, Functional Requirements, and Metadata Schema.* University of Minnesota Digital Conservancy, 2015. http://hdl.handle.net/11299/171761.

Van Tuyl, Steven, Hui Zhang, and Michael Boock. "Analysis of Challenges and Opportunities for Migrating ScholarsArchive@ OSU to a New Technical Platform: Requirements Analysis, Environmental Scan, and Recommended Next Steps." February 26, 2015. http://hdl.handle.net/1957/55221.

Watson, Carol A., James M. Donovan, and Pamela Bluh. "Implementing BePress' Digital Commons Institutional Repository Solution: Two Views from the Trenches." Presentation at the 18th Conference for Law School Computing (CALI), University of Maryland School of Law, Baltimore, MD, June 19–21, 2008. http://digitalcommons.law.uga.edu/ir/4.

Watts, Joshua. "Building tDAR: Review, Redaction, and Ingest of Two Reports Series." *Reports in Digital Archaeology,* no. 1 (June 2011). Center for Digital Antiquity, Arizona State University, Tempe, AZ. http://www.digitalantiquity.org/wp-uploads/2011/07/20110930-Building-tDAR.pdf.

Witten, Ian H., and David Bainbridge. *How to Build a Digital Library.* San Francisco: Morgan Kaufmann, 2003.

World Meteorological Organization (WMO) homepage. Accessed June 18, 2016. https://www.wmo.int.

Zhang, Allison B., and Don Gourley. *Creating Digital Collections: A Practical Guide.* Oxford: Chandos Publishing, 2014.

# Descriptive Metadata

Applying descriptive metadata to your data collection will enable users to search, discover, and retrieve data from your repository. Using a well-structured metadata schema is key. Like the documentation and contextual information gathered in *Step 3*, this step approaches description but in a more systematic way through the use of metadata standards.

According to the Digital Curation Centre, there are a number of general metadata standards used for describing data.[1] These include Common European Research Information Format, Dublin Core, DataCite Metadata Schema, Data Catalog Vocabulary (DCAT), and PREMIS. And new metadata standards for data in digital repositories are emerging, such as the Portland Common Data Model (PCDM). The intuitive Dublin Core standard is used in this chapter to illustrate some techniques for collecting and applying metadata for data in a repository.

# 5.1 Create and Apply Appropriate Metadata

In a self-deposit model, authors enter the metadata about the data set into a form, which maps the information to the metadata schema. As noted in *Step 1* case studies on page 30 (Yoo, Schneider, and Hutt) and on page 33 (Koshoffer, Hansen, and Newman), there are a number of challenges to overcome in an author-deposit model for capturing metadata. In some cases, the data curator will need to create additional metadata to supplement the metadata submitted by the depositor. This intervention has some benefits, however, as it allows for the greatest accuracy when cataloging information about the data set that will populate the record (i.e., using a metadata schema appropriately).

# Dublin Core Metadata Schema in Action

Dublin Core (DC) is a standard metadata schema used in a variety of digital repository systems, such as DSpace. As the term *Core* implies, the metadata elements in DC are intended to be basic. The Dublin Core Metadata Initiative (DCMI) is tasked with maintaining the DC elements, definitions, and properties of the standard and describes the base fifteen elements as

1. Contributor: An entity responsible for making contributions to the resource (e.g., a person, an organization, or a service).
2. Coverage: The spatial (e.g., a named place or a location specified by its geographic coordinates) or temporal (e.g., a named period, date, or date range) topic of the resource.
3. Creator: An entity primarily responsible for making the resource (e.g., a person, an organization, or a service).
4. Date: A point or period of time associated with an event in the lifecycle of the resource.
5. Description: An account of the resource (e.g., an abstract, a table of contents, a graphical representation, or a free-text account of the resource).
6. Format: The file format, physical medium, or dimensions of the resource (e.g., size and MIME type).
7. Identifier: An unambiguous reference to the resource within a given context (e.g., purl, handle, or DOI).
8. Language: A language of the resource.
9. Publisher: An entity responsible for making the resource available (e.g., a person, an organization, or a service).
10. Relation: A related resource (e.g., a version of the item).
11. Rights: Information about rights held in and over the resource (e.g., copyright statement).
12. Source: A related resource from which the described resource is derived.
13. Subject: The topic of the resource (e.g. keywords).
14. Title: A name given to the resource.
15. Type: The nature or genre of the resource (e.g., controlled vocabulary terms such as *Dataset*).[2]

On first glance, the DC metadata set is deceptively simple. However, in practice the application and use of the basic DC metadata elements can vary greatly from institution to institution.[3] To complicate matters, there are many aspects of a data set that are not clearly described by this element set. Therefore, the DC set can be expanded to include nonstandard elements at the local level. For example, see the metadata submission form screenshots (appendix 5.0 A) for the Data Repository for the University of Minnesota (DRUM, http://z.umn.edu/DRUM). DRUM was developed by Bill Tantzen and with an expanded Dublin Dore Metadata Schema (table 5.1) created by Stephen Hearn, both staff at the University of Minnesota Libraries.[4]

DRUM is part of a larger institutional repository, the University Digital Conservancy (UDC, http://conservancy.umn.edu) that functions for object types beyond data (e.g., articles, poster presentations, reports, etc.). Therefore, to retain a consistent standard across the system, DC elements were applied and expanded for the data repository specifically. In table 5.1, you will notice that core elements, such as `dc.spatial` and `dc.temporal`, are used to capture the data set descriptions for Geographic Coverage and Time Period Covered by Data respectively. In addition, an extension of DC elements, such as the `dc.contributor.contactname`, was used to collect information that is relevant to data sets (e.g., knowing who to contact with questions about the data is a key service that DRUM wanted to provide). This approach allowed DRUM to function alongside other IR elements (for searching and faceting), yet include structured metadata specific for data.

## TABLE 5.1

A selection of Dublin Core elements used by the Data Repository for the University of Minnesota (DRUM) and the submission form help text displayed to depositors for each element.

| Dublin Core (DC) Element | Record Display Label | Help Text in Submission Form |
|---|---|---|
| dc.contributor.author | Author(s) | *List the author(s) of the data set. Use complete names eg. "James Ryan Swanson"* |
| dc.contributor. contactname | Author Contact | *Email address of the principal contact for the data.* |
| dc.contributor. contactemail | Author Contact | *Name of the principal contact for the data.* |
| dc.contributor.group | Group | *If applicable for datasets produced by a group. Ex. "University of Minnesota Department of Chemistry, Crystallography Research Lab"* |
| dc.coverage.spatial | Geographic Coverage | *Do your data pertain to a specific location? Eg. Antarctica or Red Wing, MN? Or if applicable, coordinates (latitude and longitude in either degree-min-sec or decimal degree format) covered by geospatial data? If not, leave blank.* |

**TABLE 5.1** (continued)

| Dublin Core (DC) Element | Record Display Label | Help Text in Submission Form |
|---|---|---|
| dc.coverage.temporal | Time Period Covered by Data | *Do your data pertain to a specific time-period? Ex. 2006-2009 or circa 800 B.C. If not, leave blank.* |
| dc.date.available | Published Date | (Auto-populated by system) |
| dc.date.collectedbegin | Collection Period | *Beginning of time period that the data was collected. YYYY-MM-DD is the recommended format.* |
| dc.date.collectedend | Collection Period | *End of time period that the data was collected. YYYY-MM-DD is the recommended format.* |
| dc.date.completed | Date Completed | *Date the data was finalized for distribution. YYYY-MM-DD is the recommended format.* |
| dc.description | Description | *Do your data need additional explanation? Note: Documentation is required for data to be accepted into the Data Repository and these can be uploaded as files (e.g. readme files, explanations of codes used, etc.) or included here.* |
| dc.description. abstract | Abstract | *Briefly describe the data (its contents, value, and purpose) and why it is now released (recommended no more than 250 characters).* |
| dc.description. sponsorship | Sponsorship | *If applicable, enter the names of any sponsors, funding agencies, and/or funding codes.* |
| dc.description. sponsorship.funderID | Funding Agency ID | (Parsed by curator as necessary) |
| dc.description. sponsorship. fundingagency | Funding Agency | (Parsed by curator as necessary) |
| dc.description. sponsorship.grant | Sponsorship Grant | (Parsed by curator as necessary) |
| dc.format | Format | (MIME type and file size detected and verified by system) |

## TABLE 5.1 (continued)

| Dublin Core (DC) Element | Record Display Label | Help Text in Submission Form |
|---|---|---|
| dc.identifier.doi | Persistent Link to This Item | (DataCite DOI generated for each record) |
| dc.identifier.uri | Persistent Link to This Item | (Handle generated by the system) |
| dc.publisher | n/a | (Populates the Suggested Citation as Data Repository for the University of Minnesota (DRUM)) |
| dc.relation. isreferencedby | Related Publications | *Related publications that reference/use/describe the data. Paste the full citation or just include a URL. Ex. DOI:240857083.352.523.4* |
| dc.relation.isbasedon | Source Information | *Were your data generated or derived from a formerly existing data set? If you created it, then leave blank.* |
| dc.relation. isbasedonurl | n/a | |
| dc.rights | License: | *If you wish, you may add a Creative Commons License to your item. Creative Commons licenses govern what people who read your work may then do with it.* |
| dc.rights.uri | n/a | |
| dc.subject | Keyword(s) | *Use the Add More button to enter multiple subject keywords or phrases. Note: items will be full-text searchable.* |
| dc.title | Title | *Titles should be descriptive and include the what, where, when and scale of your data.* |
| dc.type | Type | (Set to "Dataset" for all records) |
| dc.type.dataset | Data Type | (Controlled vocabulary added by curators for faceting, e.g., Spatial Data, Survey Data etc.) |

# Challenges with Capturing Metadata in Data Repository Submission Forms

Some lessons learned from the DRUM metadata form have resulted in curation procedures that clean up or augment any user-supplied metadata. For example:

- Funder information is requested as one statement, to allow for user-input flexibility. Later the curator can parse this information out using additional Sponsorship fields for granting agency, grant number, funder ID, and so on.
- Related publication citations may come in a variety of citation formats. These can be normalized and a persistent DOI to the article added as a clickable URL (e.g., rather than a DOI:123.344.555).
- Spatial information can be represented in a variety of formats. Therefore, additional formatting can be applied that is consistent for the repository. Curators apply a format bounding box for GIS data if applicable. Example: "Bounding box (W, S, E, N): -93.770810, 44.468717, -92.725647, 45.303848"
- Temporal information may be scattered through the description of the record. For example, a data set description might read "The study began in 2006 to catalog the objects found between 2001 and 2004…. Later we dated the objects to the 4th Century BC…). This temporal information can be structured using the `dc.coverage.temporal` and various flavors of the `dc.date` element. Curators also reformat dates to a standard YYYY-MM-DD structure.
- Choosing what information to include in the Description versus the Abstract field can be a challenge for some authors. For DRUM purposes, the Description field is used to describe the contents of the data files and how they relate to each other, as compared to the Abstract, which describes the intent of the research. Curator adjustments to the author-supplied Abstract and Description fields are typical.

# Usability Testing of Data Repository Submission Forms

Even with help text, authors may still struggle to interpret a data repository metadata form. Some errors might occur that can be corrected by a curator, but others might be avoided altogether with small changes to the user interface. For example, based on usability testing of the Data Repository for the University of Minnesota metadata submission form, we identified the following problems and, with the help of our usability expert Erik Larson, recommended solutions:

- Multiple Values: With multiple value fields, the Add More buttons were not observed during data entry. This was problematic when adding additional authors and listing subject keywords. Instead, test users submitted keywords with commas that were entered in a single text field (e.g., "dog, canine, fido"). This resulted in user-entered keywords displaying as one long phrase, rather than as unique keywords.
  o Recommendation: Add visual clues to draw the eye towards the button. Provide a background color and include a + (plus) icon to add length.
- Help Text: Several submission steps and data-entry fields did not contain sufficient examples or help text to prevent uncertainty when entering data. This was observed when test users were adding geocoordinate data, adding temporal data, and including a description field (which served as the readme descriptive file).
  o Recommendation: Consider adding field-level help documentation and links to more detailed help near each field. Consider adding a step-by-step tutorial or guide to the start of the submission process.
- File-level descriptions: Participants desired to add more complex information to the individual file descriptions than expected. Instead of a short sentence, multiple sentences akin to a documentation readme file were included with each file-level description. Additionally, one faculty member's data set was collected over multiple year ranges at three different geographic locations, and they were uncertain where to place file-level attributes such as "1936-1950 Isle Royale National Park, MI" for one file and "1940-1968 Superior National Forest, MN" for another.
  o Recommendation: Consider changing the record display to allow for long descriptions of files. Consider allowing multiple temporal and spatial coverages (with start and end dates for individual files) with multiple collection venues or points. For added consistency, consider adding a strict date field paired alongside a textual description.[5]

# 5.2 Consider Disciplinary Metadata Standards for Data

Disciplinary metadata schemas and vocabularies used in the various fields can be essential components to a data submission, and curators should try to retain as much of this information as possible. If the data repository metadata schema is not compatible, then consider capturing and presenting disciplinary-specific metadata as a separate file alongside the data in a format that might be ingested by future information systems (e.g., XML).

The Dataverse Project repository software (http://dataverse.org) does a nice job at incorporating a growing number of domain-specific metadata schema, including for the geospatial, social science and humanities, astronomy and astrophysics, and life sciences communities.[6] Here metadata describing items in a Dataverse collection can be exported in discipline-specific metadata formats (via JSON format or XML), allowing for better operability between the general repository and more subject-specific repositories (table 5.2).

**TABLE 5.2**

Metadata schemas supported in Dataverse[a]

| Dataverse-Supported Discipline Metadata | Mapped to Related Schemas |
|---|---|
| Citation Metadata | DDI Lite, DDI 2.5 Codebook, DataCite 3.1, and Dublin Core |
| Geospatial Metadata | DDI Lite, DDI 2.5 Codebook, DataCite, and Dublin Core |
| Social Science & Humanities Metadata | DDI Lite, DDI 2.5 Codebook, and Dublin Core |
| Astronomy and Astrophysics Metadata | International Virtual Observatory Alliance's (IVOA) VO Resource Schema format, is based on Virtual Observatory (VO) Discovery and Provenance Metadata |
| Life Sciences Metadata | ISA-Tab Specification, along with controlled vocabulary from subsets of the OBI Ontology and the NCBI Taxonomy for Organisms |

a. Source: Dataverse, "Metadata Blocks," Github, accessed March 12, 2016. https://github.com/IQSS/dataverse/tree/master/scripts/api/data/metadatablocks.

For more examples of disciplinary metadata standards, the RDA Metadata Standards working group has partnered with the Digital Curation Centre to create a sustainable metadata directory (http://rd-alliance.github.io/metadata-directory/standards).

# Disciplinary-Specific Metadata in Action

The next case studies present different approaches to incorporating disciplinary metadata standards into data repositories, including the longitudinal study archive CLOSER (Jon Johnson and Gemma Seabrook) and Long Term Ecological Research Network (Jon Wheeler, Mark Servilla, and Kristin Vanderbilt).

# Modern Metadata at Scale: CLOSER Case Study

*Jon Johnson and Gemma Seabrook**

The United Kingdom is home to the world's largest and longest-running longitudinal studies. Cohort and Longitudinal Studies Enhancement Resources (CLOSER, http://www.closer.ac.uk) aims to maximize their use, value, and impact both at home and abroad. Running from 2012 to 2017, it brings together eight leading studies: the Hertfordshire Cohort Study (1930s), the National Survey of Health and Development (1946), the National Child Development Study (1958), the 1970 British Cohort Study, the Avon Longitudinal Study of Parents and Children (1990s), the Southampton Women's Survey (1998), the Millennium Cohort Study (2001), and the household study Understanding Society (2010) alongside the British Library and the UK Data Service. CLOSER works to stimulate interdisciplinary research, develop shared resources, provide training, and share expertise.

At the heart of the project is the assembly of a metadata repository encompassing the full range of information about the studies, from study description to data collection methodology, questionnaire capture, and data. Layered on top of this are controlled vocabularies and other contextual information.

The project has very specific challenges. The studies are geographically dispersed across England. Their leadership crosses scientific domains (some medical, some social science–focused) and the longevity of the studies (starting in 1946) means that the information available is inconsistently cataloged and held in various formats.

Key decisions at the outset were that

1. metadata would be generated and ingested to an existing standard for interoperability and reuse;
2. where possible existing technology would be used;
3. inputs into a metadata store would need to be tightly controlled so that standard processes were applied to all metadata;
4. there would be full discovery of the metadata for researchers; and
5. controlled vocabularies would be used for a consistent user experience.

## THE PLAN

The international Data Documentation Initiative Lifecycle standard (DDI-L, http://www.ddialliance.org/Specification/) was chosen as the underlying metadata format for use on the project. It was able to support the requirements and, at version 3.2, was sufficiently mature. Sufficient tools were also available to operationalize a major project.

Colectica Repository (http://www.colectica.com) was chosen as the metadata store as it has support for DDI-L and a software development kit (SDK). This SDK provided a straightforward development environment for creating a workflow to ingest the various metadata elements and can expose a public web portal for content discovery.

The diversity of questionnaire layout and structure meant that any programmatic extraction of information was not viable. The style, layout, and logic employed in questionnaires varies greatly across time, discipline, organization, and interview mode. DDI-L provides structures to capture the individual components of a questionnaire, for instance being able to separate out the question from interviewer instructions, and good code and category management, but judgement is required to parse and input it in a consistent manner for discovery and reuse. DDI-L captures the components and the logic of a questionnaire, not its layout, so questions that look very different but are logically the same should be rendered in the same manner. As a result, there needs to be a validation step that accounts for this.

The Centre for Longitudinal Studies (CLS), one of the partners in the collaboration, had already built a questionnaire capture tool using the Ruby on Rails web application framework (CADDIES).[7] CADDIES was intended to enable entry by a person with basic clerical skills. It was enhanced to support the latest version of DDI-L and a profile was generated to export consistent DDI-L-compliant XML from it to simplify the ingest process.

## THE REALITY CHECK

The original idea had been that CADDIES would be rolled out to each study for them to input and validate their own questionnaires. Through piloting, it became evident that the diversity of the questionnaires meant creating consistent outputs required a higher level of expertise than had been thought.

The solution was to create a centralized team who would generate the corpus of knowledge that needed to be captured and then built upon as new problems emerged. At the core of this team was a set of principles designed to summarize the aims of the work—to document and not enhance, to reproduce the thinking of the time without the benefit of hindsight.[8]

## WHAT ABOUT THE DATA?

Extraction of metadata from data sets had to take place at the studies' home institution due to data access arrangements. Several tools were evaluated for ease of use, cost, configurability, and also compatibility with IT systems at the partner organizations. SledgeHammer (http://www.mtna.us/) was selected for the range of supported input data formats, operating system support, and configurability of output.

Mapping the questions to the variables, and assigning a controlled vocabulary of topics to both questions and variables, also had to be carried out by the studies where the expertise resides. A simple web-based tool, Mapper, was developed in Ruby on Rails to facilitate this.

The final set of metadata was the high-level details. Study descriptions and information about the data collections were entered directly into Colectica Designer, providing the connecting layer.

# COMPLETING THE METADATA PUZZLE

There were now a number of pieces available. The questionnaire, the resulting response data, the mapping of topics and study metadata, and the summary data collection information were all ingested into Colectica Repository and connected together using the Colectica SDK.

In addition, further correspondence tables, which map between variables (indicating equality, similarity, and whether a variable is subset of another variable) were ingested into Colectica to support a related variables view.

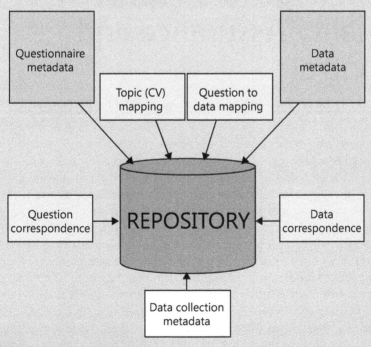

**FIGURE 5.1**
Overview of metadata components.

It was clear at the outset that the project could not provide direct access to the data for data protection reasons. Via the web portal, CLOSER Discovery (http://discovery.closer.ac.uk), users are able to see what data is available in an accessible way. They can assess the utility of the data for their research and see the full context in which that data was collected. They can extract lists to enhance data access and navigation.

Once this phase of the project is complete, the flexible nature of DDI-L and the software platform will allow us to simply add more information: for instance, the coding used in constructing derived variables, and the provenance of questions to further enrich the contextual information available.

# Beyond Discovery: Cross-Platform Application of Ecological Metadata Language in Support of Quality Assurance and Control

*Jon Wheeler, Mark Servilla, and Kristin Vanderbilt**

To support research data curation, descriptive and other types of metadata schemas may be broadly applied to administer access and reuse policies, define system requirements, or perform quality assurance and control functions. In this context, domain repositories like the Long Term Ecological Research (LTER, https://www.lternet.edu/) Network's Provenance Aware Synthesis Tracking Architecture (PASTA, https://github.com/lter/PASTA) are designed to capitalize on complex metadata schema such as the Ecological Metadata Language (EML) to perform an array of descriptive, technical, provenance, and other repository functions.[9] However, transferring data between these and more domain-agnostic systems, such as university institutional repositories (IR), can result in a loss of features when complex metadata are mapped to a more general-purpose schema, such as Dublin Core (http://dublincore.org/). For example, whereas data sets within PASTA are indexed for faceted discovery across topics including taxonomy, methods, or habitats, mapping related EML fields to Dublin Core results in a conflation of these and other attributes into a single "subject" field. Through spring and summer 2015, a collaboration between the University of New Mexico (UNM, http://library.unm.edu/) Libraries, the Sevilleta LTER program (http://sev.lternet.edu/), and the LTER Network Office (LNO, http://lternet.edu/sites/lno/) explored methods for archiving data sets with complex metadata into an IR. This brief case study describes the application of a standards-based metadata ingest process to facilitate data description and transfer across systems. By establishing and preserving documentation of EML conformance as a baseline requirement for data file properties and metadata syntax, the outcomes to date demonstrate the application of EML as a quality assurance and control resource across the data life cycle.

In 2003, an LTER Network–wide effort to better preserve and expose its data to domain scientists and the broader ecological research community led to the adoption of EML as the network's official metadata standard and the LTER Network Information System (NIS), central to which is the LNO-developed PASTA data repository.[10] PASTA is based on a service-oriented architecture design pattern[11] and exposes an open web-service end-point for data producer and consumer applications, including the LTER Network Data Portal user interface (https://portal.lternet.edu). All data packages submitted to PASTA must be described by an EML science metadata document. Because EML is an expressive metadata standard, the architects of PASTA were able to capitalize on the content and data models defined by the schema in order to enforce consistent data management practices across the LTER Network.

With the EML requirement in place, publication of Sevilleta field data in PASTA is a mediated process providing for information manager oversight and review of submitted metadata against established best practices. Scientists at the Sevilleta LTER submit their metadata to the Sevilleta information manager via a Microsoft Word template, in which they describe who was involved in creating the data set and metadata, where and how the data was collected, what each variable represents, and structural details of the data file. The metadata are then entered into the Sevilleta's instance of the Drupal Ecological Information Management System (https://www.drupal.org/project/deims). DEIMS is a web-based system for managing information products associated with an LTER site.[12] It is implemented in the Drupal content management system. Significantly, DEIMS includes a web-based metadata editor that translates the complexity of the schema into a series of user-friendly forms. Each form represents a subset of the complete metadata, such as sites, methods, people, variables, and data file structure (see appendix 5.0 B). The data, in CSV format, are also uploaded to DEIMS. Moreover, DEIMS includes a custom module that generates EML metadata that is compliant with PASTA's quality control process.

Data files and metadata are logically combined into a "data package" and uploaded to PASTA either manually by the Sevilleta information manager or automatically through DEIMS. As part of the "upload" process, PASTA analyzes the data package for compliance with LTER data management best practices by performing a series of quality checks that compare the descriptive components of the EML to the physical data. A compliance report is then generated by PASTA and is available to producers and consumers of the data package. Data packages that do not comply with critical best practices are rejected by PASTA. Compliance validation of the data package includes asserting the presence of temporal and geographic information, scientific methodologies, designation of field and record delimiters, uniqueness of data attribute identifiers, connectivity of data URLs, and, in the case of tabular data, validity of declared data types and cardinality of the table. Incorrectly recording a string variable as an integer, for instance, will cause the "data type" check to fail. In this case, the Sevilleta information manager would have to correct any errors before the data package can be successfully uploaded into PASTA. Both the EML metadata and data are stored directly in PASTA to ensure direct accessibility for consumers. For data package discovery, PASTA uses Apache Solr to index metadata attributes like key words, creator names, and temporal and geographic information, and provisions a DOI that is recorded by DataCite (https://www.datacite.org/). PASTA also takes advantage of the EML syntax to enable linked open data within the system so that users may embed linked provenance metadata to other data packages in PASTA that were used as source material during synthesis or the creation of derived data products.

In coordination with the Sevilleta LTER and the LNO, the UNM Libraries are providing an archival mirror of Sevilleta data (https://repository.unm.edu/handle/1928/29608), originally published in PASTA, within the University's DSpace-based (http://www.dspace.org/) IR, LoboVault (https://repository.unm.edu/). Archived data sets are harvested from PASTA and packaged per the Simple Archive Format specifications published by DSpace (https://wiki.duraspace.org/display/DSDOC5x/Importing+and+Exporting+Items+via+Simple+Archive+Format) for batch ingest into LoboVault. Using a desktop workflow to coordinate harvest, packaging, and upload into DSpace, the content and metadata included in each package are structured to emulate selected LTER Network Data Portal features using the data package's EML metadata. Specifically, geographic coordinates are mapped to a Darwin Core (http://rs.tdwg.org/dwc/) extension of the DSpace metadata registry and used to draw item-level maps, and a preferred citation is generated that includes the DOI of the harvested data package. While not directly published as item record metadata in LoboVault, the provenance metadata and ingest report described above are likewise harvested for inclusion as downloadable content files associated with their respective data packages. Finally, though the intellectual content of the

EML metadata exceeds the scope of the item record metadata in LoboVault, on harvest a data package's EML is serialized into HTML and likewise included as a downloadable content file. Additionally, because HTML text is fully extracted and indexed within DSpace, the content of the full EML record is thereby exposed to search and discovery features. By using EML metadata in combination with other data package components harvested via PASTA, the archival LoboVault collection supports the long-term curation of Sevilleta LTER data and carries forward the documentation of quality control processes performed by the Sevilleta information managers and within the PASTA architecture.

# Summary of Step 5.0: Descriptive Metadata

5.1 Create and Apply Descriptive Metadata: Structure author-generated metadata into the metadata schema used by your repository in order to maximize search and discovery functionality. Create and apply new metadata for the data record, including technical and provenance metadata.

5.2 Consider Metadata Standards for Disciplinary Data: When appropriate, structure and present metadata in multiple schemas to facilitate discovery and future integration into other systems.

# Appendix 5.0 A: Screenshots from the Data Repository for the University of Minnesota (DRUM) Submission Form

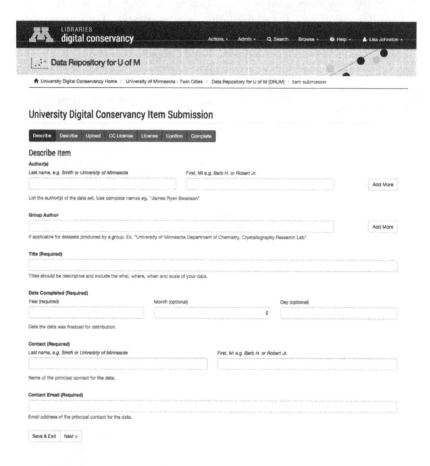

## FIGURE 5.2

The Data Repository for the University of Minnesota (DRUM) is based on a DSpace implementation that utilizes the XML-based Mirage 2 theme available for download at https://atmire.com/website/?q=contributions/dspace-mirage-2 and comes standard in DSpace (starting with version 5). The expanded DC elements, such as dc.contributor.contactname and dc.contributor. contactemail are required elements; they are captured in the first screen of the DRUM submission form.

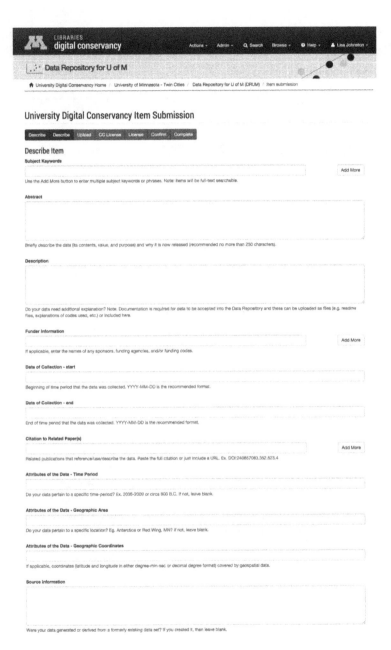

## FIGURE 5.3

The second screen of the DRUM submission form captures non-required information such `dc.coverage.temporal` and `dc.coverage.spatial`. Help text, shown in italics, suggests the type of information desired for each metadata field.

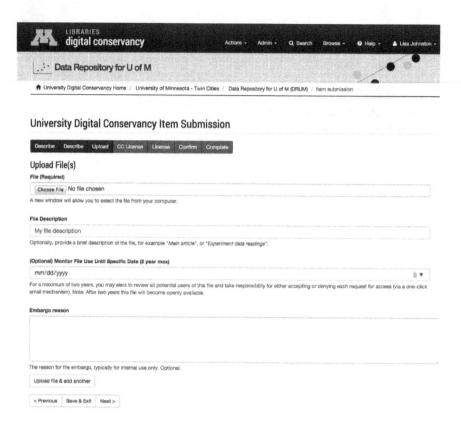

## FIGURE 5.4

The third screenshot from the DRUM submission form shows the file upload screen and the option to apply a temporary embargo (or mediate access) to one or all of the files. Curators verify that the embargo date selected fall within our two-year maximum, as the submitted will be responsible for responding to all requests for access before the files are released openly after the embargo period ends.

# Appendix 5.0 B: Screenshots from the Sevilleta LTER Program's Instance of the Drupal Ecological Information Management System (DEIMS)

*Jon Wheeler, Mark Servilla, and Kristin Vanderbilt*

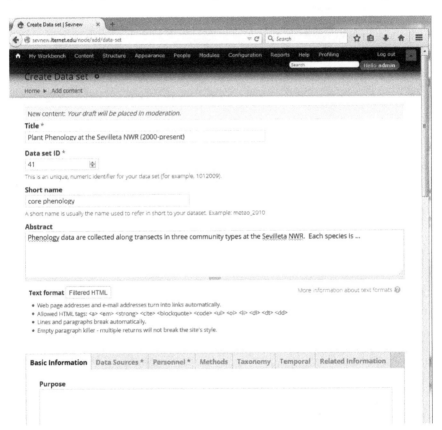

**FIGURE 5.5**

The DEIMS form to enter discovery level information about the data set captures the title, abstract, and data set identification number. The tabs at the bottom of the screen are used to enter more detailed information, such as methods, temporal and spatial domain of the data set, personnel associated with the data set, and keywords.

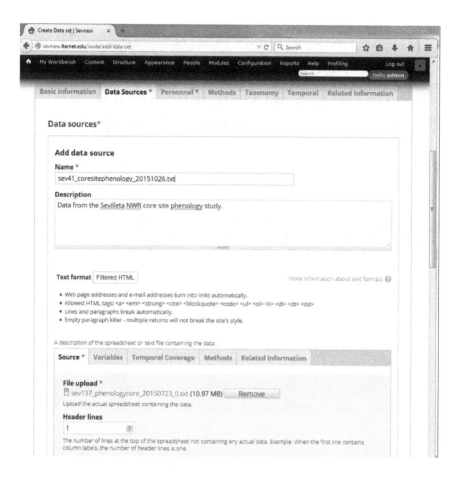

**FIGURE 5.6**

Data files are added to the data set via the Data Sources tab. Here the user can specify structural aspects of the data, such as the number of header and footer lines, the total number of data lines, and the field and line delimiters.

**FIGURE 5.7**

On the Variables tab, the user can click the button 'Parse CSV file into variables," and the variable names are autopopulated in the form. The user then enters the type of variable (date, nominal, ratio), specifies special formatting (as for dates), and enters the definition of each variable. The code used for missing values can also be entered.

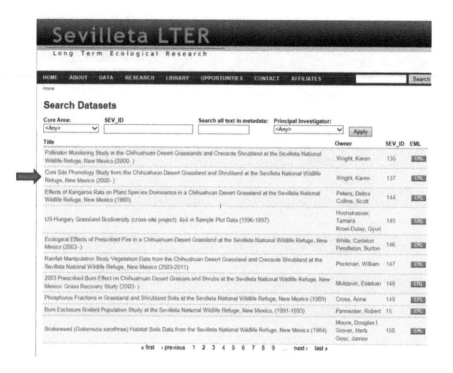

## FIGURE 5.8

The new dataset record is entered into the the DEIMS data catalog for the research site. EML can be automatically generated for the dataset.

**FIGURE 5.9**
Built-in features of Drupal can be used to manipulate the display of the metadata and link to the data.

# Notes

1. Digital Curation Centre, "General Research Data," accessed March 12, 2016, http://www.dcc.ac.uk/resources/subject-areas/general-research-data.
2. Dublin Core Metadata Initiative. "Dublin Core Metadata Element Set," version 1.1, accessed March 15, 2016, http://dublincore.org/documents/dces.
3. Mary Kurtz, "Dublin Core, DSpace, and a Brief Analysis of Three University Repositories," *Information Technology and Libraries* 29, no. 1 (March 2010): 40–46, doi:10.6017/ital.v29i1.3157.
4. The full metadata profile for DRUM is published online as University of Minnesota Libraries, *The Supporting Documentation for Implementing the Data Repository for the University of Minnesota (DRUM): A Business Model, Functional Requirements, and Metadata Schema* (University of Minnesota Libraries, 2015), http://hdl.handle.net/11299/171761.
5. The methodology and results of the usability testing were previously published as Lisa R. Johnston, Eric Larson, and Erik Moore, "Usability Testing of DRUM: What Aca-

demic Researchers Want from an Open Access Data Repository," June 9, 2015, http://hdl.handle.net/11299/172556.

6. Dataverse Project, "Appendix: Metadata References," Dataverse Project User Guide, accessed March 12, 2016, http://guides.dataverse.org/en/latest/user/appendix.html#metadata-references.

7. Claude Gierl and Jon Johnson, "How Do We Manage Complex Questions in the Context of the Large-Scale Ingest of Legacy Paper Questionnaires into DDI-Lifecycle?" (paper presented at the 5th Annual European Data Documentation Initiative User Conference, Paris, December 3–4, 2013), http://www.eddi-conferences.eu/ocs/index.php/eddi/EDDI13/paper/view/92.

8. Will Poynter and Jennifer Spiegel, "Protocol Development for Large-Scale Metadata Archiving using DDI-Lifecycle" (paper presented at the 6th Annual European Data Documentation Initiative User Conference, London, December 2–3, 2014), http://www.eddi-conferences.eu/ocs/index.php/eddi/eddi14/paper/view/168.

9. Eric H. Fegraus, Sandy Andelman, Matthew B. Jones, and Mark Schildhauer, "Maximizing the Value of Ecological Data with Structured Metadata: An Introduction to Ecological Metadata Language (EML) and Principles for Metadata Creation," *Bulletin of the Ecological Society of America* 86, no. 3 (July 2005): 158–68, doi:10.1890/0012-9623 (2005)86[158:MTVOED]2.0.CO;2.

10. William K. Michener, John Porter, Mark Servilla, and Kristin Vanderbilt, "Long Term Ecological Research and Information Management," *Ecological Informatics* 6, no. 1 (2011): 13–24, doi:10.1016/j.econinf.2010.11.005.

11. Thomas Erl, *Service-Oriented Architecture* (Upper Saddle River, NJ: Prentice Hall PTR, 2004).

12. Corinna Gries, Inigo San Gil, Kristin Vanderbilt, and Hap Garritt, "Drupal Developments in the LTER Network," *LTER Databits*, Spring 2010, http://databits.lternet.edu/spring-2010/drupal-developments-lter-network.

# Bibliography

Dataverse. "Metadata Blocks." Github. Accessed March 12, 2016. https://github.com/IQSS/dataverse/tree/master/scripts/api/data/metadatablocks.

———. "Appendix: Metadata References." *Dataverse Project User Guide. Accessed March 12, 2016.* http://guides.dataverse.org/en/latest/user/appendix.html#metadata-references.

Digital Curation Centre. "General Research Data." Accessed March 12, 2016. http://www.dcc.ac.uk/resources/subject-areas/general-research-data.

Dublin Core Metadata Initiative. "Dublin Core Metadata Element Set," version 1.1. Accessed March 15, 2016. http://dublincore.org/documents/dces.

Erl, Thomas. *Service-Oriented Architecture: A Field Guide to Integrating XML and Web Services.* Upper Saddle River, NJ: Prentice Hall PTR, 2004.

Fegraus, Eric H., Sandy Andelman, Matthew B. Jones, and Mark Schildhauer. "Maximizing the Value of Ecological Data with Structured Metadata: An Introduction to Ecological Metadata Language (EML) and Principles for Metadata Creation." *Bulletin of the Ecological Society of America* 86, no. 3 (July 2005): 158–68. doi:10.1890/0012-9623(2005)86[158:MTVOED]2.0.CO;2.

Gierl, Claude, and Jon Johnson. "How Do We Manage Complex Questions in the Context of the Large-Scale Ingest of Legacy Paper Questionnaires into DDI-Lifecycle?" Paper presented at the 5th Annual European Data Documentation Initiative User Conference, Paris, December 3–4, 2013. http://www.eddi-conferences.eu/ocs/index.php/eddi/EDDI13/paper/view/92.

Gries, Corinna, Inigo San Gil, Kristin Vanderbilt, and Hap Garritt. "Drupal Developments in the LTER Network." *LTER Databits*, Spring 2010. http://databits.lternet.edu/spring-2010/drupal-developments-lter-network.

Johnston, Lisa R., Eric Larson, and Erik Moore. "Usability Testing of DRUM: What Academic Researchers Want from an Open Access Data Repository." June 9, 2015. http://hdl.handle.net/11299/172556.

Kurtz, Mary. "Dublin Core, DSpace, and a Brief Analysis of Three University Repositories." *Information Technology and Libraries* 29, no. 1 (March 2010): 40–46. doi:10.6017/ital.v29i1.3157.

Michener, William K, John Porter, Mark Servilla, and Kristin Vanderbilt. "Long Term Ecological Research and Information Management." *Ecological Informatics* 6, no. 1 (2011): 13–24. doi:10.1016/j.econinf.2010.11.005.

Poynter, Will, and Jennifer Spiegel. "Protocol Development for Large-Scale Metadata Archiving using DDI-Lifecycle." Paper presented at the 6th Annual European Data Documentation Initiative User Conference, London, December 2–3, 2014. http://www.eddi-conferences.eu/ocs/index.php/eddi/eddi14/paper/view/168.

University of Minnesota Libraries. *The Supporting Documentation for Implementing the Data Repository for the University of Minnesota (DRUM): A Business Model, Functional Requirements, and Metadata Schema.* University of Minnesota Digital Conservancy, 2015. http://hdl.handle.net/11299/171761.

# Access

One of the more significant drivers for providing data curation services is to support access, both now and for the long term. Actions taken in *Step 6* will help ensure that data is accessible to all designated users and the metadata is disseminated as broadly as possible. When necessary, robust access controls and authentication procedures may be applicable before users can download and use.

# 6.1 Determine Appropriate Levels of Access

When determining the appropriate level of access to a particular data set, you must consider a number of factors. The overall mission of your repository (i.e. is open access as the default?), legal and cultural factors such as the sensitivity of the data set, as well as any conditions placed by the author (for any reason) at the time of deposit (see *Step 1.2*: Negotiate Deposit). It is important to consider that *discoverability* in the digital environment increases the risks of conflicting with one of these factors. For example, a scholar might feel comfortable depositing their raw data and lab notebooks to a print-based archive (with all the resulting access constraints of needing to physically visit the site to view the data set), but they might be wary of releasing their unpublished data records (and all their potential errors and mistakes) to a digital online repository without some level of access control. Therefore, as data stewards, we must weigh the desire for broad dissemination with the legal, cultural, and other potential needs that may require more restrictive access.

Dealing with the complexities of access, the University of Minnesota Libraries aimed to assist staff and potential donors in negotiating access restrictions by inventorying all the possible methods by which a data set might be deposited to the library. The "Levels of Access Options' table (displayed in table 6.1) seeks to define the various levels of digital access that the library provided for digital content. The levels will evolve as technical and financial capacities change and our mission and goals naturally shift over time.

## TABLE 6.1
Levels of access provided to digital objects stewarded by the University of Minnesota (UMN) Libraries.

**Guiding Principle**
The University Libraries will provide the widest possible access to all content to the best of our abilities and within all legal and cultural ramifications.

| Option | Definition | Examples |
|---|---|---|
| *Full Open Access* | Anyone may access the information at any time. | The IR[a] provides full-text search and discovery to content openly available for download via the web. |
| *Partial Open Access* | Access is available to a portion or subset of the content in order to protect rights or confidential information. | 1. Images and videos hosted in UMedia[b] are openly available at a lower resolution than the original, full-resolution object that is stored in the library.<br><br>2. DRUM[c] accepts a subset of data (e.g., a deidentified version of the data) for access when the original contains information that cannot be accessible due to informed consent agreements or its sensitive nature. |
| *Fixed-Term Mediated Access* | Access is mediated for a limited period of time before eventual open access. | DRUM allows authors to monitor and release access to individuals on a request basis for up to two years. |
| *Fixed-Term Embargo (Delayed Access)* | Information is held for eventual release at another access level. | Embargoed theses in the UDC that are not released or available to the public (for up to two years) after a student graduates. |
| *Traditional Circulation Access* | Content held in media is available for check-out. | Digital content held on CDs, DVDs, disks, etc., that are available for circulation. |
| *Restricted Access, Online* | Access is provided online to those with UMN-affiliated accounts or other mediated action. | Content held in the library, but rights were not granted by the authors for distribution. For example, a digital scan of in-copyright material, or archival materials for which a donor agreement prohibits open online distribution. |

**TABLE 6.1** (continued)

| Option | Definition | Examples |
|---|---|---|
| **Restricted Access, In-Library Use** | Content is not available outside of the libraries | Digital content is held on a library-controlled computer, and the material is accessible by visiting the library and using that computer, for example, Karpman Papers/Tretter collection. |
| **Restricted Access, Campus IP Range** | Content is not available outside of the campus IP network. | Digital content is held on a library-controlled network and available only to campus IP range. |
| **Not Accessible** | No access available. Content is held in the libraries for archiving and preservation purposes only. | Materials with sensitive information that cannot be made available due to legal agreements or law. |

a. The University Digital Conservancy (UDC) is the University of Minnesota's institutional repository run by the libraries. Available at http://conservancy.umn.edu.

b. UMedia is the open-access digital library for images, videos, and audio housed at the University of Minnesota Libraries. Available at http://umedia.lib.umn.edu.

c. The Data Repository for the University of Minnesota, DRUM, available at http://hdl.handle.net/11299/166578.

# 6.2 Apply the Terms of Use and Any Relevant Licenses

Another important aspect of assess is to help end users of your repository understand any freedoms and constraints to reuse the data. According to Carroll, repositories should not place the burden of obtaining permission from a data author onto third-party users because "this kind of legal uncertainty interferes with the productive reuse of research data. It can be avoided if the repository requires depositors to grant permission to downstream users or to give up any intellectual property rights they may have in the data."[1] Your data curation service has several options of providing "downstream" permission to users. This may come in the form of a Terms of Use statement that applies to all objects in your digital repository or (and possibly in addition to) the data authors might place specific reuse conditions (e.g., a data use agreement) for an individual data set. However, the more variety of data reuse options that your repository allows, the more confusing it might become for a user to navigate and responsibly use your service.

# Terms of Use for Data

A Terms of Use statement helps the consumer of a digital service understand what conditions, if any, are expected. When users access the data, any conditions or terms of use should be made readily apparent; for example, the Dataverse repository software allows curators to include a step prior to access that requires users to agree to any terms imposed by the data author before they can download the files. Its comprehensive Sample Data Use Agreement includes legal language around issues such as liability, indemnification, dispute resolution, and severability.[2] Figure 6.1 shows another example of the Terms of Use agreement that applies to each data set in the Data Repository for the University of Minnesota.

---

**Conditions**

By using or downloading the data, you signify your agreement to the conditions of use stated below:

- The user will not make any use of data to identify or otherwise infringe the privacy or confidentiality rights of individuals discovered inadvertently or intentionally in the data.

- The user will give appropriate attribution to the author(s) of the data in any publication that employs resources provided by the Data Repository.

- If your use or publication requires permission, you must contact the authors directly; administrators of the Data Repository cannot respond to requests for permission.

**Disclaimer**

Data are offered with no warranty or claim of fitness for any purpose. In no event shall the University be liable for any actual, incidental, or consequential damages arising from use of these files. The Data Repository is intended to facilitate data sharing, and the University of Minnesota Libraries staff are available to assist users with finding, accessing, and downloading the data. However, Libraries staff are limited in our ability to assist with using, analyzing, or understanding the data, and requests of this nature should be directed first to the author(s) of the data.

---

## FIGURE 6.1

Example Components for a "Terms of Use" agreement for end users of a data repository taken from the Data Repository for the University of Minnesota.

# Licenses and Copyright Notes for Data

The question of whether you can claim any copyright in a data set is complex. Sources in the United States and Australia suggest that data is factual are therefore not copyrightable.[3] However other countries, such as those in Europe and the United Kingdom may apply copyright for data compilations, such as databases.[4] In the face of uncertain legal standing for data, open-data movements and recommendations such as the Panton Principles argue that research data copyright (or lack thereof) should be removed along with all possible barriers for open reusability.[5] Ball demonstrated that a good tool to help others understand how they might legally and ethically reuse a data set is to apply a Creative Commons license (when copyright applies).[6] However, in cases where no copyright protections are available, open data licenses, such as CC0, might help others consider ways to provide attribution for a data set, even when no legal obligations exist. Yet, even in the case of non-copyrightable works, there are other intellectual property considerations that must be taken into account. Before applying licenses for access, Sims identified a number of other interrelated issues that may impact a data author's decision, such as prior contracts, grants obligations, institutional copyright and IP policies, IRB agreements, and relevant data retention policies.[7] Sims also suggested considering any stakeholders, including collaborators, colleagues, advisors, supervisors, and competitors, as well as the overall cultural practices and sharing expectations of field or lab when thinking about data-sharing access.

## Creative Commons Licenses

Many data authors will want others to share, use, and build upon their work as much as possible. This is exactly what licenses like Creative Commons (CC) can help encourage. They provide a shortcut for a conversation that might take place for any future use your work, unlike traditional copyright protections (full copyright retained), where a potential user would need to ask for permission to copy, distribute, or make derivatives of your work. If the data author plans to always say yes to these requests, then they should consider applying a CC license to the data. The CC website provides a tool to walk authors through the questions to consider for applying a CC license (such as CC licenses that approve any non-commercial use) at https://creativecommons.org/choose.

## Open Data License

Open data licenses, such as Creative Commons Zero or the Open Database License (ODL), are useful tools for releasing data as openly as possible for anyone to freely use, modify, or share.[8] The Open Definition project maintains a list of licenses that fall into this category that may be applied to data.[9] The next case study by Debra Fagan and Peggy Schaeffer will give further detail on the use and rationale behind open data license.

# Why Does Dryad Use Creative Commons Zero (CC0)?[*]

*Debra Fagan and Peggy Schaeffer[†]*

For an organization like Dryad, whose focus is on making research data underlying scholarly literature openly available and reusable, it is important that license-related barriers to accessing and reusing that data be minimized. To that end, Dryad requires that all data archived in the repository be released to the public domain under the Creative Commons Zero (CC0) Public Domain Dedication, which allows users to copy, modify, distribute, and even perform the data without seeking permission.[10] CC0 was crafted specifically to reduce legal and technical impediments to the reuse of data, such as requiring forms of attribution that cannot practically be applied in all cases. For example, tracking and satisfying attribution requirements can quickly become a problem when data is compiled from multiple sources, which in turn may have been compiled from other sources with varying attribution requirements. CC0 ameliorates this problem, which is known as "attribution stacking."

Since basic facts in and of themselves are not protected under US copyright law, making data available under CC0 generally has little or no real effect on the legal protections inherent to factual research data. However, where research data goes beyond basic facts and is eligible for copyright, CC0 waives copyright and related rights to the extent permitted by applicable law worldwide.

While CC0 does reduce legal and technical impediments, it does not exempt data users from following community norms for scholarly communication, such as the obligation to cite the original data authors. However, like other scientific norms, these expectations are best articulated and enforced by the community itself through processes such as peer review. In fact, by removing legal barriers, CC0 facilitates the discovery, reuse, and citation of that data as evidenced by the following excerpt from the Panton Principles FAQ:

---

[*] Adapted from Peggy Schaeffer, "Why Does Dryad Use CC0?" *Dryad News and Views* (blog), October 5, 2011, http://blog.datadryad.org/2011/10/05/why-does-dryad-use-cc0.

[†] This study is licensed under a Creative Commons Attribution 4.0 License, CC BY (https://creativecommons.org/licenses/by/4.0/).

Community norms can be a much more effective way of encouraging positive behaviour, such as citation, than applying licenses. A well functioning community supports its members in their application of norms, whereas licences can only be enforced through court action and thus invite people to ignore them when they are confident that this is unlikely.[11]

Overall, Dryad requires CC0 because it has some important advantages when it comes to data reuse:

- **Interoperability:** Since CC0 is both human- and machine-readable, people and indexing services will automatically be able to determine that data is available with "no rights reserved."
- **Universality:** CC0 is a single mechanism that is universal, covering all data and all countries.
- **Simplicity:** Scientists do not have to spend time making or responding to individual data reuse requests or navigating click-through reuse agreements.

What if an author does not want or is unable to place their data under CC0? While Dryad does not archive data that is not under a CC0 waiver, Dryad may provide a link to differently licensed data or software residing in an external repository. For example, authors may elect to store software packages that require version control for ongoing maintenance in a public software repository and link to that repository from Dryad.

While making data available under the CC0 waiver offers advantages, it does impact curation efforts. For example, Dryad curators take time to verify that data files do not contain licensing statements incompatible with CC0. Also, to facilitate the community norm of citation upon reuse, Dryad curators ensure correct citations for both the publication and the associated data are prominently displayed to the user.

Technology continues to advance, providing increasingly sophisticated tools scientists can use to make data openly available and reusable; however, legal issues related to licensing and copyright can present barriers to data access and reuse. CC0 provides a path around those barriers. That is why Dryad considers CC0 an integral part of achieving its vision of a world where research data from scholarly literature is openly available for reuse to advance knowledge.[12]

# 6.3 Contextualize the Data

The discovery and access environment for data should convey the reuse possibilities. This contextualization might be done in a number of ways, such as visualizing the data in a web browser, showcasing a snapshot or thumbnail of the primary data file contents to convey meaning, and linking to articles and projects that successfully use the data.

# Contextualization with Visualization

Repositories can facilitate access to data by visualizing the data or displaying the content of the data files in the browser. Fox and Hendler lamented that traditional repositories have focused their efforts on data collection and retrieval, but not exploration.[13] In their view, visualization of data is just as important as access as it gives a way to better understand the data and may help data stewards detect and fix errors.

Repositories with visualization capacity allow potential users to view and interact with the data before committing to the download for further manipulation and use. Disciplinary data repositories that house homogenous data may be in the best position to deliver data visualizations via their web-based discovery interfaces due to the consistent nature of the data file formats. For example, the Nanomaterial Registry Portal at nanoHUB.org (https://nanohub.org/groups/nanomaterialregistry) allows users to view, filter, and interact with the repository data in meaningful ways at the study level. Similarly, heterogeneous data repository platforms, such as Dataverse and Colectica, can provide data visualization for tabular and geospatial files. Basic statistical analysis can be accomplished via their customized web interfaces (filtering, formatting, or summary statistics), which can help users identify the sub-components of the data set that might fit their needs. For example, Dataverse integrates with Two Ravens, a web interface that allows users to interact with the data, therefore increasing the data's potential for download and reuse.[14]

Finally, data repositories can use web design elements to significantly alter the way that users interact with the repository. The wording and placement of links to download a data file in the repository may impact its discoverability. Usability testing will help your repository determine if users quickly see how to access and download the files. Using a visual cue, such as an icon or a thumbnail, may also indicate to users the type of data they are to expect. This thumbnail could be a screenshot of the data in its native software, a graph generated from the data contents, or an animated GIF of simulating how the data were collected.

In the next case study, Karl Benedict describes how a customized data access environment can increase exposure and reuse, while also retaining the preservation services of a local repository using API harvesting techniques.

# The Geographic Storage, Transformation and Retrieval Engine (GSToRE): A Platform for Active Data Access and Publication as a Complement to Dedicated Long-Term Preservation Systems

*Karl Benedict**

Data repositories have a mandate to preserve the data for long-term discovery and access. Yet, integrating data from all disciplines remains a challenge, both in terms of overcoming attitudinal barriers toward data sharing and the technical challenges of migrating data that, while shared, is not done so in dedicated preservation systems. This assertion is illustrated by the results of the Wiley publishing company's 2014 survey of 2,250 researchers that found that a significant proportion (29–51% depending upon discipline) of respondents who shared their data did so through web pages, such as personal, institutional, or lab-based.[15]

To support data discovery, visualization, and access across multiple projects, the Earth Data Analysis Center (EDAC) developed the Geographic Storage, Transformation and Retrieval Engine (GSToRE) platform at the University of New Mexico (UNM). In the context of the challenge described above, the EDAC system would fall into the category of a project website or resource. But the functionality built into the platform enables streamlined integration of system holdings into a long-term repository, such as the UNM's institutional repository, LoboVault (http://repository.unm.edu).

In 2008 EDAC began the development GSToRE as the successor to the geospatial data discovery and access platform for the New Mexico Resource Geographic Information System (RGIS, http://rgis.unm.edu) released in 2001. RGIS was developed as an integrated database and web interface that provided public access to tens of thousands of geospatial data sets and their associated metadata.

In recognition of the limitations of the 2001 system for reuse and interoperability with other systems and applications, GSToRE was explicitly developed as a tiered data management, discovery, and access system based on a service-oriented architecture.[16] The GSToRE architecture, illustrated in figure 6.2, is the combination of system-specific Representational State Transfer (REST) web services, web services based on externally defined open standards (i.e., the Open Geospatial Consortium), and specific external network protocols (i.e., the DataONE web application programming interface [API], https://www.dataone.org).[17]

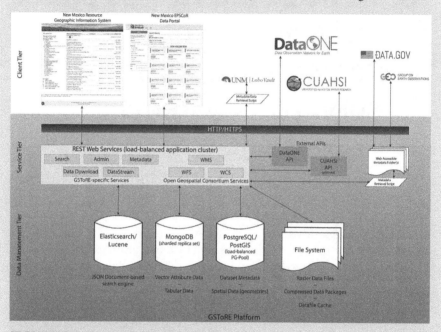

## FIGURE 6.2
The GSToRE architecture includes the underlying Data Management Tier, the Services Tier that provides web access to the Data Management Tier components, and the Client Tier that enables external client applications to interact with the data and metadata in the GSToRE system through the services provided by the Services Tier.

With the GSToRE web services in place, we can now automate the bulk integration of GSToRE data and metadata holdings into external systems, such as archival data repositories. In particular, the GSToRE API has been modified so that data sets within the system may be flagged for integration with specific repositories, such as LoboVault, advertising the intention (from the perspective of the GSToRE system) that that data and associated metadata be harvested into the target repository.[18] Based on this information, an automated integration script may be developed that allows for rapid and efficient cross-registration and assimilation of data sets and their metadata into long-term preservation systems while still providing access and value-added services through the GSToRE system. Such experimental harvesting capability is currently being developed at UNM in which specific data sets in GSToRE will be integrated into UNM's institutional repository for long-term preservation while GSToRE continues to provide data access and visualization services that complement the preservation, discovery, citation, and access capabilities of LoboVault.

## ACKNOWLEDGMENTS

The development of GSToRE has been partially funded by the National Science Foundation (Award Numbers IIA-1301346, 0814449, IIA-1329469, IIA-1329470, and IIA-1329513), NASA's ACCESS program, and the New Mexico State Legislature through the New Mexico Resource Geographic Information System Program. The GSToRE platform has been developed by a number of talented developers including Renzo Sanchez Silva, Soren Scott, William Hudspeth, Hays Barrett, and John Erickson.

## *Contextualization with Metadata*

The data record itself may incorporate contextual metadata that will help a user understand how the data fits within the landscape of scholarly objects. For example, metadata relating the data record to other holdings in the repository (e.g., version history, collection hierarchy, etc.) or metadata relating the data record to objects held elsewhere (e.g., data derived from another source, data that replaces a previously published data set) will allow the user to make decisions about how to use this data in their research.

## *Linking to Related Articles*

Linking the data set to any related publications can provide a wealth of contextual information that will support reuse. The linkage should work both ways: for example, some journals incorporate bidirectional linking between the publications with data sets housed in data repositories. The "Dryad Curation Workflows" case study (in *Step 4*) is a notable example of this, and a typical record in Dryad (shown in figure 6.2) shows the strong relationship that Dryad maintains between the journal article and the corresponding data set. Another example is Elsevier publications, which in 2010 began to incorporate links from articles to their related data sets to the earth sciences database PANGAEA.[19] Now Elsevier supports over fifty data repositories linking data to publication in meaningful ways.[20]

||||||||||||||||||||||||||||||||||||||||||||||||||||||||||||||||||||||||||||||||||||||||||||||||||||||||||||||||||||||||||||||||||||||||||||||||||

In *Curating Research Data, Volume One,* chapter 5, "Overlooked and Overrated Data Sharing: Why Some Scientists Are Confused and/ or Dismissive," Heidi J. Imker describes the importance of how traditional ways of data sharing may impact or frame data curation services.

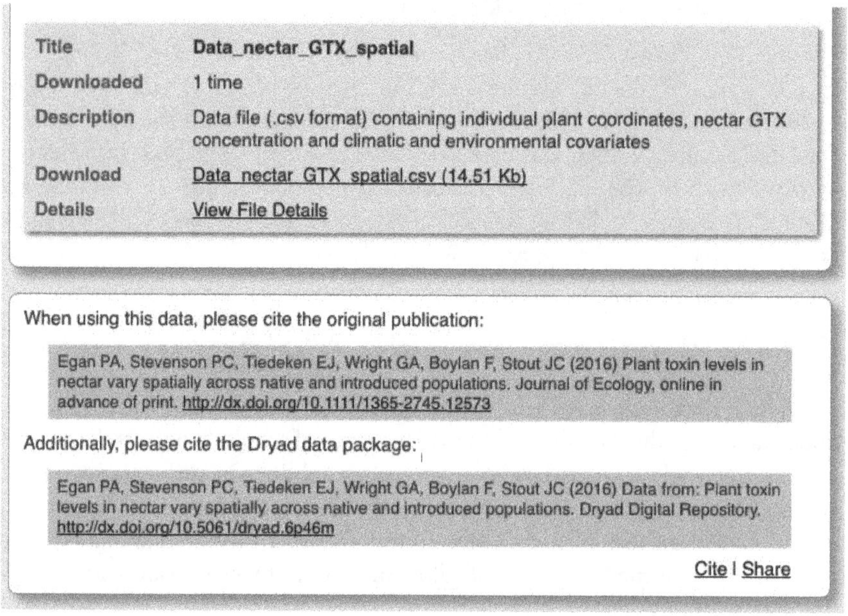

||||||||||||||||||||||||||||||||||||||||||||||||||||||||||||||||||||||||||||||||||||||||||||||||||||||||||||||||||||||||||||||||||||||||||||||||||

| | |
|---|---|
| Title | **Data_nectar_GTX_spatial** |
| Downloaded | 1 time |
| Description | Data file (.csv format) containing individual plant coordinates, nectar GTX concentration and climatic and environmental covariates |
| Download | Data_nectar_GTX_spatial.csv (14.51 Kb) |
| Details | View File Details |

When using this data, please cite the original publication:

Egan PA, Stevenson PC, Tiedeken EJ, Wright GA, Boylan F, Stout JC (2016) Plant toxin levels in nectar vary spatially across native and introduced populations. Journal of Ecology, online in advance of print. http://dx.doi.org/10.1111/1365-2745.12573

Additionally, please cite the Dryad data package:

Egan PA, Stevenson PC, Tiedeken EJ, Wright GA, Boylan F, Stout JC (2016) Data from: Plant toxin levels in nectar vary spatially across native and introduced populations. Dryad Digital Repository. http://dx.doi.org/10.5061/dryad.6p46m

Cite I Share

**FIGURE 6.3**

Data housed in the Dryad data repository is an example of directly relating to the journal article that discussed the results of the data to the archives data files.

The next case study by Elise Dunham, Elizabeth Wickes, Ayla Stein, Colleen Fallaw, and Heidi J. Imker demonstrates how the University of Illinois at Urbana-Champaign library contextualizes data sets by documenting related materials in the Illinois Data Bank.

# Pre-Metadata Counseling: Putting the DataCite relationType Attribute into Action

*Elise Dunham, Elizabeth Wickes, Ayla Stein, Colleen Fallaw, and Heidi J. Imker**

The library at the University of Illinois at Urbana-Champaign has launched an institutional data repository called the Illinois Data Bank. The Illinois Data Bank provides University of Illinois researchers with a library-based repository for research data that facilitates data sharing and ensures reliable stewardship of published data. Throughout development of the Illinois Data Bank self-deposit form, curation interface, and underlying infrastructure, we used the DataCite Metadata Schema Version 3.1 documentation as a guide for our descriptive metadata[21] so that when we mint a DataCite DOI at the end of the self-deposit process, we can register a robust set of metadata with the DataCite Metadata Store. Based on existing repository services, we anticipate that user discovery of data sets will frequently happen via harvesters and links from published papers and not directly within the Illinois Data Bank.[22] Therefore, we are committed to enhancing external discoverability and access to the data sets that we steward. Utilizing standards for data set description, like the DataCite Metadata Schema V 3.1, fulfills our commitment to following community-developed best practices for data publication and ensures that data sets are represented accurately and consistently within external discovery systems.

Our descriptive metadata schema for data sets defines relationships between data sets and other object types. The goal was to contextualize deposited data sets with related scholarly outputs, such as published papers, code, and other data sets. The functional requirements of the Illinois Data Bank that inspired this project are illustrated in table 6.2.

## TABLE 6.2
Metadata-related functional requirements for the Illinois Data Bank.

| Category | Functional Requirement of the Illinois Data Bank |
| --- | --- |
| Discoverability | Provide opportunity for end users reading a published journal article to find datasets that support conclusions of the article. |
| | Provide opportunity for end users viewing a dataset to find articles whose conclusions it supports. |
| | Provide opportunity for end users to navigate between related resources according to linked data principles.[a] |
| Provenance | Contribute to the overall record of a project's scholarly outputs. |
| | Track the life of a dataset, including its subsets and versions, over time. |
| Metrics | Position the Illinois Data Bank to be able to maintain a record of the number of times a dataset in the Illinois Data Bank is formally cited for internal and external reporting. |
| | Position the Illinois Data Bank to be able to monitor potential correlation between citation metrics and access metrics. |

a. See Christina Bizer, Tom Heath, and Tim Berners-Lee, "Linked Data: The Story So Far," *International Journal on Semantic Web and Information Systems* 5, no. 3 (July–September 2009), http://go.galegroup.com/ps/i.do?id=GALE%7CA209477051&v=2.1&u=uiuc_uc&it=r&p=AONE&sw=w&asid=fd7e52083504e596d9b86bfe8a273f7c.

Prior to implementing the DataCite Metadata Schema for the Illinois Data Bank, we reviewed the schema's `relationType` vocabulary to determine if it met our needs for linking resources. We discovered that our functional requirements and DataCite 3.1's approach were misaligned. For example, one type of relationship that we required was the connection between a data set and the article whose conclusions it supports. The DataCite `relationType` pairs that appeared to be most applicable to representing relationships between articles and data sets were

- `IsCitedBy` and `Cites`
- `IsReferencedBy` and `References`
- `IsSupplementTo` and `IsSupplementedBy`

The definitions of these relationships in DataCite 3.1 are not specific, can overlap, and do not provide guidance on their explicit differences or suggested use. There were many interpretations of these relationship definitions within our team. For example, some interpreted the `IsSupplementTo`/`IsSupplement-edBy` in a literal sense to mean that a resource must be shared in a "Supplemental Materials" section upon publication of a journal article in order for this `relationType` to apply. Others interpreted this relationship in a more abstract way to mean that a resource supplements one's understanding of a particular set of research conclusions. Our discussions about the meaning of this relationship occurred in the shadow of a wider scholarly publishing environment that has not developed consensus around definitions related to data and citation, including supplemental materials.[23] Not only did our small team's varying interpretations demonstrate just how difficult it is to navigate metadata semantics, but it also became clear that we needed a way to consistently describe a data set supporting an article regardless of how any particular author or journal decided to represent the relationship.

The troubles that we encountered with interpreting the DataCite `relationType` vocabulary definitions are indicative of the fact that the research data curation and scholarly communications fields are currently in a state of maturation on the issue of data set citation and linking of scholarly outputs.[24] As a collaborative community of practice, we see a need for solutions for linking scholarly outputs. Currently, the focus tends to be on assigning links after publication. For example, the Research Data Alliance Publishing Data Services Working Group is working to develop a common framework for cross-referencing data sets and articles that have already been published.[25] In time these efforts may feed back into the community's metadata standards and best practices to enable linking resources at the point or points of publication.

In the meantime, we developed more specific definitions of `IsSupplementTo`, `isCitedBy`, and the version and aggregation pairs based on our own interpretations (see table 6.3). We determined that the other `relationTypes` elements available in the DataCite vocabulary whose definitions were unclear to us (e.g., `IsReferencedBy`/`References` and `IsCompiledBy`/`Compiles`) would not immediately help us to achieve our goals with resource linking and therefore were not used. Through application of our limited set of the `relationType` terms, we are meeting our functional requirements in the short term and are hopeful that our definitions are flexible enough to respond to anticipated community developments surrounding issues of data set citation and linking. By developing our own clear definitions for `relationTypes` we are able to serve up our metadata consistently and in a way that fits our local needs, and by deciding to register our `relatedIdentifers` with DataCite even when our definitions do not match, we are able to represent these crucial relationships outside of our system.

**TABLE 6.3**

The DataCite relationType definitions used by the Illinois Data Bank.

| DataCite relationType | Definition | Illinois Data Bank Usage Note |
|---|---|---|
| *Is Supplement To* | The resource being described supports the conclusions of the related written work. | Use two instances of `<RelatedIdentifier>` for the same identifier when the data set whose conclusions support the paper is also formally cited in the paper:<br><br>`<RelatedIdentifier relatedIdentifierType="DOI" relationType="IsSupplementTo">10.1234/5678</RelatedIdentifier>`<br>`<RelatedIdentifier`<br><br>`relatedIdentifierType="DOI" relationType="IsCitedBy">10.1234/5678</RelatedIdentifier>` |
| *IsCitedBy* | The resource being described is formally attributed as a source in the related written work. | Use two instances of `<RelatedIdentifier>` for the same identifier when the data set whose conclusions support the paper is also formally cited in the paper:<br><br>`<RelatedIdentifier relatedIdentifierType="DOI" relationType="IsSupplementTo">10.1234/5678</RelatedIdentifier>`<br><br>`<RelatedIdentifier relatedIdentifierType="DOI" relationType="IsCitedBy">10.1234/5678</RelatedIdentifier>` |
| *IsNew VersionOf* | The resource being described is a new version of the related resource. | |
| *IsPrevious VersionOf* | The resource being described is a previous version of the related resource. | |

## TABLE 6.3 (continued)

| DataCite relationType | Definition | Illinois Data Bank Usage Note |
|---|---|---|
| *IsPartOf* | The resource being described is a member of the related aggregation. | |
| *HasPart* | The aggregation being described has the related resource as a member. | |

We are not fully satisfied with the definitions we have presented here because we believe that they are not yet specific enough to support granular, meaningful expressions of all potential relationships between articles and data sets. Even so, we have determined that it is better to move forward with a well-documented plan that enables us to, at minimum, expose links between objects and count citations than to try to solve the problem without sufficient knowledge of what we will be facing in the Illinois Data Bank. As we implement our relationship definitions for scholarly resources, we will put a system in place that will support curator efforts to capture more detail about the relationships between data sets and articles that come onto our radar in the Illinois Data Bank. A systematic approach for gathering data about resource relationships will enable future research into the many linking challenges we face in the data curation community. We will also look to the data citation community for feedback and input as we collectively move forward to address the challenges of linking digital objects within the scholarly communication landscape.

# ACKNOWLEDGMENTS

Our thanks to the DataCite Metadata Working Group for being responsive to our questions and for its continued work on the DataCite Metadata Schema.

# 6.4 Increase Exposure and Discovery

There are several ways to increase the exposure to your data holdings for discovery and access via the web. For example, evaluations of download statistics for institutional repositories (IRs) have shown that users are introduced to their objects directly from web search engines rather than via the repository search interface therefore connecting the siloed nature of IRs.[26] Subsequently, all repositories must consider a number of approaches to work directly and indirectly (e.g., via search engine optimization) with third-party indexers to maximize web exposure to your repository holdings.

*Web search engine optimization approaches for data.* For example, web search engines and services, such as Google, Bing, and Yahoo, rely heavily on text-based information to facilitate discovery. Therefore, other types of files, such as data contained in non-text-based file formats, will not register in keyword searches. If possible, enhance the data submission for discovery purposes by generating search-engine-optimized alternatives. This might be as simple as creating a ASCII text-based version of keyword rich data that are locked in file formats not indexed by your repository (e.g., disipline-specific formats) or pulling out documentation files from a zipped compression for exposure to the indexers. The structure of the content may also impact how tools like Google Scholar identify and detect the content as scholarly. A keynote address at the 2015 Open Repositories conference by a co-creator of Google Scholar (https://scholar.google.com/), Anurag Acharya, revealed a number of ways that repositories can position their content to be indexed by this web search engine mainstay.[27]

*Third-party indexing services for data discovery.* More services are designed to index and direct users to appropriate data sources in similar ways that abstract and indexing services have done for journal articles. DataCite (discussed more below), Thomson Data Citation Index, and Elsevier's DataLink (in beta) each index data in selected repositories. By applying for inclusion, your repository can help increase the exposure to the records in your holdings and benefit from auxiliary services that they might provide, such as citation count tracking.

*Data Catalogs.* Services that aim to catalog the metadata for data sets for repackaging via discovery indexes are emerging. For example, the SHared Access Research Ecosystem (SHARE, http://www.share-research.org) project aims to build an open data set of research activity in the US that includes digital research data sets as a component of scholarly output. Free access to metadata about data sets allows institutions to create robust discovery interfaces that search across a boarder body of objects. One project, the NYU Data Catalog (https://datacatalog.med.nyu.edu) does just this.

# 6.5 Apply Any Necessary Access Controls

Depending on the conditions for access and reuse, it may be necessary to place access restrictions on some or all data files in a data submission. For example, access restrictions may be due to embargoes in place with the publisher of the related journal article. Therefore, access to the data files prior to publication will be allowed only for peer reviewers of the article. Accommodating such requests by data authors will be important as more journals are requiring data sharing, and may restrict the timing of the data release to post-publication of the article.

Another consideration for repositories that allow restricted access will be to determine who is the gatekeeper of the data. If the data repository is ready to take on this role, then the access mechanisms might be reevaluated on an ongoing basis. However, if the data author is responsible (e.g., in the DSpace "request a copy" function), then this role must be clearly communicated. It may be the case that the data author is no longer able or willing to continue in this role and an alternative process must be put into place. For example, the Data Repository for the University of Minnesota (DRUM) allows authors to "monitor access" to their data sets for up to two years (an example is shown in Figure 6.4), after which the data set will be released openly. The rationale is that submitter availability to monitor and provide case-by-case data access will decrease over time as students graduate and faculty retire and therefore a time-bound limit for embargo is a necessary precaution.

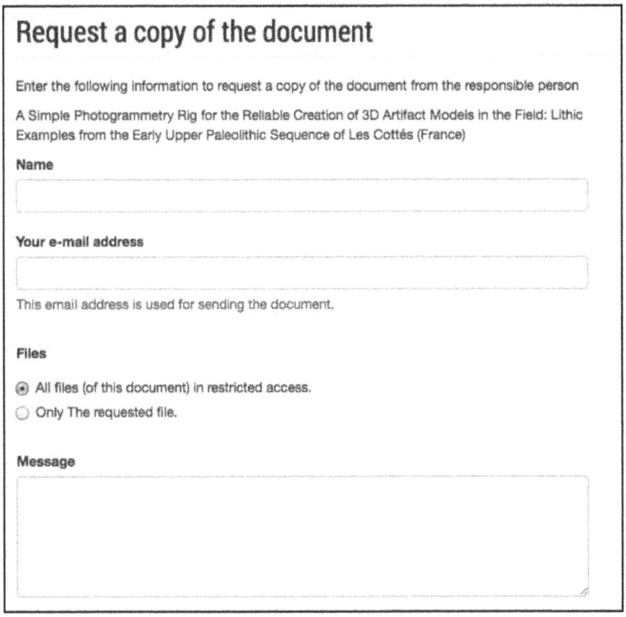

## Request a copy of the document

Enter the following information to request a copy of the document from the responsible person

A Simple Photogrammetry Rig for the Reliable Creation of 3D Artifact Models in the Field: Lithic Examples from the Early Upper Paleolithic Sequence of Les Cottés (France)

Name

Your e-mail address

This email address is used for sending the document.

Files

◉ All files (of this document) in restricted access.
○ Only The requested file.

Message

**FIGURE 6.4**
Restricted access files in DRUM appear with a lock symbol, and when clicked, users are presented with a brief request form (i.e., name, e-mail, message) that is delivered to the data submitter for approval or denial for access.

Other reasons for restricting or reducing access include
- Data that is protected by law (HIPPA, FERPA, FISMA)
- IRB restrictions that obligate you to secrecy or confidentiality
- Protect privacy of subjects
- Release data via binding agreements or de-identification
- Protect intellectual property rights
- Data with potential commercial value
- Protect digital or physical security
- From competitors, malicious attackers (student records?), or accidental release
- Before publishing a paper or releasing results (embargo)

When placing access restriction on a data set, it is important to test out this control before releasing the data, perhaps in a development test environment, to ensure that the needed restrictions are working properly. Inadvertent release of the data can have negative consequences for the reputation of the repository service.

# 6.6 Ensure Persistent Access and Encourage Appropriate Citation

In order to ensure persistent access to the data, generating a persistent identifier (e.g., a DOI) will help facilitate reliable long-term and appropriate data citation. Some repositories might consider including a "Suggested Citation" on the record to help users cite data alongside other scholarly objects (data citation practices are discussed further in *Step 8*).

The practice of assigning DOIs to data sets is on the rise. According to Austin, of the "more than six million DataCite DOIs minted since 2009, over a third have been registered in 2015."[28] DataCite (https://www.datacite.org) is an organization that relies on a distributed "registration agency" model for providing DOI-minting services worldwide. Originating from Germany in 2004, the DataCite organization now mints DOIs for over 350 agencies with registration agencies located in 16 countries.[29] The resulting metadata for each data set is searchable across the DataCite Metadata Search Tool discovery interface (http://search.datacite.org/ui). The California Digital Library's EZID service is one of the distributed services providers in the US, and for a small annual fee (between $500 and $2,500 according to their website) this service provides non-profit agencies with a web-based utility to mint custom DOIs.[30]

## Assigning Persistent Identifiers in Action

The next case study by Susan M. Braxton, Bethany Anderson, Margaret H. Burnette, Thomas G. Habing, William H. Mischo, Sarah L. Shreeves, Sarah C. Williams, and Heidi J. Imker describes how the University of Illinois is using a DOI-minting service in a novel way.

# A Participant Agreement for Minting DOIs for Data Not in a Repository

*Susan M. Braxton, Bethany Anderson, Margaret H. Burnette, Thomas G. Habing, William H. Mischo, Sarah L. Shreeves, Sarah C. Williams, and Heidi J. Imker*[*]

In 2014, the eResearch Implementation Committee[†] at the University Library, University of Illinois at Urbana-Champaign carried out a pilot study using EZID via subscription from Purdue University (http://ezid.lib.purdue.edu) to mint DataCite (https://www.datacite.org) DOIs for data upon request. The goals of the pilot were to explore researcher interest in DOIs for data on our campus and to explore the delivery of such a service by the University Library using EZID. The library-mediated service was announced via the all-faculty and staff weekly e-mail newsletter (figure 6.5) and the corresponding graduate student newsletter. The full announcement on our website specified the types of eligible resources and terms of participation (figure 6.5).

Ten individuals representing three colleges and two research institutes applied to participate between February and October 2014. Although the response was underwhelming, the unique challenge of providing DOIs for "external" resources not archived in a library repository raised questions that helped guide the development of our pilot service to production.

---

† Now the Research Data Service, or RDS Committee.

# eweek Illinois Faculty/Staff Notices

February 16, 2014

Use EZID to Obtain DOIs for Your Data

Researchers at the University of Illinois at Urbana-Champaign will soon have an opportunity to obtain Digital Object Identifiers (DOIs) for their data as part of a pilot service focused on data sharing and management. The EZID pilot is spearheaded by the University Library and will run during spring and summer 2014. It is open to faculty and staff members and students.

researchdata@library.illinois.edu • University Library

## Using EZID to obtain DOIs for your data – a pilot research data service

**Who may participate?**

Individual students, faculty and staff as well as research groups/programs at the University of Illinois at Urbana-Champaign that have created data resources are eligible to participate in the pilot.

**What types of resources are eligible for inclusion in the pilot?**

Data resources such as simple data sets (e.g., spreadsheets, CSV files), visualizations, software/code, or collections are eligible. We will exclude resources which already have DOIs, and resources that are not data resources (e.g., article preprints or reports). As a requirement of the pilot, the resource must be accessible via the World Wide Web, and the creator must supply basic metadata about the resource to include in the DOI registry. Where appropriate, participants will be strongly encouraged to deposit their data resources into our institutional repository, IDEALS, to ensure their long-term preservation. If IDEALS deposit is not an option (e.g, for data sets that are actively growing), participants will be responsible for keeping the DOI registry up to date in the event the resource is moved to a new URL.

**FIGURE 6.5**

Campus e-mail announcement and excerpt from the full description of the pilot DOI for data service.

---

We had, perhaps naively, expected requests to mint DOIs primarily for repository-ready data from completed projects. Applicants presented instead a range of resources, including several continuously updating, interactive, online databases (e.g., ongoing climate monitoring). These resources were shared by their creators via live, interactive web interfaces that would not be replicated in our institutional repository. Static files ("snapshots") deposited in the repository would be less functional for users than data in the native interface. We recognized the need to make these resources discoverable and citable, which is at the heart of DataCite's purpose.[31] It can be argued that it is precisely these types of resources that are most in need of identifiers—after all, data sets archived in repositories typically have persistent URLs and descriptive metadata already. However, we were also acutely aware of the social contract that the University Library was making to ensure the persistence of the resources, and we were reluctant to promise long-term access for resources over which we lacked curatorial control. We ultimately decided that the benefits of registering these resources with DataCite (i.e., improved discoverability through DataCite's broad dissemination of the metadata, and facilitation of citation) outweighed the risk that the DOI may fail to resolve to the resource in the future. Also, we speculated that researchers who made the effort to request DOIs and help craft descriptive metadata for the DataCite registry would be inclined to notify us if the resource moved, or if they later needed help finding a repository to preserve and create access to the resource (e.g., if the program was defunded, and they were no longer able to maintain the active instance of the resource). Finally, the ability within EZID to change the resource status to "unavailable" and redirect the DOI to a "tombstone" page displaying the metadata and reason for unavailability gave us a way to manage the DOI if the resource subsequently disappeared.[32]

In an attempt to curb dead links and subsequent accumulation of tombstones in DataCite, we developed a Participant Agreement to outline the responsibilities of the University Library and of the data creator in the creation and management of the DOI.[33] The agreement has five components: the agreement purpose, description of agreement use, definitions, general expectations, and responsibilities. Special attention was given to Creator (or designee) responsibility for resources that would live outside a trusted repository; this section is excerpted below.

### *Participant Agreement Creator (or designee) responsibilities:*

- As the creator (or designee) I certify that the descriptive metadata which I have provided to the University Library are accurate.
- As the creator (or designee), I certify that I am authorized to allow the University Library to share this descriptive metadata via the DataCite registry.
- If the resource does not reside in a trusted digital repository, then:
  - o I as the creator (or designee) take full responsibility for maintaining stable access to the resource.
  - o If the location of the resource changes (including any and all URL changes), I as the creator or designee agree to notify the University Library of the new location so that the DataCite metadata record can be updated.
  - o If contact information changes, I as the creator (or designee) agree to provide the University Library with the updated information.

o If I, as the creator or designee, am no longer able to provide access to the resource, I agree to inform the University Library and to work with the University Library to develop a plan for long-term preservation of the resource as appropriate.

o I understand that if the University Library becomes aware that access to the data has been disrupted and efforts to address the issue with the creator or designee are not resolved within a timely manner, the University Library reserves the right to edit the DataCite record to indicate unavailability (e.g. generate a "tombstone" record).

During our pilot, the agreement was integrated as a modal popup window into our DOI minting web interface* at the metadata review and approval stage, and referenced in the e-mail notice of the newly minted DOI to the requestor. The integration allowed us to retain a record of the agreement as well as an acknowledgement by the creator or designee that the metadata registered with DataCite accurately described the resource and could be made public. Although there are no repercussions for failure to comply, the agreement serves as an opportunity to emphasize the importance of DOI persistence to the requestor. Thus far we have minted thirty DataCite DOIs and 40 percent of them resolve at the request of the data creators to URLs outside of library-run repositories. We have already been notified to update DOI link resolving locations for resources in one external location when the host site URL changed. It remains to be seen how cumbersome or problematic maintaining DOIs for resources outside repositories will be. However, at this early stage in data sharing and citation, it has been a worthwhile experiment.

# ACKNOWLEDGMENTS

Thanks to Harriett Green, Karen Hogenboom, Laila Hussein, Beth Sandore Namachchivaya, Kyle Rimkus, Mary Schlembach, Ayla Stein, and Christie Wiley for input on development of the DOI Service Participant Agreement as well as work on the pilot.

---

\* A password-protected web interface to our EZID account with Purdue was developed locally to facilitate entry and management of metadata for our DOIs beyond what was possible with the standard EZID interface.

# 6.7 Release Data for Access and Notify Author

The final action in this step is to complete the data submission, or "go live," for discovery and access. This step includes a notification to the author that their data submission has been finalized. Consider providing the author with a summary list of changes that were made to the submission and a chance to correct or adjust any of the metadata before the data goes live for access. Finally, inform the author of useful post-deposit services that your repository will provide. For example you might suggest that the data author:

- Utilize the persistent identifier when citing the data set in their work.
- Link directly to the data set from any website (as opposed to uploading a new copy) to reduce versioning issues as well as save time and storage space.
- Monitor (or anticipate communications from the repository regarding) download statistics and other indicators of reuse to demonstrate the impact of their effort.
- Tie this new publication into their productivity tools, such as Google Scholar, ORCID, and SciVal Experts, and their CV to acknowledge their contribution to the scholarly record.

## *Track Effort Throughout the Process*

For the purposes of monitoring effort and workload on behalf of your repository, once the data is finalized it is useful to understand how long the curation process took. Estimating the work hours needed to curate a submission, together with other information, such as the data format and discipline, will help your repository anticipate and adjust for future staffing needs. For example, if your repository spends twice as much time on curating geospatial submissions than tabular data submissions, it may be necessary to consider staffing adjustments or bring on additional GIS experts for your repository. Note also the final completion date in your tracking spreadsheet (described in *Step 1*) to ensure that expected levels of service (e.g., turn-around time for a new submission) are within your repository goals.

## *Gather Feedback*

Another way to assess your data curation service is to gather feedback from the submitter shortly after a completed submission. Feedback, such as level of satisfaction in the curation process and degree of usefulness of your repository features, will help your service grow to better meet the targeted user needs over time.

For example, the survey displayed in figure 6.6 is delivered to Data Repository for the University of Minnesota (DRUM) submitters one to two weeks after a data submission is curated and finalized. Submitters are made aware that a survey will be delivered when the final e-mail announcing their live data record is sent and all responses are anonymous. Feedback like this helps to measure the success of the program and related marketing efforts.

# DRUM Feedback Form

Based on your recent submission, we would appreciate your anonymous feedback about your experience submitting a data set to the Data Repository for the University of Minnesota (DRUM), http://z.umn.edu/drum.

## DRUM Features

**Please rate how important the following DRUM features are to you as a researcher.**

| | Not important | Somewhat important | Very important |
|---|---|---|---|
| Obtaining a persistent identifier (DOI) | ○ | ○ | ○ |
| Obtaining data curation assistance | ○ | ○ | ○ |
| Long-term preservation of the data | ○ | ○ | ○ |
| Allowing others free access | ○ | ○ | ○ |
| Fulfilling a grant requirement | ○ | ○ | ○ |
| Adding a Creative Commons license | ○ | ○ | ○ |
| Option to monitor access to data (e.g. embargo) | ○ | ○ | ○ |
| Full-text discoverability (eg. Google) | ○ | ○ | ○ |
| Ability to track download statistics | ○ | ○ | ○ |

## Submission Process

**How easy/difficult were the following steps in the submission process?**

| | Very difficult | Somewhat difficult | Somewhat easy | Very easy | Not applicable |
|---|---|---|---|---|---|
| Finding the DRUM web site | ○ | ○ | ○ | ○ | ○ |
| Preparing the files for upload | ○ | ○ | ○ | ○ | ○ |
| Preparing data documentation | ○ | ○ | ○ | ○ | ○ |
| Submitting files using the DRUM upload form | ○ | ○ | ○ | ○ | ○ |
| Working with the DRUM curators to finalize submission | ○ | ○ | ○ | ○ | ○ |
| Navigating to view the final result in DRUM | ○ | ○ | ○ | ○ | ○ |

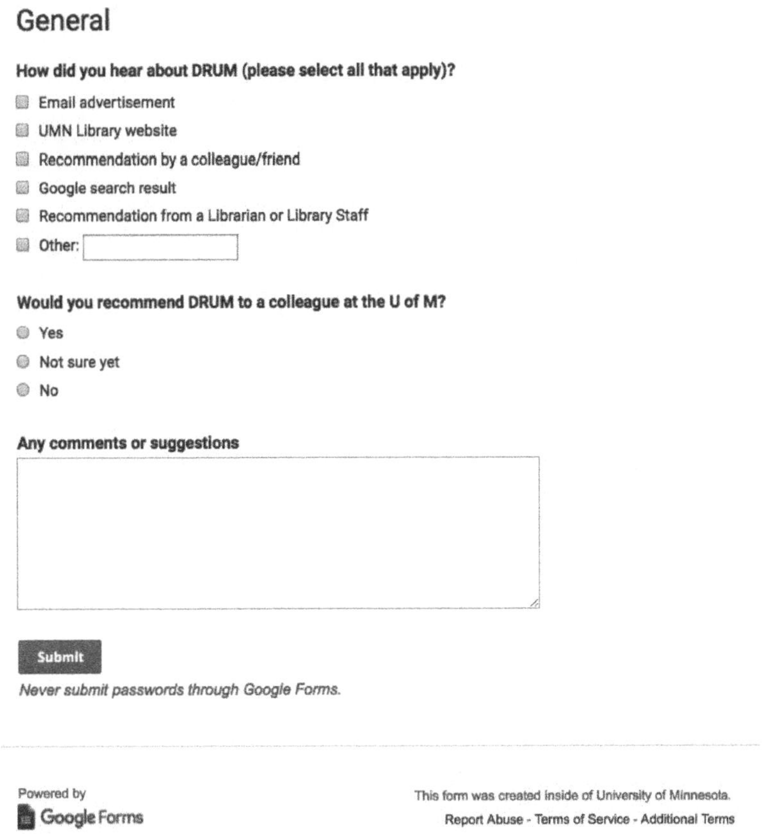

## General

**How did you hear about DRUM (please select all that apply)?**

☐ Email advertisement

☐ UMN Library website

☐ Recommendation by a colleague/friend

☐ Google search result

☐ Recommendation from a Librarian or Library Staff

☐ Other: [_____]

**Would you recommend DRUM to a colleague at the U of M?**

○ Yes

○ Not sure yet

○ No

**Any comments or suggestions**

[                                                    ]

[ Submit ]

*Never submit passwords through Google Forms.*

Powered by

🔲 Google Forms

This form was created inside of University of Minnesota.
Report Abuse - Terms of Service - Additional Terms

**FIGURE 6.6**
Screenshot of the feedback form used by the Data Repository for the University of Minnesota. This survey form is used to determine level of importance for service features and level of difficulty for using service.

# Summary of Step 6.0: Access

6.1 Determine Appropriate Access Conditions: Determine what level of access is required and how target audiences for reuse may be affected by this condition (e.g., a terms of use).

6.2 Apply the Terms of Use and Any Relevant Licenses and Copyright Notices for the Data: Work with the author to choose to apply any specific reuse conditions (e.g., a terms of use agreement), and if appropriate, apply a license, such as Creative Commons Licenses.

6.3 Contextualize the Data: The discovery and access environment for the data should convey the possibilities of reusing the data. This can be done by visualizing of the data, showcasing the primary data file contents to convey meaning, and linking to articles and projects that successfully reused the data.

6.4 Enhance the Submission to Increase Exposure and Discovery: Work directly and indirectly with third-party indexers to disseminate your repository holdings. For example, web search engines and services, such as Google, Bing, and Yahoo, rely heavily on text-based information to facilitate discovery. If possible, enhance the data submission for discovery purposes by generating search-engine-optimized formats of the data (e.g., full-text index).

6.5 Apply Any Necessary Access Controls: Depending on the conditions for access and reuse, place access restrictions on all or some of the data files.

6.6 Ensure Persistent Access: Generate a persistent identifier (e.g., a DataCite DOI) to help facilitate reliable long-term access to the data (e.g., via bibliographic citations).

6.7 Release Data for Access and Notify Author: Finalize the data submission by allowing the metadata of the data set to "go live" for discovery and access. Notify the author of this event and any further obligations that might be required of them (e.g., responding to requests for access).

# Notes

1.  Michael W. Carroll, "Sharing Research Data and Intellectual Property Law: A Primer," *PLOS Biology* 13, no. 8 (2015): e1002235, http://journals.plos.org/plosbiology/article?id=10.1371/journal.pbio.1002235.

2.  Dataverse Project, "Sample Data Usage Agreement," accessed March 18, 2016, http://best-practices.dataverse.org/harvard-policies/sample-dua.html.

3.  MacKenzie Smith, "Data Governance: Where Technology and Policy Collide," in *Research Data Management*, ed. Joyce M. Ray (West Lafayette, IN: Purdue University Press, 2014), 45–59; The Australian National Data Service defines the copyright laws related to data in Australia in Baden Appleyard and Greg Laughlin, "Copyright, Data and Licensing," The Australian National Data Service, accessed March 18, 2016, http://ands.org.au/guides/copyright-and-data-awareness.html.

4.  UK Data Archive, "Copyright and Data Sharing," accessed June 14, 2016, http://www.data-archive.ac.uk/create-manage/copyright/share.

5.  Panton Principles homepage, accessed March 18, 2016, http://pantonprinciples.org.

6.  Alex Ball, "How to License Research Data," DCC How-to Guides, February 9, 2011, revised July 17, 2014. Digital Curation Centre, http://www.dcc.ac.uk/resources/how-guides/license-research-data.

7.  Nancy Sims (University of Minnesota Copyright Specialist). "Making Decisions about Your Research Data," YouTube video, 6:38, posted by CopyrightLibn, August 28, 2012, https://youtu.be/ZuUGlGOMGjU.

8.  Creative Commons, "CC0 1.0 Universal (CC0 1.0) Public Domain Dedication," accessed March 18, 2016, https://creativecommons.org/publicdomain/zero/1.0; Open

Data Commons, "Open Data Commons Open Database License (ODbL)," accessed March 18, 2016 http://opendatacommons.org/licenses/odbl.

9. Open Definition, "Conformant Licenses," accessed March 18, 2016, http://opendefinition. org/licenses.

10. Creative Commons, "CC0 1.0 Universal (CC0 1.0)."

11. Peter Murray-Rust, Rufus Pollock, Bryan Bishop, Mike Chelen, Cameron Neylon, Daniel Mietchen, and Andy Powell, "FAQ," Panton Principles: Principles for Open Data in Science, accessed November 20, 2015, http://pantonprinciples.org/faq.

12. Dryad Digital Repository. "The Organization: Overview," last modified October 22, 2015, https://datadryad.org/pages/organization.

13. Peter Fox and James Hendler, "Changing the Equation on Scientific Data Visualization," *Science* 331, no. 6018 (2011): 705–8, doi:10.1126/science.1197654.

14. Data Science, "About TwoRavens," Institute for Quantitative Social Science, Harvard University, accessed March 18, 2016, http://datascience.iq.harvard.edu/about-tworavens.

15. Liz Ferguson, "How and Why Researchers Share Data (and Why They Don't)," *Wiley Exchanges* (blog), November 3, 2014, http://exchanges.wiley.com/blog/2014/11/03/ how-and-why-researchers-share-data-and-why-they-dont, accessed August 14, 2015; page now discontinued.

16. Jonathan Wheeler and Karl Benedict, "Functional Requirements Specification for Archival Asset Management: Identification and Integration of Essential Properties of Services Oriented Architecture Products," *Journal of Map and Geography Libraries* 11, no. 2 (2015): 155–79.

17. Roy Fielding, "Architectural Styles and the Design of Network-Based Software Architectures" (PhD diss., University of California, Irvine, 2000); DataONE, "DataONE Architecture, Version 1.2," accessed November 19, 2015, https://releases.dataone.org/ online/api-documentation-v1.2.0.

18. GSToRE V3, "Experimental API," accessed November 19, 2015, http://gstore.unm. edu/docs/experimental.html.

19. Elsevier, "Elsevier and PANGAEA Link Contents for Easier Access to Full Earth System Research," news release, February 24, 2010, https://www.elsevier.com/about/press-releases/science-and-technology/elsevier-and-pangaea-link-contents-for-easier-access-to-full-earth-system-research.

20. Elsevier, "Supported Data Repositories," accessed March 18, 2016, https://www.elsevier. com/books-and-journals/content-innovation/data-base-linking/supported-data-repositories.

21. DataCite, *DataCite Metadata Schema for the Publication and Citation of Research Data*, Version 3.1 (Hannover, Germany: DataCite, August 2015), doi:10.5438/0010.

22. According to analytics reporting at the University of Illinois Library, approximately 70% of traffic into IDEALS, the institutional repository at the University of Illinois, are visitors referred by an unpaid search engine. About 20% are referrals from external webpages and the library catalog, and direct traffic—that is, people who come to IDEALS by either typing the URL in their address bar, using a bookmark, using an e-mail link, etc.—account for the remaining 10% of the traffic. Source: Bill Ingram, e-mail to author regarding IDEALS traffic, November 6, 2015.

23. Linda Beebe, "Supplemental Materials for Journal Articles: NISO/NFAIS Joint Working Group," *Information Standards Quarterly* 22, no. 3 (Summer 2010): 33–37, http:// www.niso.org/apps/group_public/download.php/4885/Beebe_SuppMatls_WG_ISQ_ v22no3.pdf.

24. M. Martone, ed., *Data Citation Synthesis Group: Joint Declaration of Data Citation Principles—Final* (San Diego: FORCE11, 2014), https://www.force11.org/group/joint-declaration-data-citation-principles-final.

25. Research Data Alliance, "RDA/WDS Publishing Data Services WG," accessed June 14, 2016, https://rd-alliance.org/groups/rdawds-publishing-data-services-wg.html.

26. Michael K. Organ, "Download Statistics: What Do They Tell Us? The Example of Research Online, the Open Access Institutional Repository at the University of Wollongong, Australia," *D-Lib Magazine* 12, no. 11 (November 2006): 44, http://www.dlib.org/dlib/november06/organ/11organ.html; Kenning Arlitsch and Patrick S. O'Brien, "Invisible Institutional Repositories: Addressing the Low Indexing Ratios of IRs in Google Scholar," *Library Hi Tech* 30, no. 1 (2012): 60–81, doi:10.1108/07378831211213210.

27. Anurag Acharya, "Indexing Repositories: Pitfalls and Best Practices" (slides for presentation at 10th International Conference on Open Repositories, Indianapolis, IN, June 8–11, 2015), http://www.or2015.net/wp-content/uploads/2015/06/or-2015-anurag-google-scholar.pdf.

28. Tim Austin, "Towards a Digital Infrastructure for Engineering Materials Data," *Materials Discovery* (in press), doi:10.1016/j.md.2015.12.003.

29. Jan Brase, Michael Lautenschlager, and Irina Sens, "The Tenth Anniversary of Assigning DOI Names to Scientific Data and a Five Year History of DataCite," *D-Lib Magazine* 21, no. 1/2 (January/February 2015): 10, doi:10.1045/january2015-brase.

30. California Digital Library, "EZID: Pricing," accessed March 18, 2016, http://ezid.cdlib.org/home/pricing.

31. DataCite, "What Do We Do?" accessed August 6, 2015, https://www.datacite.org/about-datacite/what-do-we-do.

32. California Digital Library, "EZID Help," accessed August 6, 2015, http://ezid.cdlib.org/home/help.

33. University Library, University of Illinois at Urbana-Champaign, "University of Illinois at Urbana-Champaign DOI Service Participant Agreement," 2014, https://uofi.box.com/IllinoisDOIAgreementFinal.

# Bibliography

Acharya, Anurag. "Indexing Repositories: Pitfalls and Best Practices." Slides for presentation at 10th International Conference on Open Repositories, Indianapolis, IN, June 8–11, 2015. http://www.or2015.net/wp-content/uploads/2015/06/or-2015-anurag-google-scholar.pdf.

Appleyard, Baden, and Greg Laughlin. "Copyright, Data and Licensing." The Australian National Data Service. Accessed March 18, 2016. http://ands.org.au/guides/copyright-and-data-awareness.html.

Arlitsch, Kenning, and Patrick S. O'Brien. "Invisible Institutional Repositories: Addressing the Low Indexing Ratios of IRs in Google Scholar." *Library Hi Tech* 30, no. 1 (2012): 60–81. doi:10.1108/07378831211213210.

Austin, Tim. "Towards a Digital Infrastructure for Engineering Materials Data." *Materials Discovery*, in press. doi:10.1016/j.md.2015.12.003.

Ball, Alex. "How to License Research Data." DCC How-to Guides. February 9, 2011. Revised July 17, 2014. Digital Curation Centre. http://www.dcc.ac.uk/resources/howguides/license-research-data.

Beebe, Linda. "Supplemental Materials for Journal Articles: NISO/NFAIS Joint Working Group." *Information Standards Quarterly* 22, no. 3 (Summer 2010): 33–37. http://www.niso.org/apps/group_public/download.php/4885/Beebe_SuppMatls_WG_ISQ_v22no3.pdf.

Bizer, Christina, Tom Heath, and Tim Berners-Lee. "Linked Data: The Story So Far." *International Journal on Semantic Web and Information Systems* 5, no. 3 (July–September 2009). http://go.galegroup.com/ps/i.do?id=GALE%7CA209477051&v=2.1&u=uiuc_uc&it=r&p=AONE&sw=w&asid=fd7e52083504e596d9b86bfe8a273f7c.

Brase, Jan, Michael Lautenschlager, and Irina Sens. "The Tenth Anniversary of Assigning DOI Names to Scientific Data and a Five Year History of DataCite." *D-Lib Magazine* 21, no. 1/2 (January/February 2015): 10. doi:10.1045/january2015-brase.

California Digital Library. "EZID Help." Accessed August 6, 2015. http://ezid.cdlib.org/home/help.

———. "EZID: Pricing." Accessed March 18, 2016. http://ezid.cdlib.org/home/pricing.

Carroll, Michael W. "Sharing Research Data and Intellectual Property Law: A Primer." *PLOS Biology* 13, no. 8 (2015): e1002235. http://journals.plos.org/plosbiology/article?id=10.1371/journal.pbio.1002235.

Creative Commons. "CC0 1.0 Universal (CC0 1.0) Public Domain Dedication." Accessed March 18, 2016. https://creativecommons.org/publicdomain/zero/1.0/.

DataCite. *DataCite Metadata Schema for the Publication and Citation of Research Data*, Version 3.1. Hannover, Germany: DataCite, August 2015. doi:10.5438/0010.

———. "What Do We Do?" Accessed August 6, 2015. https://www.datacite.org/about-datacite/what-do-we-do.

DataCite homepage. Accessed March 18, 2016. https://www.datacite.org.

DataCite Metadata Search. Accessed March 18, 2016. http://search.datacite.org/ui.

DataONE. "DataONE Architecture, Version 1.2." Accessed November 19, 2015. https://releases.dataone.org/online/api-documentation-v1.2.0/.

Data Science. "About TwoRavens." Institute for Quantitative Social Science, Harvard University. Accessed March 18, 2016. http://datascience.iq.harvard.edu/about-tworavens.

Dataverse Project. "Sample Data Usage Agreement." Accessed March 18, 2016. http://best-practices.dataverse.org/harvard-policies/sample-dua.html.

Dryad Digital Repository. "The Organization: Overview." Last modified October 22, 2015. https://datadryad.org/pages/organization.

Dryad Digital Repository homepage. Last modified November 19, 2015. https://datadryad.org.

Elsevier. "Elsevier and PANGAEA Link Contents for Easier Access to Full Earth System Research." News release, February 24, 2010. https://www.elsevier.com/about/press-releases/science-and-technology/elsevier-and-pangaea-link-contents-for-easier-access-to-full-earth-system-research.

———. "Supported Data Repositories." Accessed March 18, 2016. https://www.elsevier.com/books-and-journals/content-innovation/data-base-linking/supported-data-repositories.

Ferguson, Liz. "How and Why Researchers Share Data (and Why They Don't)." *Wiley Exchanges* (blog), November 3, 2014. http://exchanges.wiley.com/blog/2014/11/03/how-and-why-researchers-share-data-and-why-they-dont. Accessed August 14, 2015; page now discontinued.

Fielding, Roy. "Architectural Styles and the Design of Network-Based Software Architectures." PhD diss., University of California, Irvine, 2000.

Fox, Peter, and James Hendler. "Changing the Equation on Scientific Data Visualization." *Science* 331, no. 6018 (2011): 705–8. doi:10.1126/science.1197654.

Google Scholar homepage. Accessed March 18, 2016. https://scholar.google.com/.

GSToRE V3. "Experimental API." Accessed November 19, 2015. http://gstore.unm.edu/docs/experimental.html.

Ingram, Bill. e-mail to author regarding IDEALS traffic. November 6, 2015.

Martone, M. ed. *Data Citation Synthesis Group: Joint Declaration of Data Citation Principles—Final.* San Diego: FORCE11, 2014. https://www.force11.org/group/joint-declaration-data-citation-principles-final.

Murray-Rust, Peter, Rufus Pollock, Bryan Bishop, Mike Chelen, Cameron Neylon, Daniel Mietchen, and Andy Powell. "FAQ." Panton Principles: Principles for Open Data in Science. Accessed November 20, 2015. http://pantonprinciples.org/faq.

nanoHUB.org. "Nanomaterial Registry Portal." Accessed March 18, 2016. https://nanohub.org/groups/nanomaterialregistry.

Open Data Commons. "Open Data Commons Open Database License (ODbL)." Accessed March 18, 2016. http://opendatacommons.org/licenses/odbl.

Open Definition. "Conformant Licenses." Accessed March 18, 2016. http://opendefinition.org/licenses.

Organ, Michael K. "Download Statistics: What Do They Tell Us? The Example of Research Online, the Open Access Institutional Repository at the University of Wollongong, Australia." *D-Lib Magazine* 12, no. 11 (November 2006). http://www.dlib.org/dlib/november06/organ/11organ.html.

Panton Principles homepage. Accessed March 18, 2016. http://pantonprinciples.org.

Research Data Alliance. "RDA/WDS Publishing Data Services WG." Accessed June 14, 2016. https://rd-alliance.org/groups/rdawds-publishing-data-services-wg.html.

Schaeffer, Peggy. "Why Does Dryad Use CC0?" *Dryad News and Views* (blog). October 5, 2011. http://blog.datadryad.org/2011/10/05/why-does-dryad-use-cc0.

Sims, Nancy. "Making Decisions about Your Research Data." YouTube video, 6:38. Posted by CopyrightLibn, August 28, 2012. https://youtu.be/ZuUGlGOMGjU.

Smith, MacKenzie. "Data Governance: Where Technology and Policy Collide." In *Research Data Management: Practical Strategies for Information Professionals.* Edited by Joyce M. Ray, 45–59. West Lafayette, IN: Purdue University Press, 2014.

UK Data Archive. "Copyright and Data Sharing." Accessed June 14, 2016. http://www.data-archive.ac.uk/create-manage/copyright/share.

University Library, University of Illinois at Urbana-Champaign. "University of Illinois at Urbana-Champaign DOI Service Participant Agreement." 2014. https://uofi.box.com/IllinoisDOIAgreementFinal.

University of Minnesota Libraries. "Data Repository for the University of Minnesota." Accessed March 18, 2016. http://hdl.handle.net/11299/166578.

———. "Umedia." Accessed March 18, 2016. http://umedia.lib.umn.edu.

———. "University Digital Conservancy." Accessed March 18, 2016. http://conservancy.umn.edu.

Wheeler, Jonathan, and Karl Benedict. "Functional Requirements Specification for Archival Asset Management: Identification and Integration of Essential Properties of Services Oriented Architecture Products." *Journal of Map and Geography Libraries* 11, no. 2 (2015): 155–79.

# Preservation of Data for the Long Term

The same data files that were originally submitted to your repository will not stay intact forever. They will erode at the bit level, and over time their degree of usability will decrease and disappear at the rate at which available operating systems, software programs, and the necessary hardware can no longer interpret them. All digital files that we create today are at risk of becoming obsolete, and digital data is no exception. Digital preservation strategies can help mitigate these risks through planning and a long-term commitment to maintaining access to the information contained within the digital files. Therefore a data curation service must actively monitor the integrity and reusability of the data files it stewards and use all available software and tools for ongoing digital preservation.

## 7.1 Preservation Planning for Long-Term Reuse

The delivery and reuse of the data that your service curates will rely on long-term preservation planning that anticipates format obsolescence and storage failures. Preservation planning can be expressed through policy, but it also requires practical strategies for action. A digital preservation framework, such as the one outlined by McGovern, provides an organization with the justification for the staffing, resources, and time involved with digital data curation.[1]

The University of Minnesota Libraries developed a digital preservation framework in 2012 that outlines three levels of technical support for a variety of digital objects.[2] The framework is general; therefore, a long-term preservation plan for particular data file formats is expressed in the various preservation policies of the organization. See table 7.1 for an example of how the framework's three technical

231

levels of support map to the digital preservation policy of data file types housed in the institutional repository. Note that the designation of support does not solely reflect the openness of the format (e.g., limited support for proprietary vs. full support for open formats) and takes into account other sustainability factors such as adoption and disclosure.[3] For example, Real Audio files are proprietary (Real Networks), yet the software needed to run the files (RealPlayer) is freely downloadable and this format was widely used for many years to stream music over the Internet, but is now in decline. To make your own policy determinations about file formats, the Library of Congress Recommended Formats Statement, recently updated for 2016-2017, provides an authoritative source.[4]

## TABLE 7.1

**Digital preservation framework of the University of Minnesota Libraries mapped to example data file formats housed in the University Digital Conservancy.**

| Technical Levels of Support | Description | Example Data File Formats[a] |
|---|---|---|
| Level 2: Comprehensive (Full) Support | All effort will be made to ensure long-term preservation for digital objects identified under this stewardship level. A high level of available resources (staff, technologies, funding) will be considered for use. In addition to Level 1 treatment, strategies here may include migration, emulation, normalization, and the development of material-specific solutions. | PDF<br>Comma Separated Value (.csv)<br>Plain Text (.txt)<br>XML-based (.xml, .sgml)<br>JPEG image (.jpg)<br>TIFF image (.tif)<br>Wave Audio (.wav) |
| Level 1: Fundamental (Limited) Support | All reasonable effort will be made to ensure long-term preservation for digital objects identified under this stewardship level. A moderate level of available resources (staff, technologies, funding) will be considered for use. Treatment strategies will be selected from widely available best practices and may include fixity, validation, geographic replication, and others as developed. | Microsoft Excel (.xls, .xlsx)<br>Rich Text (.rtf)<br>Bitmap image (.bmp)<br>GIF image (.gif)<br>JPEG 2000 (.jp2)<br>Photoshop (.psd)<br>MP3 audio (.mp3)<br>Real Audio (.ra, .rm, .ram)<br>Windows Media Audio (.wma)<br>AVI (.avi)<br>MPEG (.mp1, .mp2, .mp4)<br>QuickTime (.mov)<br>Windows Media Video (.wmv) |

**TABLE 7.1** (continued)

| Technical Levels of Support | Description | Example Data File Formats[a] |
|---|---|---|
| Level 0: Non-Supported | No preservation efforts will be made for digital objects outside the collection's stewardship scope and existing collecting policy of the Libraries. | Does not apply |

a. Based on the Preservation Policy of the University Digital Conservancy, the IR service run by the University of Minnesota Libraries.

Some additional digital preservation policies to consult include

- The ICPSR Digital Preservation Policy Framework, developed by Nancy Y. McGovern, April 2007, last revised June 2012. http://www.icpsr. umich.edu/icpsrweb/content/datamanagement/preservation/policies/ dpp-framework.html.
- The National Library of Australia's, "Digital Preservation Policy," 4rd ed. 2013. http://www.nla.gov.au/policy-and-planning/digital-preservation-policy.
- Purdue University Research Repository's, "PURR Digital Preservation Policy" from 2012. https://purr.purdue.edu/legal/digitalpreservation,
- The UK Data Archive's *Preservation Policy* (Colchester, UK: University of Essex, 2012). http://www.data-archive.ac.uk/media/54776/uk-da062-dps-preservationpolicy.pdf.

# Practical Approaches to Digital Preservation

As the next case study will show, even with the best intentions, planning for digital preservation must take into account real-world use of the data. Some practical aspects to consider for effective data preservation planning include

- Secure Storage: Storing the data in a safe place is the first defense against deterioration. Hardware devices (e.g., magnetic tape, disk, etc.) have optimal environmental conditions and a life expectancy that will help determine when a media refresh is needed.[5]
- Redundancy: Keep several identical (copied at the bit level) but separate copies of the files stored on geographically separated and technologically diverse devices.[6]

- Disaster planning. Determine the risks if some or all of the backups fail. Could the data be recovered (e.g., digital forensic approaches applied) and at what costs?[7]
- Partnerships: There are a number of programs emerging to help organizations preserve digital objects across multiple institutions that are applicable for data preservation—notably the Lots of Copies Keep Stuff Safe (LOCKSS) initiative (http://www.lockss.org) and the Digital Preservation Network (DPN, http://www.dpn.org). These dark archives provide the necessary protection of digital content in the event of administrative or physical failures. In the case of the DPN, users access the network through nodes, like the DuraCloud Vault (http://duracloud.org/duracloud-vault) service from Duraspace, for safely depositing their digital content.

This next case study by Christine Mayo will further illustrate practical approaches to preservation with specific emphasis on the challenges with the heterogeneous file types for data.

# Balancing Digital Preservation Standards with Data Reusability

*Christine Mayo*[*]

The Dryad Digital Repository is a curated resource that makes research data underlying scientific and medical publications discoverable, freely reusable, and citable.[8] Dryad has submission requirements that purposefully do not exceed publisher data policies, since it is an archive of the scholarly record, rather than a filter of that record. Dryad hosts many types of research data that are not served by more specialized repositories, and data from a wide variety of disciplines. As a result, the repository hosts data files in a wide variety of formats, including some that are proprietary. While Dryad has preservation practices in place to ensure bitstream-level preservation of all the files it hosts, ensuring long-term scientific reusability for such a diversity of formats is more of a challenge. This case study addresses specifically Dryad's curation policies concerning file format and bitstream curation, which present unique challenges separate from those of metadata curation.

When a Dryad curator accesses a data package, they first and foremost ensure that all of the files are operable (i.e., are not corrupted) and that they generally match any descriptive metadata provided, including readme files. Currently, Dryad very specifically does not engage in preservation reformatting of files, either during curation or after deposit, because of the potential for loss of information posed by reformatting, particularly flattening, specialty scientific data formats. There are, however, a few exceptions to this rule, and while Dryad most often respects the author's choice of file formats, curators will sometimes request that an author resubmit a file in a different format. This primarily happens in one of three situations:

1.  when the data is in a proprietary format for which there is no open-source reader available,
2.  when data is machine-actionable (e.g., software code) but is instead presented in a display format such as Portable Document Format (PDF), or
3.  when a file requires a piece of software that is demonstrably becoming obsolete.

**Files with no open-source alternative:** Dryad can accept files in proprietary formats, but curators tend to contact submitters to ask for alternatives if the format does not have a readily available open-source alternative (e.g., OpenOffice for MS Word, PSPP for SPSS). This is both because Dryad aims to minimize technical barriers to data accessibility for users and because curators may be unable to open the file to verify its contents if there is no open-source viewer available.

**Inappropriate use of PDF:** Although PDF and PDF/A are generally considered low risk in terms of digital preservation, Dryad encourages authors to limit their use of PDF for actionable materials and instead use PDF only for pictorial data or diagrams. Actionable materials such as code and numerical tables can be difficult to extract from PDF, and this poses an unnecessary technical barrier to reusability.

**Clear obsolescence risk:** Dryad occasionally receives files produced by researchers using older versions of software that are no longer readily available, or with which newer versions of the software are incompatible. If a file is effectively obsolete, curators typically ask the submitter to provide a different format for archiving. However, care must be taken in doing so, since there is potential for information to be lost during format migration. Thus, Dryad aims to educate and work with authors to ensure that data files are useful both today and into the future.

# 7.2 Monitor Preservation Needs and Take Action

This section will outline some appropriate software tools and strategies for digital preservation. The *Digital Preservation Handbook* is another good place to explore in more depth ways to actively monitor and sustain the integrity of your data files.[9]

## Tools for Active Monitoring and Management

There are a number of tools to use when implementing the preservation step, and more are under development.[10] Here are few examples that practitioners may find immediately useful. For more examples, the US Library of Congress website (http://digitalpreservation.gov) offers a directory of tools and publishes the latest research in file format standards and approaches for preservation.

*Data Accessioner:* This tool transfers files from one location to another using MD5 checksums that work like fingerprints to verify that the migration was perfect. Kussman notes, "In addition to copying files, an XML file about the transfer is generated that documents associated (entered) descriptive metadata and collected technical metadata about the files."[11] Data Accessioner was made possible by the POWERR project and is available for free download at http://dataaccessioner.org.[12]

*DROID:* Used for generating MD5 checksums and for returning file format identification reports, DROID links to the PRONOM registry (https://www.nationalarchives.gov.uk/PRONOM/Default.aspx) to validate technical information. Available for free download at http://digital-preservation.github.io/droid.

*JHOVE/JHOVE2:* Used for file format identification, JHOVE identifies, validates (based on the binary header information), and gathers representation metadata for the file such as file pathname or URI, last modification date, byte size, format, format version, MIME type, format profiles, and more. Available for free download at https://bitbucket.org/jhove2/main/wiki/Home.

## Data Preservation Strategies

Harvey's second edition of *Preserving Digital Materials* describes a range of strategies to preserve digital objects. Relevant to research data are the following solutions:[13]

- Format migration: Move the contents of a data file from one format to another so that the information remains intact and accessible using whatever software is current. Often the original file is retained.

- Format standardization (or normalization): Convert the data files into a consistent (often nonproprietary and prevalent) format that will continue to be read by software for a long time (e.g., ASCII-based text files) or by a wider audience.
- Encapsulation: Recreate data in a persistent format, such as XML, with ample metadata (using standards such as PREMIS [Preservation Metadata Implementation Strategies, http://www.loc.gov/standards/premis]) to describe the original object.
- Emulation: Create a virtual computing environment that simulates the original system or software required to run an obsolete data format (e.g., digital art objects).[14]
- Preserve the old technology: Maintain the obsolete technology (software and hardware) in order to access the data in their native environment. (Note that Harvey (p.132) warns this approach is "…'ultimately a dead end' because obsolete technology cannot be maintained in a functional condition indefinitely.")[15]

## *Data Preservation in Action*

The next two case studies, the first by Chiu-chuang (Lu) Chou and Charlie Fiss and the second by Robin Burgess, provide two views of how data repositories must seek out long-term solutions for the unique digital data that their repositories house.

# Archiving Three Waves of the National Survey of Families and Households

*Chiu-chuang (Lu) Chou and Charlie Fiss*

During the 1970s and early 1980s, American families experienced significant changes. Divorce rates rose, more couples chose to cohabitate rather than marry, more women joined in the labor force, and the fertility rate of women declined considerably.[16] These changes had significant effects on family life and household structure. The federal government wanted to better understand these social changes in order to formulate public policies to address them. In 1983, the Center for Population Research of the National Institute of Child Health and Human Development (NICHD) issued a Request for Proposal (REF No.

NICHD-DBS-83-8) for a large-scale data collection to study the causes and consequences of the changes happening in the families and households in the United States. A research team from the Center for Demography and Ecology (CDE) at the University of Wisconsin-Madison responded with a proposal to design a national study covering many aspects of family experiences and life course events. NICHD awarded a three-year, $4.8 million grant to CDE to conduct the National Survey of Families and Households (NSFH) starting on January 1, 1986.[17]

The main NSFH sample was a national, multi-stage area probability sample containing about 17,000 housing units drawn from 100 sampling areas in the 48 contiguous states in the United States.

The sample included a main cross-section sample of 9,643 households. The oversample of blacks, Puerto Ricans, Mexican Americans, single-parent families and families with stepchildren, cohabiting couples, and recently married was accomplished by doubling the number of households selected within the 100 sampling areas. Wave 1 interviews were conducted in 1987–1988 with 13,017 respondents.[18] A five-year follow-up interview in 1992–1994 gathered data on life events including marriages, divorces, births, work experiences, and other transitions.[19] Interviews were conducted with 10,007 respondents from wave 1. In addition, separate interviews were conducted with the respondent's current spouse or partner, the respondent's partner at wave 1 (if no longer together), one of the respondent's children, and one of the respondent's parents. Wave 3 interviews were conducted in 2001–2003. Due to budgetary constraints, only a sub-sample of the original wave 1 sample was selected for interviewing at wave 3. This sub-sample included parents of young adult children and mid-to-later-life adults. A total of 4,600 wave 1 respondents were interviewed as part of wave 3.[20]

NSFH has a very broad scope of data on family living arrangements; kin contact; life histories including marriage, cohabitation, education, and fertility; employment; and economic and psychological well-being. These issues are important to several disciplines and sub-disciplines. NSFH data over the years has been used to test different hypotheses related to various aspects of American families. The impact of the NSFH is demonstrated by its use in 1,087 scholarly publications (633 journal articles, 206 theses, 190 reports, 35 book sections, 13 conference proceedings, and 10 books).[21]

The NSFH project website (http://www.ssc.wisc.edu/nsfh) was created in 1999 to disseminate data and relevant information to researchers in a timely fashion. It was redesigned in 2005, when wave 3 data and documentation files were released. NSFH funding ended in 2006. The Center for Demography of Health and Aging (CDHA) at the University of Wisconsin-Madison assumed the custodian role of the NSFH project website and continues to provide support to NSFH users.

Three waves of NSFH data and documentation files at the project website were created over a span of almost two decades. The files exist in a variety of formats that reflect the evolution of software used by the project over time. As technology continues to advance, these files need to be preserved to ensure their usability for future researchers. In 2012, CDHA submitted a grant proposal to the National Institute on Aging (NIA) to seek funding to archive the NSFH study data and documentation files at its project website. In August of 2013, CDHA was awarded an NIA grant to appraise the public-use data and documentation files at the NSFH project website, preserve them, and archive them in publicly accessible archives. Preservation of the NSFH website is not covered by this grant. Nevertheless, CDHA will maintain this website as long as its NIA P30 Aging Center grant continues.

## NSFH WEBSITE CONTENT APPRAISAL

The process of content evaluation and file preparation for archiving was performed systematically according to the guidelines described in the *Guide to Social Science Data Preparation and Archiving: Best Practice throughout the Data Life Cycle*, 5th edition, published by the Inter-university Consortium for Political and Social Research (ICPSR).[22] There are over 600 files at the NSFH project website. Many are HTML files, image files, and utility files related to the function and design of the website. An inventory list of files was created. These files were thoroughly examined and appraised. Essential data and documentation files in the three waves of the NSFH study were identified for preservation.

## FILE TYPES AND ORGANIZATION

The three waves of NSFH documentation files exist in various formats: ASCII text, WordPerfect, Microsoft Word, and PDF. At the NSFH website, they are grouped in ten areas: notes to users, content outlines, introductory files, methodology reports, codebook files, indices, appendices, questionnaires, layout files, and skip maps. To standardize file format over all the waves, our team converted all documentation files to Microsoft Word and Adobe PDF. Microsoft Word is chosen because it maintains the layout and format in the original documentation files. PDF is a format that ICPSR uses to distribute its study documentation files. To provide adequate information for the NSFH data files, we classified these documentation files into five types: methodology, codebook, questionnaire, skip map, and record layout. In the case of wave 1, thirty-five documentation files at the NSFH website are now organized into five files. Tables of contents were created to assist users in navigating within these consolidated documentation files.

The NSFH website distributed wave 1 and wave 2 data in ASCII text format and wave 3 data as SPSS system (.sav) files. Our project retained ASCII text data files for waves 1 and 2. The wave 3 SPSS system (.sav) data files were converted to ASCII text data files using SledgeHammer (http://www.mtna.us/?page_id=1232), a data management tool distributed by Metadata Technology North America (MTNA). ASCII text is portable across platforms, systems, and time. It is a standard format for preserving social science data at ICPSR. We ran frequencies tests on subsets of variables to insure that the wave 3 data in the new ASCII files produced the same results as the original SPSS version of the data.

An ASCII text data file is primitive (see figure 7.1). To analyze an ASCII text data file, a researcher first needs to create a statistical statement file (see figure 7.2), including column locations of the variables, variable labels, and variable value labels in order to read in the data correctly. All the variable level information is stored in a codebook file. In the case of wave 1 data, 4,300 variables are documented in its codebook file. A researcher first needs to locate such information in the codebook for selected variables in his or her analysis on wave 1 data. To aid researchers, we wrote SPSS and SAS statement files for all the ASCII text data files in waves 1 and 2. SledgeHammer ingested wave 3 SPSS system data files and exported them as ASCII text data files with SAS and SPSS setup files. These statistical statement files are a time saver for researchers as the files can be readily edited to conduct their analysis in SAS or SPSS.

All three waves of data files are now available in ASCII text format with accompanying SAS and SPSS programming statement files. Providing data in ASCII text format with SAS and SPSS statement files is a standard practice in social science data archives in the United States and around the world. To facilitate longitudinal analyses of NSFH data, we compiled SAS and SPSS setup files to show users how to merge data from all three waves in these two statistical packages.

```
00008R10387020394203
00024R20387061093102039117032120604959 5       015    55
00040R10387062494106019406012121200009 5       015    55
00061R20387113093133989830999 5  959595         985    55
00079R10387042893101119101 95    1201959595     015    55
00095R20387010594103068701054 5  00951899       015    55
00218R10387092193102039206012124295959 5       015    55
```

**FIGURE 7.1**
Raw ASCII text data file.

```
FILE HANDLE DATA / NAME="R:\nsfh\sample.txt".
DATA LIST FILE=DATA/
       MCASEID   001-005(F)
       ZZ1A      006(A)
       ZZ2       007-007(F)
       ZZ401     012-013(F).
VARIABLE LABELS
       MCASEID   'CaseID'
       ZZ1A      'INTERVIEW TYPE INDICATOR'
       ZZ2       'RESPONDENT'S SEX'
       ZZ401     'MONTH OF INTERVIEW' .
VALUE LABELS
       ZZ1A
                 'R' 'Respondent'
                 /
       ZZ2
                 1 'MALE'
                 2 'FEMALE'
                 /
       ZZ401
                 1 'January'
                 2 'February'
                 3 'March'
                 4 'April'
                 5 'May'
                 6 'June'
                 7 'July'
                 8 'August'
                 9 'September'
                 10 'October'
                 11 'November'
                 12 'December'.
EXECUTE.
```

**FIGURE 7.2**
SPSS statement file for the first few variables in the ASCII data file.

# ADDITIONAL FILES FOR WAVE 3

In 2006, the NSFH research team did not have the time or funding to create survey questionnaires or skip maps for the wave 3 data. As part of our project, we acquired the CASES q files that the University of Wisconsin Survey Center

(UWSC) used to create the Computer Aided Telephone Interview (CATI) instruments for the NSFH. In order to facilitate usability, we choose to eliminate as many of the complex instructions as possible. For example, the system included a number of complex instructions to determine the wording of question (e.g., determining whether to refer to the respondent as *he* or *she* in a question). Where possible, we added this wording to the question and left out the coding language from the CASES system. We also added the variable names assigned to the data gathered for each question to assist users in their understanding of how the data was produced.

We then used the completed questionnaire files to create skip maps. A skip map provides users with a means to visualize how the interviewer would proceed through an interview based on the responses given to a particular question. We chose to include the variable name and a brief description of the variable for each question in the interview. We added the major instructions that interviewers were given by the CASES system on how to proceed based on the response to a particular question. While the questionnaires and skip maps lack the detail from the CASES system, we felt that given the limited resources and time available for our project, we needed to sacrifice some of the detail in order to provide the user with resources that were not previously available.

There is an existing FAQ page on the NSFH website, and since 2006 CDHA has answered many NSFH-related questions from researchers. We incorporated these answers into a new and expanded FAQ appendix and added it to all codebooks to provide quick tips for researchers who are not familiar with NSFH.

## METADATA DOCUMENTS

NSFH metadata files were created by Nesstar Publisher 4.0 (http://nesstar.com/software/publisher.html), a metadata-authoring tool in compliance with Data Documentation Initiative (DDI)-codebook standard.[23] We first created SPSS system (.sav file extension) files for waves 1 and 2 waves of data files. Wave 3 data files are SPSS system files, and they were ready to be imported. These NSFH SPSS system data files were imported to Nesstar Publisher, which retrieved variable-level information such as variable name, value labels for all responses, and summary statistics for each variable into its variable metadata fields. Question text was manually entered into Nesstar Publisher for the first two NSFH waves. For Wave 3, the UWSC provided copies of the question text in XML format, which facilitated adding the question text to Nesstar Publisher. Study-level and document-level metadata were created by our team. These metadata files are deposited with ICPSR and NACDA, which can import these files to their Survey Documentation and Analysis (SDA) (http://sda.berkeley.edu/) online tool. SDA allows users to browse and search data documentation, create cross-tabulations, and download data. These XML files can be utilized by other developers and archives to build new tools for data discovery and online analyses of the NSFH data because they can be easily ingested and modified by other established data analysis tools like Nesstar and Colectica (http://www.colectica.com/).

DDI-C was chosen for our project because DDI-Life Cycle (DDI-L) standard requires resources beyond the scope of our NIA grant. NSFH project ended in 2006, and its research team members either retired or left CDE. Without their expertise, it is not feasible to use DDI-L in this project.

## GEOGRAPHIC DATA MERGING SERVICE

Over the years, researchers have asked if they can request a geo-merge on wave 3 data. The NSFH project ended before a geocode file was created for wave 3 respondents. With NIA funding for this project, we were able to fill this need and create a geocoded file for wave 3 respondents. This new geocode file was created with collaboration from the UWSC and the Applied Population Laboratory.

To protect respondents' confidentiality, no geographical data collected from respondents is included in the NSFH public-use data files. Geographic code files for wave 1, 2, and 3 responses (based on the address provided by the respondent) are stored in a secured space at CDHA. The geographic levels in these restricted geocode files range from state to census tract (census tracts are geographic areas composed of between 1,200 and 8,000 people).[24] Researchers who need to combine geographical characteristics with NSFH data in their projects can contact CDHA and request our NSFH geographic merge service. This service adds researchers' geographical contextual data, such as unemployment rate in census tracts, to NSFH respondents. To start a geo-merge request, a researcher is required to obtain an approval from his or her institutional review board (IRB) and prepares a data protection plan for his or her geo-merged NSFH data in a mandatory confidentiality agreement (http://www.ssc.wisc.edu/nsfh/624649EB.pdf) before we can perform a geographic data merging service.

## ARCHIVING THE NSFH DATA

This project appraised and prepared all public-use data and documentation files at the National Survey of Families and Households (NSFH) project website (http://www.ssc.wisc.edu/nsfh) and archived them in publicly accessible archives at the National Archive of Computerized Data on Aging (NACDA), the Inter-university Consortium for Political and Social Research (ICPSR), and the Data and Information Services Center (DISC) at the University of Wisconsin-Madison.

Descriptive documents in Microsoft Word for all three waves of NSFH study were created for the receiving archives to facilitate the creation of NSFH study records in their archive holdings. In addition, we compiled a list of recent NSFH publications published from 2008 to 2015. This list is arranged by waves and was sent to ICPSR to update its NSFH bibliography.

NSFH is a prominent longitudinal study on family life in the United States. Three waves of surveys were conducted in 1987–1988, 1992–1994, and 2001–2003. A total of $14.5 million in federal grant funds were awarded to field NSFH surveys over time. The goal of our project is to ensure the accessibility of all three waves of the NSFH for current and future researchers studying family-related issues. To accomplish this goal, we worked diligently—especially in the case of the wave 3 data—to get the data into standard archival format and to reformat the documentation to make it more user-friendly. One of the things we discovered during the course of the project is the difficulty in going back in time to standardize documentation and data in a consistent manner. Preserving and archiving research data is a meticulous and important process. We hope the tools and procedures mentioned in this paper can be useful for other research data curators.

# ACKNOWLEDGMENTS

The first wave of the National Survey of Families and Households was funded by a grant (HD21009) from the Center for Population Research of the National Institute of Child Health and Human Development, and the second and third waves were funded jointly by this grant and a grant (AG10266) from the National Institute on Aging. NSFH was designed and carried out at the Center for Demography and Ecology at the University of Wisconsin-Madison under the direction of Larry Bumpass and James Sweet. The field work for the first two waves was done by the Institute for Survey Research at Temple University, and for the third wave by the University of Wisconsin Survey Center. This NIA grant (AG R03 AG045503) made archiving three waves of NSFH document and data files at NSFH project website (http://www.ssc.wisc.edu/nsfh) possible. The Center for Demography of Health and Aging (grant number P30 AG017266) at University of Wisconsin-Madison has maintained NSFH project website and provided user support to NSFH researchers since 2006, when the NSFH project ended.

# From KAPTUR to VADS4R: Exploring Research Data Management in the Visual Arts

*Robin Burgess**

Across the higher education sector, research councils, organizations, teams, and researchers are under pressure to make publicly funded research data freely available, and in line with the Research Councils UK guidance. Publication of data resulting from the research is increasingly a requirement of funding. Equally important is data transparency and the ability for researchers to access data in order to test the validity and reliability of the research outputs and methods; to reinterpret and reuse data, thereby adding value to publicly funded research; and, ultimately, to access the data in the longer term.

By its very nature, research in the visual arts is highly complex and varied, often comprising a wide variety of outputs and formats that present researchers, information managers, and technology teams with many discipline-specific issues. Examples include sketch books, paintings, architectural plans and buildings, physical artifacts, and complex modelling algorithms. Additionally, the methods and processes that generate this type of research information are just as varied and complex. Research in the visual arts relies heavily on sketchbooks, logbooks, journals, and workbooks. Alongside this data, a wide range of related research documentation and protocols (such as "how-to guides" and methodology reports) are also created. The physical nature of research in the arts presents researchers and curators with significant problems with security and preservation issues while also greatly increasing the risk of data loss and deterioration. Issues arise, for example, in the field of architecture. When data is locked up in the physical building that has been created as the output, how can this information be preserved and managed?

Therefore, appropriate curation and management of research data in the visual arts is essential to

- satisfy funding requirements and demands for open access;
- limit the issue that production of data can be extremely time-consuming and therefore costly;
- reduce its lack of discoverability or loss;
- enable other researchers to test the reliability and validity of the data and the research method;

- enable greater impact of research and make tracking more accurate; and
- extend collaborative opportunities between researchers and teams working on similar and related data sets to create new research opportunities.

# INTRODUCING THE KAPTUR PROJECT

Led by the Visual Arts Data Service (VADS), a Research Centre of the University for the Creative Arts (UCA), in collaboration with the Glasgow School of Art; Goldsmiths, University of London; and University of the Arts London, and supported by JISC, the KAPTUR project (2011–2013) sought to address these problems. Each partner institute had been engaged in projects together such as KULTUR and shared a common need for managing research data in the arts and therefore joined forces for the KAPTUR project. A steering group was set up to help manage the continuation of the project, and each institute provided a project officer to carry out the required work for the project. Regular meetings were held between the partners, alternating between locations—Glasgow and London. A project website was set up to help capture the work that was being undertaken and to share this with the wider community.

Visual arts research data is a valuable resource and, with appropriate curation and management, it has much to offer in learning, teaching, research, knowledge transfer, and consultancy in the visual arts. From the outset in 2011, the KAPTUR project team noted that very little was known about the curation and management of this data: none of the specialist arts institutions (e.g., the partners involved in the project, like Glasgow School of Art, and other arts-based institutes) had research data management policies or infrastructure in place, and evidence suggested that curation practice was ad hoc and left to individual researchers with little support or guidance. In addition, the curation and management of such diverse and complex digital and physical resources presented unique challenges. These challenges were associated both with the curation (management, handling, storing the data) and the preservation of the data for reuse—such as collecting numerical data and algorithms that constitute the modeling of the human body as demonstrated by the work done by the Digital Design Studio at The Glasgow School of Art, or capturing the processes and ephemeral thoughts created during a dance performance.

The objectives of the KAPTUR project were two-fold: first, to investigate the role of research data in the visual arts; and second, to consider the application of technology to support collection, discovery, use and reuse, and preservation of research data in the arts. To support this, a number of policies, procedures, and systems were reviewed and case studies were developed to assess and understand existing tools, knowledge, and practices regarding research data management more generally.

The project began with an environmental assessment that considered issues of terminology, the role of the visual arts researcher (within the institute and externally), and how visual arts research data is created, used, and preserved (the researchers role in this process). Next, a technical review considered two questions: first, what did researchers need to support effective research data management in the visual arts? and second, what was the most appropriate technology solution to facilitate the appropriate management of research data in the visual arts? Regarding the first question, each KAPTUR partner considered the types of data that it collects and manages, disk space requirements, where the data was stored (such as shared drives and remote servers), operating environments, the cloud (whether this would be a reliable option for storage and access to data, and its sustainability as a resource), authentication methods, tracking of research data (in relation to its production and ultimate use within the research project workflows), backup procedures, and required support for the technical aspects of data management. Once the requirements were identified, a variety of potential technical solutions were identified for piloting and review. These solutions presented themselves via the repository platforms that were available to the project partners, such as ePrints and DSpace, but also alternative data management tools, including figShare and CKAN, that the team had researched.

The technical report highlighting findings and methodology for this process can be accessed here: http://www.vads.ac.uk/kaptur/outputs/Kaptur_technical_analysis.pdf.

Finally the team developed two training sessions (which were part of the original project scope, to help disseminate findings), each one hour in duration. The first looked at the basic principles of research data management in the visual arts, and the second focused on the creation of a research data management plan. These were further developed by each partner into a pilot course using appropriate content and resources from their respective institutions with reference to their particular organizational practices, processes, and disciplinary areas. Each partner worked with different stakeholders (to help develop the training, but also to take part in it). Participants included early-career researchers, research students, established researchers, and professional support staff from a range of departmental perspectives (administrators, IT, library, etc.). Feedback from attendees was favorable, and evaluation results indicated that participants' understanding of research data management had improved or improved considerably. The criteria for assessing this were solely reliant on the perception of those attending the training and how they felt the sessions went and what they had learned. These training materials were then published freely to the higher education community.

Details of the training sessions and the findings include

- Training plans: http://www.slideshare.net/kaptur_mrd/kaptur-rdm-trainingplan
- GSAs institutional workshop: http://www.slideshare.net/kaptur_mrd/tag/gsardmtraining
- Outputs and Toolkits: http://www.vads.ac.uk/kaptur/outputs/index.html

# VISUAL ARTS DATA SKILLS FOR RESEARCHERS (VADS4R) PROJECT

Following the work of the KAPTUR project, the Visual Arts Data Skills for Researchers (VADS4R) project extended this work by tailoring these learning materials for use with early-career researchers and postgraduate students in the visual arts to inform, support, and embed appropriate research data management practice across the visual arts. Led by the Centre for Digital Scholarship (formerly known as VADS) at the University for the Creative Arts (UCA) and in collaboration with Falmouth University and Glasgow School of Art, VADS4R has developed, delivered, and evaluated training programs at each partner institution. VADS4R ran from February 2013 to July 2014 and was funded by the Arts and Humanities Research Council (AHRC). The approach, method, and lessons learned from the project can be accessed from the project website, http://www.vads4r.vads.ac.uk/p/welcome.html. Here you can access the training packages that were developed (using XERTE software) as a significant output from the project. These looked at:

- How to avoid a data disaster
- Writing an AHRC technical plan
- Introduction to research data
- Data management planning
- Managing the material
- Principles of research data management in the visual arts
- The discoverability and reuse of visual arts data

These training packages can be found at http://www.vads4r.vads.ac.uk/p/online-learning.html. Also here you can see the additional material used as part of the training programs developed and the findings determined during some of the sessions run at the partnering institutes. Research in this area of data management in the visual arts continues between UCA and GSA, and new methods and approaches will be shared.

In conclusion, research data in the visual arts can be characterized as tangible and intangible, digital and physical, heterogeneous and infinite, and complex and complicated. It does not always fit into the natural scheme of data management. However, the development of policies, procedures, systems, and training can provide an innovative and flexible approach for this data, which is iterative and open to interpretation. These approaches support appropriate curation and management of data to alleviate the issues surrounding funder requirements, elements of time and discoverability, and at the same time improve the impact of research and create new collaborative opportunities for the institutes.

# Summary of Step 7.0: Preservation of Data for the Long Term

7.1 Plan for Long-Term Reuse: The delivery and use of the data will rely on long-term preservation planning that anticipates format obsolescence and storage failures.

7.2 Monitor Preservation Needs and Take Action: Actively monitor the integrity and reusability of the data files using appropriate software, and apply digital preservation strategies.

# Notes

1.  Daniel W. Noonan, "Digital Preservation Policy Framework: A Case Study," *Educause Review*, July 28, 2014, http://er.educause.edu/articles/2014/7/digital-preservation-policy-framework-a-case-study; Nancy McGovern, "Digital Preservation Management Model Document," Version 3.0, Digital Curation and Preservation Framework: Outline, last revised September 2014, http://www.dpworkshop.org/workshops/management-tools/policy-framework/model-document.

2.  The pdf version and the web version are available online: University of Minnesota Libraries, "Digital Preservation Framework," last updated January 2014, https://www.lib.umn.edu/dp/digital-preservation-framework.

3.  Read about sustainability factors used by the Library of Congress's Digital Formats website: Library of Congress, "Sustainability Factors," Sustainability of Digital Formats, Planning for Library of Congress Collections, accessed March 15, 2016, http://www.digitalpreservation.gov/formats/sustain/sustain.shtml.

4.  Library of Congress, "Recommended Formats Statement, 2016–2017," accessed August 7, 2016, http://www.loc.gov/preservation/resources/rfs/RFS%202016-2017.pdf.

5.  For environmental storage conditions for magnetic tape, CD-ROM, and DVD, see Ross Harvey, *Preserving Digital Materials* (Berlin: Walter de Gruyter, 2005), 125–26.

6.  Note that replication is not the same as backup. In a typical storage backup system, a copy of the data is replicated at multiple locations. When a change is made to one copy, that change gets mirrored to the other locations according to the backup schedule (e.g., nightly). Therefore, if one copy is compromised, perhaps through bitrot deterioration, then all copies will be replaced with this corrupt version.

7.  Such as those found in the BitCurator Environment (BitCurator homepage, accessed

March 15, 2016, http://www.bitcurator.net). Some more examples are presented in this keynote address by the creator of BitCurator: Christopher A. Lee, "Digital Forensics Meets the Archivist (and They Seem to Like Each Other)," *Provenance, Journal of the Society of Georgia Archivists* 30, no. 1 (2012): 2, http://digitalcommons.kennesaw.edu/provenance/vol30/iss1/2.

8. Dryad Digital Repository homepage, last modified November 19, 2015, https://data-dryad.org.

9. Available freely online: Digital Preservation Coalition, *Digital Preservation Handbook*, 2nd ed. (Digital Preservation Coalition, 2015), http://www.dpconline.org/advice/preservationhandbook.

10. For example, a roundup of digital preservation projects for data in the United Kingdom was published in a blog post: Jenny Mitcham, "Addressing Digital Preservation Challenges through Research Data Spring," *Digital Archiving at the University of York* (blog). December 8, 2015, http://digital-archiving.blogspot.com/2015/12/the-research-data-spring-projects.html.

11. Carol Kussmann, "Quick Reference Guide for Tools to Manage and Protect Your Digital Content," University of Minnesota Libraries, accessed March 15, 2016, https://drive.google.com/a/umn.edu/file/d/0B8MvBJV_5_s5MlpBNUNTNlZvemM/view. Detailed guides for additional preservation tools are also available from University of Minnesota Libraries, "Digital Preservation, Guides," accessed July 9, 2016, https://www.lib.umn.edu/dp/guides.

12. The Preserving Digital Objects with Restricted Resources (POWRR) project team researched scalable digital preservation (DP) solutions for small and mid-sized institutions. (Preserving Digital Objects with Restricted Resources [POWRR] homepage, accessed March 15, 2016, http://digitalpowrr.niu.edu). The project is described in Amanda Kay Rinehart, Patrice-Andre Prud'homme, and Andrew Reid Huot, "Overwhelmed to Action: Digital Preservation Challenges at the Under-resourced Institution," *OCLC Systems and Services* , no. 1 (2014): 28–42, http://digitalpowrr.niu.edu/wp-content/uploads/2014/05/Overwhelmed-to-action.rinehart_prudhomme_huot_2014.pdf, and in the final report, Jaime Schumacher, *Digital POWRR—Preserving Digital Objects with Restricted Resources: A Final Report to the Institute of Museum and Library Services,* February 2015, http://hdl.handle.net/10843/13678.

13. Harvey, *Preserving Digital Materials.*

14. Tim Murray, Desiree Alexander, Oya Y. Rieger, Liz Muller, Dianne Dietrich, Michelle Paolillo, Madeleine Casad, and Jason Kovari, *Preserving and Emulating Digital Art Objects*, white paper submitted to the National Endowment for the Humanities (Ithaca, NY: Cornell University Library, November 2015), http://hdl.handle.net/1813/41368.

15. Harvey, *Preserving Digital Materials*, 132.

16. Larry L. Bumpass, "What's Happening to the Family? Interactions between Demographic and Institutional Change," *Demography* 27, no. 4 (1990): 483–98.

17. James Sweet, Larry Bumpass, and Vaughn Call, *The Design and Content of the National Survey of Families and Households*, NSHF Working Paper no. 1 (Madison, WI: Center for Demography and Ecology, 1988), http://www.ssc.wisc.edu/cde/nsfhwp/nsfh1.pdf.

18. Ibid.

19. Elaine Trull and Lisa Famularo, "Appendix N: ISR Field Report," *National Survey of Families and Households Wave 2 Field Report* (Philadelphia: Institute for Survey Research, 1996), ftp://elaine.ssc.wisc.edu/pub/nsfh/cmapp_n.001.

20. Debra Wright, *National Survey of Families and Households Wave 3 Field Report* (Madison: University of Wisconsin Survey Center, July 15, 2003), http://www.ssc.wisc.edu/nsfh/wave3/fieldreport.doc.
21. According to an October 26, 2015 search (http://www.icpsr.umich.edu/icpsrweb/ICPSR/biblio/series/00193/resources?sortBy=1) in the Inter-university Consortium for Political and Social Research (ICPSR). Data-Related Literature Database, http://www.icpsr.umich.edu/icpsrweb/ICPSR/citations/index.jsp.
22. Inter-university Consortium for Political and Social Research (ICPSR), *Guide to Social Science Data Preparation and Archiving*, 5th ed. (Ann Arbor, MI: ICPSR, 2012), http://www.icpsr.umich.edu/files/ICPSR/access/dataprep.pdf.
23. DDI Alliance, "DDI Codebook 2.1 Specification," accessed October 29, 2015, http://www.ddialliance.org/Specification/DDI-Codebook/2.1/.
24. US Bureau of the Census, "Geographic Terms and Concepts: Census Tract," accessed February 5, 2016, http://www.census.gov/geo/reference/gtc/gtc_ct.html.

# Bibliography

BitCurator homepage. Accessed March 15, 2016. http://www.bitcurator.net.

Bumpass, Larry L. "What's Happening to the Family? Interactions between Demographic and Institutional Change." *Demography* 27, no. 4 (1990): 483–98.

Colectica homepage. Accessed October 29, 2015. http://www.colectica.com/.

DDI Alliance. "DDI Codebook 2.1 Specification." Accessed October 29, 2015. http://www.ddialliance.org/Specification/DDI-Codebook/2.1/.

Digital Preservation Coalition. *Digital Preservation Handbook,* 2nd ed. Digital Preservation Coalition, 2015. http://www.dpconline.org/advice/preservationhandbook.

Dryad Digital Repository homepage. Last modified November 19, 2015. https://datadryad.org.

Harvey, Ross. "Environmental Storage Conditions for Magnetic Tape, CD-ROM, and DVD." In *Preserving Digital Materials*, 125–6. Berlin: Walter de Gruyter, 2005.

Inter-university Consortium for Political and Social Research (ICPSR). Data-Related Literature Database. Accessed October 26, 2015. http://www.icpsr.umich.edu/icpsrweb/ICPSR/citations/index.jsp.

———. *Guide to Social Science Data Preparation and Archiving: Best Practice throughout the Data Life Cycle*, 5th edition. Ann Arbor, MI: ICPSR, 2012. http://www.icpsr.umich.edu/files/ICPSR/access/dataprep.pdf.

Kussmann, Carol. "Quick Reference Guide for Tools to Manage and Protect Your Digital Content." University of Minnesota Libraries. Accessed March 15, 2016. https://drive.google.com/a/umn.edu/file/d/0B8MvBJV_5_s5MlpBNUNTNlZvemM/view.

Lee, Christopher A. "Digital Forensics Meets the Archivist (and They Seem to Like Each Other)." *Provenance, Journal of the Society of Georgia Archivists* 30, no. 1 (2012): 2. http://digitalcommons.kennesaw.edu/provenance/vol30/iss1/2.

Library of Congress. "Recommended Formats Statement, 2016–2017." Accessed August 7, 2016. http://www.loc.gov/preservation/resources/rfs/RFS%202016-2017.pdf.

———. "Sustainability Factors." Sustainability of Digital Formats, Planning for Library of Congress Collections. Accessed March 15, 2016. http://www.digitalpreservation.gov/formats/sustain/sustain.shtml.

McGovern, Nancy. "Digital Preservation Management Model Document." *Version 3.0, Digital Curation and Preservation Framework: Outline.* Last revised September 2014. http://www.dpworkshop.org/workshops/management-tools/policy-framework/model-document.

Metadata Technology North America. "SledgeHammer." Accessed October 29, 2015. http://www.mtna.us/?page_id=1232.

Mitcham, Jenny. "Addressing Digital Preservation Challenges through Research Data Spring." *Digital Archiving at the University of York* (blog). December 8, 2015. http://digital-archiving.blogspot.com/2015/12/the-research-data-spring-projects.html.

Murray, Tim, Desiree Alexander, Oya Y. Rieger, Liz Muller, Dianne Dietrich, Michelle Paolillo, Madeleine Casad, and Jason Kovari. *Preserving and Emulating Digital Art Objects.* White paper submitted to the National Endowment for the Humanities. Ithaca, NY: Cornell University Library, November 2015. http://hdl.handle.net/1813/41368.

National Archives. "The Technical Registry: PRONOM." Accessed March 15, 2016. https://www.nationalarchives.gov.uk/PRONOM/Default.aspx.

Noonan, Daniel W. "Digital Preservation Policy Framework: A Case Study." *Educause Review.* July 28, 2014. http://er.educause.edu/articles/2014/7/digital-preservation-policy-framework-a-case-study.

Norsk Senter for Forskningsdata. "Nesstar Publisher." Accessed October 20, 2015. http://nesstar.com/software/publisher.html.

Preserving Digital Objects with Restricted Resources (POWRR) homepage. Accessed March 15, 2016. http://digitalpowrr.niu.edu.

Rinehart, Amanda Kay, Patrice-Andre Prud'homme, and Andrew Reid Huot. "Overwhelmed to Action: Digital Preservation Challenges at the Under-resourced Institution." *OCLC Systems and Services,* no. 1 (2014): 28–42. http://digitalpowrr.niu.edu/wp-content/uploads/2014/05/Overwhelmed-to-action.rinehart_prudhomme_huot_2014.pdf.

Schumacher, Jaime. *Digital POWRR—Preserving Digital Objects with Restricted Resources: A Final Report to the Institute of Museum and Library Services.* February 2015. http://hdl.handle.net/10843/13678.

SDA: Survey Documentation and Analysis homepage. Accessed October 29, 2015. http://sda.berkeley.edu/.

Sweet, James, Larry Bumpass, and Vaughn Call. *The Design and Content of the National Survey of Families and Households.* NSHF Working Paper no. 1. Madison, WI: Center for Demography and Ecology, 1988. http://www.ssc.wisc.edu/cde/nsfhwp/nsfh1.pdf.

Trull, Elaine, and Lisa Famularo. "Appendix N: ISR Field Report." *National Survey of Families and Households Wave 2 Field Report.* Philadelphia: Institute for Survey Research, 1996. ftp://elaine.ssc.wisc.edu/pub/nsfh/cmapp_n.001.

University of Minnesota Libraries. "Digital Preservation Framework." Last updated January 2014. https://www.lib.umn.edu/dp/digital-preservation-framework.

———. "Digital Preservation, Guides." Accessed July 9, 2016. https://www.lib.umn.edu/dp/guides.

University of Wisconsin Madison. National Survey of Families and Households confidentiality agreement. Accessed February 5, 2016. http://www.ssc.wisc.edu/nsfh/624649EB.pdf.

US Bureau of the Census. "Geographic Terms and Concepts: Census Tract." Accessed February 5, 2016. http://www.census.gov/geo/reference/gtc/gtc_ct.html.

Wright, Debra. *National Survey of Families and Households Wave 3 Field Report.* Madison: University of Wisconsin Survey Center, July 15, 2003. http://www.ssc.wisc.edu/nsfh/wave3/fieldreport.doc.

# Reuse

All of the valuable time and energy involved in data curation is in anticipation that the data will be useful beyond its original purpose. Therefore, in one respect, reuse is the ultimate end goal of data curation. The actions taken in this step will aid in demonstrating the value or impact of data reuse. This demonstration has several goals. First, the awareness of how used or impactful a data set has become can be a positive benefit that rewards researchers for their efforts to deposit and publish their data. Second, by monitoring the challenges encountered of data reusers, we can detect and possibly resolve any data quality issues post-ingest. Third, by providing ongoing services for the data as long as needed, your data repository can monitor the value of the data and make ongoing determinations for retention. The final actions for the data curation life cycle include reappraisal and disposal when the data ceases to be useful.

||||||||||||||||||||||||||||||||||||||||||||||||||||||||||||||||||||||||||||||||||||||||||||||||||||||||||||||||||||||||

Cynthia Hudson Vitale explores how this far end of the spectrum is emerging and compares thirteen linked data repositories, their underlying missions, and their technical approaches to federating data search and discovery in *Curating Research Data, Volume One*, chapter 11, "The Current State of Linked Data Repositories: A Comparative Analysis."

||||||||||||||||||||||||||||||||||||||||||||||||||||||||||||||||||||||||||||||||||||||||||||||||||||||||||||||||||||||||

# 8.1 Monitor Data Reuse

Use indicators (e.g., downloads, citations, etc.) tracked for a each data set may help your repository determine their value over time as well as provide the data author with a tool to measure the impact of their data-sharing efforts. Traditional impact measures (such as article citation counts) and altmetrics (such as the number of Tweets or Mendeley Reads an article receives) can also be used to track the individual impact of data.[1] But these assessment metrics are not without their flaws, as highlighted in the June 17, 2010 *Nature* issue on research assessment.[2]

Attention (traditional or alt) to a particular data set may represent quality and reuse, or as Madlock-Brown and Eichmann have shown, it might represent concerns, such as using it as an example to point out quality issues, thus resulting in a "negative citation."[3] Just as some articles have been shown to attract more citations even after the article was retracted, it is possible that these assessment issues will similarly impact data use metrics.[4]

# Impact Measures for Tracking Data Reuse

Caveats aside, monitoring, tracking, and displaying a variety of data reuse indicators for a data set in your repository is a value-add service that will support the needs of authors and end users, as well as aid in the assessment of the repository itself. Use indicators such as data set citations, file downloads, page views, requests for access, and other factors might indicate the value of data overtime and influence decisions about retention and deselection.

## Data Citations

The number of citations to a data set is a key traditional metric, yet a difficult one to track. One reason why is that the practice of citing data as a scholarly object in the bibliography is not yet common practice across all disciplines, and Brase and colleagues rightly argued that data citations must be elevated out of the methods section or literature review and hold equal status as what they described as a "first-class object for bibliographic purposes" similar to any other cited object (article, book, etc.).[5] Data citation best practices are available, and the FORCE11 project and the W3C provide good reference points.[6] For example Ball and Duke suggested that a data citation should include all the relevant information about who created the data (the authors), the location (the publisher name and access URL), and any uniquely identifying information (the title, release date, and granularity information that might point to a specific aspect or subset of the data).[7] Ideally the data citation should point to a stable location for access, such as a DOI. To help track the citations to data, indexes such as the Thomson Reuters Data Citation Index and INSPIRE, are counting formal references to data sets housed in their databases.[8] Tools like these will make it easier for data repositories to link data sets to publications that reference the data, thus creating a scholarly chain of record indicating data reuse.

The next case study by Christine Mayo illustrates how one repository is helping its reusers make good citation choices in order to best measure the long-term impact of the data.

# Facilitating Good Data Citation Practice

*Christine Mayo**

In recent years, a coalition of influential organizations has recommended that data not only be formally cited when reused in the scholarly literature, but that data citations be structurally similar to citations for written works.[9] Dryad, a curated general-purpose repository of data underlying scientific publications, asks users to cite both the publication and the data package should they reuse the data in new work. To encourage that practice, both types of citations are displayed prominently on every data package's landing page.

Dryad includes the following elements in a data citation: author(s), publication date, title, publisher of the data package, and persistent identifier (in this case, a DOI). For a given data package, the publication and data citations tend to be quite similar, since all data packages are closely linked to a specific publication by design. While the author list is identical by default, it may be modified at submission since the contributors to the data package can differ. Authors may be added or subtracted from the publication author list, and order may be rearranged, in order to appropriately credit those who contributed, as illustrated by the following example:

Publication:

> Chave J, Coomes DA, Jansen S, Lewis SL, Swenson NG, Zanne AE (2009) Towards a worldwide wood economics spectrum. Ecology Letters 12(4): 351-366. http://doi.org/10.1111/j.1461-0248.2009.01285.x.

Data package:

> Zanne AE, Lopez-Gonzalez G, Coomes DA, Ilic J, Jansen S, Lewis SL, Miller RB, Swenson NG, Wiemann MC, Chave J (2009) Data from: Towards a worldwide wood economics spectrum. Dryad Digital Repository. http://doi.org/10.5061/dryad.234.

Furthermore, different files within the same data package may list different authors, a feature that is most commonly used to distinguish authors of code and scripts from those who collected data. Fewer than 10 percent of authors take advantage of these features, which are presented when the author fills out descriptive metadata for their data package and data files during the submission process.

Dryad uses DataCite Digital Object Identifiers (DOIs), registered through the California Digital Library EZID service, as persistent identifiers. A base DOI is "minted," or created, for a given data package. The component files in that data package share the same base DOI, followed by the sequence of the file within the package. For example, http://doi.org/10.5061/dryad/234/2 would be the second file in the data package from the above example, which has base DOI http://doi.org/10.5061/dryad/234. While data file DOIs enable a user to provide persistent links to individual files, only the data package DOI is intended to be used as part of the formal citation.

In addition, the citation should be specific to a given version of the data package. Versions may be created by Dryad curators at author request, for example, to add a corrected file after publication. As a matter of repository trustworthiness and transparency, any changes made to files after a data package has been published are done in the form of a new version. If any file in the data package is versioned, the data package as a whole is also versioned. To enable persistent identification, Dryad mints a unique DOI for each file version and each data package version. For example, http://doi.org/10.5061/dryad/1234.2 refers to the second version of the data package discussed above. Each DOI is registered with metadata that specifies the relation between the data package and its component data files, as well as the relationship among versions. Use of the original base DOI will lead users to the landing page for the most recent version of the data package, and this page contains links to all previous versions.

With these conventions, Dryad aims to make it easy for those who reuse data to formulate a data citation that follows recommended practice, and for readers to unambiguously identify the specific version of data used in a given study.

## Altmetrics for Data

There are several alternatives to formal citation in which the impact of data might be measured such as:

- how often individuals share the data set URL via social media tools (e.g., Twitter, Mendeley, or Facebook),
- how often the page is visited (e.g., page views), or
- how many times the files are downloaded (download tracking).

Data repositories, either natively or using add-ons built for displaying the impact of a data set, can track these altmetrics and communicate them to authors and potential users. Konkiel and Scherer discussed the built-in metrics available in three repository platforms (Digital Commons, DSpace, and EPrints) and concluded that these indicators "can reflect both scholarly and popular impact, show readership, reflect an institution's output, justify tenure and promotion and indicate direction for collection management."[10] Several altmetric-tracking techniques are discussed below.

*Download Tracking.* The number of times a file is downloaded from a repository can be a powerful indicator of interest and impact. Download counts for data sets can demonstrate use, or more accurately, the intent to use. Unfortunately, download statistics for data files will be subject to the same issues that article-based repositories face—how to determine when a download is legitimate. Hackers, search engine bots, and mass downloads can easily raise the download count of a particular item in a digital repository. Some repositories, like bepress, have built-in statistics that attempt to filter out nefarious download counts for items.[11] Other repositories have implemented tools like Google Analytics to make decisions about how they are tracking this impact indicator. Fortunately the COUNTER Code of Practice provides a standard for tracking downloads that can also be applied to data repositories.[12] New projects, such as 2016 Jisc project IRUSdataUK and the Research Dataset-Level Metrics (DLM) interest group of CASRAI, are also developing ways to increase the reliability of data download metrics.[13]

*Page Views.* How often a data set record, or page, is visited and the circumstances related to it (e.g., referring source, search terms used, country of origin, timestamp, etc.) can demonstrate reusability interest in a data set. A greater level of sophistication of page views may be needed in a data repository architecture that facilitates browser-level manipulation of the data set (e.g., DataVerse allows users to interact with tabular data without first needing to download the files. See more in *Step 6*: Access). In this sense, how users interact with the data may be captured and new insights gained from this monitoring.

*Altmetric Services.* Beyond built-in repository software features for tracking downloads and page views, Ball and Duke described several external services that could be harnessed for measuring research data impact:[14]

- Lagotto (http://www.lagotto.io) is the open-source software used by PLOS journals to track article-level altmetrics and can be adapted for data repositories. Related to this is the Making Data Count Project (http://mdc.lagotto.io), which brings together PLOS, Dataone, and the CDL to better understand how data can fit into the article-centric landscape of citation metrics.
- PlumX (https://plu.mx) is a pay-to-use service by PlumAnalytics that captures altmetrics for data sets, including Mendeley.com saves, blog mentions, and Github.com references.
- Altmetric (https://www.altmetric.com) is a free service for researchers to bring together metrics from a variety of sources, similar to PlumX. Institutions can pay to use this tool in their repository.

- Impactstory (https://impactstory.org) is a tool aimed at the individual researcher (~$60/year) and includes statistics for data from sources such as such as Figshare.com and Github.com.
- Mendeley Data (https://data.mendeley.com) and figShare (https://figshare.com) are data repositories that do a good job at tracking data set downloads and views in ways that increase the value-proposition for researchers to share their data.
- Also of note are ResearchGate, Google Scholar, and Microsoft Academic Search, which are used for tracking data publications (e.g., *Scientific Data*), but their focus is primarily on research articles.

*Requests for Access.* For restricted-use data, the number of times that access to data is requested may also indicate impact. Placing data behind access barriers is sometimes necessary (e.g., legal restrictions on the data content to project privacy). However, it is still unclear if access restrictions may deter data reuse. Repositories that do require access credentials may be in a better position to follow up with the user to determine if they successfully reused the data. The next case study by Arun Mathur, Johanna Davidson Bleckman, and Jared Lyle illustrates how one repository is helping its reusers make good citation choices in order to best measure long-term impact of the data.

# Reuse of Restricted-Use Research Data

*Arun Mathur, Johanna Davidson Bleckman, and Jared Lyle**

As described in the *Step 1* case study on page 24, the Inter-university Consortium for Political and Social Research (ICPSR) makes restricted-use data available through three highly secure, highly controlled data access mechanisms: ICPSR's virtual data enclave, ICPSR's physical enclave, or using the researcher's approved computing environment with appropriate precautions taken.

Interested parties may apply for restricted-use data electronically via an online request system, which enables ICPSR user support staff to manage individual collection's data use agreements with users.[15] This process includes verifying initial requests (including ensuring system security), transmitting data, tracking data use, and terminating access.

# VERIFYING INITIAL REQUESTS

After researchers apply for data access through an online application system, ICPSR staff review the application submission. This includes ensuring that

- The credentials of applicants match their online identities in institutional directories
- All sections of the application have been completed and the application has been signed by an authorized institutional representative
- For studies that require it, IRB review documentation for the project has been submitted
- The data is a good fit for their research plan; for example, the study is plausible

# ENSURING SYSTEM SECURITY

One additional, and important, point of verification for initial access requests involves reviewing the users' security plans for accessing the data. ICPSR provides security plan templates, through which applicants attest that

- Work with the data can be completed only in a secure office by authorized users
- Users may not discuss the restricted-use data in nonsecure or public locations
- Under no circumstances can any unauthorized person be allowed to access or view the restricted-use data, including through windows or doors
- The computer on which the data is viewed must be password-protected and locked if the user leaves, even momentarily
- The computer on which the data is viewed is physically disconnected from the Internet and protected against malware
- Restricted data cannot be copied or duplicated; this includes not taking screenshots or handwritten notes
- If required, users of the virtual and physical enclaves will submit all statistical outputs and results from the restricted-use data to ICPSR for a disclosure review prior to sharing outputs with unauthorized persons
- Users may disseminate only aggregated (i.e., nonconfidential) information from the restricted-use data to anyone not named in the research plan

# TRANSMITTING DATA

Once the application is reviewed and all of the criteria are met, the data is then distributed to the user through one of the restricted-use data access mechanisms: via the virtual data enclave (VDE), via the physical enclave, or through a one-time secure download to a researcher's secure environment.

## VIRTUAL DATA ENCLAVE (VDE)

A virtual machine is launched from the researcher's local desktop, but the software and data files are operated on ICPSR's server, similar to remotely logging into another physical computer. The virtual machine is isolated from the user's physical desktop computer, restricting the user from downloading files or parts of files to their physical computer. The virtual machine also restricts external access, preventing users from e-mailing, copying, or otherwise moving files outside of the secure environment, either accidentally or intentionally. Available options of the VDE include file sharing among project team members and vetting of output for disclosure risk.

## PHYSICAL ENCLAVE

Data is accessible for analysis on-site at the ICPSR building in Ann Arbor, Michigan, in a secure, monitored room. This data is of the highest sensitivity and may contain personal information collected from, for example, victims of violence. When using the enclave, investigators must use non-networked computers provided by ICPSR. The computer cannot send e-mail or access the Internet, and the external media ports (e.g., USB) are disabled. An ICPSR staff member is present at all times when a researcher is using the enclave. The monitor inspects and approves all material brought in or taken out of the enclave, and all output (notes and other material) must be submitted for disclosure review before leaving the physical enclave.

## RESEARCHER'S SECURE ENVIRONMENT

Data is provided to the researcher by one-time secure download or by encrypted compact disk. The data must be stored and used only in the computing environment agreed to in the researcher's approved data security plan. The lead researcher is responsible for ensuring that all research team members comply with the security plan and terms of the particular collection's data use agreement. As a security precaution, ICPSR makes each data file unique to the researcher in order to prevent unauthorized dissemination.

# TRACKING AND TERMINATING DATA ACCESS

Restricted-use data users accessing data through the VDE or their secure environment are tracked by the online application system. VDE licenses are for one year, with the possibility of renewal. If access is about to expire, the system sends an e-mail notifying users that they may renew access by uploading an annual report and by obtaining IRB approval for an extension, or that they must close out the access agreement.

Upon the end date, VDE remote access is turned off and the user's log-in credentials no longer work. User files are retained for one year to preserve an opportunity for the user to seamlessly renew at a later time. For physical enclave users, work is limited to on-site visits. As mentioned above, usage is closely monitored in person.

Researchers with access via their secure local environment must use a secure erasure program to wipe restricted-use data files and any files containing confidential content from their computer. If the data was transmitted on encrypted compact disk, they must securely destroy the media. Finally, researchers must send ICPSR a signed and notarized affidavit of destruction to attest that all files with confidential data have been destroyed.

# SUMMARY

Restricted-use data is available at ICPSR through highly secure, highly controlled data access mechanisms, including a virtual data enclave and a physical enclave. Similar systems are used at other repositories, such as the National Opinion Research Center (NORC) Data Enclave housed at the University of Chicago.[16] Key elements of a request access system include verifying initial requests (including ensuring system security), transmitting data, tracking data users, and verifying end of access.

# 8.2 Collect Feedback about Data Reuse and Quality Issues

When data is reused, new information is generated about the quality, usefulness, and challenges inherent to the data. Consider incorporating post-ingest review techniques into your repository and curation services that allow others, the general public or subject matter experts, to provide feedback on the data. This process may provide additional post-ingest quality control or aid in the presentation or design of your digital repository.

For example, an informal review mechanism might request input from users in order to provide quality assurances for data housed in your repository. Imagine a digital badge for data sets that have been certified "Successfully Reused" by another researcher. Another possibility is to allow users to recommend changes to the data set. Perhaps a qualified user might be in a good position to upload a "cleaned" version of the data set, based on their efforts to understand and reuse the files. This derivative of the data set might closely resemble the original, but with additional modifications to the documentation and notations when errors are discovered that might facilitate the next user's experience. Finally, a rating system could be put into place in your repository that allows potential future users of the data to review previous users comments. Similar to 5-star rating tools in Amazon.com or Google Play, this sort of simple review system would aid in understanding how past users either approved or disapproved of the quality of the data, supplementing the record and providing additional context.

## Facilitate the Peer Review of Data

A more formal model of peer review might be implemented by the repository at the point of ingest. Lawrence and colleagues described the function of the data peer review procedure, saying that it "must ensure that all metadata is as complete as possible, but it must also address other qualities expected of Publication class material, such as the data's internal self-consistency, the merit of the algorithms used, the data importance, and its potential impact."[17] However they went on to point out that "[Peer review] of scientific quality must be done by domain experts, and hence is out of scope for the data archive staff, though they may be able to make judgments about the dataset's technical quality (suitability of format, completeness of metadata etc.)."[18] Co-author Sarah Callahan, in her Wiley blog *Exchanges*, recommended several considerations to take (as cited by Murphy) "by whoever is commissioning the review—depending on a number of variables. These include: what use the data are to be put to, and what aspects need to be checked (e.g. technical, scientific or accessibility issues). This in turn influences who should be approached to provide the review, and then what questions they should be encouraged to ask of the dataset."[19] There are a growing number of journals that are including data as part of the peer review process for scholarly articles and many "data journals" are considering peer-review of the data as part of the publication process (e.g., *Nature's Scientific Data* and the *Biodiversity Data Journal*).[20] The Peer Review for Publication and Accreditation of Research Data in the Earth Sciences (PREPARDE) project looked at this issue in detail, and its project report by Meyernik and colleagues found that

> Peer review can increase trust in scientific data and results and enable datasets to be evaluated and certified for quality. Data

assessment processes and software, however, are often very specific to data types, experimental designs, and systems. In addition, scientists, data managers, and software engineers all have different expertise applicable to data peer review. Few reviewers would be qualified to review all aspects of a dataset.[21]

Lawrence and colleagues offered a helpful data review checklist that might be adapted by data repositories seeking external peer-review support for their data holdings.[22]

## Data Review in Action

The next case by Limor Peer illustrates one archive's ground-breaking efforts to implement a peer review process for data.

# Enabling Scientific Reproducibility with Data Curation and Code Review

*Limor Peer*[*]

Much of science these days is computational and involves both data and code. For example, a recent survey found that about 70 percent of UK researchers say they would not be able to do their research without software.[23] Most researchers rely on data—broadly defined here—and increasingly on code for their research. Computing, by virtue of its digital medium, makes it possible for researchers to share their data and code. That is very good news for science because it allows research results to be reviewed, verified, and reproduced by others.[24]

While sharing data and code is technically feasible, it is not so simple.[25] Notwithstanding technical conditions, cultural and behavioral barriers, and legal and ethical constraints, there are questions about how to share data and code so that they are interpretable and usable in the long term. When we created the Institution for Social and Policy Studies (ISPS) Data Archive at Yale University in 2010, we decided to make usability a high priority. Following the footsteps of established social science data archives such as the Inter-university Consortium for Political and Social Science (ICPSR) and the UK Data Archive (UKDA), we have implemented a data curation workflow that aims to ensure that data is well documented and usable. In addition, we subject all code files to a review process intended to ensure that the code executes properly* and that, in the context of a research project, it interacts with input data as reported by the researcher; that is, that the analysis can be reproduced. By applying rigorous data curation and code review practices, we aim to release files that have passed the first test of reproducibility and that will remain usable for the long term.

The ISPS Data Archive (http://isps.yale.edu/research/data) is a digital repository for research produced by scholars affiliated with ISPS, with special focus on experimental design and methods. Associated data is primarily quantitative and gathered from a combination of administrative records, surveys, and observations. The archive was launched in September 2010 as a pilot at Yale. At present it contains nearly 1,400 files, associated with about 80 studies, and is 10 GB in size. The archive provides free and public access to research materials and accepts content for distribution only under a Creative Commons license. The archive is managed by a full-time professional with knowledge of the specific research domain, and graduate student research assistants handle most of the data curation.

The data held in the archive is intended for scholars to use for research and educational purposes. Scholars may examine data files, scrutinize data transformations and analysis procedures, perform replication and meta-analysis, and otherwise benefit and learn from the transparent presentation of the particular study's research process. This deep learning can serve as a stepping stone for additional research and analyses and, as the collection grows, for more interactive reuse. Achieving these goals hinges on the accessibility and long-term usability of the archive's content.

For our purposes, we think of reproducibility as the ability of "another researcher using the same methods ...to reach the same results."[26] Reproducibility presents data sharing (and preservation) with a concrete purpose, as well as prescribes particular steps for the data curation and code review. Put another way, data curation and code review enable accessibility and usability, which pave the way for reproducibility (figure 8.1).

At the ISPS Data Archive we subject all deposits to rigorous appraisal.[27] To be considered for inclusion in the archive, a study must be conducted with support, financial or otherwise, from ISPS. Many studies involve field experiments in the social sciences. Deposits are organized by study and include much of the research output—data, metadata, statistical code, codebooks, research materials, and description files—from each study. Upon deposit, study-level and file-level

---

* The ISPS Data Archive currently captures basic metadata for code files (i.e., file name, file size, file format, file version, PID) and is consulting standards as they evolve. The archive does not currently archive versions of the software but is in conversations with the library's preservation department about possible solutions.

metadata is collected and a link to the published article is established. When deposits are made before an article has been published, the archive affords researchers quality review prepublication, as well as an option for meeting some journals' data-sharing requirements.

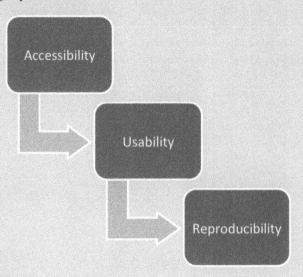

**FIGURE 8.1**
Accessibility, usability, and reproducibility.

Research assistants access files from a secure storage location following file check-in and -out procedures and currently conduct their work on local machines loaded with statistical software. Quality checks are conducted throughout the process via regular communication among archive staff. All changes made to the files are documented. With respect to data files, curation includes confirming all variables and values are labeled, standardizing missing values, creating and augmenting documentation, and assessing and minimizing disclosure risk by applying techniques such as recoding, masking, or removal of variables, and assigning persistent links. The review of code files—statistical and other programming scripts—includes verifying that the code executes and that the published scientific results can be reproduced with the given code and data. The data and code review processes include an assessment of the quality of documentation and contextual information necessary for long-term usability (for example, a codebook, a readme file, a commented code). In cases where these are found lacking or insufficient, the archive works with researchers on remedial actions. All files formats are normalized (including migrating software-specific data files to flat file formats such as ASCII, text, or comma delimited, and rewriting code written using licensed statistical software such as SPSS to open-source statistical languages such as R). All files are assigned a unique identifier (handle), and files sets have citation information.

In 2014, ISPS joined Innovations for Poverty Action (IPA), a nonprofit network of researchers conducting field experiments in economics and based in New Haven, Connecticut, to develop curation software to formalize and automate data curation and code review.[28] The new tool is modular and open-source to account for the changing needs of an archive such as encountering new research methods, moving to new dissemination platforms, and incorporating new preservation solutions. It leverages the DDI Lifecycle* for machine-readable metadata production at the study level, the file level, and the variable level and focuses on key curation and review tasks designed to ensure usability, and therefore, reproducibility mentioned above (see figures 8.2 and 8.3).†

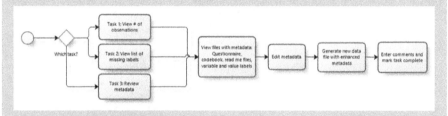

**FIGURE 8.2**
Curation tasks 1–3.

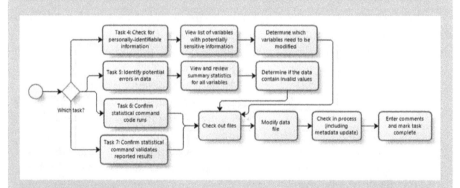

**FIGURE 8.3**
Curation tasks 4–7.

---

* Also known as DDI 3.2, available at http://www.ddialliance.org/Specification/DDI-Life-cycle.

† See software documentation, available at http://docs.colectica.com/curation.

We think that our approach, and specifically the new curation tool, can support sharing of quality data by providing a layer of "mediation" to help ensure that deposits meet certain accessibility and usability standards. Meeting these standards ultimately contributes to more reproducible science. It is in the interest of the scientific community that data curation and code review practices become the norm throughout the research life cycle.

# 8.3 Provide Ongoing Support as Long as Necessary

Data has been shown to be useful long after its original intended purpose. New curation needs will arise over the life span of the data that your repository houses: some foreseeable (such as new versions to the data) and some not. It is possible that for many types of data, their ideal digital curation and retention period will be *indefinite*. For example, an astronomical image captured to a glass plate in the 1880s represents data that can never be observed again.[29] The same will be true for a sophisticated space telescope image taken today, and one to be taken 100 years from now. The medium, resolution, and quality of that image may advance, but the uniqueness of the data stays constant. In the reuse step, it is important to consider the possible versioning challenges that data may pose. For example, will the data be replaced by new "better" data? Will you retain every version of the data or only the newest? How will your service respond to questions if the original version is no longer available? How will access to the data versions indicate long-term value and influence retention? Your repository should provide services that meet the evolving needs of the data over the anticipated life or usefulness of the data.

What happens to the data in the long term? A data rescue effort, and the challenges encountered, is addressed in *Curating Research Data, Volume One*, chapter 12, "Curation of Scientific Data at Risk of Loss: Data Rescue and Dissemination" by Robert R. Downs and Robert S. Chen.

Tools like Git (https://git-scm.com) and the Open Science Framework (http://osf.io) do a good job at tracking the evolution of revisions over time, and one project called DataHub (https://datahub.io) attempts to improve on this model by using more efficient compression methods for tracking version history.[30] Similarly, your repository might consider ways to link the version history of a data set together via metadata relationships. For example, Dataverse software (starting with 4.0) allows users to not only track the versions of their data in small release (e.g., from version 1.1 to version 1.2) and large releases (e.g., from version 1.2 to version 2.0), but it also allows users to compare data versions to see their differences.[31] Finally consider how the version history of the data set will be expressed through the persistent identifier. The DataCite metadata schema, for example, allows for version history to be captured in the metadata using the `IsNewVersionOf` and `IsPreviousVersionOf` properties.[32] And tracking these versions at the DOI level can also be an important step. For example, see Mayo's case study on how Dryad versions their DOIs (presented earlier in this *Step 8*).

# 8.4 Cease Data Curation

A final act of data curation will be to plan for when and how you will ultimately terminate access to the data. Yet, as persistence is one of the key tenets of the Force 11 data citation principles, retaining the metadata that the data once existed is key. The persistence principle states, "Unique identifiers, and metadata describing the data, and its disposition, should persist—even beyond the lifespan of the data they describe."[33] In light of this, your repository should consider using tombstones to retain the metadata of the data set and allow for a permanent home for the identifier to resolve. This tombstone should also detail the circumstances of the data's removal and the date it was deselected from your repository.

Reuse metrics might aid in your decision-making process for data deselection. For example, the University of Michigan's Deep Blue Data Repository states that after ten years the data will be reviewed by the repository staff to "determine if a dataset should be retained and will be subject to further, periodic, reviews thereafter."[34] Based on the metrics of reuse (e.g., how often was the data downloaded, cited, etc.) and the policies for data retention (institutional, legal, contractual), curators must decide if and when data in your repository should be withdrawn. Other factors to consider are whether the data has been replaced or has become obsolete.

|||||||||||||||||||||||||||||||||||||||||||||||||||||||||||||||||||||||||||||||||||||||||||||||||||||||||||||||||||||||||||||||||||||||||

> *Curating Research Data, Volume One*, chapter 10, "Open Exit: Reaching the End of the Data Life Cycle," by Andrea Ogier, Natsuko Nicholls, and Ryan Speer, makes the case that deselection decisions for data must take place across the data life cycle.

|||||||||||||||||||||||||||||||||||||||||||||||||||||||||||||||||||||||||||||||||||||||||||||||||||||||||||||||||||||||||||||||||||||||||

Finally, a contingency plan should be in place for the possibility that your repository may need to discontinue services and shut down. If the repository is no longer supported financially or institutionally, how will you migrate the data holdings to another data repository? This was recently the case with the

National Virtual Observatory (NVO), an astronomical digital data repository in the United States (http://www.usvao.org/support-community/science-definition-for-the-virtual-observatory; site now discontinued). Originally conceived in 2001 with direct funding support by the National Science Foundation, the NVO functioned as a data repository for a wide variety of space-based telescope image files, including those from the Hubble Space Telescope, the Chandra X-ray Observatory, and the Spitzer Space Telescope. The repository was officially shut down in October 2014 and, according to the closeout website, their plan included a migration of all the data and software to archival websites for retention.[35]

# Summary of Step 8.0: Reuse

8.1 Monitor Data Reuse: Track any requests for access, file downloads, data set citations, and other factors that might indicate the reuse value of data over time.

8.2 Consider Post-ingest Review Techniques: Allow others, public or experts, to provide feedback on the data in order to provide additional post-ingest quality control. Consider peer-review mechanisms to track input and provide quality measures for data housed in your repository.

8.3 Provide Ongoing Support as Long as Necessary: Provide services that meet the evolving needs of the data over the anticipated usefulness of the data, such as new versions, supplemental file additions, and user-generated documentation.

8.4 Cease Data Duration: Plan for any contingencies that will ultimately terminate access to the data, such as loss of funding for the repository. For example, how will you respond to takedown requests and deselection (e.g., provide tombstones)?

# Notes

1. For a review of the history and a comparison of scholarly impact measures, see Johan Bollen, Herbert Van de Sompel, Aric Hagberg, and Ryan Chute, "A Principal Component Analysis of 39 Scientific Impact Measures," *PloS ONE* 4, no. 6 (2009): e6022, doi:10.1371/journal.pone.0006022; Mike Thelwall, Stefanie Haustein, Vincent Larivière, and Cassidy R. Sugimoto, "Do Altmetrics Work? Twitter and Ten Other Social Web Services," *PloS ONE* 8, no. 5 (2013): e64841, doi:10.1371/journal.pone.0064841; Stefanie Haustein, Vincent Larivière, Mike Thelwall, Didier Amyot, and Isabella Peters, "Tweets vs. Mendeley Readers: How Do These Two Social Media Metrics Differ?" *IT—Information Technology* 56, no. 5 (2014): 207–15, doi:10.1515/itit-2014-1048.

2. The editorial overview of this special issues is available as "Assessing Assessment," *Nature* 465, no. 845 (June 17, 2010), doi:10.1038/465845a. The entire issue is available online at http://www.nature.com/news/specials/metrics/index.html.

3. Charisse R. Madlock-Brown and David Eichmann, "The (Lack of) Impact of Retraction on Citation Networks," *Science and Engineering Ethics* 21, no. 1 (2015): 127–37, doi:10.1007/s11948-014-9532-1.

4. Ivan Oransky, "Top 10 Most Highly Cited Retracted Papers," Retraction Watch, December 28, 2015, http://retractionwatch.com/the-retraction-watch-leaderboard/top-10-most-highly-cited-retracted-papers.

5. Jan Brase, Yvonne Socha, Sarah Callaghan, Christine L. Borgman, Paul F. Uhlir, and Bonnie Carrol, "Data Citation: Principles and Practice," in *Research Data Management: Practical Strategies for Information Professionals*, ed. Joyce M. Ray (West Lafayette, IN: Purdue University Press, 2014), 167, 171.

6. M. Martone, ed., *Data Citation Synthesis Group: Joint Declaration of Data Citation Principles* (San Diego: FORCE11, 2014) https://www.force11.org/datacitation; Bernadette Farias Lóscio, Eric G. Stephan, and Sumit Purohit, eds., "Data on the Web Best Practices: Dataset Usage Vocabulary," W3C Working Draft, accessed March 24, 2016, https://www.w3.org/TR/vocab-duv.

7. Alex Ball and Monica Duke, "How to Cite Datasets and Link to Publications," DCC How-to Guides, Edinburgh, UK: Digital Curation Centre, 2015, http://www.dcc.ac.uk/resources/how-guides/cite-datasets.

8. Web of Science, "The Data Citation Index," accessed March 24, 2016, http://wokinfo.com/products_tools/multidisciplinary/dci; INSPIRE, "HEP Search: High-Energy Physics Literature Database," accessed March 24, 2016, http://inspirehep.net; According to Herterich and Dallmeier-Tiessen (Patricia Herterich and Sünje Dallmeier-Tiessen, "Data Citation Services in the High-Energy Physics Community," *D-Lib Magazine* 22, no. 1/2 [January/February 2016], http://www.dlib.org/dlib/january16/herterich/01herterich.html), "INSPIRE will expand the citation counts to research data and in doing so become one of the first providers of a data citation count."

9. Martone, *Data Citation Synthesis Group*.

10. Stacy Konkiel and Dave Scherer, "New Opportunities for Repositories in the Age of Altmetrics." *Bulletin of the American Society for Information Science and Technology* 39, no. 4 (2013): 22, doi:10.1002/bult.2013.1720390408.

11. bepress, "Download Statistics Matter," accessed March 24, 2016, http://www.bepress.com/download_counts.html.

12. COUNTER, "COUNTER Code of Practice, release 4" January 1, 2004, https://www.projectcounter.org/wp-content/themes/project-counter-2016/pdfs/COUNTER-code-of-practice.pdf?v=1470610624.

13. Jisc, "Research Data Metrics for Usage: Understanding How Research Data Is Downloaded and Used," accessed March 24, 2016, https://www.jisc.ac.uk/rd/projects/research-data-metrics-for-usage; CASRAI, "Research Dataset-Level Metrics," accessed March 24, 2016, http://ref.casrai.org/Research_Dataset-Level_Metrics.

14. Alex Ball and Monica Duke, "How to Track the Impact of Research Data with Metrics," DCC How-to Guides, Edinburgh, UK: Digital Curation Centre, 2015, http://www.dcc.ac.uk/resources/how-guides/track-data-impact-metrics.

15. As of February 2016, ICPSR's archival holdings include 1,256 restricted-use data collections; ICPSR staff manage over 3,400 active data use agreements.

16. The NORC Data Enclave "archives, curates, and indexes the data; provides researchers remote and onsite secure access to the data; and statistically protects confidential information." (NORC, "Data Enclave," accessed February 8, 2016, http://www.norc.org/Research/Capabilities/Pages/data-enclave.aspx.)

17. Bryan Lawrence, Catherine Jones, Brian Matthews, Sam Pepler, and Sarah Callaghan, "Citation and Peer Review of Data: Moving towards Formal Data Publication," *International Journal of Digital Curation* 6, no. 2 (2011): 11, doi:10.2218/ijdc.v6i2.205.

18. Ibid., 11.

19. Sarah Callaghan. "Starting Something New—The Beginnings of Peer Review of Data," *Wiley Exchanges. Our Ideas, Research and Discussion Blog*, posted January 26, 2016, https://hub.wiley.com/community/exchanges/discover/blog/2016/01/26/starting-something-new-the-beginnings-of-peer-review-of-data; Fiona Murphy, "An Update on Peer Review and Research Data." *Learned Publishing* 29, no. 1 (January 2016): 51–53. doi:10.1002/leap.1005.

20. *Scientific Data*, "About," accessed March 24, 2016, http://www.nature.com/sdata/about; *Biodiversity Data Journal*, "About," accessed March 24, 2016, http://biodiversitydata-journal.com/about.

21. Matthew S. Mayernik, Sarah Callaghan, Roland Leigh, Jonathan Tedds, and Steven Worley, "Peer Review of Datasets: When, Why, and How," *Bulletin of the American Meteorological Society* 96, no. 2 (2015): 192, doi:10.1175/BAMS-D-13-00083.1.

22. Lawrence et al., "Citation and Peer Review of Data," 13–15.

23. Simon Hettrick, "It's Impossible to Conduct Research without Software, Say 7 Out of 10 UK Researchers," Software Sustainability Institute, December 4, 2014, http://www.software.ac.uk/blog/2014-12-04-its-impossible-conduct-research-without-software-say-7-out-10-uk-researchers.

24. Roger Peng, Francesa Dominici, and Scott Segar, "Reproducible Epidemiologic Research," *American Journal of Epidemiology* 163, no. 9 (2006): 783–89, doi:10.1093/aje/kwj093; Victoria Stodden, "The Legal Framework for Reproducible Scientific Research: Licensing and Copyright," *Computing in Science and Engineering* 11, no. 1 (2009): 35–40, doi:10.1109/MCSE.2009.19; Victoria Stodden, "Open Data Dead on Arrival," *Victoria Stodden* (blog), February 3, 2010, http://blog.stodden.net/2010/02/03/open-data-dead-on-arrival.

25. Limor Peer, "Why 'Intelligent Openness' Is Especially Important When Content Is Disaggregated," *Lux et Data: ISPS Blog*, December 22, 2014, http://isps.yale.edu/news/blog/2014/12/why-intelligent-openness-is-especially-importantwhen-content-is-disaggregated; Limor Peer, "Mind the Gap in Data Reuse: Sharing Data Is Necessary but Not Sufficient for Future Reuse," *The Impact Blog*, London School of Economics and Political Science, March 28, 2014, http://blogs.lse.ac.uk/impactofsocialsciences/2014/03/28/mind-the-gap-in-data-reuse.

26. Richard G. Anderson, William H. Greene, B. D. McCullough, and H. D. Vinod, "The Role of Data/Code Archives in the Future of Economic Research," *Journal of Economic Methodology* 15, no. 1 (2008): 100, doi:10.1080/13501780801915574.

27. Limor Peer, "Building an Open Data Repository: Lessons and Challenges," Social Science Research Network, September 15, 2011, http://ssrn.com/abstract=1931048, doi:10.2139/ssrn.1931048; Limor Peer, Ann Green, and Elizabeth Stephenson, "Committing to Data Quality Review," *International Journal of Digital Curation*, 9, no. 1 (2014): 263–91, doi:10.2218/ijdc.v9i1.317; Peer, Limor, and Ann Green, "Building an Open Data Repository for a Specialized Research Community: Process, Challenges and Lessons," *International Journal of Digital Curation* 7, no. 1 (2012): 151–62, doi:10.2218/ijdc.v7i1.222.

28. Limor Peer and Stephanie Wykstra, "New Curation Software: Step-by-Step Preparation of Social Science Data and Code for Publication and Preservation," *IASSIST Quarterly*, 39, no. 4 (2015): 6-13, http://www.iassistdata.org/sites/default/files/vol_39_4_peer.pdf.

29. Centers like the Pisgah Astronomical Research Institute (PARI) rescue and house astronomical plates for ongoing research and reuse (Pisgah Astronomical Research Institute [PARI] homepage, accessed March 24, 2016, http://www.pari.edu).

30. Rufus Pollock, "Git (and Github) for Data," *Open Knowledge Blog*, July 2, 2013, http://blog.okfn.org/2013/07/02/git-and-github-for-data; This blog post (Amol Deshpande, "Why Git and SVN Fail at Managing Dataset Versions," *UMD Data-intensive Systems Blog*, June 26, 2015, http://www.cs.umd.edu/~amol/DBGroup/2015/06/26/datahub.html) described in more general terms the results of this research paper (Souvik Bhattacherjee, Amit Chavan, Silu Huang, Amol Deshpande, and Aditya Parameswaran, "Principles of Dataset Versioning: Exploring the Recreation/Storage Tradeoff," *Proceedings of the VLDB Endowment* 8, no. 12 (2015): 1346–57, doi:10.14778/2824032.2824035).

31. Data Science, "Dataset Versioning in Dataverse 4.0 Beta," *Data Science* blog, June 6, 2014, http://datascience.iq.harvard.edu/blog/dataset-versioning-dataverse-40-beta.

32. DataCite. *DataCite Metadata Schema for the Publication and Citation of Research Data, Version 3.1.* Hannover, Germany: DataCite, August 2015. doi:10.5438/0010.

33. Martone, *Data Citation Synthesis Group*.

34. Deep Blue Data, "Retention," accessed March 24, 2016. https://deepblue.lib.umich.edu/data/retention.

35. US Virtual Astronomical Observatory, "VAO Closeout Repository," September 10, 2014, http://www.usvao.org/2014/09/10/vao-closeout-repository (site now discontinued).

# Bibliography

Altmetric homepage. Accessed March 24, 2016. https://www.altmetric.com.

Anderson, Richard G., William H. Greene, B. D. McCullough, and H. D. Vinod. "The Role of Data/Code Archives in the Future of Economic Research." *Journal of Economic Methodology* 15, no. 1 (2008): 99–119. doi:10.1080/13501780801915574.

Ball, Alex, and Monica Duke. "How to Cite Datasets and Link to Publications." DCC How-to Guides. Edinburgh: Digital Curation Centre, 2015. http://www.dcc.ac.uk/resources/how-guides/cite-datasets.

———. "How to Track the Impact of Research Data with Metrics." DCC How-to Guides. Edinburgh: Digital Curation Centre, 2015. http://www.dcc.ac.uk/resources/how-guides/track-data-impact-metrics.

bepress. "Download Statistics Matter." Accessed March 24, 2016. http://www.bepress.com/download_counts.html.

Bhattacherjee, Souvik, Amit Chavan, Silu Huang, Amol Deshpande, and Aditya Parameswaran. "Principles of Dataset Versioning: Exploring the Recreation/Storage Tradeoff." *Proceedings of the VLDB Endowment* 8, no. 12 (2015): 1346–57. doi:10.14778/2824032.2824035.

*Biodiversity Data Journal.* "About." Accessed March 24, 2016. http://biodiversitydatajournal.com/about.

Bollen, Johan, Herbert Van de Sompel, Aric Hagberg, and Ryan Chute. "A Principal Component Analysis of 39 Scientific Impact Measures." *PloS ONE* 4, no. 6 (2009): e6022. doi:10.1371/journal.pone.0006022.

Brase, Jan, Yvonne Socha, Sarah Callaghan, Christine L. Borgman, Paul F. Uhlir, and Bonnie Carrol, "Data Citation: Principles and Practice." In *Research Data Management: Practical Strategies for Information Professionals*. Edited by Joyce M. Ray, 167–186. West Lafayette, IN: Purdue University Press, 2014.

Callaghan, Sarah. "Starting Something New—the Beginnings of Peer Review of Data." *Wiley Exchanges. Our Ideas, Research and Discussion Blog*. Posted January 26, 2016. https://hub.wiley.com/community/exchanges/discover/blog/2016/01/26/starting-something-new-the-beginnings-of-peer-review-of-data.

CASRAI. "Research Dataset-Level Metrics." Accessed March 24, 2016. http://ref.casrai.org/Research_Dataset-Level_Metrics.

DataCite. *DataCite Metadata Schema for the Publication and Citation of Research Data, Version 3.1*. Hannover, Germany: DataCite, August 2015. doi:10.5438/0010.

Datahub homepage. Accessed March 24, 2016. https://datahub.io.

Data Level Metrics Project. "Making Data Count: Project to Develop Data-Level Metrics." Accessed March 24, 2016. http://mdc.lagotto.io.

Data Science. "Dataset Versioning in Dataverse 4.0 Beta." *Data Science* blog. June 6, 2014. http://datascience.iq.harvard.edu/blog/dataset-versioning-dataverse-40-beta.

Deep Blue Data. "Retention." Accessed March 24, 2016. https://deepblue.lib.umich.edu/data/retention.

Deshpande, Amol. "Why Git and SVN Fail at Managing Dataset Versions." *UMD Data-intensive Systems Blog*. June 26, 2015. http://www.cs.umd.edu/~amol/DB-Group/2015/06/26/datahub.html.

Dryad Digital Repository homepage. Last modified November 19, 2015. https://datadryad.org.

Farias Lóscio, Bernadette, Eric G. Stephan, and Sumit Purohit, eds. "Data on the Web Best Practices: Dataset Usage Vocabulary." W3C Working Draft. Accessed March 24, 2016. https://www.w3.org/TR/vocab-duv.

figshare homepage. Accessed March 24, 2016. https://figshare.com.

Haustein, Stefanie, Vincent Larivière, Mike Thelwall, Didier Amyot, and Isabella Peters. "Tweets vs. Mendeley Readers: How Do These Two Social Media Metrics Differ?" *IT—Information Technology* 56, no. 5 (2014): 207–15. doi:10.1515/itit-2014-1048.

Herterich, Patricia, and Sünje Dallmeier-Tiessen. "Data Citation Services in the High-Energy Physics Community." *D-Lib Magazine* 22, no. 1/2 (January/February 2016). http://www.dlib.org/dlib/january16/herterich/01herterich.html.

Hettrick, Simon. "It's Impossible to Conduct Research without Software, Say 7 Out of 10 UK Researchers." Software Sustainability Institute, December 4, 2014. http://www.software.ac.uk/blog/2014-12-04-its-impossible-conduct-research-without-software-say-7-out-10-uk-researchers.

Impactstory homepage. Accessed March 24, 2016. https://impactstory.org.

INSPIRE. "HEP Search: High-Energy Physics Literature Database." Accessed March 24, 2016. http://inspirehep.net.

Jisc. "Research Data Metrics for Usage: Understanding How Research Data Is Downloaded and Used." Accessed March 24, 2016. https://www.jisc.ac.uk/rd/projects/research-data-metrics-for-usage.

Konkiel, Stacy, and Dave Scherer. "New Opportunities for Repositories in the Age of Altmetrics." *Bulletin of the American Society for Information Science and Technology* 39, no. 4 (2013): 22–26. doi:10.1002/bult.2013.1720390408.

Lagotto. "About Lagotto." Accessed March 24, 2016. http://www.lagotto.io.

Lawrence, Bryan, Catherine Jones, Brian Matthews, Sam Pepler, and Sarah Callaghan. "Citation and Peer Review of Data: Moving towards Formal Data Publication." *International Journal of Digital Curation* 6, no. 2 (2011): 4–37. doi:10.2218/ijdc.v6i2.205.

Madlock-Brown, Charisse R., and David Eichmann. "The (Lack of) Impact of Retraction on Citation Networks." *Science and Engineering Ethics* 21, no. 1 (2015): 127–37. doi:10.1007/s11948-014-9532-1.

Martone, M., ed. *Data Citation Synthesis Group: Joint Declaration of Data Citation Principles.* San Diego: FORCE11, 2014. https://www.force11.org/datacitation.

Mayernik, Matthew S., Sarah Callaghan, Roland Leigh, Jonathan Tedds, and Steven Worley. "Peer Review of Datasets: When, Why, and How." *Bulletin of the American Meteorological Society* 96, no. 2 (2015): 191–201. doi:10.1175/BAMS-D-13-00083.1.

Mendeley Data homepage. Accessed March 24, 2016. https://data.mendeley.com.

Murphy, Fiona. "An Update on Peer Review and Research Data." *Learned Publishing* 29, no. 1 (January 2016): 51–53. doi:10.1002/leap.1005.

*Nature.* "Assessing Assessment." Editorial. *Nature* 465, no. 845 (June 17, 2010). doi:10.1038/465845a.

NORC. "Data Enclave." Accessed February 8, 2016. http://www.norc.org/Research/Capabilities/Pages/data-enclave.aspx.

Oransky, Ivan. "Top 10 Most Highly Cited Retracted Papers." Retraction Watch. December 28, 2015. http://retractionwatch.com/the-retraction-watch-leaderboard/top-10-most-highly-cited-retracted-papers.

Peer, Limor. "Building an Open Data Repository: Lessons and Challenges." Social Science Research Network. September 15, 2011. http://ssrn.com/abstract=1931048. doi:10.2139/ssrn.1931048.

———. "Mind the Gap in Data Reuse: Sharing Data Is Necessary but Not Sufficient for Future Reuse." *The Impact Blog*, London School of Economics and Political Science. March 28, 2014. http://blogs.lse.ac.uk/impactofsocialsciences/2014/03/28/mind-the-gap-in-data-reuse.

———. "Why 'Intelligent Openness' Is Especially Important When Content Is Disaggregated." *Lux et Data: ISPS Blog.* December 22, 2014. http://isps.yale.edu/news/blog/2014/12/why-intelligent-openness-is-especially-importantwhen-content-is-disaggregated.

Peer, Limor, and Ann Green. "Building an Open Data Repository for a Specialized Research Community: Process, Challenges and Lessons." *International Journal of Digital Curation* 7, no. 1 (2012): 151–62. doi:10.2218/ijdc.v7i1.222.

Peer, Limor, Ann Green, and Elizabeth Stephenson. "Committing to Data Quality Review." *International Journal of Digital Curation*, 9, no. 1 (2014): 263–91. doi:10.2218/ijdc.v9i1.317.

Peer, Limor, and Stephanie Wykstra. "New Curation Software: Step-by-Step Preparation of Social Science Data and Code for Publication and Preservation." *IASSIST Quarterly*, 39, no. 4 (2015): 6-13. http://www.iassistdata.org/sites/default/files/vol_39_4_peer.pdf.

Peng, Roger, Francesa Dominici, and Scott Segar. "Reproducible Epidemiologic Research." *American Journal of Epidemiology* 163, no. 9 (2006): 783–89. doi:10.1093/aje/kwj093.

Pisgah Astronomical Research Institute (PARI) homepage. Accessed March 24, 2016. http://www.pari.edu.

Plum Analytics. Accessed March 24, 2016. http://plumanalytics.com/ (site now discontinued).

Pollock, Rufus. "Git (and Github) for Data." *Open Knowledge Blog*. July 2, 2013. http://blog.okfn.org/2013/07/02/git-and-github-for-data.

*Scientific Data*. "About." Accessed March 24, 2016. http://www.nature.com/sdata/about.

Stodden, Victoria. "The Legal Framework for Reproducible Scientific Research: Licensing and Copyright." *Computing in Science and Engineering* 11, no. 1 (2009): 35–40. doi:10.1109/MCSE.2009.19.

———. "Open Data Dead on Arrival." *Victoria Stodden* (blog). February 3, 2010. http://blog.stodden.net/2010/02/03/open-data-dead-on-arrival.

Thelwall, Mike, Stefanie Haustein, Vincent Larivière, and Cassidy R. Sugimoto. "Do Altmetrics Work? Twitter and Ten Other Social Web Services." *PloS ONE* 8, no. 5 (2013): e64841. doi:10.1371/journal.pone.0064841.

US Virtual Astronomical Observatory. "Science Definition for the Virtual Observatory." Accessed March 24, 2016. http://www.usvao.org/support-community/science-definition-for-the-virtual-observatory (site now discontinued).

———. "VAO Closeout Repository." September 10, 2014. http://www.usvao.org/2014/09/10/vao-closeout-repository (site now discontinued).

Web of Science. "Data Citation Index." Accessed March 24, 2016. http://wokinfo.com/products_tools/multidisciplinary/dci.

Wiley. *Wiley Exchanges. Our Ideas, Research and Discussion Blog*. Accessed March 24, 2016. http://exchanges.wiley.com/blog.

# Brief Concluding Remarks and a Call to Action

*Curating Research Data, Volume Two: A Handbook of Current Practice* guides you across the data life cycle through the practical strategies and techniques for curating research data in your digital repository setting. The eight data curation steps for receiving, appraising and selecting, processing, ingesting and storing, describing (with approprate metadata), facilitating access, preserving, and reusing digital research data (see appendix on page xviii in the Foreword for a detailed list) are explored and over 50 library, archives, and information science specialists contributed to cases studies providing a snap shot of their current practice. Yet if each author here continued to improve upon and create new best practices for effectively curating data at each of their institutions, I'd say we are only halfway toward achieving our goals. Instead, we must strive to not only share, as this book does, our efforts and best practices with colleagues, but partner in more meaningful ways if we are to successfully approach the full gamut of digital research data generated by scholars today and going forward. Though partnership and collaboration we might pool our resources to develop robust technological infrastructure, build greater expertise in our curation staff, and voice our ideas and concerns to relevant stakeholders more effectively. A united data curation community may more effectively advocate to policy makers the necessary components that data curation brings to the emerging practices and polices of data sharing.

The broader ecosystem and historical context for interlinking data repositories is further explored by Karen S. Baker and Ruth E. Duerr in Chapter 1 "Research and the Changing Nature of Data Repositories" in *Curating Research Data, Volume One.*

For this level of partnership I look to several national examples of data curation such as the Portage network, developed by the Canadian Association of Research Libraries (CARL), which aims to integrate existing research data repositories within a robust national discovery and preservation infrastructure network and bring together library-based experts in order to share data management consultation and curation services across a broader network.[1] Or the JISC-funded Research Data Management Shared Service Project, which aims to develop a lightweight service framework that can scale to all UK institutions and result in efficiencies by "relieving burden from institutional IT and procurement staff."[2] In the US, partnerships on technological infrastructure are booming. The Hydra Sofia project, which builds upon the DuraSpace Fedora framework, has been co-developed by numerous institutions that seek to create a better digital repository infrastructure for data.[3] And the Hydra-in-a-Box project (led in part by another partnership success story for disseminating archival materials, the Digital Public Library of America) aims to provide a feature-rich platform for repository services that will scale for institutions big and small.[4] Another inspiring example is the Research Data Alliance, which provides an incubator for collaboration around a range of data-related topics. RDA projects to track include the Publishing Data Workflows working group and the newly formed Research Data Repository Interoperability working group.[5]

Finally, partnerships do not necessarily need to start at the national level. Several smaller-scale partnerships underway for sharing curation staff expertise across institutions include the Digital Liberal Arts Exchange, which facilitates data-related problem solving and communication amongst peers as well as providing hosting services that allow digital humanities projects to be run on shared infrastructure.[6] And the DataQ Project, which provides a virtual online forum for expert data staff to discuss and provide solutions for data issues in a collaborative way.[7] Additionally, the Data Curation Network project (which I am spearheading) will develop a model for sharing expert curation staff across a 'network of expertise.'[8] Our project recognized that every academic library couldn't realistically hire a data curator for every data type (e.g., GIS, spreadsheet/tabular, statistical/survey, video/audio, computer code) or discipline-specific data set (genomic sequence, chemical spectra, biological image). Similarly, each type of data curation expertise might only be needed occasionally depending on the disciplinary makeup at each institution. Therefore the Data Curation Network will enable partner institutions to specialize in a few key disciplinary areas of data curation and then share that expertise across the network to help accommodate the heterogeneous and diverse data types an institutional data curation service typically receives.[9]

By partnering on data curation efforts like these we will move beyond disseminating our current strategies toward what I hope will become a robust data curation field where resources as well as dialogue are shared to develop new and improved processes for curating research data. In doing so, research data curation will demonstrate the continuing role that library and archives professionals have to play in the broader scholarly process.

# Notes

1.  Portage network homepage, accessed August 6, 2016, https://portagenetwork.ca/.
2.  JISC-funded Research Data Management Shared Service Project, accessed August 4, 2016. https://www.jisc.ac.uk/rd/projects/research-data-shared-service.
3.  See for example the University of Michigan's Deep Blue Data homepage, accessed August 11, 2016, https://deepblue.lib.umich.edu/data, which runs on Sofia 7 by the Project Hydra, accessed August 11, 2016, https://projecthydra.org, as described in the poster by Amy Neeser, "Expanding Research Data Services with Deep Blue Data," June 2016, https://deepblue.lib.umich.edu/handle/2027.42/120431.
4.  Hydra in a Box homepage, accessed August 11, 2016, http://hydrainabox.projecthydra. org.
5.  Research Data Alliance homepage, accessed August 11, 2016, https://rd-alliance.org; RDA/WDS Publishing Data Workflows WG homepage, accessed August 11, 2016, https://rd-alliance.org/groups/research-data-repository-interoperability-wg.html; Research Data Repository Interoperability WG homepage, accessed August 11, 2016, https://rd-alliance.org/groups/research-data-repository-interoperability-wg.html.
6.  The Digital Liberal Arts Exchange (DLaX) homepage, accessed August 11, 2016, https://dlaexchange.wordpress.com.
7.  DataQ Project homepage, accessed August 11, 2016, http://researchdataq.org.
8.  Data Curation Network project homepage, accessed August 11, 2016, https://sites. google.com/site/datacurationnetwork; A network of expertise model is defined by Joy Kirchner, José Diaz, Geneva Henry, Susan Fliss, John Culshaw, Heather Gendron, and Jon E. Cawthorne, "The Center of Excellence Model for Information Services," CLIR Publication No. 163, Council on Library and Information Resources, http://www. clir.org/pubs/reports/pub163 as "…a way to implement and sustain new information services for research…. Through this method, existing organizations will start to change as they integrate experts more fully into the daily work and as a greater number of information professionals share knowledge" (p.16) and "a shared approach to address specialized information needs or to solve a common problem" (p17).
9.  In order to better understand the capacity and limitations of accepting and curating data in the Digital Conservancy the University of Minnesota libraries ran a successful Data Curation Pilot in 2013. Data sets from five faculty in diverse fields provided a draft workflow model for data curation in the libraries. The full report and recommendation from this pilot provided a roadmap for implementing these services is published as Lisa R. Johnston  (2014). A Workflow Model for Curating Research Data in the University of Minnesota Libraries: Report from the 2013 Data Curation Pilot. University Digital of Minnesota Conservancy. Retrieved from the University of Minnesota Digital Conservancy, http://hdl.handle.net/11299/162338.

# Bibliography

Data Curation Network project homepage. Accessed August 11, 2016. https://sites.google.com/site/datacurationnetwork.

DataQ Project homepage. Accessed August 11, 2016. http://researchdataq.org.

Digital Liberal Arts Exchange (DLaX) homepage. Accessed August 11, 2016. https://dlaexchange.wordpress.com.

Hydra in a Box homepage. Accessed August 11, 2016. http://hydrainabox.projecthydra.org.

Johnston, Lisa R. "A Workflow Model for Curating Research Data in the University of Minnesota Libraries: Report from the 2013 Data Curation Pilot." University Digital of Minnesota Conservancy. January 2014. http://hdl.handle.net/11299/162338.

Kirchner, Joy, José Diaz, Geneva Henry, Susan Fliss, John Culshaw, Heather Gendron, and Jon E. Cawthorne. "The Center of Excellence Model for Information Services." CLIR Publication No. 163, Council on Library and Information Resources. http://www.clir.org/pubs/reports/pub163.

Neeser, Amy. "Expanding Research Data Services with Deep Blue Data." June 2016. https://deepblue.lib.umich.edu/handle/2027.42/120431.

Portage Network homepage. Accessed August 6, 2016. https://portagenetwork.ca.

Project Hydra homepage. Accessed August 11, 2016. https://projecthydra.org.

Research Data Alliance homepage. Accessed August 11, 2016. https://rd-alliance.org.

———."Publishing Data Workflows WG." Accessed August 11, 2016. https://rd-alliance.org/groups/research-data-repository-interoperability-wg.html.

———."Research Data Repository Interoperability WG." Accessed August 11, 2016. https://rd-alliance.org/groups/research-data-repository-interoperability-wg.html.

Research Data Management Shared Service Project homepage. Accessed August 4, 2016. https://www.jisc.ac.uk/rd/projects/research-data-shared-service.

University of Michigan. "Deep Blue Data." Accessed August 11, 2016. https://deepblue.lib.umich.edu/data.

# Bibliography

3D-ICONS. "Guidelines." 2014. http://3dicons-project.eu/eng/Guidelines-Case-Studies/ Guidelines2.

Acharya, Anurag. "Indexing Repositories: Pitfalls and Best Practices." Slides for presentation at 10th International Conference on Open Repositories, Indianapolis, IN, June 8–11, 2015. http://www.or2015.net/wp-content/uploads/2015/06/or-2015-anurag-google-scholar.pdf.

Adolph, Karen E. "Social and Motor Play on a Playground." *Databrary*. 2014. Accessed November 10, 2015. doi:10.17910/B77P4V.

Akgun, Mahir, and Patricia Hswe. "A Tale of Redaction." Digital Stewardship (blog). December 1, 2015. http://stewardship.psu.edu/2015/12/01/a-tale-of-redaction.

Albright, Jeremy J., and Jared A. Lyle. "Data Preservation through Data Archives." *PS: Political Science and Politics* 43, no. 1 (January 2010):17–21. doi:10.1017/S1049096510990768.

Alliance of Digital Humanities Organizations (ADHO) homepage. Accessed June 18, 2016. http://adho.org.

Altmetric homepage. Accessed March 24, 2016. https://www.altmetric.com.

Anderson, Richard G., William H. Greene, B. D. McCullough, and H. D. Vinod. "The Role of Data/Code Archives in the Future of Economic Research." *Journal of Economic Methodology* 15, no. 1 (2008): 99–119. doi:10.1080/13501780801915574.

Appleyard, Baden, and Greg Laughlin. "Copyright, Data and Licensing." The Australian National Data Service. Accessed March 18, 2016. http://ands.org.au/guides/copyright-and-data-awareness.html.

Archaeology Data Service/Digital Antiquity. "Data Selection: Preservation Intervention Points." In *Guides to Good Practice*. York, UK: Archaeology Data Service, 2011. http://guides.archaeologydataservice.ac.uk/g2gp/ArchivalStrat_1-3.

Arlitsch, Kenning, and Patrick S. O'Brien. "Invisible Institutional Repositories: Addressing the Low Indexing Ratios of IRs in Google Scholar." *Library Hi Tech* 30, no. 1 (2012): 60–81. doi:10.1108/07378831211213210.

Armbruster, Chris, and Laurent Romary. "Comparing Repository Types: Challenges and Barriers for Subject-Based Repositories, Research Repositories, National Repository Systems and Institutional Repositories in Serving Scholarly Communication." Social Science Research Network. November 23, 2009. http://ssrn.com/abstract=1506905.

Austin, Tim. "Towards a Digital Infrastructure for Engineering Materials Data." *Materials Discovery*, in press. doi:10.1016/j.md.2015.12.003.

Austin, Tony, and Jenny Mitcham. *Preservation and Management Strategies for Exceptionally Large Data Formats: "Big Data."* York, UK: Archaeology Data Service, 2007. http://archaeologydataservice.ac.uk/research/bigData.

Australian National University Library. *Data Management Manual: Managing Digital Research Data at the Australian National University*, 10th ed. Data Service Data Literacy guide. Canberra: Australian National University, 2016. https://services.anu.edu.au/files/DataManagement.pdf.

Averkamp, Shawn, Xiaomei Gu, and Ben Rogers. "Data Management at the University of Iowa: A University Libraries Report on Campus Research Data Needs." Annual Report. February 28, 2014. University of Iowa Libraries Staff Publications. http://ir.uiowa.edu/lib_pubs/153.

AVPreserve. "Exactly." Accessed March 14, 2016. https://www.avpreserve.com/tools/exactly.

Bakeman, Roger, and Vicenç Quera. "Behavioral Observation." In *APA Handbook of Research Methods in Psychology, Vol 1: Foundations, Planning, Measures, and Psychometrics*. Edited by H. Cooper, P. M. Camic, D. L. Long, A. T. Panter, D. Rindskopf, and K. J. Sher, 207–25. Washington, DC: American Psychological Association, 2012. doi:10.1037/13619-013.

Ball, Alex. "How to License Research Data." DCC How-to Guides. February 9, 2011. Revised July 17, 2014. Digital Curation Centre. http://www.dcc.ac.uk/resources/how-guides/license-research-data.

Ball, Alex, and Monica Duke. "How to Cite Datasets and Link to Publications." DCC How-to Guides. Edinburgh: Digital Curation Centre, 2015. http://www.dcc.ac.uk/resources/how-guides/cite-datasets.

———. "How to Track the Impact of Research Data with Metrics." DCC How-to Guides. Edinburgh: Digital Curation Centre, 2015. http://www.dcc.ac.uk/resources/how-guides/track-data-impact-metrics.

Barnes, Adam, "Close-Range Photogrammetry: A Guide to Good Practice." In *Guides to Good Practice*. York, UK: Archaeology Data Service, 2011. http://guides.archaeologydataservice.ac.uk/g2gp/Photogram_2-1.

Barton, Mary R., and Margaret M. Waters. Creating an Institutional Repository: LEADIRS Workbook. Cambridge, MA: MIT Press, 2004. http://hdl.handle.net/1721.1/26698.

Beebe, Linda. "Supplemental Materials for Journal Articles: NISO/NFAIS Joint Working Group." *Information Standards Quarterly* 22, no. 3 (Summer 2010): 33–37. http://www.niso.org/apps/group_public/download.php/4885/Beebe_SuppMatls_WG_ISQ_v22no3.pdf.

bepress. "Download Statistics Matter." Accessed March 24, 2016. http://www.bepress.com/download_counts.html.

Bhattacherjee, Souvik, Amit Chavan, Silu Huang, Amol Deshpande, and Aditya Parameswaran. "Principles of Dataset Versioning: Exploring the Recreation/Storage Tradeoff." *Proceedings of the VLDB Endowment* 8, no. 12 (2015): 1346–57. doi:10.14778/2824032.2824035.

*Biodiversity Data Journal*. "About." Accessed March 24, 2016. http://biodiversitydatajournal.com/about.

BitCurator homepage. Accessed March 15, 2016. http://www.bitcurator.net.

Bizer, Christina, Tom Heath, and Tim Berners-Lee. "Linked Data: The Story So Far." *International Journal on Semantic Web and Information Systems* 5, no. 3 (July–September 2009). http://go.galegroup.com/ps/i.do?id=GALE%7CA209477051&v=2.1&u=uiuc_uc&it=r&p=AONE&sw=w&asid=fd7e52083504e596d9b86bfe8a273f7c.

Bollen, Johan, Herbert Van de Sompel, Aric Hagberg, and Ryan Chute. "A Principal Component Analysis of 39 Scientific Impact Measures." *PLOS ONE* 4, no. 6 (2009): e6022. doi:10.1371/journal.pone.0006022.

Borgman, Christine L. *Big Data, Little Data, No Data: Scholarship in the Networked World.* Cambridge, MA: MIT Press, 2015.

Bradley, Kevin. "Chapter 6.1.9: Trusted Digital Repositories (TDR) and Institutional Responsibility." *Guidelines on the Production and Preservation of Digital Audio Objects,* 2nd ed. International Association of Sound and Audiovisual Archives, 2009. http://www. iasa-web.org/tc04/trusted-digital-repositories-tdr-and-institutional-responsibility.

Brandt, Scott. "Data Management for Undergraduate Researchers: File Naming Conventions." Purdue Libraries, Last modified December 8, 2015. http://guides.lib.purdue. edu/c.php?g=353013&p=2378293.

Brase, Jan, Michael Lautenschlager, and Irina Sens. "The Tenth Anniversary of Assigning DOI Names to Scientific Data and a Five Year History of DataCite." *D-Lib Magazine* 21, no. 1/2 (January/February 2015): 10. doi:10.1045/january2015-brase.

Brase, Jan, Yvonne Socha, Sarah Callaghan, Christine L. Borgman, Paul F. Uhlir, and Bonnie Carrol, "Data Citation: Principles and Practice." In *Research Data Management: Practical Strategies for Information Professionals.* Edited by Joyce M. Ray, 167–186. West Lafayette, IN: Purdue University Press, 2014.

Brickley, Dan, and Libby Miller. "FOAF Vocabulary Specification 0.99." Accessed November 11, 2015. http://xmlns.com/foaf/spec/.

Briney, Kristin, Abigail Goben, and Lisa Zilinski. "Do You Have an Institutional Data Policy? A Review of the Current Landscape of Library Data Services and Institutional Data Policies." *Journal of Librarianship and Scholarly Communication* 3, no. 2 (2015): eP1232. doi:10.7710/2162-3309.1232.

Briney, Kristin. *Data Management for Researchers: Organize, Maintain and Share Your Data for Research Success.* Exeter, UK: Pelagic Publishing, 2015.

Budapest Open Access Initiative. *Guide to Institutional Repository Software,* 3rd ed. New York: Open Society Institute, August 2004. http://www.budapestopenaccessinitiative.org/ pdf/OSI_Guide_to_IR_Software_v3.pdf.

Bumpass, Larry L. "What's Happening to the Family? Interactions between Demographic and Institutional Change." *Demography* 27, no. 4 (1990): 483–98.

Callaghan, Sarah. "Starting Something New – the Beginnings of Peer Review of Data." *Wiley Exchanges. Our Ideas, Research and Discussion Blog.* Posted January 26, 2016. https:// hub.wiley.com/community/exchanges/discover/blog/2016/01/26/starting-something-new-the-beginnings-of-peer-review-of-data.

California Digital Library. "EZID Help." Accessed August 6, 2015. http://ezid.cdlib.org/ home/help.

———. "EZID: Pricing." Accessed March 18, 2016. http://ezid.cdlib.org/home/pricing.

Canadian Institutes of Health Research. CIHR Best Practices for Protecting Privacy in Health Research. Ottawa, Ontario: Public Works and Government Services Canada, 2005. http://www.cihr-irsc.gc.ca/e/documents/et_pbp_nov05_sept2005_e.pdf.

Carlson, Jake R. "The Use of Life Cycle Models in Developing and Supporting Data Services." In *Research Data Management: Practical Strategies for Information Professionals.* Edited by Joyce M. Ray, 63–86. West Lafayette, IN: Purdue University Press, 2014.

Carroll, Michael W. "Sharing Research Data and Intellectual Property Law: A Primer." *PLOS Biology* 13, no. 8 (2015): e1002235. http://journals.plos.org/plosbiology/article?id=10.1371/journal.pbio.1002235.

CASRAI. "Research Dataset-Level Metrics." Accessed March 24, 2016. http://ref.casrai.org/ Research_Dataset-Level_Metrics.

Center for Human Resource Research. "Guide to the NLSY97 Data." in NLSY97 User's Guide: A guide to the Rounds 1–3 Data, National Longitudinal Survey of Youth 1997. (Columbus: Ohio State University, 2001). https://web.archive.org/web/20100727011626/http://www.nlsinfo.org/nlsy97/97guide/chap3.htm.

Center for Research Libraries (CRL) and Online Computer Library Center (OCLC). Trustworthy Repositories Audit and Certification (TRAC): Criteria and Checklist. Chicago: CRL and Dublin, OH: OCLC, 2007. https://www.crl.edu/sites/default/files/d6/attachments/pages/trac_0.pdf.

Code Sector. "TeraCopy for Microsoft Windows." Accessed March 14, 2016. http://www.codesector.com/teracopy.

Colectica homepage. Accessed October 29, 2015. http://www.colectica.com/.

Columbia University Libraries. "Depositing Data in Academic Commons." Accessed March 14, 2016. http://scholcomm.columbia.edu/data-management/depositing-data-in-academic-commons.

Columbia University. "Academic Commons." Accessed March 14, 2016. http://academic-commons.columbia.edu.

Committee on Future Career Opportunities and Educational Requirements for Digital Curation; Board on Research Data and Information; Policy and Global Affairs; National Research Council. *Preparing the Workforce for Digital Curation*. Washington, DC: National Academies Press, 2015. http://www.nap.edu/catalog.php?record_id=18590.

Consortia Advancing Standards in Research Administration Information (CASRAI). "Repository." Accessed July 9, 2016. http://dictionary.casrai.org/Repository.

Consultative Committee for Space Data Systems. Audit and Certification of Trustworthy Digital Repositories. Recommended Practice, CCSDS 652.0-M-1, Magenta Book, Issue 1 Washington, DC: CCSDS Secretariat, September 2011. http://public.ccsds.org/publications/archive/652x0m1.pdf.

———. Reference Model for an Open Archival Information System (OAIS). Recommended Practice, CCSDS 650.0-M-2, Magenta Book, Issue 2. Washington, DC: CCSDS Secretariat, June 2012. http://public.ccsds.org/publications/archive/650x0m2.pdf.

Converse, Philip E. "A Network of Data Archives for the Behavioral Sciences." *Public Opinion Quarterly* 28, no 2 (Summer 1964): 273–86. http://www.jstor.org/stable/2746992.

Corrado, Edward M., and Heather Lea Moulaison. *Digital Preservation for Libraries, Archives, and Museums.* Lanham, MD: Rowman & Littlefield, 2014.

Costello, Kaitlin Light, and Michael E. Brown. "Preliminary Report on the 2010–2011 DigCCurr Professional Institute: Curation Practices for the Digital Object Lifecycle." *D-Lib Magazine* 16, no. 11/12 (November/December 2010): 6. http://www.dlib.org/dlib/november10/costello/11costello.html.

Coughlin, Dan, and Mike Giarlo. "Architecting ScholarSphere: How We Built a Repository App That Doesn't Feel Like Yet Another Janky Old Repository App." Presentation, code{4}lib conference, Chicago, IL, February 11–14, 2013. http://code4lib.org/conference/2013/coughlin-giarlo.

Creative Commons. "CC0 1.0 Universal (CC0 1.0) Public Domain Dedication." Accessed March 18, 2016. https://creativecommons.org/publicdomain/zero/1.0/.

Crow, Raym. SPARC Institutional Repository Checklist and Resource Guide. Washington, DC: Scholarly Publishing and Academic Resources Coalition, 2002. http://sparcopen.org/wp-content/uploads/2016/01/IR_Guide__Checklist_v1_0.pdf.

CyArk homepage. Accessed June 18, 2016. http://www.cyark.org/.

Daries, Jon P., Justin Reich, Jim Waldo, Elise M. Young, Jonathan Whittinghill, Daniel Thomas Seaton, Andrew Dean Ho, and Isaac Chuang. "Privacy, Anonymity, and Big Data in the Social Sciences." *acmqueue* 12, no. 7 (July 14, 2014). http://queue.acm.org/detail.cfm?id=2661641.

Data Curation Network project homepage. Accessed August 11, 2016. https://sites.google.com/site/datacurationnetwork.

Data Documentation Initiative (DDI) homepage. Accessed June 18, 2016. http://www.ddialliance.org.

Data Level Metrics Project. "Making Data Count: Project to Develop Data-Level Metrics." Accessed March 24, 2016. http://mdc.lagotto.io.

Data Seal of Approval. "Extension to the Current Data Seal." News release, February 3, 2016. http://datasealofapproval.org/en/news-and-events/news/2016/2/3/extension-current-data-seal.

DataAccessioner homepage. Accessed March 14, 2016. http://www.dataaccessioner.org.

DataCite homepage. Accessed March 18, 2016. https://www.datacite.org.

DataCite. *DataCite Metadata Schema for the Publication and Citation of Research Data*, Version 3.1. Hannover, Germany: DataCite, August 2015. doi:10.5438/0010.

———. "What Do We Do?" Accessed August 6, 2015. https://www.datacite.org/about-datacite/what-do-we-do.

DataCite Metadata Search. Accessed March 18, 2016. http://search.datacite.org/ui.

DataCite. *DataCite Metadata Schema for the Publication and Citation of Research Data, Version* 3.1. Hannover, Germany: DataCite, August 2015. doi:10.5438/0010.

Datahub homepage. Accessed March 24, 2016. https://datahub.io.

DataONE. "DataONE Architecture, Version 1.2." Accessed November 19, 2015. https://releases.dataone.org/online/api-documentation-v1.2.0/.

DataQ Project homepage. Accessed August 11, 2016. http://researchdataq.org.

Data Science. "About TwoRavens." Institute for Quantitative Social Science, Harvard University. Accessed March 18, 2016. http://datascience.iq.harvard.edu/about-tworavens.

———. "Dataset Versioning in Dataverse 4.0 Beta." Data Science blog. June 6, 2014. http://datascience.iq.harvard.edu/blog/dataset-versioning-dataverse-40-beta.

Dataverse. "Metadata Blocks." Github. Accessed March 12, 2016. https://github.com/IQSS/dataverse/tree/master/scripts/api/data/metadatablocks.

Dataverse Project. "Sample Data Usage Agreement." Accessed March 18, 2016. http://best-practices.dataverse.org/harvard-policies/sample-dua.html.

———. "Appendix: Metadata References." Dataverse Project User Guide. Accessed March 12, 2016. http://guides.dataverse.org/en/latest/user/appendix.html#metadata-references.

Datavyu homepage. Accessed November 16, 2015. http://www.datavyu.org/.

DDI Alliance. "DDI Codebook 2.1 Specification." Accessed October 29, 2015. http://www.ddialliance.org/Specification/DDI-Codebook/2.1/.

Dearborn, Carly C., Amy J. Barton, and Neal A. Harmeyer. "The Purdue University Research Repository: HUBzero Customization for Dataset Publication and Digital Preservation." OCLC Systems and Services 30, no. 1 (2014): 15–27. doi:10.1108/OCLC-07-2013-0022.

Deep Blue Data. "Retention." Accessed March 24, 2016. https://deepblue.lib.umich.edu/data/retention.

Deshpande, Amol. "Why Git and SVN Fail at Managing Dataset Versions." UMD Data-intensive Systems Blog. June 26, 2015. http://www.cs.umd.edu/~amol/DB-Group/2015/06/26/datahub.html.

Digital Curation Centre. "General Research Data." Accessed March 12, 2016. http://www.dcc.ac.uk/resources/subject-areas/general-research-data.

———. "What Is Digital Curation?" Accessed June 14, 2016. http://www.dcc.ac.uk/digital-curation/what-digital-curation.

Digital Humanities Data Curation. "DH Curation Guide." Accessed April 5, 2016. http://guide.dhcuration.org/contents.

Digital Liberal Arts Exchange (DLaX) homepage. Accessed August 11, 2016. https://dlaexchange.wordpress.com.

Digital Preservation Coalition. Digital Preservation Handbook, 2nd ed. Digital Preservation Coalition, 2015. http://www.dpconline.org/advice/preservationhandbook.

Dryad Digital Repository. "Dryad Metadata Application Profile (Schema)." Last modified February 27, 2013. http://wiki.datadryad.org/Metadata_Profile.

———. "Dryad REST API Technology." Last modified November 10, 2015. http://wiki.datadryad.org/Dryad_REST_API_Technology.

———. "Journal Metadata Processing Technology." Last modified November 17, 2015. http://wiki.datadryad.org/Journal_Metadata_Processing_Technology.

———. "Submission Integration: Overview." Last modified January 15, 2016. http://wiki.datadryad.org/Submission_Integration.

———. "Terms of Service." Last modified August 22, 2013. https://datadryad.org/pages/policies.

———. "The Organization: Overview." Last modified October 22, 2015. https://datadryad.org/pages/organization.

Dryad Digital Repository homepage. Last modified November 19, 2015. https://datadryad.org.

Dublin Core Metadata Initiative homepage. Association for Information Science and Technology. Accessed November 11, 2015. http://dublincore.org/.

Dublin Core Metadata Initiative. "Dublin Core Metadata Element Set," version 1.1. Accessed March 15, 2016. http://dublincore.org/documents/dces.

Elsevier. "Elsevier and PANGAEA Link Contents for Easier Access to Full Earth System Research." News release, February 24, 2010. https://www.elsevier.com/about/press-releases/science-and-technology/elsevier-and-pangaea-link-contents-for-easier-access-to-full-earth-system-research.

———. "Supported Data Repositories." Accessed March 18, 2016. https://www.elsevier.com/books-and-journals/content-innovation/data-base-linking/supported-data-repositories.

Ember, Carol, and Robert Hanisch. "Sustaining Domain Repositories for Digital Data: A White Paper." Output of the workshop "Sustaining Domain Repositories for Digital Data," Ann Arbor, MI, June 24–25, 2013. doi:10.3886/SustainingDomainRepositoriesDigitalData.

Ember, Carol, Robert Hanisch, George Alter, Helen Berman, Margaret Hedstrom, and Mary Vardigan. "Sustaining Domain Repositories for Digital Data: A White Paper." December 11, 2013. http://datacommunity.icpsr.umich.edu/sites/default/files/WhitePaper_ICPSR_SDRDD_121113.pdf.

Erl, Thomas. *Service-Oriented Architecture: A Field Guide to Integrating XML and Web Services*. Upper Saddle River, NJ: Prentice Hall PTR, 2004.

Erway, Ricky, and Amanda Rinehart. If You Build It, Will They Fund? Making Research Data Management Sustainable. Dublin, OH: OCLC, 2016. http://www.oclc.org/content/dam/research/publications/2016/oclcresearch-making-research-data-management-sustainable-2016.pdf.

Erway, Ricky. "What Is Actually Happening Out There in Terms of Institutional Data Repositories?" Hangingtogether.org (blog). July 27, 2015. http://hangingtogether.org/?p=5342.

Eschenfelder, Kristin R., and Andrew Johnson. "Managing the Data Commons: Controlled Sharing of Scholarly Data." *Journal of the Association for Information Science and Technology* 65, no. 9 (2014): 1757–74.

Estlund, Karen, and Anna Neatrour. "Utah Digital Repository Initiative: Building a Support System for Institutional Repositories." *D-Lib Magazine* 13, no. 11/12 (November/December 2007). http://www.dlib.org/dlib/november07/neatrour/11neatrour.html.

European Parliament, Council of the European Union. "Directive 95/46/EC of the European Parliament and of the Council of 24 October 1995 on the Protection of Individuals with Regard to the Processing of Personal Data and on the Free Movement of Such Data." EUR Lex. Accessed November 20, 2015. http://eur-lex.europa.eu/legal-content/EN/TXT/?uri=CELEX:31995L0046.

EZID. "The EZID API, Version 2." Accessed February 10, 2015. http://ezid.cdlib.org/doc/apidoc.html.

Fabricius, William. "Absence of Construct Validity in Standard False Belief Tasks." *Databrary*. 2014. Accessed November 10, 2015. doi: 10.17910/B7Z300.

Farias Lóscio, Bernadette, Eric G. Stephan, and Sumit Purohit, eds. "Data on the Web Best Practices: Dataset Usage Vocabulary." W3C Working Draft. Accessed March 24, 2016. https://www.w3.org/TR/vocab-duv.

Fearon, David Jr., Betsy Gunia, Barbara E. Pralle, Sherry Lake, and Andrew L. Sallans. Research Data Management Services: SPEC Kit 334. Washington, DC: Association of Research Libraries, 2013. http://publications.arl.org/Research-Data-Management-Services-SPEC-Kit-334.

Federal Committee on Statistical Methodology. Statistical Policy Working Paper 22 (Second Version, 2005): Report on Statistical Disclosure Limitation Methodology. Washington, DC: Office of Management and Budget, 2005.

Federer, Lisa. "The Librarian as Research Informationist: A Case Study." *Journal of the Medical Library Association 101*, no. 4 (January 2013): 298–302.

Fegraus, Eric H., Sandy Andelman, Matthew B. Jones, and Mark Schildhauer. "Maximizing the Value of Ecological Data with Structured Metadata: An Introduction to Ecological Metadata Language (EML) and Principles for Metadata Creation." *Bulletin of the Ecological Society of America* 86, no. 3 (July 2005): 158–68. doi:10.1890/0012-9623(2005)86[158:MTVOED]2.0.CO;2.

Ferguson, Liz. "How and Why Researchers Share Data (and Why They Don't)." Wiley Exchanges (blog), November 3, 2014. http://exchanges.wiley.com/blog/2014/11/03/how-and-why-researchers-share-data-and-why-they-dont. Accessed August 14, 2015; page now discontinued.

Fernie, Kate, and Julian D. Richards, eds. Creating and Using Virtual Reality: A Guide for the Arts and Humanities. AHDS Guides to Good Practice. London: Arts and Humanities Data Service, 2002. http://www.vads.ac.uk/guides/vr_guide/.

Fielding, Roy. "Architectural Styles and the Design of Network-Based Software Architectures." PhD diss., University of California, Irvine, 2000.

figshare homepage. Accessed March 24, 2016. https://figshare.com.

File Information Tool Set (FITS). Accessed March 14, 2016. http://projects.iq.harvard.edu/fits.

Fox, Peter, and James Hendler. "Changing the Equation on Scientific Data Visualization." Science 331, no. 6018 (2011): 705–8. doi:10.1126/science.1197654.

Galeazzi, Fabrizio, Holley Moyes, and Mark Aldenderfer. "Defining Best 3D Practices in Archaeology: Comparing Laser Scanning and Dense Stereo Matching Techniques for 3D Intrasite Data Recording." Advances in Archaeological Practice 2, no. 4 (2014): 353–65. doi: 10.7183/2326-3768.2.4.353.

German Social Science Infrastructure Services (GESIS). Accessed July 8, 2016, http://www.gesis.org/en/services/archiving-and-registering/data-archiving.

Giarlo, Michael J. "Academic Libraries as Data Quality Hubs." Journal of Librarianship and Scholarly Communication 1, no. 3 (March 2013): 1–10. doi:10.7710/2162-3309.1059.

Gibbons, Susan. "Establishing an Institutional Repository." Library Technology Reports 40, no. 4 (July/August 2004). doi:10.5860/ltr.40n4.

Gierl, Claude, and Jon Johnson. "How Do We Manage Complex Questions in the Context of the Large-Scale Ingest of Legacy Paper Questionnaires into DDI-Lifecycle?" Paper presented at the 5th Annual European Data Documentation Initiative User Conference, Paris, December 3–4, 2013. http://www.eddi-conferences.eu/ocs/index.php/eddi/EDDI13/paper/view/92.

Gierveld, Heleen. "Considering a Marketing and Communications Approach for an Institutional Repository." Ariadne, no. 49 (2006). http://www.ariadne.ac.uk/issue49/gierveld.

GitHub homepage. Accessed March 14, 2016. https://github.com.

Globus homepage. Accessed March 14, 2016. https://www.globus.org.

Google Scholar homepage. Accessed March 18, 2016. https://scholar.google.com/.

Green, Ann G., and Myron P. Gutmann. "Building Partnerships among Social Science Researchers, Institution-Based Repositories, and Domain Specific Data Archives." OCLC Systems and Services: International Digital Library Perspectives 23 (2007): 35–53. http://hdl.handle.net/2027.42/41214.

Green, Ann, JoAnn Dionne, and Martin Dennis. Preserving the Whole: A Two-Track Approach to Rescuing Social Science Data and Metadata. CLIR Publication 83. Washington, DC: Council on Library and Information Resources, 1999. http://www.clir.org/pubs/reports/pub83/contents.html.

Gries, Corinna, Inigo San Gil, Kristin Vanderbilt, and Hap Garritt. "Drupal Developments in the LTER Network." LTER Databits, Spring 2010. http://databits.lternet.edu/spring-2010/drupal-developments-lter-network.

Griffiths, Aaron. "The Publication of Research Data: Researcher Attitudes and Behaviour." International Journal of Digital Curation 4, no. 1 (2009): 46–56.

Group on Earth Observations (GEO) homepage. Accessed June 18, 2016. https://www.earthobservations.org.

GSToRE V3. "Experimental API." Accessed November 19, 2015. http://gstore.unm.edu/docs/experimental.html.

Gutmann, Myron P., Kevin Schürer, Darrel Donakowski, and Hilary Beedham. "The Selection, Appraisal, and Retention of Digital Social Science Data." *Data Science Journal* 3, (2006): 209–21. doi:10.2481/dsj.3.209.

Hanson, Karen, Alisa Surkis, and Karen Yacobucci. "Data Sharing and Management Snafu in Three Short Acts." YouTube video, 4:40. Posted by New York University Health Sciences Library, December 19, 2012. https://www.youtube.com/watch?v=N2zK3sA-tr-4.

Harvey, Ross. "Appraisal and Selection." Curation Reference Manual. Digital Curation Centre. June 2006. http://www.dcc.ac.uk/resource/curation-manual/chapters/appraisal-and-selection.

———. "Environmental Storage Conditions for Magnetic Tape, CD-ROM, and DVD." In *Preserving Digital Materials*, 125–6. Berlin: Walter de Gruyter, 2005.

HathiTrust Digital Library. "Technological Profile." Accessed July 9, 2016. https://www.hathitrust.org/technology.

Haustein, Stefanie, Vincent Larivière, Mike Thelwall, Didier Amyot, and Isabella Peters. "Tweets vs. Mendeley Readers: How Do These Two Social Media Metrics Differ?" *IT—Information Technology* 56, no. 5 (2014): 207–15. doi:10.1515/itit-2014-1048.

HeavenTools Software. "Malware Code Analysis Made Easy." PE Explorer data sheet. 2007. http://www.heaventools.com/files/11hFgnI0s/PE.Explorer.datasheet.pdf.

Heidorn, P. Bryan. "The Emerging Role of Libraries in Data Curation and E-Science." *Journal of Library Administration* 51, no. 7/8 (October 2011): 662–72. doi:10.1080/0193 0826.2011.601269.

Henry, Charles. "Introduction." In The Problem of Data, by Lori Jahnke, Andrew Asher, and Spencer D. C. Keralis, 1–2. CLIR publication no. 154. Washington, DC: Council on Library and Information Resources, 2012. http://www.clir.org/pubs/reports/pub154/pub154.pdf.

Herterich, Patricia, and Sünje Dallmeier-Tiessen. "Data Citation Services in the High-Energy Physics Community." *D-Lib Magazine* 22, no. 1/2 (January/February 2016). http://www.dlib.org/dlib/january16/herterich/01herterich.html.

Hettne, Kristina M., Katherine Wolstencroft, Khalid Belhajjame, Carole A. Goble, Eleni Mina, Harish Dharuri, David De Roure, Lourdes Verdes-Montenegro, Julián Garrido, and Marco Roos. "Best Practices for Workflow Design: How to Prevent Workflow Decay." In SWAT4LS 2012: Semantic Web Applications and Tools for Life Sciences. Proceedings of the 5th International Workshop on Semantic Web Applications and Tools for Life Sciences, Paris, November 28–30, 2012. Edited by Adrian Paschke, Albert Burger, Paolo Romano, M. Scott Marshall, and Andrea Splendiani. Aachen, Germany: CEUR Workshops Proceedings, 2012. http://ceur-ws.org/Vol-952/paper_23.pdf.

Hettrick, Simon. "It's Impossible to Conduct Research without Software, Say 7 Out of 10 UK Researchers." Software Sustainability Institute, December 4, 2014. http://www.software.ac.uk/blog/2014-12-04-its-impossible-conduct-research-without-software-say-7-out-10-uk-researchers.

Higgins, Sarah. "The DCC Curation Lifecycle Model." *International Journal of Digital Curation* 3, no. 1 (2008): 134–40. doi:10.2218/ijdc.v3i1.48.

Holdren, John P. "Increasing Access to the Results of Federally Funded Scientific Research." Memorandum for the Heads of Executive Departments and Agencies, Office of Science and Technology Policy, Executive Office of the President, February 22, 2013. http://www.whitehouse.gov/sites/default/files/microsites/ostp/ostp_public_access_memo_2013.pdf.

Humphrey, Chuck. "Canada's Long Tale of Data." Preserving Research Data in Canada: The Long Tale of Data. December 5, 2012. http://preservingresearchdataincanada.net/category/introduction.

———. "The Long Tail of Data Wagging the Institutional Repository." Slides for presentation, Open Repositories Conference, Charlottetown, Prince Edward Island, Canada, July 8–12, 2013. http://or2013.net/sites/or2013.net/files/slides/OR2013_Workshop_Humphrey_0/index.pdf.

Hunt, David. "'Save Everything' Data Retention: Why It's a Problem." The C2C Blog. July 1, 2013. https://web.archive.org/web/20150424052232/http://www.c2c.com/save-everything-data-retention-why-its-a-problem/.

Hydra in a Box homepage. Accessed August 11, 2016. http://hydrainabox.projecthydra.org.

IANUS. "3D und Virtual Reality." In IANUS IT-Empfehlungen. Berlin: Deutsches Archäologisches Institut, 2015. http://www.ianus-fdz.de/it-empfehlungen/3d.

Impactstory homepage. Accessed March 24, 2016. https://impactstory.org.

Indiana University. "Secure Data Removal." Accessed March 14, 2016. https://protect.iu.edu/online-safety/protect-data/data-removal.html.

Ingram, Bill. e-mail to author regarding IDEALS traffic. November 6, 2015.

INSPIRE. "HEP Search: High-Energy Physics Literature Database." Accessed March 24, 2016. http://inspirehep.net.

Inter-university Consortium for Political and Social Research (ICPSR). "Additional ICPSR Services." Accessed June 18, 2016. http://www.icpsr.umich.edu/icpsrweb/content/datamanagement/lifecycle/services.html.

———. "Data Deposit Form." Accessed March 14, 2016. https://www.icpsr.umich.edu/cgi-bin/ddf2?inbox=NAHDAP.

———. "Data Enclaves." Accessed June 18, 2016. http://www.icpsr.umich.edu/icpsrweb/content/icpsr/access/restricted/enclave.html.

———. Data-Related Literature Database. Accessed October 26, 2015. http://www.icpsr.umich.edu/icpsrweb/ICPSR/citations/index.jsp.

———. "Disclosure Risk Training—For Public-Use or Not for Public Use, That Is the Question." YouTube video, 43:36, posted October 8, 2014. https://www.youtube.com/watch?v=9vdWseLay9g&feature=youtu.be&list=PLqC9lrhW1VvaKgzk-S87WwrlS-MHliHQo6%22.

———. "Find Publications." Accessed June 18, 2016. https://www.icpsr.umich.edu/icpsrweb/ICPSR/citations/index.jsp.

———. *Guide to Social Science Data Preparation and Archiving: Best Practice throughout the Data Life Cycle*, 5th edition. Ann Arbor, MI: ICPSR, 2012. http://www.icpsr.umich.edu/files/ICPSR/access/dataprep.pdf.

———. "ICPSR Collection Development Policy." Accessed June 17, 2016, http://www.icpsr.umich.edu/icpsrweb/content/datamanagement/policies/colldev.html.

———. "Preserving Respondent Confidentiality." Accessed November 20, 2015. https://www.icpsr.umich.edu/icpsrweb/content/deposit/confidentiality.html.

———. "Restricted-Use Data Management at ICPSR." Accessed March 14, 2016. http://www.icpsr.umich.edu/icpsrweb/content/icpsr/access/restricted/index.html.

———. "Search/Compare Variables." Accessed June 18, 2016. https://www.icpsr.umich.edu/icpsrweb/ICPSR/ssvd/.

International Council for Science World Data System (ICSU WDS) homepage. Accessed June 18, 2016. https://www.icsu-wds.org.

International Organization for Standardization. "ISO 16363:2012: Space Data and Information Transfer Systems—Audit and Certification of Trustworthy Digital Repositories." February 15, 2012. http://www.iso.org/iso/catalogue_detail.htm?csnumber=56510.

———. "ISO 14721:2012: Space Data and Information Transfer Systems—Open Archival Information System (OAIS)—Reference Model." September 1, 2012. http://www.iso.org/iso/catalogue_detail.htm?csnumber=57284.

International Social Science Council (ISSC) homepage. Accessed June 18, 2016. http://www.worldsocialscience.org.

International Society for Environmental Ethics (ISEE) homepage. Accessed June 18, 2016. http://enviroethics.org.

Jisc. "Research Data Metrics for Usage: Understanding How Research Data Is Downloaded and Used." Accessed March 24, 2016. https://www.jisc.ac.uk/rd/projects/research-data-metrics-for-usage.

Johnston, Lisa R. "A Workflow Model for Curating Research Data in the University of Minnesota Libraries: Report from the 2013 Data Curation Pilot." University Digital of Minnesota Conservancy. January 2014. http://hdl.handle.net/11299/162338.

Johnston, Lisa R., Eric Larson, and Erik Moore. "Usability Testing of DRUM: What Academic Researchers Want from an Open Access Data Repository." June 9, 2015. http://hdl.handle.net/11299/172556.

Joint Task Force on Library Support for E-Science. Agenda for Developing E-science in Research Libraries. Final Report and Recommendations to the Scholarly Communication Steering Committee, the Public Policies Affecting Research Libraries Steering Committee, and the Research, Teaching, and Learning Steering Committee. Washington, DC: Association of Research Libraries, November 2007. http://www.arl.org/storage/documents/publications/arl-escience-agenda-nov07.pdf.

Jones, Sarah, Graham Pryor, and Angus Whyte. How to Develop Research Data Management Services: A Guide for HEIs. DCC How-to Guides. Edinburgh, UK: Digital Curation Centre, 2013. http://www.dcc.ac.uk/resources/how-guides/how-develop-rdm-services.

Kellam, Lynda, and Kristi Thompson, eds. Databrarianship: The Academic Data Librarian in Theory and Practice. Chicago: American College and Research Libraries, 2016.

Kanous, Alex, and Elaine Brock. "Contractual Limitations on Data Sharing." Report prepared for ICPSR as part of the Building Community Engagement for Open Access to Data project. George Alter, principal investigator. March 31, 2015. doi:10.3886/ContractualLimitationsDataSharing.

———. "Model Data Sharing Agreement." Customizable model created as part of the Building Community Engagement for Open Access to Data project. George Alter, principal investigator. August 31, 2015. doi:10.3886/ModelDataSharingAgreement.

Keralis, Spencer D. C. "Data Curation Education: A Snapshot." In The Problem of Data, by Lori Jahnke, Andrew Asher, and Spencer D. C. Keralis, 32–43. CLIR publication no.

154. Washington, DC: Council on Library and Information Resources, 2012. http://www.clir.org/pubs/reports/pub154/pub154.pdf.

Kirchner, Joy, José Diaz, Geneva Henry, Susan Fliss, John Culshaw, Heather Gendron, and Jon E. Cawthorne. "The Center of Excellence Model for Information Services." CLIR Publication No. 163, Council on Library and Information Resources. http://www.clir.org/pubs/reports/pub163.

Konkiel, Stacy, and Dave Scherer. "New Opportunities for Repositories in the Age of Altmetrics." *Bulletin of the American Society for Information Science and Technology* 39, no. 4 (2013): 22–26. doi:10.1002/bult.2013.1720390408.

Kozlowski, Wendy. "Guidelines for Writing 'readme' Style Metadata." Research Data Management Services Group, Cornell University Library. Last updated May 30, 2014. http://data.research.cornell.edu/sites/default/files/SciMD_ReadMe_Guidelines_v4_1_0.pdf.

Krier, Laura, and Carly A. Strasser. *Data Management for Libraries: A Lita Guide.* Chicago: ALA TechSource, 2013.

Kurtz, Mary. "Dublin Core, DSpace, and a Brief Analysis of Three University Repositories." *Information Technology and Libraries* 29, no. 1 (March 2010): 40–46. doi:10.6017/ital.v29i1.3157.

Kussmann, Carol. "HashMyFiles Evaluation." May 2012. Minnesota Historical Society. http://www.mnhs.org/preserve/records/legislativerecords/carol/docs_pdfs/HashMyFilesEvaluation.pdf.

———. "Quick Reference Guide for Tools to Manage and Protect Your Digital Content." University of Minnesota Libraries. Accessed March 15, 2016. https://drive.google.com/a/umn.edu/file/d/0B8MvBJV_5_s5MlpBNUNTNlZvemM/view.

Lagotto. "About Lagotto." Accessed March 24, 2016. http://www.lagotto.io.

Language Archive. "ELAN." Accessed November 16, 2015. https://tla.mpi.nl/tools/tla-tools/elan/.

Lavoie, Brian F. "The Open Archival Information System Reference Model: Introductory Guide." *Microform and Imaging Review* 33, no. 2 (2004): 68–81. doi:10.7207/twr14-02.

Lawrence, Bryan, Catherine Jones, Brian Matthews, Sam Pepler, and Sarah Callaghan. "Citation and Peer Review of Data: Moving towards Formal Data Publication." *International Journal of Digital Curation* 6, no. 2 (2011): 4–37. doi:10.2218/ijdc.v6i2.205.

Leahey, Amber, Peter Webster, Claire Austin, Nancy Fong, Julie Friddell, Chuck Humphrey, Susan Brown, and Walter Stewart. "Research Data Repository Requirements and Features Review," v. 4. Standards and Interoperability Committee. February 24, 2015. http://hdl.handle.net/10864/10892.

Lee, Christopher A. "Digital Forensics Meets the Archivist (and They Seem to Like Each Other)." *Provenance, Journal of the Society of Georgia Archivists* 30, no. 1 (2012): 2. http://digitalcommons.kennesaw.edu/provenance/vol30/iss1/2.

Library of Congress. "Bagit-java." Github. Accessed March 14, 2016. https://github.com/LibraryOfCongress/bagit-java.git.

———. "National Digital Stewardship Residency." Digital Preservation. Accessed March 14, 2016. http://www.digitalpreservation.gov/ndsr.

———. "Recommended Formats Statement, 2016–2017." Accessed August 7, 2016. http://www.loc.gov/preservation/resources/rfs/RFS%202016-2017.pdf.

———. "Sustainability Factors." Sustainability of Digital Formats, Planning for Library of Congress Collections. Accessed March 15, 2016. http://www.digitalpreservation.gov/formats/sustain/sustain.shtml.

———. "VRA Core Schemas and Documentation." Accessed November 11, 2015. http://www.loc.gov/standards/vracore/schemas.html.

Lord, Philip, Alison Macdonald, Liz Lyon, and David Giaretta. "From Data Deluge to Data Curation." In Proceedings of the UK e-Science All Hands Meeting 2004. Edited by Simon J. Cox, 371–75. Swindon, UK: EPSRC, 2004. http://www.allhands.org.uk/2004/proceedings/papers/150.pdf.

Lynch, Clifford A. "Institutional Repositories: Essential Infrastructure for Scholarship in the Digital Age." ARL Bimonthly Report, no. 226 (February 2003): 1–7. http://www.arl.org/storage/documents/publications/arl-br-226.pdf.

Mackie, Christopher, and Norman Bradburn, eds. *Improving Access to and Confidentiality of Research Data: Report of a Workshop.* Washington, DC: National Academies Press, 2000.

Madlock-Brown, Charisse R., and David Eichmann. "The (Lack of) Impact of Retraction on Citation Networks." *Science and Engineering Ethics* 21, no. 1 (2015): 127–37. doi:10.1007/s11948-014-9532-1.

MailChimp homepage. Accessed March 14, 2016. http://mailchimp.com.

manez. "Research Data in Islandora." Islandora blog, December 2, 2014. http://islandora.ca/content/research-data-islandora.

Mangold International. "INTERACT: The Professional Software for Behavioral Research Studies." Accessed November 16, 2015. http://www.mangold-international.com/software/interact/what-is-interact.html.

Marshall, Brianna, Katherine O'Bryan, Na Qin, and Rebecca Vernon. "Organizing, Contextualizing, and Storing Legacy Research Data: A Case Study of Data Management for Librarians." *Issues in Science and Technology Librarianship*, no. 74 (Fall 2013). doi:10.5062/F4K07270.

Martinez-Uribe, Luis, and Stuart MacDonald. "User Engagement in Research Data Curation." In Research and Advanced Technology for Digital Libraries, *Lecture Notes in Computer Science*, vol. 5714, 309–14. New York: Springer, 2009. doi:10.1007/978-3-642-04346-8_30.

Martone, M., ed. Data Citation Synthesis Group: Joint Declaration of Data Citation Principles. San Diego: FORCE11, 2014. https://www.force11.org/datacitation.

Matthews, Courtney Earl, and Michael Witt. "The Purdue University Research Repository (PURR): An Institutional Data Management Service with a Virtual Research Environment, Data Publication, and Archiving." Poster presented at Open Repositories conference, Helsinki, Finland, June 10–12, 2014. http://docs.lib.purdue.edu/lib_fspres/52.

Mayernik, Matthew S., Sarah Callaghan, Roland Leigh, Jonathan Tedds, and Steven Worley. "Peer Review of Datasets: When, Why, and How." *Bulletin of the American Meteorological Society* 96, no. 2 (2015): 191–201. doi:10.1175/BAMS-D-13-00083.1.

Mayernik, Matthew, G. Sayeed Choudhury, Tim DiLauro, Elliot Metsger, Barbara Pralle, Mike Rippin, and Ruth Duerr. "The Data Conservancy Instance: Infrastructure and Organizational Services for Research Data Curation." *D-Lib Magazine* 18, no. 9/10 (September/October 2012): 2. doi:10.1045/september2012-mayernik.

McGrory, John. "Excel Archival Tool User Guide." Github. April 24, 2015. https://github.com/mcgrory/ExcelArchivalTool/blob/master/UserGuide.pdf.

———. "Poster for 'Excel Archival Tool: Automating the Spreadsheet Conversion Process.'" Presented at the 2015 Research Data Access and Preservation Summit, Minneapolis, MN, April 23, 2015. http://hdl.handle.net/11299/171966.

McGovern, Nancy. "Digital Preservation Management Model Document." Version 3.0, Digital Curation and Preservation Framework: Outline. Last revised September 2014. http://www.dpworkshop.org/workshops/management-tools/policy-framework/model-document.

McHenry, Kenton, and Peter Bajcsy. An Overview of 3D Data Content, File Formats and Viewers. Technical report isda08-002. Urbana, IL: National Center for Supercomputing Applications, 2008. http://isda.ncsa.illinois.edu/drupal/sites/default/files/NCSA-ISDA-2008-002.pdf.

Mendeley Data homepage. Accessed March 24, 2016. https://data.mendeley.com.

Metadata Technology North America. "SledgeHammer." Accessed October 29, 2015. http://www.mtna.us/?page_id=1232.

Michener, William K, John Porter, Mark Servilla, and Kristin Vanderbilt. "Long Term Ecological Research and Information Management." *Ecological Informatics* 6, no. 1 (2011): 13–24. doi:10.1016/j.econinf.2010.11.005.

Mitcham, Jenny. "Addressing Digital Preservation Challenges through Research Data Spring." Digital Archiving at the University of York (blog). December 8, 2015. http://digital-archiving.blogspot.com/2015/12/the-research-data-spring-projects.html.

Moss, Elizabeth, Christin Cave, and Jared Lyle. "Sharing and Citing Research Data: A Repository's Perspective." *Big Data, Big Challenges in Evidence-Based Policy Making.* Edited by H. Kumar Jayasuriya and Kathryn A. Ritcheske, Chapter 4, 1-17. American Casebook Series. St. Paul, MN: West Academic Publishing, 2015.

Muenchen, Robert. "The Popularity of Data Analysis Software." r4stats.com. Last updated October 17, 2015. Accessed November 6, 2015. http://r4stats.com/articles/popularity/.

Murphy, Fiona. "An Update on Peer Review and Research Data." *Learned Publishing* 29, no. 1 (January 2016): 51–53. doi:10.1002/leap.1005.

Murray-Rust, Peter, Rufus Pollock, Bryan Bishop, Mike Chelen, Cameron Neylon, Daniel Mietchen, and Andy Powell. "FAQ." Panton Principles: Principles for Open Data in Science. Accessed November 20, 2015. http://pantonprinciples.org/faq.

Murray, Tim, Desiree Alexander, Oya Y. Rieger, Liz Muller, Dianne Dietrich, Michelle Paolillo, Madeleine Casad, and Jason Kovari. Preserving and Emulating Digital Art Objects. White paper submitted to the National Endowment for the Humanities. Ithaca, NY: Cornell University Library, November 2015. http://hdl.handle.net/1813/41368.

nanoHUB.org. "Nanomaterial Registry Portal." Accessed March 18, 2016. https://nanohub.org/groups/nanomaterialregistry.

National Addiction & HIV Data Archive Program (NAHDAP). "IRBs and Data Sharing." Accessed June 17, 2016. http://www.icpsr.umich.edu/files/NAHDAP/irbs-data-sharing.pdf.

———. Restricted-Use Data Deposit and Dissemination Procedures, October 2015. http://www.icpsr.umich.edu/files/NAHDAP/NAHDAP-RestrictedDataProcedures_Revised_Oct2015.pdf.

———. "Restricted Data Use Agreement for Confidential Data." Accessed June 17, 2016. http://www.icpsr.umich.edu/files/NAHDAP/GenericRDAAgreement.pdf.

———. "Restricted Data Use Agreement for Use of Confidential Data through the ICPSR Virtual Data Enclave." Accessed June 17, 2016. http://www.icpsr.umich.edu/files/NAHDAP/NAHDAPGenericVDERDUA.pdf.

National Archives and Records Administration. "Toolkit for Managing Electronic Records." Accessed June 15, 2015. http://www.archives.gov/records-mgmt/toolkit/#list.

National Archives. "The Technical Registry: PRONOM." Accessed March 15, 2016. https://www.nationalarchives.gov.uk/PRONOM/Default.aspx.

National Institutes of Health. "How Can Covered Entities Use and Disclose Protected Health Information for Research and Comply with the Privacy Rule?" HIPAA Privacy Rule: Information for Researchers. Accessed March 14, 2016. https://privacyrule-andresearch.nih.gov/pr_08.asp.

National Library of Medicine Digital Repository Working Group. "Digital Repository Policies and Functional Requirements," v. 1. Revised March 16, 2007. https://www.nlm.nih.gov/digitalrepository/NLM-DigRep-Requirements-rev032007.pdf.

Nature. "Assessing Assessment." Editorial. *Nature* 465, no. 845 (June 17, 2010). doi:10.1038/465845a.

Neeser, Amy. "Expanding Research Data Services with Deep Blue Data." June 2016. https://deepblue.lib.umich.edu/handle/2027.42/120431.

Noldus. "Event Logging Software: The Observer XT." Accessed November 16, 2015. http://www.noldus.com/human-behavior-research/products/the-observer-xt.

Noonan, Daniel W. "Digital Preservation Policy Framework: A Case Study." Educause Review. July 28, 2014. http://er.educause.edu/articles/2014/7/digital-preservation-policy-framework-a-case-study.

NORC. "Data Enclave." Accessed February 8, 2016. http://www.norc.org/Research/Capabilities/Pages/data-enclave.aspx.

Norsk Senter for Forskningsdata. "Nesstar Publisher." Accessed October 20, 2015. http://nesstar.com/software/publisher.html.

Odum Institute for Research in Social Science. "Data Deposit Form." Accessed July 8, 2016. http://www.odum.unc.edu/content/pdf/OdumDepositForm.pdf.

Olesen, Sarah. ANDS Guide to Publishing and Sharing Sensitive Data. Melbourne, Australia: Australian National Data Service, 2014. http://ands.org.au/guides/sensitivedata.pdf.

Open Data Commons. "Open Data Commons Open Database License (ODbL)." Accessed March 18, 2016. http://opendatacommons.org/licenses/odbl.

Open Definition. "Conformant Licenses." Accessed March 18, 2016. http://opendefinition.org/licenses.

OpenOASIS. "Establishing a Repository." Accessed March 14, 2016. http://www.openoasis.org/index.php?option=com_content&view=article&id=161&Itemid=354.

Oransky, Ivan. "Top 10 Most Highly Cited Retracted Papers." Retraction Watch. December 28, 2015. http://retractionwatch.com/the-retraction-watch-leaderboard/top-10-most-highly-cited-retracted-papers.

Organ, Michael K. "Download Statistics: What Do They Tell Us? The Example of Research Online, the Open Access Institutional Repository at the University of Wollongong, Australia." *D-Lib Magazine* 12, no. 11 (November 2006). http://www.dlib.org/dlib/november06/organ/11organ.html.

Panton Principles homepage. Accessed March 18, 2016. http://pantonprinciples.org.

Payne, Angie, "Laser Scanning for Archaeology: A Guide to Good Practice." In *Guides to Good Practice*. York, UK: Archaeology Data Service, 2011. http://guides.archaeology-dataservice.ac.uk/g2gp/LaserScan_1-1.

PE Explorer download page. Accessed March 14, 2016. http://www.pe-explorer.com/peexplorer-download.htm.

Pearce-Moses, Richard, ed. *A Glossary of Archival and Records Terminology*. Chicago: Society of American Archivists, 2005. Accessed May 8, 2015, http://www2.archivists.org/glossary/terms/a/appraisal.

Peer, Limor. "Building an Open Data Repository: Lessons and Challenges." Social Science Research Network. September 15, 2011. http://ssrn.com/abstract=1931048. doi:10.2139/ssrn.1931048.

———. "Mind the Gap in Data Reuse: Sharing Data Is Necessary but Not Sufficient for Future Reuse." The Impact Blog, London School of Economics and Political Science. March 28, 2014. http://blogs.lse.ac.uk/impactofsocialsciences/2014/03/28/mind-the-gap-in-data-reuse.

———. "Why 'Intelligent Openness' Is Especially Important When Content Is Disaggregated." Lux et Data: ISPS Blog. December 22, 2014. http://isps.yale.edu/news/blog/2014/12/why-intelligent-openness-is-especially-importantwhen-content-is-disaggregated.

Peer, Limor, and Ann Green. "Building an Open Data Repository for a Specialized Research Community: Process, Challenges and Lessons." *International Journal of Digital Curation 7*, no. 1 (2012): 151–62. doi:10.2218/ijdc.v7i1.222.

Peer, Limor, and Stephanie Wykstra. "New Curation Software: Step-by-Step Preparation of Social Science Data and Code for Publication and Preservation." *IASSIST Quarterly*, 39, no. 4 (2015): 6-13. http://www.iassistdata.org/sites/default/files/vol_39_4_peer.pdf.

Peer, Limor, Ann Green, and Elizabeth Stephenson. "Committing to Data Quality Review." *International Journal of Digital Curation 9*, no. 1 (2014): 263–91. doi:10.2218/ijdc.v9i1.317.

Peng, Roger, Francesa Dominici, and Scott Segar. "Reproducible Epidemiologic Research." *American Journal of Epidemiology* 163, no. 9 (2006): 783–89. doi:10.1093/aje/kwj093.

Pisgah Astronomical Research Institute (PARI) homepage. Accessed March 24, 2016. http://www.pari.edu.

Piwowar, Heather A., and Todd J. Vision. "Data Reuse and the Open Data Citation Advantage." *PeerJ 1* (2013): e175. doi:10.7717/peerj.175.

Piwowar, Heather A., Roger S. Day, and Douglas B. Fridsma. "Sharing Detailed Research Data is Associated with Increased Citation Rate." *PLOS ONE* 2, no. 3 (2007): e308. doi:10.1371/journal.pone.0000308.

*PLOS ONE*. "Guidelines for Specific Study Types: Human Subjects Research." Submission Guidelines. Accessed November 20, 2015. http://journals.plos.org/plosone/s/submission-guidelines#loc-guidelines-for-specific-study-types.

Plum Analytics. Accessed March 24, 2016. http://plumanalytics.com/ (site now discontinued).

Pollock, Rufus. "Git (and Github) for Data." *Open Knowledge Blog*. July 2, 2013. http://blog.okfn.org/2013/07/02/git-and-github-for-data.

Portage Network homepage. Accessed August 6, 2016. https://portagenetwork.ca.

POWRR Project homepage. Accessed March 14, 2016. http://digitalpowrr.niu.edu.

Poynter, Will, and Jennifer Spiegel. "Protocol Development for Large-Scale Metadata Archiving using DDI-Lifecycle." Paper presented at the 6th Annual European Data Documentation Initiative User Conference, London, December 2–3, 2014. http://www.eddi-conferences.eu/ocs/index.php/eddi/eddi14/paper/view/168.

Preserving Digital Objects with Restricted Resources (POWRR) homepage. Accessed March 15, 2016. http://digitalpowrr.niu.edu.

Project Hydra homepage. Accessed August 11, 2016. https://projecthydra.org.

Pryor, Graham, Sarah Jones, and Angus Whyte, eds. *Delivering Research Data Management Services: Fundamentals of Good Practice*. London: Facet Publishing, 2014.

R Core Team. R Project for Statistical Computing homepage. R Foundation for Statistical Computing. 2015. http://www.R-project.org/.

Raboin, Regina, Rebecca C. Reznik-Zellen, and Dorothea Salo. "Forging New Service Paths: Institutional Approaches to Providing Research Data Management Services." *Journal of eScience Librarianship 1*, no. 3 (2013): e1021. doi:10.7191/jeslib.2012.1021.

Rasheed, Abdul, and Mohamed Mohideen. "Fedora Commons with Apache Hadoop: A Research Study." *code4lib*, no. 22 (October 14, 2013). http://journal.code4lib.org/articles/8988.

Ray, Joyce M., ed. *Research Data Management: Practical Strategies for Information Professionals*. West Lafayette, IN: Purdue University Press, 2014.

Registry of Research Data Repositories homepage. Accessed March 14, 2016. http://www.re3data.org.

Repositories Support Project. "Briefing Papers." Accessed March 14, 2016. http://www.rsp.ac.uk/help/publications/#briefing-papers.

Research Data Alliance Data Foundation and Terminology Working Group (RDA DFT-WG). "Edit RDA: digital repository." Accessed July 9, 2016. http://smw-rda.esc.rzg.mpg.de/index.php/Special:FormEdit/RDA/digital_repository.

Research Data Alliance. "Publishing Data Workflows WG." Accessed August 11, 2016. https://rd-alliance.org/groups/research-data-repository-interoperability-wg.html.

———. "RDA/WDS Publishing Data Services WG." Accessed June 14, 2016. https://rd-alliance.org/groups/rdawds-publishing-data-services-wg.html.

———. "Research Data Repository Interoperability WG." Accessed August 11, 2016. https://rd-alliance.org/groups/research-data-repository-interoperability-wg.html.

Research Data Alliance homepage. Accessed August 11, 2016. https://rd-alliance.org.

Research Data Management Shared Service Project homepage. Accessed August 4, 2016. https://www.jisc.ac.uk/rd/projects/research-data-shared-service.

Research Libraries Group. Trusted Digital Repositories: Attributes and Responsibilities. An RLG-OCLC report. Mountain View, CA: Research Libraries Group, May 2002. http://www.oclc.org/content/dam/research/activities/trustedrep/repositories.pdf.

Rice, Robin. "On Being a Cog Rather Than Inventing the Wheel: Edinburgh DataShare as a Key Service in the University of Edinburgh's RDM Initiative." Workshop: Institutional Repositories Dealing with Research Data, hosted by the DCC, IASSIST, and COAR. Open Repositories conference, Charlottetown, Prince Edward Island, Canada, July 8, 2013. http://www.slideshare.net/edinadocumentationofficer/or2013-workshoprice-0.

Rinehart, Amanda Kay, Patrice-Andre Prud'homme, and Andrew Reid Huot. "Overwhelmed to Action: Digital Preservation Challenges at the Under-resourced Institution." OCLC Systems and Services, no. 1 (2014): 28–42. http://digitalpowrr.niu.edu/wp-content/uploads/2014/05/Overwhelmed-to-action.rinehart_prudhomme_huot_2014.pdf.

Rocca-Serra, Philippe, Susanna-Assunta Sansone, and Marco Brandizi. "Specification Documentation: Release Candidate 1, ISA-TAB 1.0." 2008. http://isatab.sourceforge.net/docs/ISA-TAB_release-candidate-1_v1.0_24nov08.pdf.

Roche, Dominique G., Loeske E. B. Kruuk, Robert Lanfear, and Sandra A. Binning. "Public Data Archiving in Ecology and Evolution: How Well Are We Doing?" *PLOS Biology* 13, no. 11 (2015): e1002295. doi:10.1371/journal.pbio.1002295.

Rothstein, Mark A. "Is Deidentification Sufficient to Protect Health Privacy in Research?" *American Journal of Bioethics* 10, no. 9 (2010): 3–11. doi:10.1080/15265161.2010.494215.

Royal Society. "Data Sharing and Mining: Open Data Policy." *Publishing Ethics and Policies.* Accessed November 20, 2015. https://royalsociety.org/journals/ethics-policies/data-sharing-mining.

RunMyCode homepage. Accessed March 14, 2016. http://www.runmycode.org.

Sabharwal, Arjun. *Digital Curation in the Digital Humanities: Preserving and Promoting Archival and Special Collections.* Cambridge: Chandos Publishing, 2015.

Schaeffer, Peggy. "Why Does Dryad Use CC0?" Dryad News and Views (blog). October 5, 2011. http://blog.datadryad.org/2011/10/05/why-does-dryad-use-cc0.

Schumacher, Jaime. Digital POWRR—Preserving Digital Objects with Restricted Resources: A Final Report to the Institute of Museum and Library Services. February 2015. http://hdl.handle.net/10843/13678.

Scientific Data. "About." Accessed March 24, 2016. http://www.nature.com/sdata/about.

Scottish Ten homepage. Accessed June 18, 2016. http://www.scottishten.org/.

SDA: Survey Documentation and Analysis homepage. Accessed October 29, 2015. http://sda.berkeley.edu/.

Selden, Robert Z. Jr., Bernard K. Means, Jon C. Lohse, Charles Koenig, and Stephen. L. Black. "Beyond Documentation: 3D Data in Archaeology." *Texas Archaeology* 58, no. 4 (Fall 2014): 20–24.

Shaw, Seth. "DataAccessioner." Github. Accessed March 14, 2016. https://github.com/seth-shaw/DataAccessioner.

Shoshani, Arie, and Doron Rotem, eds. *Scientific Data Management: Challenges, Technology, and Deployment.* Boca Raton, FL: CRC Press, 2010.

Sigurðsson, Kristinn. "To ZIP or Not to ZIP, That Is the (Web Archiving) Question." Kris's blog, January 28, 2016. http://kris-sigur.blogspot.ca/2016/01/to-zip-or-not-to-zip-that-is-web.html.

Sims, Nancy. "Making Decisions about Your Research Data." YouTube video, 6:38. Posted by CopyrightLibn, August 28, 2012. https://youtu.be/ZuUGlGOMGjU.

Smith, MacKenzie. "Data Governance: Where Technology and Policy Collide." In *Research Data Management: Practical Strategies for Information Professionals.* Edited by Joyce M. Ray, 45–59. West Lafayette, IN: Purdue University Press, 2014.

Smithsonian X 3D homepage. Accessed June 18, 2016. http://3d.si.edu/.

Society for the Preservation of Natural History Collections. "Publications." Accessed April 5, 2016. http://www.spnhc.org/19/publications.

Society of American Archivists. "Digital Archives Specialist (DAS) Curriculum and Certificate Program." Accessed March 14, 2016. http://www2.archivists.org/prof-education/das.

Stanford University. "Data Classification, Access, Transmittal, and Storage." Accessed March 14, 2016. https://uit.stanford.edu/security/dataclass.

Stanford University Libraries. "Case Study: File Naming Done Well." Accessed March 14, 2016. https://library.stanford.edu/research/data-management-services/case-studies/case-study-file-naming-done-well.

———. "Stanford Digital Repository Terms of Deposit." Accessed January 10, 2016. http://www.stanford.edu/group/sdr/SDR-Terms-of-Deposit-v13.pdf.

———. "Stanford Digital Repository." Accessed March 14, 2016. https://library.stanford.edu/research/stanford-digital-repository.

Starr, Joan, Perry Willett, Lisa Federer, Claudia Horning, and Mary Linn Bergstrom. "A Collaborative Framework for Data Management Services: The Experience of the University of California." *Journal of eScience Librarianship 1*, no. 2 (2012): e1014. http://escholarship.umassmed.edu/jeslib/vol1/iss2/7.

State Archives of North Carolina. "BagIt Tutorials." YouTube playlist. Accessed March 14, 2016. https://www.youtube.com/playlist?list=PL1763D432BE25663D.

Stodden, Victoria. "The Legal Framework for Reproducible Scientific Research: Licensing and Copyright." *Computing in Science and Engineering* 11, no. 1 (2009): 35–40. doi:10.1109/MCSE.2009.19.

———. "Open Data Dead on Arrival." Victoria Stodden (blog). February 3, 2010. http://blog.stodden.net/2010/02/03/open-data-dead-on-arrival.

Storino, Christine M. "Identifying Sensitive, Private, or Legally Protected Data in DRUM Submissions." University of Minnesota Digital Conservancy. 2015. http://hdl.handle.net/11299/171825.

"SUNScholar/Practical Guidelines for Starting an Institutional Repository (IR)." Libopedia wiki. Accessed March 14, 2016. http://wiki.lib.sun.ac.za/index.php/SUNScholar/Practical_guidelines_for_starting_an_institutional_repository_(IR).

Supporting Repositories Project. "Promotion of Repositories." 2011. http://www.rsp.ac.uk/documents/briefing-papers/repoadmin-promotion.pdf.

Swan, Alma. "The Business of Digital Repositories." In A DRIVER's Guide to European Repositories. Edited by Kasja Weenink, Loe Waaijers, and Karen van Godtsenhoven, 14–26. Amsterdam: Amsterdam University Press, 2007.

Sweet, James, Larry Bumpass, and Vaughn Call. The Design and Content of the National Survey of Families and Households. NSHF Working Paper no. 1. Madison, WI: Center for Demography and Ecology, 1988. http://www.ssc.wisc.edu/cde/nsfhwp/nsfh1.pdf.

Takao, Hidemasa, Naoto Hayashi, and Kuni Ohtomo. "Brain Morphology Is Individual-Specific Information." *Magnetic Resonance Imaging* 33, no. 6 (2015): 816–21. doi:10.1016/j.mri.2015.03.010.

Tamis-LeMonda, Catherine. "Language, Cognitive, and Socio-emotional Skills from 9 Months until Their Transition to First Grade in U.S. Children from African-American, Dominican, Mexican, and Chinese Backgrounds." *Databrary*. October 2013. Accessed November 16, 2015. doi: 10.17910/B7CC74.

Tenopir, Carol, Suzie Allard, Kimberly Douglass, Arsev Umur Aydinoglu, Lei Wu, Eleanor Read, Maribeth Manoff, and Mike Frame. "Data Sharing by Scientists: Practices and Perceptions." *PLOS ONE* 6, no. 6 (2011): e21101. doi:10.1371/journal. pone.0021101.

Thelwall, Mike, Stefanie Haustein, Vincent Larivière, and Cassidy R. Sugimoto. "Do Altmetrics Work? Twitter and Ten Other Social Web Services." *PloS ONE* 8, no. 5 (2013): e64841. doi:10.1371/journal.pone.0064841.

Thomson, Sara Day. "Technical Solutions: Preserving Databases." Preserving Transactional Data. DPC Technology Watch Report 16, May 2, 2016. http://dx.doi.org/10.7207/ twr16-02.

Transana home page. Accessed November 16, 2015. http://www.transana.org/.

Trull, Elaine, and Lisa Famularo. "Appendix N: ISR Field Report." National Survey of Families and Households Wave 2 Field Report. Philadelphia: Institute for Survey Research, 1996. ftp://elaine.ssc.wisc.edu/pub/nsfh/cmapp_n.001.

UK Data Archive. "Copyright and Data Sharing." Accessed June 14, 2016. http://www. data-archive.ac.uk/create-manage/copyright/share.

———. "How We Curate Data: Our Preservation Policy." Accessed June 18, 2016. http:// www.data-archive.ac.uk/curate/preservation-policy.

UK Data Service. Collections Development Policy. January 19, 2016. https://www.ukdataservice.ac.uk/media/398725/cd227-collectionsdevelopmentpolicy.pdf.

University of Edinburgh. "Checklist for Deposit." Accessed March 14, 2016. http://www. ed.ac.uk/information-services/research-support/data-library/data-repository/checklist.

University of Illinois at Urbana-Champaign Library. "University of Illinois at Urbana-Champaign DOI Service Participant Agreement." 2014. https://uofi.box.com/Illinois-DOIAgreementFinal.

University of Michigan. "Deep Blue Data." Accessed August 11, 2016. https://deepblue.lib. umich.edu/data .

University of Minnesota Libraries. "Data Repository for the University of Minnesota." Accessed March 18, 2016. http://hdl.handle.net/11299/166578.

———. "Digital Preservation Framework." Last updated January 2014. https://www.lib. umn.edu/dp/digital-preservation-framework.

———. "Digital Preservation, Guides." Accessed July 9, 2016. https://www.lib.umn.edu/dp/ guides.

———. "Managing Sensitive Data." Accessed March 11, 2016. https://www.lib.umn.edu/ datamanagement/sensitive.

———. "Submission Checklist for DRUM." Accessed August 6, 2016. https://www.lib. umn.edu/datamanagement/drum.

———. "The Supporting Documentation for Implementing the Data Repository for the University of Minnesota (DRUM): A Business Model, Functional Requirements, and Metadata Schema." University of Minnesota Digital Conservancy, 2015. http://hdl. handle.net/11299/171761.

———. "Umedia." Accessed March 18, 2016. http://umedia.lib.umn.edu.

———. "University Digital Conservancy." Accessed March 18, 2016. http://conservancy. umn.edu.

University of Minnesota Libraries Digital Conservancy. "Deposit License." In "DRUM Policies and Terms of Use." Accessed March 14, 2016. https://conservancy.umn.edu/ pages/drum/policies/#deposit-license.

University of Minnesota Libraries Facebook page. Accessed March 14, 2016. https://www. facebook.com/umnlib.

University of North Carolina. "DigCCurr Professional Institute: Curation Practices for the Digital Object Lifecycle." Accessed March 14, 2016. http://ils.unc.edu/digccurr/institute.html.

University of Texas at Austin. "Information Researchers to Create Digital Archives from Central Lunatic Asylum for Colored Insane." UT News, news release, April 8, 2015. http://news.utexas.edu/2015/04/08/information-researchers-to-create-digital-archives.

University of Wisconsin Madison. National Survey of Families and Households confidentiality agreement. Accessed February 5, 2016. http://www.ssc.wisc.edu/nsfh/624649EB.pdf.

US Bureau of the Census. "Geographic Terms and Concepts: Census Tract." Accessed February 5, 2016. http://www.census.gov/geo/reference/gtc/gtc_ct.html.

US Department of Health and Human Services, Office for Civil Rights. "45 CFR Parts 160 and 164: Standards for Privacy of Individually Identifiable Health Information. Final Rule." Federal Register 67, no.157. August 14, 2002. DOCID:fr14au02-32. http://www.gpo.gov/fdsys/pkg/FR-2002-08-14/pdf/02-20554.pdf.

US Department of Health and Human Services. "Frequently Asked Questions: Data Sharing." National Institutes of Health, Office of Extramural Research. Revised February 16, 2004. http://grants.nih.gov/grants/policy/data_sharing/data_sharing_faqs.htm.

———. "Health Information Privacy: Guidance Regarding Methods for De-identification of Protected Health Information in Accordance with the Health Insurance Portability and Accountability Act (HIPAA) Privacy Rule." Office of Civil Rights. Accessed November 20, 2015. http://www.hhs.gov/ocr/privacy/hipaa/understanding/coveredentities/De-identification/guidance.html.

US Geological Survey Earth Resources Observation and Science Center. "Records Appraisal Tool Questions." Accessed June 15, 2015. http://eros.usgs.gov/government/ratool.

US Virtual Astronomical Observatory. "Science Definition for the Virtual Observatory." Accessed March 24, 2016. http://www.usvao.org/support-community/science-definition-for-the-virtual-observatory (site now discontinued).

———. "VAO Closeout Repository." September 10, 2014. http://www.usvao.org/2014/09/10/vao-closeout-repository (site now discontinued).

Van den Eynden, Veerle, Louise Corti, Matthew Woollard, Libby Bishop, and Laurence Horton. *Managing and Sharing Data: Best Practice for Researchers*, 3rd ed. Essex: UK Data Archive, 2011. http://www.data-archive.ac.uk/media/2894/managingsharing.pdf.

Van Tuyl, Steven, Hui Zhang, and Michael Boock. "Analysis of Challenges and Opportunities for Migrating ScholarsArchive@ OSU to a New Technical Platform: Requirements Analysis, Environmental Scan, and Recommended Next Steps." February 26, 2015. http://hdl.handle.net/1957/55221.

Watson, Carol A., James M. Donovan, and Pamela Bluh. "Implementing BePress' Digital Commons Institutional Repository Solution: Two Views from the Trenches." Presentation at the 18th Conference for Law School Computing (CALI), University of Maryland School of Law, Baltimore, MD, June 19–21, 2008. http://digitalcommons.law.uga.edu/ir/4.

Watts, Joshua. "Building tDAR: Review, Redaction, and Ingest of Two Reports Series." *Reports in Digital Archaeology*, no. 1 (June 2011). Center for Digital Antiquity, Arizona State University, Tempe, AZ. http://www.digitalantiquity.org/wp-uploads/2011/07/20110930-Building-tDAR.pdf.

Web of Science. "Data Citation Index." Accessed March 24, 2016. http://wokinfo.com/products_tools/multidisciplinary/dci.

Wheeler, Jonathan, and Karl Benedict. "Functional Requirements Specification for Archival Asset Management: Identification and Integration of Essential Properties of Services Oriented Architecture Products." *Journal of Map and Geography Libraries* 11, no. 2 (2015): 155–79.

Whyte, Angus, and Andrew Wilson. *How to Appraise and Select Research Data for Curation.* Working level guide. Acton, Australia: Digital Curation Centre, Australian National Data Service, 2010.

Whyte, Angus. "Five Steps to Decide What Data to Keep: A Checklist for Appraising Research Data," version 1. Edinburgh, UK: Digital Curation Centre, 2014. http://www.dcc.ac.uk/resources/how-guides/five-steps-decide-what-data-keep#sthash.Zrx3J3N3.dpuf.

Wickham, Jackie. "Institutional Repositories: Staff and Skills Set." Draft RSP Document, 3rd ed. October 5, 2011. http://www.rsp.ac.uk/documents/Repository_Staff_and_Skills_Set_2011.pdf

Wiley. *Wiley Exchanges. Our Ideas, Research and Discussion Blog.* Accessed March 24, 2016. http://exchanges.wiley.com/blog.

Witten, Ian H., and David Bainbridge. *How to Build a Digital Library.* San Francisco: Morgan Kaufmann, 2003.

World Medical Association (WMA). *WMA Declaration of Helsinki: Ethical Principles for Medical Research Involving Human Subjects.* Fortaleza, Brazil: 64th WMA General Assembly, 2013. http://www.wma.net/en/30publications/10policies/b3.

World Meteorological Organization (WMO) homepage. Accessed June 18, 2016. https://www.wmo.int.

Wright, Debra. National Survey of Families and Households Wave 3 Field Report. Madison: University of Wisconsin Survey Center, July 15, 2003. http://www.ssc.wisc.edu/nsfh/wave3/fieldreport.doc.

Zhang, Allison B., and Don Gourley. *Creating Digital Collections: A Practical Guide.* Oxford: Chandos Publishing, 2014.

# Biographies

## Author Biography

**Lisa R. Johnston** is an Associate Librarian at the University of Minnesota, Twin Cities. Johnston serves as the libraries' Research Data Management/Curation Lead and as Co-Director of the University Digital Conservancy, the University of Minnesota's institutional repository. In 2014, Johnston led the team that developed and launched the Data Repository for the University of Minnesota (DRUM), http://hdl.handle.net/11299/166578. She serves as principal investigator of the multi-institution collaboration, the Data Curation Network project, which launched in 2016 with funding from the Alfred P. Sloan Foundation. Johnston has presented internationally on topics of academic library services for research data management, authored research articles on data management topics, and co-edited the book *Data Information Literacy: Librarians, Data, and the Education of a New Generation of Researchers* (Purdue University Press, eds. Carlson and Johnston, 2015), which details a variety of educational approaches used in data management training for STEM graduate students. Prior to becoming a librarian, Johnston was a science writer and assistant editor for *Sky & Telescope* magazine. Johnston holds a master of library science and bachelors of science in astrophysics, both from Indiana University, and was certified by the Society of American Archivists as a Digital Curation Specialist in 2014. Her ORCID is http://orcid.org/0000-0001-6908-9240.

## Case Study Author Biographies

**Karen E. Adolph** is Professor in the Department of Psychology and the Center for Neuroscience at New York University. Adolph leads the Databrary.org project to enable open video data sharing and reuse among developmental scientists. She is an expert in coding infant and child behavior from video and developed the Datavyu video coding tool. She is a Fellow of the American Psychological Association and American Psychological Society and President of the Interna-

303

tional Congress of Infant Studies. She received a Cattell Sabbatical Award, Fantz Memorial Award, Boyd McCandless Award, ICIS Young Investigator Award, FIRST and MERIT awards from NICHD, and five teaching awards from NYU. Adolph's research has been continually funded by NIH and NSF since 1991. She studies the effects of body growth, exploratory activity, environmental and social supports, and culture on perceptual-motor learning and development.

**Bethany Anderson** is an Archival Operations and Reference Specialist in the University Archives at the University of Illinois at Urbana-Champaign. Prior to Illinois, she worked at the Dolph Briscoe Center for American History at the University of Texas at Austin and the William L. Clements Library at the University of Michigan. She holds an MSIS from the University of Texas at Austin, an MA in Near Eastern languages and civilizations from the University of Chicago, and a BA in anthropology from the University of Michigan. She is the Reviews Editor for *The American Archivist* and has presented her research internationally.

The **Archaeology Data Service (ADS)** is the national digital data archive for archaeology in the United Kingdom. It was founded in 1996, as part of the Arts and Humanities Data Service, but is now an independent, self-sustaining, trusted digital repository, hosted by the University of York, with a twelve-strong staff. It hosts an online catalogue of over 1.3 million items, 35,000 unpublished fieldwork reports, 20,000 journal articles, and over 900 rich data archives. In 2010 it was awarded the Data Seal of Approval (renewed 2014), and in 2012 it won the Digital Preservation Coalition's Decennial Award for the most outstanding contribution to digital preservation over the last decade. The ADS works with the US-based Digital Antiquity organization to maintain an online series of guidelines and metadata standards in support of the long-term preservation of the wide variety of data types used in archaeological research.

**Karen S. Baker,** after careers in oceanography and long-term data management, is a graduate student at University of Illinois Urbana-Champaign at the School of Information Sciences. Having worked as an information manager with the Long-Term Ecological Research program, Karen has done work that has stretched from multidisciplinary bio-optics and field science to interdisciplinary ecology and ultimately the information sciences. Her interests are in study of the data ecosystem and how data practices can inform development of a web-of-repositories that supports research. Her work explores the continuing development of information infrastructures and information environments that in turn facilitate collaborative work and collective learning.

**Karl Benedict**, PhD, is an Associate Professor and Director of Research Data Services in the College of University Libraries and Learning Sciences at the University of New Mexico. Dr. Benedict has worked since 1986 in parallel tracks of geospatial information technology, data management and analysis, and archaeology. Previously he was the Director of the Earth Data Analysis Center (EDAC) and Research Assistant Professor in the Department of Geography and in CUL&LS at UNM and worked for the US Forest Service, National Park Service, and in the private sector conducting archaeological research, developing geospatial databases, performing geospatial and statistical analyses, and developing web-based information delivery applications. His work within the library focuses on managing the Research Data Services program to support UNM's researchers' abilities to manage their data during the research process and maximize the discovery, access, and use of their data products long after the end of their projects.

**Susan M. Braxton** is the Prairie Research Institute Librarian at the University of Illinois at Urbana-Champaign, providing support to institute staff with emphasis on scholarly communications and publishing, researcher information services, repository services, and data stewardship. Prior positions included Science Librarian at Illinois State University and Technical Information Specialist for the Biological Control Documentation Center at the US Department of Agriculture. She has a bachelor's degree in botany from the University of Florida, a master's degree in ecology from North Carolina State University, and an MLS from the University of Illinois at Urbana-Champaign.

**Robin Burgess,** PhD, is the Manager of Repository and Digitisation Services at The University of Sydney. Prior to this, he was the Research Information Manager at The Glasgow School of Art, where he wrote the case study contained in this book. Robin's research interests lie in the application of research data management (RDM) techniques and in analysis and the development of RDM strategies and systems for the visual arts and other creative fields. Robin has developed repositories, tool kits, and advisory documentation for researchers and students and used EPrints and DSpace repository technologies to develop suitable systems for the management of the research data and research outputs. Currently Robin is focused on the integration of repositories, data management systems, digitization techniques, and educational resources to form a single Enterprise System at The University of Sydney. Robin is a PhD-qualified expert research and data analyst who enjoys developing and delivering innovative solutions to real-world problems.

**Margaret H. (Peg) Burnette** is Assistant Professor and Biomedical Sciences Librarian at the University of Illinois at Urbana-Champaign. Peg's current research explores the convergence of knowledge management and library and information science (LIS) with an emphasis on the concept of expertise, the role of tacit knowledge, and tacit knowledge transfer and transformation. Prior to joining the

University of Illinois at Urbana-Champaign, Peg was at the University of Illinois at Chicago College of Medicine-Peoria, where she built expertise in the areas of biomedical informatics, evidence-based practice, knowledge management, health literacy, and curriculum-integrated instruction.

**Chiu-chuang (Lu) Chou** is a Senior Special Librarian in the Data and Information Services Center (DISC) at the University of Wisconsin in Madison. She is also a Senior Data Librarian in the Center for Demography of Health and Aging (CDHA), one of the thirteen P30 demography centers on aging funded by the National Institute on Aging. She helps users identify and locate data sets for their research. She maintains CDHA and DISC websites, DISC collection databases, and the BADGIR online data archive. She helps researchers at the University of Wisconsin-Madison prepare their studies for archives like DISC, National Archive of Computerized Data on Aging (NACDA), and the Inter-university Consortium for Political and Social Research (ICPSR).

**Erin Clary** is a curator at Dryad Digital Repository, through the Metadata Research Center, College of Computing and Informatics, Drexel University. She studied library science at the University of North Carolina, Chapel Hill, and biology at the College of Charleston.

**Johanna Davidson Bleckman** serves as Manager of the Education and Child Care Data Archive at the Inter-university Consortium for Political and Social Research (ICPSR), where she oversees the day-to-day operations, including restricted-data contract maintenance and administration. Ms. Bleckman received her undergraduate degree in philosophy from Carlow University in Pittsburgh, Pennsylvania, and her master's degree in social policy and evaluation from the University of Michigan, Ann Arbor. Her background is in program evaluation and data management.

**Ruth E. Duerr** is a generalist with interests in nearly everything from music and art to science, data, and policy, with stops for many other things along the way. She has been actively involved in earth and space sciences, together with the information and data sciences, for many years. She has a passion for encouraging researchers to become better data managers, demonstrated in part through teaching courses, developing and presenting a variety of workshops, and editing of the Federation of Earth Science Information Partners (ESIP) peer-reviewed Data Management short course (learning modules that are freely available online for self-paced learning). Her lectures at meetings and conferences introduce audiences (from various disciplines in earth and space sciences, social sciences, and computing and information sciences) to data management issues and solutions. She also teaches about data management at the University of Illinois at Urbana-Champaign, contributing to the expertise of new data management practitioners.

**Elise Dunham** is a Data Curation Specialist for the Research Data Service at the University of Illinois at Urbana-Champaign. She holds an MLS from the Simmons College Graduate School of Library and Information Science, where she specialized in archives and metadata. She contributes to the development of the Illinois Data Bank in areas of metadata management, repository policy, and workflow development. Currently she co-chairs the proposed Research Data Alliance Archives and Records Professionals for Research Data Interest Group and is leading the DACS workshop revision working group of the Society of American Archivists Technical Subcommittee for Describing Archives: A Content Standard.

**Debra Fagan** is a Curation and Technical Specialist with the Dryad Digital Repository. Prior to joining Dryad, she held positions as a librarian and as a software engineer. She holds a master of science in library and information science from the University of Illinois at Urbana-Champaign and a bachelor of science in computer science from the University of Central Florida.

**Colleen Fallaw** is a Research Programmer for the Research Data Service at the University Library of the University of Illinois at Urbana-Champaign. As the primary programmer for the emerging Illinois Data Bank, she draws on library school coursework, web development experience in the publishing industry, and technical involvement in HathiTrust Research Center projects to implement the vision of the Research Data Service Team in an integrated way with other university repository initiatives.

**John Faundeen** has worked at the US Geological Survey (USGS) Earth Resources Observations and Science (EROS) Center as the EROS Archivist since 2001. His current role involves policy, oversight, and guidance for the observational, cartographic, and elevation data created and maintained at EROS. John allocates most of his time to preservation and appraisal functions. The preservation activity includes environmentally managing a 20,000-square-foot archive containing 100,000 rolls of analog film and thousands of magnetic tapes. Establishing an off-site archive containing petabytes of electronic data continues to be a centerpiece of EROS's data management risk mitigation strategy. Memorandums of Understanding (MOUs) with the US National Archives and Records Administration were established based upon proven data management capabilities. ORCID http://orcid.org/0000-0003-0287-2921.

**Charlie Fiss** is a Senior Information Manager at the University of Wisconsin Center for Demography of Health and Aging and the Center for Demography and Ecology. He is the co-editor of a daily aging news clipping service and internet resource blog for the Center for Demography of Health and Aging. He also assists users in locating and utilizing data resources available at the University of Wisconsin, and he assists users in acquiring restricted data resources for their research.

**Jon Johnson** is the Senior Database Manager at the University of London UCL Institute of Education. Jon provides technical oversight and leadership on the development of the CLOSER (Cohorts and Longitudinal Studies Enhancement Resource) discovery platform. He is a member of the DDI Alliance Technical Committee and a co-investigator of the ESRC Resource Centre at the Centre for Longitudinal Studies.

**Amy Koshoffer** is currently the Science Informationist for the University of Cincinnati Libraries, where her work focuses on providing data management support for researchers and developing new research data services. Amy holds a BS in biology focusing on ecology from the University of Illinois, an MS in mathematics from the University of Cincinnati and an MLIS from Kent State University. Prior to joining UC Libraries, Amy worked as a senior research assistant in the UC College of Medicine Department of Cancer Biology and most recently the Department of Dermatology. Her research focus was on understanding melanocyte biology, especially the mechanisms that trigger vitiligo and other hypopigmentary disorders.

**Andrew S. Gordon** is Data Curator for the Databrary.org project. In this role, he performs outreach to Databrary data contributors, helping them to prepare their data for ingestion. This includes management, cleaning, and creation of metadata, automating ingest processes, and informing workflows and interfaces that help researchers on Databrary to find and reuse this data. He also assists researchers in the behavioral and learning sciences on how to bring the tools Databrary provides into their day-to-day research data management practices. Andrew received a master of science in information and bachelor of arts in anthropology from the University of Michigan.

**Thomas G. Habing** is the Interim Director of Information Technology and Manager of the Software Development Group for the University of Illinois at Urbana-Champaign Library. With the library for nearly twenty years, he has contributed technical expertise and leadership to numerous digital library projects. Prior to Illinois, he worked as a Senior Computing Methods and Technology Engineer for the Boeing Company in Seattle, Washington. He holds an MS in mechanical engineering from Purdue University and a BS in mechanical engineering from the University of Illinois at Urbana-Champaign.

**Carolyn Hansen** is Metadata Librarian at the University of Cincinnati, where her responsibilities include the creation and management of metadata for physical materials and digital collections. She has previously worked for Eastern Washington University, the Brooklyn Historical Society, ProQuest, and the American Geographical Society Library. She holds an MLIS from the University of Wisconsin-Milwaukee and an MA in European history from Marquette University.

**Alicia Hofelich Mohr** is a Research Data Manager in the College of Liberal Arts at the University of Minnesota. She provides support and consultation to researchers around quantitative methodology, data management, reproducible research, and open data. She works closely with the University of Minnesota Libraries and is a social science curator for the Data Repository at the University of Minnesota (DRUM). She holds a PhD in Cognitive Psychology and an MA in Statistics from the University of Michigan, as well as a BA in psychology from Hope College.

**Arwen Hutt** is a Metadata Librarian and head of the Digital Object Metadata Management unit in the Metadata Services Program at University of California (UC) San Diego Library. In this role she coordinates and manages metadata work for the UC San Diego Library's digital repository, which includes research data and cultural heritage materials. She works closely with the Research Data Curation Program to coordinate and develop services and has been actively involved with previous UC San Diego Library digital preservation and research curation projects.

**Heidi J. Imker** is the Director of the Research Data Service (RDS) at the University of Illinois at Urbana-Champaign. The RDS is a campus-wide service headquartered in the University Library that provides the Illinois research community with the expertise, tools, and infrastructure necessary to manage and steward research data. Prior to joining the library, Heidi was the Executive Director of the Enzyme Function Initiative, a large-scale collaborative center involving nine universities, funded by the National Institutes of Health, and located in the Institute for Genomic Biology. Heidi holds a PhD in biochemistry from the University of Illinois and did her postdoctoral research at the Harvard Medical School.

**Jared Lyle** is an Associate Archivist at the Inter-university Consortium for Political and Social Research (ICPSR), where he is responsible for developing and maintaining a comprehensive approach to data management and digital preservation policy. Mr. Lyle directs the ICPSR Curation Services Unit, which is responsible for metadata, data-related publications, and digital preservation. He also serves as Director of the Data Documentation Initiative (DDI), an international effort to establish a metadata standard for the social and behavioral sciences.

**Kaye Marz** is Archive Manager for the National Addiction & HIV Data Archive Program (NAHDAP), a data repository funded by the National Institute on Drug Abuse. NAHDAP is hosted by the Inter-university Consortium for Political and Social Research (ICPSR), which is part of the University of Michigan's Institute for Social Research. Ms. Marz has been with ICPSR since 1991. Her responsibilities include acquisitions outreach, support for depositors, data-processing plans and implementation, web and technical outreach, and user support. She has supervised the processing and release of public-use and restricted-use social science data sets on a variety of sensitive topics (e.g., criminal justice, addiction, HIV, health and risk behaviors), as well as those obtained from vulnerable populations. Ms. Marz holds an MS in criminal justice from the Michigan State University and a BA in psychology from the University of Michigan, Ann Arbor.

**Arun Mathur** is responsible for managing data support activities at the Inter-university Consortium for Political and Social Research (ICPSR). His responsibilities include managing restricted-use data agreements, including providing restricted-use data to researchers. Mr. Mathur received his undergraduate degree in political science from the University of Michigan and his master's degree in political science from the University of Washington.

**Christine Mayo** served as an Assistant Curator and then Curator at the Dryad Data Repository between March 2013 and October 2015. She is currently the Digital Production Librarian at Boston College. Her interests include the creation and management of all kinds of digital content, as well as repository assessment metrics and open access. She currently lives in Boston, where she shares her apartment and her life with a software engineer, a parakeet, and too many balls of yarn.

**William H. Mischo** is Head, Grainger Engineering Library Information Center, and the Berthold Family Professor of Information Access and Discovery at the University of Illinois at Urbana-Champaign (UIUC) Library. He has been involved in numerous grant-funded digital library projects, including the NSF Digital Library Initiative, IMLS National Leadership grants, Mellon Foundation grants, and NSF NSDL (National Science Digital Library) grants. Bill has published and presented widely in the field of library and information science. He was elected an AAAS (American Association for the Advancement of Science) Fellow in 2015 and was the recipient of the 2009 Frederick G. Kilgour Award for Research in Library and Information Technology from ALA/OCLC and the 2001 Homer I. Bernhardt Distinguished Service Award from the American Society for Engineering Education Engineering Libraries Division.

**Linda Newman** is Head of Digital Collections and Repositories for the University of Cincinnati Libraries. One of her assignments is to lead the agile software development team that supports the open-source development of Scholar@UC (https://scholar.uc.edu). Linda brings over thirty years of experience in libraries, including support of library systems, digitization, and software development. She holds a BA in philosophy from Denison University and an MLIS from the University of Kentucky. She remembers when BITNET and 3270 terminals were cool. She's addicted to the word puzzles known as acrostics.

**Limor Peer,** PhD, is Associate Director for Research at the Institution for Social and Policy Studies (ISPS) at Yale University. She oversees research infrastructure and process at ISPS, including the Field Experiment Initiative, which encourages field experimentation and interdisciplinary collaboration in the social sciences at Yale. In this capacity, she has led the creation of a specialized research data repository (the ISPS Data Archive) and is currently involved in campus-wide efforts relating to research data sharing and preservation. Prior to joining ISPS, Peer was Research Director at Northwestern University's Media Management Center and Readership Institute, which focuses on applied research primarily in the areas of media audience, content, and management strategy. At Northwestern University, she was also Associate Professor (clinical) at the Medill School of Journalism and held a courtesy appointment in the Department of Communication Studies. Her research interests include the media's role in democracy and in the public opinion process.

**Tina Na Qin** is a Science Librarian at Michigan State University Libraries in East Lansing, Michigan. She began this professional position in August 2013 after completing a master of library science degree with a chemical information specialization from Indiana University in July 2013. She also holds an MS degree in paper and chemical engineering from Miami University, Oxford, Ohio. In her second year as a Science Librarian, she focuses on gaining experience and exploring opportunities to be an effective liaison with and enhance services to the faculty and students. She is also interested in data management and text mining of chemistry literature.

**Peggy Schaeffer** served as Dryad Communications Coordinator from shortly after the repository's inception in 2008 until 2014. She has a background as a librarian in medical and pharmaceutical libraries and strong interests in facilitating open science, medical informatics education, international library development, and literacy education.

**Sara Scheib** is the Sciences Reference & Instruction Librarian at the University of Iowa Sciences Library. She serves as the liaison librarian to the biology, chemistry, earth and environmental sciences, mathematics, physics and astronomy, and statistics and actuarial sciences departments, providing reference and research assistance to students, faculty, and staff and offering instruction services. Sara is one of the founding members of the UI Libraries' Research Data Interest Group, working collaboratively with other offices such as the Division of Sponsored Programs, Information Technology Services, and the Iowa Informatics Initiative to develop comprehensive research data services on the UI campus. She works closely with her colleague, Marina Zhang, on several projects related to research data services, including the development of a data management curriculum for researchers, focusing specifically on graduate students and senior undergraduates.

**Juliane Schneider** is a metadata expert who develops ontologies and tools to maximize discovery of information, manages projects, does outreach on data curation, and instructs on annotation and OpenRefine. She has worked in all kinds of environments, from an insurance library near Wall Street to Countway Library at Harvard Medical School. She is currently a Metadata Specialist with the Research Data Curation Program, UC San Diego.

**Gemma Seabrook** is the Project Manager for Data and Metadata Enhancement at the University of London UCL Institute of Education. Gemma is the Project Manager for the Uniform Search Platform element of the CLOSER (Cohorts and Longitudinal Studies Enhancement Resource) project. She is also responsible for enhancing legacy data resources at the Centre for Longitudinal Studies.

**Mark Servilla** is an active member of the Long Term Ecological Research (LTER) Network as an informatics scientist and is the Lead Scientist for the LTER Network Information System (NIS), a service-oriented architecture framework for data discovery and preservation. In addition, Mark has been a member of the DataONE Core Cyberinfrastructure Team since the project's inception and currently provides technical support to new and existing DataONE member nodes. Prior to his current position at the LTER Network Office and DataONE, Mark worked in the private sector as a technical manager at Photon Research Associates (PRA), Inc. During his seven years at PRA, Mark participated in numerous software development projects and was involved in the startup of an Internet company that utilized satellite imagery for commercial agriculture. Mark holds a PhD in earth and planetary sciences (volcanology) and an MS in computer science, both from the University of New Mexico.

**Sarah L. Shreeves** is Associate Dean for Digital Strategies at the University of Miami Libraries, where she provides leadership and direction for the UML digital infrastructure and technology planning. Previously she was Coordinator for the Illinois Digital Environment for Access to Learning and Scholarship (IDEALS), a set of services and collections supporting scholarly communication including the institutional repository at the University of Illinois at Urbana-Champaign. She serves on the Digital Library Federation Advisory Committee and the Open Repositories Steering Committee.

**Lisa Steiger** is the Community Liaison and Project Manager of the Databrary. org project. She holds a BA in sociology from Bethel University and an MA in international education from New York University. She has overseen the development of Databrary's policy framework. As Community Liaison, she interfaces with researchers who use Databrary, working closely with them to help them fulfill data management requirements and ensure that their video data complies with research ethics policies that enable sharing with other researchers.

**Ayla Stein** is a Metadata Librarian at the University of Illinois at Urbana-Champaign. She holds a BA in East Asian studies from the University of Arizona and an MS of information from the University of Michigan.

**Jennifer L. Thoegersen** is an Assistant Professor and Data Curation Librarian at the University of Nebraska-Lincoln. Thoegersen instructs and consults on data management planning and contributes to the preservation of digital assets at UNL Libraries. She earned her MLIS through a joint program between Høgskolen i Oslo og Akershus, Tallinna Ülikool, and Università degli Studi di Parma. In 2013, Thoegersen contributed to the open-source digital library project Greenstone as part of a Fulbright fellowship at the University of Waikato.

**Kristin Vanderbilt** is a Research Associate Professor in the Department of Biology at the University of New Mexico. She has served as the information manager for the Sevilleta Long-Term Ecological Research (LTER) program since 2000. She has collaborated extensively with members of the International LTER Network on information management research and training activities.

**Jon Wheeler** is a Data Curation Librarian within the University of New Mexico's College of University Libraries and Learning Sciences. As a member of the libraries' Research Data Services program, he has a principal focus on the development of research data ingest, packaging, and archiving workflows that facilitate preservation and compliance with funder requirements. His ORCID is http://orcid.org/0000-0002-7166-3587.

**Elizabeth Wickes** is a Data Curation Specialist for the Research Data Service at the University Library of the University of Illinois at Urbana-Champaign. She is an MS student at the School of Information Sciences where she completed coursework in data curation and analytics. She currently co-organizes a Python user group, is a Software Carpentry instructor, and has previously worked as the Curation Manager for Wolfram|Alpha.

**Sarah C. Williams** is the Life Sciences Data Services Librarian at the University of Illinois at Urbana-Champaign. Focusing on the research data needs of life scientists on campus, she conducts training, provides individualized consultations, reviews data management plans, and develops web resources. Her research concentrates on data practices in the life sciences and services that can facilitate better data practices. She has a bachelor's degree in soil and crop science from Purdue University, an MLS from Indiana University, and a master's degree in information systems from Illinois State University.

**Ho Jung S. Yoo** is a Technical Analyst in the Research Data Curation Program at UC San Diego Library. One of her primary roles is to work directly with researchers to produce highly reusable data collections for the library's data repository. She also strategizes with members of her team to provide relevant data curation services to the campus. Prior to joining the library, she conducted ecological research on insect populations in citrus orchards, soybean fields, and a coastal sand dune habitat. She earned her doctorate in ecology from UC Santa Barbara, held a postdoctoral research associate position in entomology at Purdue University, and worked as an assistant project scientist for the Division of Biological Sciences at UC San Diego.

**Qianjin (Marina) Zhang** is the Engineering & Informatics Librarian at University of Iowa Lichtenberger Engineering Library. Her work focuses on providing data management support and developing library research data services. As a subject librarian, she also provides instruction, reference, and consultation services for the engineering faculty and students. Marina holds an MA in information resources and library science from the University of Arizona and a BS in biotechnology from Jiangsu University of Science and Technology in Zhenjiang, China.

Finally, the case study "Marking the Case for Institutional Repositories" was crowdsourced with the leadership of **Cynthia R. H. Vitale** (Data Services Coordinator in Data & GIS Services at Washington University in St. Louis), with contributions by the following academic library professionals: **Jacob Carlson** (Research Data Services Manager, University of Michigan, Ann Arbor), **Amy E. Hodge** (Science Data Librarian, Stanford University), **Patricia Hswe** (Digital Content Strategist and Head ScholarSphere User Services, Penn State University), **Erica Johns** (Research Data and Environmental Sciences Librarian, Cornell University), **Lisa R. Johnston** (Data Management and Curation Lead, University of Minnesota Twin Cities), **Wendy Kozlowski** (Data Curation Specialist, Cornell University), **Amy Nurnberger** (Research Data Manager, Columbia University), **Jonathan Petters** (Data Management Consultant, Johns Hopkins University), **Elizabeth Rolando** (formerly the Research Data Librarian, Georgia Institute of Technology, now with MailChimp in Atlanta, GA), **Yasmeen Shorish** (Physical & Life Sciences Librarian, James Madison University), **Juliane Schneider** (Metadata Specialist of the Research Data Curation Program, University of California San Diego), and **Lisa Zilinski** (Research Data Consultant, Carnegie Mellon University).